Race and Class in the Colonial Bahamas, 1880–1960

UNIVERSITY PRESS OF FLORIDA

Florida A&M University, Tallahassee
Florida Atlantic University, Boca Raton
Florida Gulf Coast University, Ft. Myers
Florida International University, Miami
Florida State University, Tallahassee
New College of Florida, Sarasota
University of Central Florida, Orlando
University of Florida, Gainesville
University of North Florida, Jacksonville
University of South Florida, Tampa
University of West Florida, Pensacola

RACE AND CLASS IN THE

Colonial Bahamas,

1880–1960

GAIL SAUNDERS

Foreword by Bridget Brereton

UNIVERSITY PRESS OF FLORIDA

Gainesville / Tallahassee / Tampa / Boca Raton

Pensacola / Orlando / Miami / Jacksonville / Ft. Myers / Sarasota

This book may be available in an electronic edition.

22 21 20 19 18 17   6 5 4 3 2 1

First cloth printing, 2016
First paperback printing, 2017

Library of Congress Cataloging-in-Publication Data
Names: Saunders, Gail, author. | Brereton, Bridget, 1946– author of foreword.
Title: Race and class in the colonial Bahamas : 1880–1960 / Gail Saunders ;
foreword by Bridget Brereton.
Description: Gainesville : University Press of Florida, [2016] | 2016 |
Includes bibliographical references and index.
Identifiers: LCCN 2015047890 | ISBN 9780813062549 (cloth: alk. paper)
ISBN 9780813064512 (pbk.)
Subjects: LCSH: Bahamas—Race relations—History. | Social classes—
Bahamas—History. | Bahamas—Social conditions—History. | Bahamas—History.
Classification: LCC F1660.A1 S28 2016 | DDC 305.80097296—dc23
LC record available at http://lccn.loc.gov/2015047890

The University Press of Florida is the scholarly publishing agency for the State
University System of Florida, comprising Florida A&M University, Florida Atlantic
University, Florida Gulf Coast University, Florida International University, Florida
State University, New College of Florida, University of Central Florida, University
of Florida, University of North Florida, University of South Florida,
and University of West Florida.

University Press of Florida
15 Northwest 15th Street
Gainesville, FL 32611-2079
http://upress.ufl.edu

To the memory of my late husband, Winston V. Saunders,
and my late parents, Basil and Audrey North,
for their love and encouragement.

Contents

Figures

Figures appear after page 143.

Gail Saunders, the author of *Race and Class in the Colonial Bahamas, 1880–1960*, has made a unique contribution to the writing of the history of her native country. As the founding and long-serving director of the National Archives of the Bahamas, she did more than anyone else to ensure the preservation, organization, and acquisition of the original records of the nation's past. As an acknowledged expert on the heritage of these islands, she has worked for decades to safeguard the nation's built and artistic patrimony and to disseminate knowledge about and appreciation of the national history and culture through museums and art galleries, exhibitions, newspaper articles, lectures, and publications.

As an academic historian, Saunders has authored, co-authored, or edited many publications on Bahamian history. Her books deal with a wide range of subjects and chronological periods: the era of slavery, the post-slavery period and the twentieth century; the historical heritage sites of Nassau; sources and documents illustrating the national history; and school texts. From an academic point of view, I would single out the important two-volume study of Bahamian social history, co-authored with Michael Craton and titled *Islanders in the Stream*; and her *Bahamian Society after Emancipation*.[1]

Ten years ago I wrote the foreword to the third edition of this last named book. In that short piece I noted the important contribution it made to our knowledge of Bahamian history in the period between the 1830s and the 1950s. I also commented on how this work, along with others, had helped to locate Bahamian history within the context of the historiography of the Caribbean, especially the Anglophone subregion. The essays it contained pointed to the commonalities between the Bahamian and the Caribbean historical experience but also to the uniqueness, the singularities, of the former.

The majority of the essays in *Bahamian Society after Emancipation* deal with the late nineteenth and the first half of the twentieth centuries, and the last one (chapter 14) might be seen as a brief survey of the subject of the present book. But the earlier work is a compilation of articles and papers written as separate essays, previously published or presented at conferences. As with all such books, it presents episodes in the nation's past rather than a sustained and coherent narrative and interpretation. It is a collection of discrete pieces (all valuable, of course), not a monograph.

Race and Class in the Colonial Bahamas is a major academic monograph on Bahamian social history between the 1880s and the 1960s, with a focus on race relations. The author brings to it her own personal experience as a middle-class, mixed-race Bahamian who grew up in the last decades of co-lonialism (the 1940s to 1960s). It is based on a wide range of original archival sources, held mainly in the National Archives of the Bahamas and of the United Kingdom. These include the unpublished (manuscript) records of the Colonial Office in London and of the colonial government in Nassau; local newspapers and other periodicals; contemporary published works; church records and publications; papers of the local legislature; personal papers such as those of the Chamberlain family; anthropological and ethnographic studies; government reports and statistical compilations like the *Colonial Annual Reports* and *Bahamas Blue Books*—and more. Saunders supplements this impressive range of documentary sources with material from oral his-tory interviews, conducted since the 1970s with many Bahamians, both those who had been engaged in public life and others. Of course, she also cites and incorporates the insights and information generated in the secondary works relevant to her subject.

This is a meticulously researched study of its subject. Saunders provides insights into the dynamics of the Bahamian social system and its develop-ment through detailed "case studies" of individuals, of episodes, and of social or political movements—what the anthropologists call "thick description," or perhaps micro-history. All this is subjected to analysis and interpretation, informed by social scientific theory, especially the work of Colin Hughes.[2] Also invoked is the considerable literature on Anglophone Caribbean social history in the post-emancipation period and the twentieth century.[3]

This book does not focus on the immediate post-emancipation period (1830s to 1860s–70s), which has been fairly well studied in the case of the Ba-hamas, as elsewhere in the Caribbean. Chapters 1 to 5 in volume 2 of Craton and Saunders's *Islanders in the Stream* deal with this period, as do many of the essays in Howard Johnson's valuable 1996 collection, *The Bahamas from Slavery to Servitude*.[4] Moreover, Whittington Johnson has recently published a detailed work on post-emancipation race relations in the Bahamas, taking his account up to the mid-1860s.[5] Instead, Saunders deals with the decades between 1880 and 1960, an "in between" era, between the much-researched post-emancipation years and the period of independence and postcolonial development. Saunders has written on this period before, in chapters 6 to 9 of the second volume of *Islanders in the Stream* and, as already noted, in her *Bahamian Society after Emancipation*. But this is the first significant scholarly monograph on Bahamian social history in this period.

Typical of social history, the book moves between a chronological and thematic structure, for this genre does not generally employ straightforward narrative. Within each chapter, different themes or topics are considered. But they follow a chronological line from the late nineteenth century (chapters 1–3) and early twentieth (3 and 4), to the 1930s (5), World War II and its aftermath (6), and the 1950s and run-up to the 1962 general elections (7). The concluding two chapters provide a snapshot of the state of social and race relations in the 1960s just before independence in 1973.

Though this is primarily a work of social history, it contains much of relevance to Bahamian political and economic history in the period addressed. Students and readers interested mainly in the Bahamas will find this book one of the most important scholarly contributions to its history published in recent years. But Caribbeanists in general will find much of interest too; it encourages comparisons with the rest of the region and especially with the British-colonized territories, of which the Bahamas were always a part, certainly in the view of the Colonial Office in London.

Unlike most of the British colonies in the region, the Bahamas had a deeply rooted, relatively large creole white community, more than 10 percent of the population at least up to the 1950s. This group had been present in the islands since the late eighteenth century, or even earlier in the case of some families. By 1880 the more important families, based in Nassau and mainly involved in trade, maintained a strong grip on the colony's social and economic life. Politically they were well entrenched, in control of the legislature and the organs of local government. This was recognized in London, which generally deferred to the oligarchs at least up to the 1950s. This is why the elected House of Assembly, tightly controlled by the Nassau white elite, was allowed to survive when other colonies lost theirs, and why the transition to adult suffrage and self-government came later to the Bahamas than to the other British colonies.

In all this the Bahamas most closely resembled Barbados, and this is a fruitful comparison to make. But economically the two colonies were very different. Barbados was the classic one-crop sugar plantation economy, while the Bahamas had neither sugar nor significant plantations. Its economy during the period Saunders deals with was based on marine exploitation, notably sponging, trade, subsistence farming, and, by the 1920s, tourism from the United States.

As Saunders shows, the Bahamian pattern of race relations was closer to the U.S. model than to that of the rest of the Caribbean, again with the probable exception of Barbados. Entrenched segregation in most spheres of life, though extra-legal, lasted at least up to the 1950s. The mixed-race and black middle stratum was relatively weak in the first half of the twentieth century, in comparison with that in Jamaica or Trinidad. The working class, overwhelmingly rural, was unorganized and fairly quiescent; trade unions and labor-based parties came late to the Bahamas. There were no significant labor protests in the 1930s, and even the 1942 Nassau riot was tame compared with what happened in Jamaica, Trinidad, and Barbados in 1937–38. (Hence the Moyne Commission did not bother to visit Nassau during its travels around the region in 1938–39.)

The racist attitudes of the white elite hardened in the early twentieth century, as the colony came ever more closely under American influence through migration to Florida, U.S. tourists, and the liquor smuggling business during Prohibition (1919–33). Segregation in public places was made more rigid to cater to the tourists, many of them from the U.S. South. In response, a small group of middle-class mixed-race and black Bahamians found in Garveyism and similar ideologies a way of confronting this situation. But Saunders makes it clear that no effective challenge to white racism and exclusive control was mounted before the 1950s.

One other important difference between the Bahamas and the other British colonies deserves mention: the dichotomy between New Providence and Nassau, on the on hand, and the Out Islands (now called the Family Islands), on the other. Nassau, and in effect the whole of the small island where the capital is situated, was very much the "metropolis" in comparison to the impoverished, underdeveloped, and often remote Out Islands. Other colonies had smaller "dependent" appendages—such as Trinidad and Tobago or St. Kitts-Nevis-Anguilla. But in 1880 the Out Islands contained about three quarters of the total colonial population, and this made the Bahamian situation unique.

The book moves easily between Nassau, which from 1900 onward increasingly acquiring the trappings of modernity and the amenities of a tourist destination, and the Out Islands. These, up to the 1950s, remained remote, sparsely populated, cash-poor places, where subsistence farming was combined with sponging and small-scale fishing. Most black people were sharecroppers with uncertain tenure, but most whites were miserably poor too, even if they maintained rigid segregation and endogamy in their enclaves in Harbour Island, Eleuthera, Abaco, and elsewhere. Little cash circulated, and most people who farmed or crewed the sponging boats were trapped in the notorious truck system. Occasional attempts to establish commercial farming for export (sisal, pineapples) or forestry on Andros proved unsustainable. The existence of the Out Islands—somewhat similar to other very small, non-plantation islands like the Grenadines, the British Virgin Islands, Barbuda and Anguilla, but in the Bahamian case containing the majority of the whole population during the period the book covers—certainly points to the unique features in the country's geography and history.

Race and Class in the Colonial Bahamas is valuable both to those mainly concerned with the national history and to others with a broader interest in the Caribbean region. Advanced pupils in the secondary schools as well as university undergraduate and postgraduate students will profit from the book, and so will general readers. Because it is comprehensively annotated with full bibliographical references and citations to primary sources, it will be welcomed by researchers. In my view, Saunders has made yet another important contribution to the development of Bahamian and Caribbean historiography.

Bridget Brereton, Professor Emerita of History
University of the West Indies, St. Augustine, Trinidad and Tobago
January 2014

Acknowledgments

I thank the following individuals and agencies for their assistance with this project.

The Right Honourable Perry Christie, LLB, M.P., Prime Minister
Mr. Alfred Sears, BA, MIA, M.Phil., JD, CLE, Chairman of the Council, College of the Bahamas
Dr. Rodney Smith, Ph.D., President, College of the Bahamas
Dr. Keva Bethel, Ph.D., former President, College of the Bahamas
Mrs. Janeen Hodder, former President, College of the Bahamas
Mrs. Betsy Voge-Boze, former President, College of the Bahamas
Dr. Tracey Thompson, College of the Bahamas
Ms. Virginia Balance, College of the Bahamas
Professor Bridget Brereton, Ph.D., University of the West Indies
Amanda Coulson and staff of the National Art Gallery of the Bahamas
Mrs. Pamela Burnside
Ms. Erika Stevens, Acquisitions Editor, University Press of Florida
Ms. Stephanye Hunter, Acquisitions Assistant, University Press of Florida
Ms. Catherine-Nevil Parker, Project Editor, University Press of Florida
Mrs. Elaine Toote, Director, Bahamas Archives
Mrs. Sherriley Strachan, Chief Archivist, Bahamas Archives
The staff of the Research Room, Bahamas Archives
The staff of the University of Cambridge Library, Cambridge, U.K.
Dr. Keith Tinker, Director, Antiquities, Monuments and Museums Corporation
Dr. Grace Turner, Antiquities, Monuments and Museums Corporation
Ms. Sally Antrobus, Independent Editor

INTRODUCTION

The Bahamas archipelago comprises about seven hundred limestone islands, cays, and rocks. Mainly flat terrain, they stretch some five hundred miles southeastward from just off Florida to Cape Haitien in Haiti. The island of New Providence where the capital Nassau is situated has always been the major center of population. All the other islands were collectively called the Out Islands and are now referred to as the Family Islands. Geographically, the Bahamas is isolated from the rest of the West Indies. It was one of the least important of an insignificant group of colonies and was also one of the most remote and perhaps poorest parts of the British Empire. The entire archipelago covers an area of 5,400 square miles. Described as an "Atlantic outpost" because of the absence of sugar, the Bahamas historically was not regarded as part of the West Indies and traditionally was not accepted as "a member of the family."[1]

The soil is sparse and much of it infertile. Rainfall patterns divide the islands into three geographical zones: the wetter northwestern islands, the central islands, and extreme southern islands where the rainfall is about half that of New Providence in the north.

The islands are surrounded by mainly shallow water in the west, north, and southeast. However, these shallows are punctuated by several deep channels or passages. A temperate climate prevails, and there are rarely sudden changes in temperature. In summer the temperature rises above 90 degrees Fahrenheit, and in winter it seldom falls below 60 degrees Fahrenheit. Although the humidity is high, the sea breezes and northeast trade winds compensate for the summer heat.

The population centers are widely distributed on the islands, some on the calm and sheltered leeward side, as at Cat Island, while others face north and northeast and are exposed to the northeast trades, as in the case of the Abaco

Cays. Main settlements, however, usually occur where there is a natural harbor or at least accessibility to shipping.

Largely owing to the poor soil, the population of the Bahamas has never been large. However, it more than doubled from 17,862 people at emancipation in 1838 to 43,521 in 1881. This growth in population was the result of a healthy rate of natural increase and, in the years up to 1860, the arrival of liberated Africans. (Britain banned the Atlantic slave trade as of 1808; slavery persisted in the Bahamas until its Abolition Act in 1831, with some conditions taking effect in 1834, and slavery was abolished in all British colonies in 1838.) But although the upward population trend continued, the rate of natural increase "until the mid-twentieth century was never higher than during the late slave period and declined markedly between 1860 and 1890."[2] The serious downturn in population growth was caused by recurrent epidemics (especially cholera in 1852–53) and the steady deterioration of work and living conditions that followed the boom years of the American Civil War.[3]

There were few immigrants in the early 1880s. In 1881 about 90 percent of the population had been born in the Bahamas. The indigenous creole population comprised former slaves, free blacks and browns, and the descendants of liberated Africans, early white settlers, and white Loyalists. According to the 1881 census, there were very few immigrants from Britain, Europe, Canada, America, the West Indies, the East Indies, and Africa. Unfortunately, no breakdown by color was made after 1851 because the executive council wished "not to offend any portion of the population."[4] The white population was estimated at about 25 percent of the total in 1888.[5]

In 1881 the Bahamas population was spread over twenty-one inhabited islands. About a quarter of the population was concentrated on New Providence Island (11,653 people). Most people on New Providence lived in Nassau, the capital city. The white population in New Providence lived mainly in the town between the harbor and the summit of the ridge that rises less than a hundred feet some one hundred yards inland and parallel to the harbor. Nassau in the 1880s was usually quiet and fairly free from violence and noise.[6] The houses of the white inhabitants usually had their own gardens, adorned by a variety of the colorful flowering plants and creepers so vividly captured in Winslow Homer's watercolor studies, such as *On the Way to Market, Bahamas, 1885*. On Bay Street, the main street that ran along the edge of the harbor, many inhabitants of the town had their businesses. The majority probably lived above their shops or places of business.

Residential segregation was not laid down by law but accepted by custom.

Brown and black people, with few exceptions, lived apart from the whites, occupying suburbs of the city and distant settlements such as Fox Hill, Adelaide, Carmichael, and Gambier. The latter were settled mainly by liberated Africans and their descendants. However, the majority of blacks, creoles, and liberated Africans lived behind the town ridge (that is, Over-the-Hill) south of Nassau in Grant's Town, Bain Town, or the more mixed southwestern suburb of Delancey Town, which was not strictly black. Some wealthy whites also lived in the area, which was laid out in 1789 by Chief Justice Stephen Delancey, who purchased 150 acres from the Honorable John Brown. After Delancey's death it was divided, and the allotments were bought both by affluent members of white society and by black and brown persons. Black Loyalists established Bethel Baptist Chapel in 1801, and some settled nearby. The area later became a high-class brown residential area.[7] The suburbs thrived because they were located near Nassau and the Public Market, where the inhabitants sold their produce and poultry.

Many mixed-race people, some very nearly white, lived in the racially mixed eastern suburbs of Nassau between Victoria Avenue and the Eastern Parade. The minister of Ebenezer Baptist Chapel in 1899, for example, characterized his congregation as an "intermediate class." He described the whites as poor artisans "with a distant coloured strain," while the majority were "actually coloured people."[8] Some wealthier whites also lived in the area, mainly on Victoria Avenue and opposite the Eastern Parade Ground. Brown and black people also lived in the area known as the Pond, to the east of Church Street. It was practically a marsh in 1800 but was reclaimed and settled by Governor Dowdeswell.[9] Farther east, between Church Street and Fort Montagu, "families engaged in fishing, sponging, and other maritime employments" lived along the shore.[10]

Brown and black people on New Providence generally lived in small wooden houses, although some were constructed of limestone. The better-off people had shingled roofs, while others used thatch. Glass windows were rare. Instead, board shutters were used. Each house usually had a garden where fruit, vegetables, and flowers grew. If the yard was large enough, there was an outside kitchen building. Cooking for poor blacks, however, was usually done outdoors using dead wood gathered in the forest. Rock walls, usually plastered, surrounded the garden.[11]

The majority of the Bahamas population (about 75 percent) lived on the Out Islands, which were isolated and more rural in character than New Providence. In a sense, the whole of the Bahamas could be considered rural, as much of New Providence was under agricultural cultivation. Being the chief town, Nassau served as the market for produce brought from the outlying districts of New Providence and also by boat from the other islands.

The most populous islands besides New Providence in 1881 were Eleuthera (7,010), Cat Island (4,226), Abaco (3,610), and Andros (3,434).[12] Eleuthera was the home of the early settlers known as the "Eleutherian Adventurers"—Englishmen and independent Puritans from Bermuda. After drawing up the Articles and Orders of the Company of Eleutherian Adventurers in July 1647 and led by Captain William Sayle, they set off for the Bahamas in the summer of 1648. Landing at Cigateo, which they renamed Eleuthera from the Greek word for freedom, they established a settlement probably near Governor's Bay and Preacher's Cave and had the longest relationship with Nassau. By the 1880s Eleuthera still contained quite a large percentage of whites in settlements such as Governor's Harbour, Rock Sound, and the Current. Cat Island, on the other hand, had a predominantly black population, which was concentrated mainly in the Bight, Arthurs Town, Bennett's Harbour, the Bluff, Port Howe, and Bayley Town. There were also smaller settlements. Abaco, among the northern islands, was settled mainly by "Yankee" Loyalists (supporters of Britain who fled the newly independent United States) and had settlement patterns that differed from those in the southern islands.[13]

As Cyrus Sharer explained, the northwestern islands were more compact and geared toward maritime activities, while the southeastern islands tended to have communities more densely settled and spread farther apart, being almost entirely oriented toward agriculture. The former held 85 percent of the European-descended population; the latter were predominantly black.[14]

Older northern settlements, such as Governor's Harbour on Eleuthera and Dunmore Town on Harbour Island, had large mixed populations. Dunmore Town, for example, had 1,472 people in 1891.[15] Governor's Harbour had slightly over a thousand in 1889.[16] The all-white settlement of Spanish Wells, on the other hand, had a smaller population of only 440 in 1881.[17] Governor's Harbour and Harbour Island had a long and close connection with Nassau mainly because of trade. North Eleuthera had a long tradition of relative agricultural success.

Post-Loyalist settlers preferred the cays off the island of Abaco. Early settlement had taken place on the mainland, but the cays were settled soon afterward because they were less mosquito-ridden and were adjacent to the resources of the sea. The inhabited cays that lie off the eastern side of Great Abaco include Green Turtle Cay, Man-O-War Cay, Elbow Cay (or Hope Town), and Cherokee Sound. Green Turtle Cay had a 60:40 white to black ratio, and Hope Town contained only two or three families of blacks. The other two settlements were exclusively white.

The white Loyalists and their descendants had neat, well built houses with gardens. In the Current settlement in North Eleuthera, which Stark described as containing many light-skinned brown people, there were "houses well built and much above the average." In contrast, however, some of the blacks in the settlement lived in huts made entirely of palmetto thatch.[18]

In the southern Bahamian Islands settled mainly by Loyalists and their slaves from the southern United States and abandoned for the most part by whites, the patterns of settlement were very different. They resembled what Erna Brodber described in urban Kingston, Jamaica, more closely than the northern Bahama Islands.[19] The people usually lived not in a single house surrounded by a garden but in a "yard" and compound. The yard itself was a living space.[20] Bahamian households in the southern islands, mainly made up of the descendants of slaves, did not consist of one structure or house. There was usually a main house, primarily for sleeping; and accompanying it were a kitchen with a wood-burning stove for food preparation; a washing room; an outside privy; and two or three sheds for storage, a well, and chicken coop or crab pen. Much of the day was spent out of doors and there was usually an area under a large tree for recreation such as storytelling or just relaxing. This pattern existed also in the black settlements or suburbs of Nassau in New Providence.[21]

Some family compounds actually became settlements; for example, Seymour's at Cat Island and Simms on Long Island. Different yards often made up a settlement, parts of which would retain a family surname; for example, Darling Yard in Colonel Hill, Crooked Island. Important persons in these Out Island settlements were the resident justice or commissioner, the priest or minister, and the school teacher. There was usually a highly respected older man of the village and there might be a midwife and an elderly woman held in high esteem.

Most Out Island settlements were self-contained and isolated and might have more contact with Nassau, the metropolis, for trade purposes, than with a neighboring village. Just as each island was quite a distance from the others, so too was each settlement, and in the 1880s, intercommunication was difficult. There was a lack of good roads except in Nassau, and transportation between the distant settlements was by foot, horseback, small sail boat, or schooner.

It was difficult to reach Out Island settlements. Travel in the late nineteenth century was mainly by sailing vessel. Fortnightly steam ship communication had been established between Nassau and several of the principal Out Islands: Abaco, Eleuthera, Cat Island, Long Island, and Inagua, but the majority of people still traveled by sailing vessel, especially the mail boat.[22] The mail boat was a vessel chartered by the government to carry the post. However, it conveyed much more than correspondence and parcels. Its decks were usually packed with all sorts of produce—sheep, pigs, fowls, barrels of sisal and sponge—as well as people. Difficult conditions such as a head wind, calm, or scorching sun made the sea journey tedious and often led to delays.

On arrival at an island settlement, passengers usually disembarked into a small row boat, which conveyed them to land. Docks and jetties were rare, and if the tide was too low to accommodate the boat, passengers were often carried for the last part of the journey on the back or in the arms of a strong local man. Once at the settlements, onward transportation was difficult because of roughly built and overgrown roads, or none at all, and the lack of bridges. Out Islanders walked miles to schools, churches, and to visit friends in other villages. The leading men of the settlement occasionally traveled on horseback or in a small sail boat.

This study examines the nature of the Bahamian society, race relations, and the interactions among the major groups—white, brown, black creoles, and liberated Africans—between the 1880s and the early 1960s. Before beginning with a brief outline of the immediate post-emancipation period, I should define some of the terms used.

White refers to people of British or American descent, including British-born persons and locally born individuals, and including both the New Providence oligarchy and poorer whites in Nassau and the Out Islands. *Brown* or *mixed race* refers to an individual who is of mixed European and African descent. A *black* person is one who appears to be of predominantly African descent. *African* describes persons born in Africa.

Liberated Africans were differentiated from creole blacks. However, their children were considered creole. Following the abolition of the slave trade in 1807, approximately 3,375 Africans liberated from foreign ships were landed in the Bahamas between 1811 and 1838. About one fifth were recruited into the Second West India Regiment or the British Navy, while the remainder were placed in the hands of the chief customs officer and apprenticed to "prudent and humane masters or mistresses" for between seven and fourteen years. The ostensible aim was to encourage them to learn a skill or trade and prepare them to make a living.

Creole is a concept described by Kamau Brathwaite for Jamaica as meaning persons of British, European, or West African descent, or a combination of these, who lived, worked, and were born in Jamaica, adapting themselves to a new environment and to one another. A new creole society with its own characteristics or culture resulted.[23] The term is not used in the Bahamas as extensively as in Trinidad, but it describes locally born persons in the society.

As Bridget Brereton has explained, there are difficulties in writing about race and class in the complex West Indian society of the late nineteenth century. However, by the 1870s, views on the pattern of race relations had become established and "would not be significantly changed until perhaps the 1930s."[24]

Brereton warned that serious difficulties apply not so much in identifying "acts of racial discrimination" as in addressing the "ideas and prejudices behind the actions." Not all racial happenings were publicized, and there is no way of knowing the thoughts and attitudes about race of those persons who had passed on. In the present study, information about the subject has been gleaned from official documents, travelogues, newspapers, and, for the more modern period, oral history interviews. It was particularly difficult to record the attitudes of the black masses who had emerged from slavery, as they left few written accounts of their activities. Historians must depend on accounts written by the elites and middle stratum as well as on folkloric and official records, taking care to differentiate nineteenth-century beliefs and attitudes from those of a century later.[25]

An important legacy of enslavement in the British Caribbean was the strictly stratified color and class system. The pyramidal structure delineating positions of the white, brown, and black groups in descending order of power and influence ensured the continuation of white dominance in post-emancipation years. Color was extremely important in the Bahamas, especially in Nassau, the capital, and in the all-white and biracial settlements on the Out Islands.

From the post-emancipation period until the 1870s, Bahamian society comprised a white, brown, and black population, including liberated Africans. In the late nineteenth and early twentieth centuries, the population was augmented by relatively small numbers of immigrant groups including Chinese, Greek, Lebanese, and Jewish people, groups who soon became involved in commercial activities, thus competing with local merchants.

The society at emancipation was thus divided by race and national origin. It was also a segmented society dominated by the white elite, who controlled the political and constitutional machinery and also the land resources. The pro-British Loyalist merchants and their descendants in Nassau had prospered from the import and export trade and formed a white oligarchy. This "agro-commercial bourgeoisie" had been given land grants on the Out Islands, where they established cotton plantations. Following the decline of cotton, many planters emigrated, leaving the merchants as the dominant group.[26] The white merchant elite dominated the legislature and occupied most of the civil service posts as well as those in the judiciary. Office holders and members of the House of Assembly and Legislative Council were usually related. Although the British officials usually allied themselves with the local elites, there was some friction between them. White Bahamian elites often felt contempt for the British officials sent to the Bahamas. Heskett Bell, British receiver general in the Bahamas during the late nineteenth century, felt that although "liked and respected, Englishmen were considered 'foreigners' and their appointments were often resented."[27] The House of Assembly purposely kept their salaries low to discourage English officials.

Most British settlers and officials "shared the racial prejudices of the Bahamian whites."[28] They saw nonwhites as "child-like, dependent," and "irresponsible loafers in the sun."[29] Like the local elite, the British held certain values cherishing hard work, thrift, ownership of property, Christian marriage, and the subordinate position of women.[30] They were patriotic and loyal subjects and were usually Anglican or Methodist. Through control of the oppressive labor systems, such as sharecropping, tenant farming, and the credit and truck system, the local white oligarchy—although not always wealthy—was able to dominate the lower classes, including the poor whites. Poor whites also engaged in seafaring activities, including piloting, fishing, and boat building. Some were tradesmen and craftsmen in Nassau. They lived in the eastern suburbs of Nassau and in white and biracial settlements on the Out Islands. Despite their poverty, they despised nonwhites and were, in turn, held in contempt by brown and black people.

A small brown and black middle class had emerged at emancipation. It held an ambiguous position in the strictly stratified society in Nassau between the white elite at the top and the black laboring class at the bottom. The middle class comprised free persons of mixed race who had risen out of enslavement, those who were products of European and African ancestry born into a free society, and upwardly mobile liberated Africans. The majority of the brown middle class generally had no business experience, although there were notable exceptions, such as successful black merchant William Parliament Adderley. Most, however, worked for wages or fees as artisans or tradesmen, with a few in the lower ranks of the civil service. Some browns sought political positions. Two men of mixed race were elected to the House of Assembly in 1834 for the town of Nassau: Stephen Dillet, a tailor, who was born in Haiti and brought to Nassau as a young child, and Thomas Minns, a businessman. In the same election, attorney Samuel Minns was elected for the Island of Andros. The brown middle class admired European culture and were patriotic supporters of the British monarch. Most belonged to the Anglican Church. They did not completely reject their African heritage, and some had a keen sense of race consciousness. Aspiring mixed-race men attempted to obtain a good education, secure good jobs, own land, attend the "right" churches, and enter politics. While attempting to acquire white values, members of the brown middle class created social distance between themselves and the black laboring class, although some had relatives in that group and attended the same churches, and their children attended the same schools.

The majority of the Bahamian black creole population at emancipation lived on the Out Islands. Most were illiterate. The formerly enslaved in the Bahamas, as in the Caribbean generally, were eager to own land because of its value as a vital source of food through peasant farming. Official policy, however, made it difficult for freed slaves to obtain ownership of property. Many former slaves therefore became squatters, having no legal tenure. Land tenure was further confused by the existence of "commonage land" and "generation property."[31] While wage labor existed in New Providence, it was limited in the Out Islands.

Black creoles who lived in New Providence were hired as domestics, seamstresses, gardeners, stable hands, and laborers at other menial tasks. Some also farmed small plots and sold their produce in the Grant's Town and Nassau markets. The black laboring class differed from the brown middle class in their views about the choice of an occupation and what was considered a good education. Their ideas on morality, marriage, and religion also distinguished them. The black creole masses celebrated their African culture in dance, song, storytelling, and the John Canoe Christmas festival.

The influx of liberated Africans into the Bahamas after 1811 caused "fear and apprehension of the white community," who saw the new arrivals as a threat "to their lives and property" and as competition for their slaves in the town.[32] Liberated Africans, under the apprenticeship system, worked at tasks similar to those of the formerly enslaved but now freed black population. Howard Johnson argues by 1828 an African peasantry existed "with access to land rather than ownership of it." Additionally, a freehold peasantry had emerged among the liberated Africans whose indentures had expired.[33] The Bahamian government from the early 1820s acquired land at Headquarters (Carmichael), some seven miles from the town of Nassau, and laid out Grant's Town, just over the hill from Nassau, to accommodate freed slaves and liberated Africans who moved from Carmichael Village in order to be near the Nassau market where they sold their crops. Other African settlements included Bain Town, developed by black businessman Charles Bain just west of Grant's Town in the 1840s. African villages settled or expanded in the 1830s and 1840s included Delancey Town, Adelaide, Gambier, and Fox Hill/Sandilands Village. Some settlers were able to purchase plots of land, some of which were quite substantial. Liberated Africans preserved their ethnic origins in establishing societies to assist in promoting African solidarity and to provide benefits for the sick, aged, widowed, and orphaned; such organizations also ensured decent burials for their members.[34] The first one to be formed was the Grant's Town Friendly Society, established by both liberated Africans and former slave apprentices. Liberated Africans joined churches and also reinforced African customs such as drumming, ring dances, John Canoe, storytelling, styles of food preparation, and *asue* or *su su* (collective savings clubs, discussed in chapter 2).

This brief introduction to the geography and population of the Bahamian archipelago and Nassau's key role sets the stage for closer examination of race relations in the colonial Bahamas. Well into the twentieth century the white elite controlled the political, social, and economic life of the colony. Discrimination and racial segregation were rife.

Chapter 1 briefly examines the apprenticeship system, land tenure, and labor arrangements including labor tenancy, sharecropping, and the truck system. It also gives a brief account of business and tourism, political and constitutional developments, religion, and an underfunded educational system in the late nineteenth and early twentieth centuries. With the work of Colin Hughes in mind, chapter 2 explores in some detail the Bahamian experience, the complex structure of Bahamian society, and how it differed from the norm of the British Caribbean.

Chapter 3 scans worldwide advances in science and technology that transformed twentieth-century life, including in the Bahamas. The British West Indies and the Bahamas, with its sufferings from the legacy of slavery and the indifference of the home government, entered the twentieth century in dire economic straits. However, as elsewhere in the Caribbean during this period, black and mixed-race Bahamians expressed a sense of racial pride and identity. A small group of nonwhite Bahamians organized a black nationalist movement and identified with Pan-Africanism, advocating awakening of racial consciousness.

In chapter 4 Garveyism and Prohibition are examined with emphasis on race relations during the World War I period. Though Bahamians were eager to join the war effort, at the beginning of the war the British government was unwilling to accept nonwhite colonials in the armed forces and refused to appoint them as commissioned officers. News of this pernicious racial discrimination dampened Bahamians' enthusiasm.

The economic depression of the 1930s as experienced by Bahamians is the focus of chapter 5. The era saw development of the tourism industry but also brought social unrest, although this was more isolated than in the West Indies. In the Bahamas change was slower in coming. Tourism, while boosting the economy, worsened the racial situation and hardened the existing color line. A new consciousness experienced in the 1930s provoked labor restlessness and the setting up of the anti-establishment *Herald* newspaper and a labor union. Disturbances occurred in Inagua and in Nassau led by Milo Butler, calling for the introduction of the secret ballot during a 1937 by-election.

Between 1940 and 1945 the Bahamas assumed strategic importance as an aircraft staging and antisubmarine base, as described in chapter 6. New Providence became a training ground for air crews. Edward, Duke of Windsor, the former king and emperor who served as governor of the Bahamas between 1940 and 1945, was abroad when the Nassau riot occurred in June 1942. A labor program known as "the Project" or "the Contract" was negotiated with the American government, exposing Bahamian laborers to legally enforced Jim Crow segregation in the American South. Nassau was developing into an important offshore banking center.

Chapter 7 describes the establishment of the Citizens' Committee in 1950, consisting mainly of nonwhite middle-class professionals concerned with the extreme discrimination upheld by the white elite, many of whom were wealthy. During this time political parties were founded: the Progressive Liberal Party and the Bahamas Democratic League. Both were critical of racial discrimination and inequalities.

The dispute that led to the General Strike of 1958 is the pivot of chapter 8. It involved a scheme whereby the local bus company and meter cab firm, controlled by Bay Street representatives, would be given "franchises" to convey passengers between the airport and the hotels. The scheme was to increase the seating capacity of hotel vehicles and would dent business for members of the Taxi-Cab Union. The Women's Suffrage Movement, established in 1957, is also reviewed.

Chapter 9 examines the society in the 1950s and 1960s via demographic characteristics of both New Providence and the Out (Family) Islands. Racial categories in 1943 and 1953 census showed a decrease of self-defined blacks and quadrupling of the number calling themselves mixed. Discriminatory practices still existed in certain residential areas, and an overview of society in the early 1960s revealed that attitudes toward race had not changed fundamentally.

Thus the system of racial discrimination inherited from the institution of enslavement persisted into the 1960s. Attitudes toward race by the white, mixed-race, and black middle class had not changed significantly. Despite some upward mobility of mixed-race and black Bahamians, the economy continued to be dominated by the white elite. Secondary education, although limited to those who could afford it, was the route to salvation for nonwhite Bahamians, as it led to mixed-race and black persons studying in professional fields and brought rising political consciousness. This book is the story of how racial discrimination persisted until at last squarely challenged by the majority of Bahamians.

1

The Bahamas in the Post-Emancipation Period

The Bahamas has been described as a marginal non-plantation colony, which never grew sugar commercially. It did however, have a short-lived cotton industry that had collapsed by 1800. Despite this, the ruling white elite opposed attempts to ameliorate slave conditions and, later, the abolition of enslavement. Like other West Indian colonies, however, and in keeping with the spirit of the British legislation, the Bahamas passed its own Abolition Act, which stipulated certain conditions that were to take effect on 1 August 1834.[1] It was left to colonial assemblies to grant complete freedom or to adopt the apprenticeship system. Apprenticeship was intended to act as an easy transition from enslavement into freedom, guaranteeing the planters a labor supply for a time and assisting the formerly enslaved in their new responsibilities as free citizens.[2] Bahamian slave owners, like those in all British West Indians colonies except Antigua, opted to introduce the apprenticeship system partly because of fearing social disorder but chiefly to maintain the power structure founded on ownership.

Apprenticeship

Apprenticeship failed to fulfill many of its aims. Former slaves were forced to work not for themselves but for their former owners. In reality the formerly enslaved remained subordinate to their former owners, and apprenticeship was nothing more than a modified form of slavery.[3] It ensured, for four years, the retention of economic, political, and social domination by former Caribbean and Bahamian slave owners who feared social uprisings and were reluctant to surrender control over their enslaved laborers.[4]

Michael Craton and Gail Saunders posit that the transition of 1834–38 was made easier because of "an experimental system of apprenticeship" that had already been "tried and proven since 1811," having been applied "to Africans liberated from foreign slavers and landed in the Bahamas after abolition of the British slave trade in 1808."[5] They further note that the "immediate transition out of chattel slavery was thus smooth, and the apprenticeship as in the West Indies generally, was ended two years early on 1 August 1838." Early optimism, which marked the ending of formal enslavement and the immediate post-emancipation period, soon evaporated. The former enslaved and apprentices were free, but oppressive labor systems and the difficulties of acquiring land resulted in the steady worsening of their working conditions and material welfare. Additionally, the former slave owners, allied in some instances with the brown middle class, "tightened their control over both the political system and the mercantile economy."[6]

Land Tenure

Traveling was made difficult by the fact that large areas of the Bahamas were unsettled and uncultivated. The post-emancipation years witnessed a lack of interest by the Crown, and by the end of the nineteenth century the system of land tenure would become "extremely confused."[7] The former enslaved in the Bahamas, as in the British West Indies generally, were eager to own land. It was valuable not because of its monetary worth but as a vital source of food through peasant farming. Official policy, however, made it difficult for freed slaves to obtain ownership of property. Regulations governing the sale of Crown land "served to thwart the ex-slaves' ambitions to own land" immediately following emancipation.[8]

An 1839 land act tightened legislation, allowing magistrates to eject settlers lacking title from any land, including Crown land, and to imprison those who resisted.[9] The law did make exception for those who had enjoyed "quiet possession" for at least five years. However, forcible ejection of squatters proved impracticable, especially from Crown lands, and the 1839 legislation was amended within a year to except those who had enjoyed "quiet possession" for at least twelve months.[10] The Crown protected itself from "unlawful alienation" by decreeing that "unauthorized settlers" could gain title by "squatters' right" on Crown land after sixty years of unchallenged occupation and after twenty years for private land.

Government policy concerning Crown land, influenced by the ideas of Edward Gibbon Wakefield, dictated that it was to be sold only to those who could afford a "sufficient price," thus maintaining a "proper balance between land and capital, leaving those without capital as a reservoir of landless labour."[11] Many of the former enslaved therefore came within the category of squatters, having no legal tenure. While some peasants managed to purchase land, the prevalence of squatting continued, especially on the Out Islands. The practice of rotational slash-and-burn agriculture and overcropping of the cleared area soon exhausted the soil and the field was abandoned, being replaced with a newly prepared one. Peasant farmers were therefore obliged to move fields every one or two years, as no one piece of land had a lengthy farm value. Many squatters did not realize that they needed to occupy a tract of land beneficially (in its totality and not merely isolated fields) for sixty years in order to establish legal title to Crown Land or for twenty years in the case of private land.[12]

An institution with roots in Africa that emerged out of enslavement in the British West Indies was the concept of "family" land.[13] In the Bahamas there were similarities but also significant differences, as Nicolette Bethel and Michael Craton have demonstrated.[14] Jean Besson argued that family land is "a dynamic Afro-Caribbean cultural creation by peasantries themselves in response and resistance to the plantation system."[15] Whereas Bahamian generation property resembles Caribbean family land, Bethel observes that "the origin of Bahamian lands and those of the West Indies is different." While the communities Besson studied originally consisted for the most part of "small holdings by ex-slaves during the post-emancipation period . . . in the Bahamas, the majority of generation property consists of the original estates themselves." She added that "the rights to generation property are not limited to the descendants of slaves." Bahamian generation property may be owned not only by the descendants of the enslaved but also by white and brown Bahamians.[16]

Even where former slave owners in the Bahamas continued to hold legal title to the land, however, "the former enslaved residents often developed a communal sense of attachment, belonging, that was quasi-proprietorial."[17] Many of the former enslaved adopted the names of their previous owners and sometimes retained the names of the former estates as the names of their subsequent settlements of free black peasant farmers. Once the former master's family left, those descendants of the former enslaved who remained on the land for generations claimed it by custom, if not in law. This practice became known as commonage, meaning that it belonged to the community; that is, these were lands held in common by the community. Individuals tracing their roots back to the area can apply for land to farm and build a house. Generation land, however, was usually kept within the family and passed down from generation to generation. The title might have lapsed, or been long forgotten, or been claimed by a mixed-race descendant of the original owner, but it was almost invariably challenged by all family heads still living in the settlement.

It can be argued that "the senses of community reinforced by actual or fictive kinship, of an attachment to a particular location amounting to a communal quasi-proprietorship, and of being what Sidney Mintz has termed proto-peasants rather than praedial slaves occurred even earlier, . . . on the increasingly large number of Out Island plantations owned by absentees."[18]

Even under the management of a poor white or free colored person, these operations were concerned with making a profit from cotton or salt, and tensions developed between managers and the enslaved. However, the sense of community among the enslaved was aided by their isolation, a common ethnicity, and ever-tightening kinship ties. As profits faded, the enslaved, although constrained to live within a limited area on the owners' estate, were left increasingly on their own and encouraged to subsist for themselves by slash-and-burn agriculture and raising small stock, resulting in a close replication of "an African-style village-based peasantry."[19]

The best known case was that of the Rolle estates on Great Exuma, owned by Lord John Rolle, an absentee owner. His slaves served a nominal apprenticeship and, when fully free on 1 August 1838, took over Rolle's five tracts on Exuma, setting up "a well-regulated system of commonage based on the villages of Rolleville, Steventon, Mount Thompson, Ramsey's, and Rolletown, even though they had no formal deed of conveyance from their former owner." The former enslaved also took the surname Rolle. From that time to the present, anyone with the surname Rolle, and who could prove descent from a Rolle on either the male or female side, could claim a plot of land on which to build and farm. Commonages occurred in other Out Islands, where the former enslaved tended to form villages based on the old plantations. In Eleuthera, however, the original commonage dated back to the early English settlement, but this was not deeded until 1842.[20] Many problems persisted into the late nineteenth century owing to the lack of proper control and management, uncertain boundaries, and questionable titles. Finally, in order to resolve some of the legal problems, a Commonage Act was passed in 1896.[21] Lands held in common are defined as "any lands which have been granted to more than twenty people and not partitioned." Authentic commonages were listed, rules were made as to who was entitled to occupy or use common land, and machinery for managing the commonages was established.

As noted, generation land was similar to but also distinct from commonage. A shifting form of peasant farming, the prevailing vagueness about other persons' titles and boundaries, and the general availability of unused land re-inforced the African traditions that all land was for common use according to need and that the land belonged equally to members of the user group. Moreover, this informal tenure existed within the family from "generation to generation," and the land was not to be divided. Even when a single family had title, that party held the land in trust for the family at large, and any member of the family might be the user. Even in cases when wills gave priority to one descendant, all descendants including "illegitimate" or "outside" children retained a fundamental claim.[22] The government, in tune with the sensitive feelings surrounding land ownership, was reluctant to interfere in either generation property or commonages. The thorny problem of generation property, especially in Cat Island and Long Island, remained unsolved into modern times. Until certain complicated and lengthy transactions took place, generation property was considered "untitled private land" and could not be sold. Much land in the Bahamas was therefore occupied and utilized by persons having no legal claim and who were in fact considered squatters.

The Economy

Labor Systems: Labor Tenancy and Sharecropping

At emancipation in 1834, the mainstays of the colony's economy were salt and wrecking industries. Because of general poverty and the lack of a viable industry, wrecking—that is, the salvaging of goods from ships in trouble—was still practiced. By that period cotton had failed as a viable export.[23] Most Out Islanders worked as cultivators farming corn, peas, sweet potatoes, and other vegetables, and pineapples were grown later in the nineteenth century. Some livestock was also raised, notably goats. Salt continued as a staple even after the Turks and Caicos Islands were separated from the Bahamas in 1848 due to pressure from Turks Islanders, who resented being taxed and generally neglected by the Bahamas government. Salt production was moved to Inagua, and the Heneaga Salt Pond Company was established in 1849 to develop salt ponds on that island. Wage labor existed in New Providence but was limited on the Out Islands where the majority of Bahamians lived. As Howard Johnson has demonstrated, new labor arrangements developed between the ending of slavery and complete emancipation. These included two main systems: labor tenancy and sharecropping. In the former, African apprentices, the enslaved, and later ex-slaves worked part of the week in the fields of their holders or owners and part of it on their provision grounds, the products of which sustained them and their families.[24] In the operation of the share system, the former enslaved and liberated Africans were considered tenants, remaining on the land of their former owners or employers who "supplied the land" while the tenants provided labor. The landlord received a share of the crop, usually a third of the produce. In the latter part of the nineteenth century some landlords who grew pineapples received half rather than a third of the proceeds.[25] The sharecroppers were entitled to the "remainder." Howard Johnson states that the "absence of a staple crop to replace cotton," and the shortage of capital, meant that wages did not generally "result."[26] This trend continued into the twentieth century. By 1847 the tenancy agreements were "firmly established by custom." In at least one case, the former Charles Farquharson estate of Prospect Hill on Watlings Island (later renamed San Salvador), a written contract was drawn up, in 1865, stating that the tenants were expected to give one third of everything grown on the land to the manager of the estate.[27] It also stipulated that a sharecropping agreement binding them to it would have to be signed.

The share system, while benefiting the landlords by the avoidance of high labor costs, also benefited the ex-slaves and their descendants by giving them legal access to some of the fertile tracts on the islands at the price of a third of their labor. However, sharecroppers became increasingly dependent on advances offered by the merchant landlords. The pineapple industry (components of which included plantations as well as canning factories) developed during the mid-nineteenth century. It was controlled by relatively few landowners, who still operated on the share system in order to maximize profits by benefiting from cheap labor, which included the tenants' families. Howard Johnson also noted that sisal, initially cultivated by wage earners at the beginning of the twentieth century, was grown on San Salvador (Cat Island) by share tenants.[28]

The Truck System

Peasant farming operated on a sharecropping basis because it was increasingly affected by the truck system. Owning no land, many sharecroppers depended on the landowner for advances in cash and provisions. Interest rates on cash advances were high. The landlord received one-third of the crop harvested. But the advances in cash and kind were subtracted from the sale of the pineapples produced, and prices varied.[29] The laborer often ended up in debt to the landlord.

By the late 1860s external demand for local Bahamian commodities such as salt, pineapples, and sponges led to the tightening of control of the already harsh labor systems. As Howard Johnson notes, "control mechanisms . . . enabled a white mercantile minority to recruit and retain labourers and thus consolidate its position as ruling elite in the post emancipation period."[30] This "agro-commercial bourgeoisie," comprising Loyalist merchants and some descendants of the early English settlers, came to dominate the import and export trades in Nassau. By the abolition of slavery in 1834, these merchants dominated the Bahamas House of Assembly, a domination that would last until the 1960s.

The mechanism used to control labor mirrored that used in pre-emancipation years. By providing credit, the merchants dominated the "poor white population politically."[31] Governor William Colebrook noted in 1836 that "a commercial interest had grown up by the dependence of the poorer classes on the Merchants for their necessary supplier, and the debts they had thus generally contracted."[32] The practice of paying in truck had occurred during enslavement among the liberated African apprentices. Howard Johnson suggested that "the truck system of the post emancipation years was nothing more than the wider application of a practice used in connection with the free Africans during slavery."[33]

Payment in wages in the early post-emancipation period was usually limited to the growing of pineapples and salt raking. Post-emancipation laborers who worked in leading industries such as wrecking and sponging, with the exception of sisal, were usually paid "on a profit-sharing basis rather than a wage basis." The laborers therefore came to depend on credit from the merchants and landowners who were intimately involved with the "major economic activities."[34] The Nassau merchant class in pre-emancipation years also used the credit system with the poor white communities in the northern islands, and they in turn became dependent on the shopkeepers in the capital. Craton and Saunders have suggested that this dependency after emancipation led to an alliance between the white Out Islanders and the agro-commercial elite. Although instances of exploitative wage labor and dependence on advances lingered on in the poorer white communities to the end of the nineteenth century in ship building, wrecking, and fishing, the poorest whites always found it easier to obtain minor government employment, to borrow money, to be self-employed, and to avoid wage labor than did the black majority because the poor whites' growing sense of racial superiority gave them an identification with the interests of the ruling class.[35]

White and black laborers were exploited by the merchants, who were "able to manipulate the transition out of slavery and apprenticeship and the mechanics of the trade system to avoid actually having to pay cash wages."[36]

Blacks, however, were numerically in the majority. Control and exploitation occurred in the salt industry at Mathew Town, Inagua, and in the pineapple and sponging industries, upon which the economy was based in the late nineteenth century. The truck system ensured dependency of the tenants on the merchants. Pineapple farmers, who lived mainly in Eleuthera, Cat Island, and Long Island, needed credit to support themselves between the planting and harvesting of the fruit, usually within an eighteen-month period. Merchants advanced credit in the form of pineapple slips and fertilizers, provisions, and sometimes cash. The debts incurred were usually paid following the sharing of the "proceeds of the crop." Very often, tenants remained in debt to the merchants at the end of the session. The system was slightly different for peasants, as they were usually paid in kind. Laborers in the pineapple canning factories set up in Nassau and Eleuthera by J. S. Johnson, a member of the House of Assembly, were also exploited, being paid "in the form of tokens," which initially could be "exchanged for goods" at any local store, "but eventually only at the company and store during the canning season."[37]

The sponging industry, which had begun on a small scale as early as the 1840s, was the foremost industry in the Bahamas by the end of the nineteenth century. It offered steady employment, operating on the credit and truck system, to at least one eighth of the population and was to sustain the Bahamian economy for three-quarters of a century.

Before 1896 credit was usually given to the fisherman in the form of goods rather than cash. The merchants supplied not only the food taken on the voyage by the sponge fisherman but also the provisions he left with his wife and family. These goods were often supplied at high profit to the merchant, being recorded at high rates of interest and thus rendering it almost impossible for the fisherman to make an economic return. Furthermore, the outfitter sometimes took advantage of the illiteracy of the typical Bahamian sponger by listing the same item under different guises. As L. D. Powles demonstrated in *The Land of The Pink Pearl*, the outfitter often supplied provisions in kind such as flour, sugar, tobacco, and articles of clothing, which the fisherman might not necessarily want. Needing the money to leave with his family, he often sold the goods at about half price.[38] Reaction to this obvious exploitation of sponge fisherman drove them to sell either a portion or the entire catch to persons who had established depots in Andros and the main sponging center by 1884. But following pressure from the merchants, this practice was stopped by 1886 legislation. From that year onward sponges could be sold only to the Nassau Sponge Exchange, thus establishing merchant control. The act did give some concessions to the sponge fishermen, however. They were no longer paid shares in truck, and the value of advances to the captains and seamen was limited. Sponge fishermen remained in debt to the merchants because of "large advances of provisions and cash at higher interest rates."[39]

As Howard Johnson explained, sponge fishermen were "in debt to the merchants for trips interrupted by bad weather." After weeks at sea, the spongers often had a "fling" when returning to land, and as most were illiterate, they were often cheated by the merchants, to whom they remained indebted.[40] During the late nineteenth century early twentieth, some Nassau merchants were able to accumulate capital and expand their influence and control over Bahamian society as a result of the sponge trade, blockade running (1861–65), and bootlegging (1919–33).[41]

The use of the truck system was pervasive. Governor William Haynes-Smith noted in 1896 that "the spirit of the truck system appears to saturate every transaction."[42] The truck system was employed also in minor industries, such as shipbuilding and pilotage. In Bimini the white population was regularly employed in piloting and was paid in provisions. Howard Johnson stated that the "credit and truck systems were not primarily racial in orientation but were key elements in a machinery of class slavery in which merchants dominated with whites and blacks." Merchants had replaced the enslaved "with a dependent laboring population" whom they controlled economically and socially. Johnson further argues that the "decline" of the credit and truck system "was largely the result of developments in the export sector." New opportunities for "profitable wage labor" in Florida and New Providence opened up in the early twentieth century.[43]

The Effects of the American Civil War on the Bahamas

Soon after the outbreak of the American Civil War, President Lincoln ordered a blockade of southern ports of the United States. Despite Britain's neutrality, Nassau, due to its strategic position and proximity to ports in the South such as Charleston and Wilmington, became a transshipment area where goods bound for Europe and Confederate ports were traded. Between 1861 and 1865 Nassau experienced a significant increase in trade, which resulted in improvements and construction growth in Nassau. Its population also profited from an increase in wages and general prosperity. There was, however, a corresponding increase in the price of rents, food, and goods, the last two of which were imported.

When the Civil War ended the colony's economy fell into a slump and was once more dependent on its agricultural products and sponge fishing. The beneficiaries of this brief prosperity were the "foreign commercial agents and captains and gang leaders who left as soon as the brittle affluence of the Atlantic (bubble) burst."[44] Benefiting the most locally was the white merchant class, which included Nassauvians, British residents, and landed proprietors who had previously lived in the Out Islands and had moved to Nassau. The company John S. George, for example—established in 1859 by Englishman John Saffrey George who had arrived in Nassau in the mid-1840s—expanded during the 1860s and survived the depression that followed. Some men of color also profited and were able to expand their businesses; among these men was the building contractor J. E. Dupuch.

Generally, though, the vast majority of the black population, quite a number of poor whites, and even some white elites remained extremely poor. Even so, the blockade-running era helped to underline the social divisions in Nassau society, which were based mainly on race. It also had a profound effect on the moral tone of the society, which had once again profited from activities that were generated from the outside and were illegal.[45] Many Out Islanders who had migrated to Nassau during the "boom" period returned to their homes and to farming and fishing. The Bahamian government made no effort to develop farming on a systematic basis, and most Out Islanders were locked out of the legal ownership of land and continued to operate under the sharecropping and truck systems for many years to come.

Business and Tourism

Business in the Bahamas in the 1880s, as in nineteenth-century Trinidad, consisted of import and export agencies and large dry goods stores.[46] These were located in Nassau on Bay Street, the commercial center where most professional work and the main trade of the colony were concentrated. The economy was dominated by the mercantile community or agro-commercial bourgeoisie, which was mainly white but included some brown and black merchants with businesses on or near Bay Street, all of whom found it cheaper and more profitable to import foodstuffs from the United States, and to a lesser degree Great Britain, than to subsidize the local economy. Importing foodstuffs and manufactured goods nominally boosted the local economy, as the bulk of the colony's revenue derived from indirect taxation; that is, from import duties, which were levied on nearly every class of import, including basic foodstuffs such as rice, lard, sugar, salt, meat, fish, flour, cornmeal, and hominy.[47] Three quarters of the imports came from the United States, as they were being produced more cheaply than in the United Kingdom or were conveyed less expensively. Bahamians therefore developed a preference for American goods, even if, as Governor Haynes-Smith later claimed, they were inferior to the British counterparts.[48] The slowly developing tourist industry also made the importation of foreign goods a necessity since foreign visitors demanded nonlocal products.

As early as 1740 Nassau had gained a reputation as a winter health resort for "invalids" and others from North America and Canada seeking refuge from the cold north. It was not until the mid-1850s that the Bahamian government began actively promoting tourism. In 1851 the government signed a contract with a New York steamship company, but the steamer that arrived was destroyed by fire. Renewed efforts were made in 1857, when a Steam Navigation Act was passed to provide steam navigation between Nassau and New York. Two years later an act was passed to build a hotel, and the government purchased a site in the center of Nassau.[49] Additionally, in 1859 the first contract for steamship service between Nassau and New York was made with Canadian-born pioneer Samuel Cunard. This included Nassau on a monthly voyage between New York and Havana.

The Cunard service began with the arrival of the SS *Corsica* in November 1859 and prompted the government to begin building the Bahamas' first hotel, the Royal Victoria, in 1860. This coincided with the upswing in the economy spurred by the American Civil War. The Royal Victoria opened in 1863 with the blockade trade at its height. The last blockade runner arrived in Nassau in 1865, and during the next year the Royal Victoria was offered for sale without success. When the contract with Cunard expired in 1867, a new contract was made with the Atlantic Mail Ship company.

The 1870s saw the beginning of the modern tourism industry in the Bahamas. In 1870 a large number of guests visited, filling the Royal Victoria for the season. Nassau experienced its most successful season in the winter of 1873, when nearly five hundred tourists arrived. Several other contracts were signed, the most significant being in 1879 with the Ward Line, which provided service between New York and Nassau, and in 1882 with a direct line of twin-screw steamships between London, Nassau, and Belize.[50]

Political and Constitutional Developments

Unlike most British islands, which had become Crown colonies by the end of the nineteenth century, the Bahamas, Bermuda, and Barbados retained the old representative system in the post-emancipation era. In the Bahamas, a governor appointed by the British monarch was responsible for the administration of the colony. He was assisted by a nominated council and an elected House of Assembly. In 1840, Royal Letters Patent established separate executive and legislative councils for the Bahamas.[51] The Executive Council, which the governor appointed and chaired, included three members appointed by the Crown—that is, government officials—usually but not always the colonial secretary, attorney general, and receiver general. The holders of these posts were *ex-officio* members of the Executive Council, holding their seats by virtue of their position. The governor could appoint, at most, six unofficial members.[52]

The Legislative Council, also nominated by the governor, had a membership of nine, including Bahamians and British colonial officials, and in 1844 officials were in the majority. It initiated and amended legislation, except money bills. Each council had a quorum of three. Between 1840 and 1880 significant changes took place in the composition of the councils. White Bahamian males dominated both councils, which were white except for occasional men of color, who included attorney Thomas M. Mathews and merchant W. E. Armbrister. Both fair-skinned mixed-race men who passed for white, they were also invited to all-white events and seem to have been accepted by the Nassau white elite. Members of the House of the Assembly, after the passage of the 1840 legislation, could serve on the Executive Council but not the Legislative Council.[53] Members could not serve on both councils simultaneously. In this way the governor increased the power of the executive in the House but was sometimes controlled by the Executive Council's decisions, which he had to follow before taking action.[54] The House of Assembly in 1834 had twenty-nine members elected from fifteen districts, and three of the members were nonwhites. To qualify, candidates and electors had to be male, free, twenty-one years of age, and residents of the Bahamas for at least a year. Candidates were required to own an estate of at least fifty acres or property to the value of £200. Electors had to be freeholders in possession of property to the value of £20 or in possession of fifty acres of land "under active cultivation."[55] Although privileged free blacks and mixed-race men were given the right to vote in 1807, it was not until after the passage of the 1830 act to extend voting rights to free nonwhites that men of color were elected.

However, the numbers of nonwhites elected remained small well into the twentieth century, as open voting, inequitable constituencies, lack of unity among nonwhites, and a franchise that favored the propertied class stymied their progress. Moreover, the majority of blacks and those of mixed race, as well as poor whites, were impoverished and dependent on the white merchants, who usually controlled their votes. The House of Assembly from the early eighteenth century controlled finances, despite the fact that the Legislative Council "claimed the right" to do so. Money bills "invariably" originated in the House of Assembly.[56] Social and educational reforms that would benefit the lower classes were chronically underfunded.

Religion

Religious denominations also assisted in socializing the society. The Anglican Church was the oldest denomination established in the Bahamas. Its advent in the islands dated to the arrival of the Eleutherian Adventurers in 1648, the first European population to settle permanently in the Bahamas. As early as 1729 the Anglican Church was recognized as the Established and Endowed Church of England in the Bahamas and was supported financially by the government, answering to the bishop of London and enjoying the patronage of the governor of the Bahamas.

Later the Anglican Church was placed under the See of Jamaica, established in 1824, and remained a part of it until 1861, when the Bahamas became a separate See. Christ Church was subsequently elevated to the status of a cathedral and Nassau was declared a city.

During enslavement, partly due to the shortage of priests (the Society for the Propagation of the Gospel was almost bankrupt and unable to supply any missionaries between 1807 and 1835), the Anglican Church did not actively proselytize the enslaved or free blacks, nor did it promote abolition.

The Anglicans therefore began to lose ground, and it was not until the 1860s and 1870s—after Addington Venables, a ward of Sir Robert Peel and an "adherent to the Oxford movement," was consecrated as bishop in 1863—that its influence and prestige heightened. Indeed, it was the governor's church and that of many white officials in Nassau. During Venables's tenure the number of clergymen was increased, and more effort was made to evangelize the Bahamian masses in New Providence and the Out Islands. With its High Church ritual and its educational policies, the Anglican church was appealing increasingly to nonwhites, especially at St. Agnes in Grant's Town and St. Anne's in Fox Hill. By 1870 the Anglicans had established thirteen parishes in the far flung Bahamian diocese, which also included St. George in the Turks and Caicos Islands. Popular among Anglicans were the Sunday schools and its operation of day schools for a large percentage of the population.[57]

Methodists had a presence in the Bahamas by the end of the eighteenth century. Joseph Paul, a black Loyalist who arrived in the Bahamas around 1784, set up a school for blacks and the enslaved and also built a Methodist chapel in 1793 at the western end of the town of Nassau. Following Paul's defection to the Anglican Church, the Manchester Methodist Conference dispatched William Turton, a mixed-race Barbadian. He and other missionaries, mainly British, successfully converted a large number of the poor whites in Harbour Island, Eleuthera, and Abaco. This departed from the pattern established in the Caribbean, where blacks and browns dominated membership in Methodist churches. Some blacks joined as well and became a part of the English Conference.

The Methodist conversion of free blacks and the enslaved led white legislators, who were at the time mainly Anglican, to control rigorously all forms of Non-conformist activity among Bahamian blacks. Restrictive legislation was passed limiting the holding of services by dissenting ministers and the hours when services could be held.[58] Despite these restrictions, due to the dedication over time of English missionaries the Methodist Church grew by attracting whites and nonwhites. Before emancipation in 1831, British missionary Charles Penny established a chapel (later known as Wesley) in Grant's Town to accommodate mainly liberated Africans and black creoles. By 1865 Methodist membership in the Bahamas numbered 7,270, with substantial congregations in Nassau, Eleuthera, and Harbour Island, all with sizable white populations. Racial divisions resulted. As early as 1838 a Methodist missionary chairman acknowledged: "I am sorry to say that there is a vast deal of prejudice of colour in the circuit."[59] Racial tensions and prejudice within the Methodist Church in the Bahamas persisted into the twentieth century.

Baptists, who were present in the Bahamas from the 1780s, also competed with Anglicans for members. Black Loyalists Amos Williams, Prince Williams, Sharper Morris, and Samuel Scriven were among the early Anabaptists who began preaching during the 1790s in Delancey Town, New Providence. In 1801 the Baptists purchased two lots in Delancey Town on which they built their first chapel, a wooden structure called Bethel. Samuel Scriven was pastor until his death, being succeeded by Prince Williams around 1822.

After several years of schism in the Bethel congregation, and with the need to have "white missionary supervisors in order to gain official sanction and respectability," the majority of the congregation voted to become a part of the Baptist Missionary Society, London, England, then represented by Joseph Burton.[60] Prince Williams and some of his followers objected to the agreement, and between 1833 and 1834 he purchased land about three hundred yards west of Bethel on Meeting Street, establishing the St. John's Particular Church of Native Baptists Society. Shortly afterward Burton purchased land in the town on the corner of East and Shirley streets and built a chapel, named Zion Baptist, which opened in 1835. Bethel and Zion were considered one congregation by the Baptist Missionary Society.[61] However, in the mid-1860s, this situation changed, and following the 1866 hurricane when Bethel was destroyed and rebuilt "with state funds," Bethel allied itself with St. John's Society of Native Baptists.[62]

The Baptist churches, especially the "Native Baptist" churches, rapidly gained members because they combined the attractions of a native black ministry, black management, and participation at all levels with the appeal of "traditional, evangelical and fundamentalist forms of Christianity with revivalism and spiritualism."[63] Also popular among the black population in the 1880s was the United States-originated African Methodist Episcopal Church, or "Shouter Chapel."[64] Located in Grant's Town, it was presided over in the mid to late nineteenth century by Bishop Venables Eneas, the son of a Yoruba liberated African. It was probably the forerunner of the Pentecostal or "Jumper" churches, which proliferated in the twentieth century.

Very different in tone was the Presbyterian Church in the Bahamas, the Established Church of Scotland, organized by the St. Andrews Society. By 1810 the Presbyterian Kirk had been established. However, like the Anglican Church during enslavement, the Kirk took little interest in the black population. It attracted not only those of Scottish descent but also the commercial elite, who were predominantly white. Its congregation at the end of the nineteenth century was exclusively white. It did, however, assist in the early 1890s in establishing the Kirk's Quarry Mission School to serve the black community in Delancey Town.[65]

During the late 1840s and the 1860s, the Anglican Church was embroiled in the "burial ground dispute" and questions of disestablishment and disendowment. The Methodists and Baptists resented the Anglican Church's status as the "established Church," which gave it access to public funds, and also the Anglicans' privileged status regarding public burial grounds. They were also offended by the High Church practices in the Anglican Church, which they saw as "semi-Romanish" doctrines. Matters came to a head because of these views and several other factors, including the financial slump following the American Civil War, the devastating effects of the 1866 hurricane and the distress that followed, compounded by the hotly contested 1868 elections. The disendowment controversy developed into a political issue, with mainly white electors of Dunmore Town in Harbour Island—a Wesleyan stronghold—siding with the "Liberals" who were opposed to endowment. Governor Rawson W. Rawson reported that the "question of colour had been raised." The Anglican Church, aware of the racial divisions within the Methodist Church, particularly in Harbour Island, asserted that the Anglican Church "provided for the poor and has a toleration and sympathy for the coloured race."[66] Following a general policy of the Colonial Office to disestablish Anglican churches in the colonies, an Act to amend the Ecclesiastical Laws of the Colony and for other purposes was passed and assented to on 1 June 1869, disestablishing the Anglican and Presbyterian churches. Financial aid did not cease immediately. Incumbents were permitted to retain their salaries during their lifetime, and a system of "concurrent endowment" was introduced whereby all Christian churches received state aid according to the number of communicants.[67]

Education

During enslavement, British West Indian planters, for the most part, did not educate their enslaved. Only in exceptional circumstances were slave children educated in any way. By the age of six most slave children were working at some task, in either the field or household.[68] There were occasional advocates of education for the enslaved, exceptional planters such as Codrington in Barbados and Wylly in the Bahamas, whose own religion and outlook made them willing for the enslaved on the estates to receive instruction in Christianity.

As already noted, missionary societies such as the Society for the Propagation of the Gospel (SPG), Anglicans, Methodists, and Baptists were active in educating white, brown, and free black children during the eighteenth and early nineteenth centuries and beyond. The government and the Society for the Propagation of the Gospel formed a partnership in 1746 (the date of the first Education Act), catering to whites and free blacks. Although the results of this union were limited, children were usually taught the "three Rs"—reading, writing, and arithmetic—and religion in the schools established by the government and the SPG.

The Anglican Church controlled the colony's schools for most of the nineteenth century, even after its disestablishment in 1869. Day schools and Sunday schools, the latter attached to churches, taught "sound Christian principles." An 1804 Education Act provided for the establishment of a high school, which proved short-lived. The act also encouraged the establishment of several schools in Eleuthera and Abaco, started on the initiative of the settlement's population, who petitioned the government annually for funds to pay the teacher's salary. This was probably the beginning of the grant-in-aid system, which lasted well into the twentieth century. Abolitionist governor Sir James Carmichael Smyth in 1832, before being forced out of the Bahamas in the following year, used Crown funds to establish schools at the liberated African villages of Carmichael and Adelaide.[69] At emancipation the Anglican Church still dominated education. There was only one public school, Dr. Bray's Associates School, located in Nassau under the control of the rector of Christ Church, and a few private schools existed. There were four public schools in the widely scattered Out Islands. Indeed, a large number of children were not educated in the mid-nineteenth century. Where schools existed they were underfunded, short of school supplies, and lacking in good teachers.[70]

There was little public education until emancipation, when the colonial government granted to the British West Indies £30,000 a year for five years and then decreased the grant each year until it ended in 1845.[71]

The Bahamas' first allocation was £550, which was granted to the SPG missionaries. An act was passed in 1836 to set up a "Board of Public Instruction," which would administer the minuscule allocation to the Bahamas from the colonial education grant, with power to make rules and regulations for all public schools and to establish schools to support teachers.[72] The board's effectiveness was stymied due to financial woes and its unwieldy structure: it had sixty members—men of different denominations—and suffered from a bitter power struggle that raged between the Anglicans and the Non-conformists.[73] In 1838 the board's annual report listed fourteen schools and 935 pupils.[74] The government grant for 1838–39 totaled £1,690, of which £1,138 were expended on salaries for teachers. In 1839 the board was dissolved and reconstituted with a smaller number of members but remained interdenominational, which led to continued discord and the removal of all clergymen from the board in 1841.[75]

Three years later Archdeacon John Trew "insinuated himself onto the Board causing another clash with the Baptists, Methodists and Presbyterians who opposed the Anglican insistence that the Liturgy of the Church of England and the Catechism be taught to all pupils," which again resulted in the removal of all clergymen.[76] The change in 1847 occurred under pressure, when an act was passed establishing "a Board of Education comprising the Governor and five members of his choosing." The act stipulated that the board, with the assistance of a fulltime secretary and an inspector of Schools, would be responsible for establishing schools, regulating them, and appointing and training local teachers. During 1846, however, the colonial education grant had been revoked, leaving the colony's government responsible for its own expenditures. The explanation offered was that the grant's purpose of the "civilizing" the former enslaved had been accomplished. Removal of the subsidy hindered expansion and slowed the development of secular and popular education in the Bahamas. Additionally, it "placed educational policy more firmly in the hands of the local regime."[77]

The partnership between the Anglican Church and the government was dissolved in 1847. Government took over the schools that had been operated by the Anglicans, except the Bray's Associates School. However, the church established schools of its own, focusing particularly on areas where black creoles and liberated Africans lived, such as Grant's Town and Bain Town.

Established in 1849, St. Agnes School in Grant's Town was personally financed by Reverend Woodcock, and its students numbered between four hundred and five hundred children by 1854. With funds raised in honor of Woodcock, a second school for black boys, girls, and infants was established in Bain Town at the end of 1849, and shortly after Woodcock's death in December 1851 a third school was built at the western edge of St. Agnes Parish, financed by a memorial fund. Two years later, more than three hundred children were attending the Woodcock schools every day, and many adults attended literacy classes in the evenings. Although Woodcock's schools flourished, he was highly critical of the deficiencies of the Bahamian educational system and bitterly attacked the Board of Education.[78]

Despite weak and underfunded public education, some progress was made. The Educational Committee was able, with the help of the officers appointed, to establish or redesignate twenty-one board schools, including six in New Providence. The most productive was the Boys Central School in Nassau Court, New Providence, established in 1847, with a curriculum consisting of "Arithmetic, Geography, Writing, Spelling, Grammar, Handicrafts, Vocal music and Prayers."[79] Opened to boys and later some girls, the school succeeded in training teachers in the colony. It employed the monitorial system, whereby the more capable older students taught the younger children.

On the downside, Governor Gregory reported that due to the "lack of support from the Assembly" five of the twenty-six schools that operated in 1850 were forced to close.[80] The Board of Education was again dissolved in 1864 and was replaced by a new board comprising the governor and five other members appointed by him.[81] By that date only 1,570 children out of a population of 36,000 attended board schools. A total of £1,920 was the entire bill for teachers, and schools continued to rely on the monitorial system. Although highly criticized in England in the 1840s, it was still used in some of the more remote Bahamian Islands until the 1960s.[82]

Some improvements were made in education between the 1870s and 1890s. In 1875 a revised code for board schools, requiring the use of more rigid curriculum and set examination standards, classified teachers according to ability and laid down rules of conduct for teachers and monitors. Three years later, however, due to massive nonattendance, compulsory education was introduced for children aged between six and twelve years.[83]

Improved standards were evident when George Cole, "father of Bahamian education," was appointed headmaster of the Boys Central School in 1871. Many black, brown, and white boys were educated there, served as monitors, and received a sound basic education. By the early 1890s at least three of the head teachers of the six New Providence schools were nonwhites, as were a number of teachers in the Out Islands. George Cole was appointed inspector of schools in 1881, and a commission was appointed to investigate education in the colony. Besides the perennial problem of truancy, the commission report revealed that in Nassau the Anglicans, through their Sunday schools and day schools at St. Mary's and St. Agnes, educated as many children as did the board.[84]

Up until 1925 secondary education was mostly provided by the churches. Efforts had been made by the Board of Education between 1835 and 1864 to provide public secondary (or higher) education, but because of the lack of funds, these attempts had all failed. King's College School, established in 1835 and mainly catering to elite boys, was founded on the principle of shares and gained the patronage of the king. Its curriculum included classical subjects like Greek, Latin, and French in addition to the three Rs, history, geography, literature, elocution, and composition. The school closed in 1849 due to the lack of finance. Several years later, in 1854, the Grammar School was founded as a replacement for King's College School, but it too failed after ten years. More successful was the Anglican-established Nassau Grammar School organized by Bishop Addington Venables in 1864. The school accepted boys of color and functioned until 1922.

The Methodists also provided secondary education by establishing the Bahamas Collegiate School (the forerunner of Queen's College), which catered to white boys and girls though admitting a few light-skinned nonwhite children. St. Hilda's, a grammar school for girls, was established by the Anglican Church in 1886, closing in 1931 during the Great Depression. It was primarily a white school, but a few fair-skinned brown girls were admitted.[85]

The majority of Bahamian children (black, brown, and white) in the nineteenth and early twentieth centuries obtained only a primary education. They were taught in small (usually one-room) schools that were badly equipped. Teachers for the most part were untrained or poorly trained, and the monitorial system continued to be used until well into the twentieth century. The archipelagic nature of the Bahamas, with settlements on about twenty islands and some of these hundreds of miles from the capital, negatively affected the Out Islands. Some of the more remote islands had no schools or educational facilities. Inspector of Schools Blair reported in 1870: "The Social, moral and intellectual condition of many people in the Out-Islands is a disgrace to any British Colony."[86] The Board of Education's annual report for 1875 noted that there were 10,924 children in the colony. Less than a third of these attended board schools. Those 1,900 pupils in denominational and private schools were taught by teachers who were barely literate, some being described as "unable to write and in one or two cases . . . to read."[87]

This brief account of key social indicators, from labor systems and land tenure to education, provides a profile of the post-emancipation period as difficult in many respects in the Bahamas. Some changes were tried but failed, some were welcomed, and some were resisted. Some were simultaneously advocated by one segment of society but challenged by another. Transition to a functional free society involved major adjustments for everyone, and progress was painfully slow.

2

BAHAMIAN SOCIETY IN THE LATE NINETEENTH AND EARLY TWENTIETH CENTURIES

Class, Race, and Ethnicity

Bahamian society in the late nineteenth and early twentieth centuries was deeply divided by race. Despite the gradual changes that occurred in post-emancipation years, the fundamental structure of the society had not been altered. The black majority remained dominated and socially ignored by the white officials and elite mercantile class. New Providence had an expanding middle class that was largely disregarded by the ruling clique yet in turn looked down on the laboring black classes. This chapter explores the complex structure of this society and the interrelationships between Bahamian classes in the late nineteenth and early twentieth centuries.

Colin Hughes, in his penetrating monograph *Race and Politics in the Bahamas,* refines Braithwaite's hierarchical model, M. G. Smith's refinement of Furnivall's concept of the "plural society," and Lowenthal's theory of "class hierarchy," "social pluralism," and "cultural pluralism."[1] Hughes argues that "the Bahamian experience is too deviant, even from the norm of the British Caribbean, to support any attempt to establish new theory or even to go very far towards endorsing established theory."[2] He finds that within M. G. Smith's distinction of five dimensions of the color concept, *structural color*—that is, "an abstract analytic category reflecting the distributions and types of power, authority, knowledge, wealth which together define and constitute the social framework"—is the most important for examining political change in the Bahamas.[3] Because social change has in fact depended to a large extent on political change, Hughes's contention can be accepted in examining the social history of the Bahamas. He further asserted that among the variables listed by Smith, "wealth has had pre-eminent place in the Bahamas," especially after Prohibition.[4]

Wealth attracted power and authority, and therefore in the Bahamas racial differences were linked to economic relationships. Racial difference rather than class difference "determined the predominant features of social, economic, and political relationships."[5]

Nassau

In analyzing Bahamian society it is necessary to distinguish between that of Nassau, the "miniature metropolis," and that of the Out Islands, rural in character. The Out Islands settlements themselves showed variations and need to be examined separately according to racial distribution.

Of all the nineteenth-century writers, Liston D. Powles, British stipendiary and circuit magistrate, perhaps gave the most penetrating account of social life in Nassau at that time. He vividly described how the society in the mini-metropolis revolved around Government Hill. The governor was the most important man in the colony, and the woman who presided at Government House, whether his wife, sister, or daughter, was recognized as the leader of the colony's social life. Powles explained that Nassau society could be divided into the "Upper ten," those eligible for invitation to Government House on all occasions, and the "lower Upper ten," those invited only on state occasions. Occasionally members of the respectable middle class (whites and browns) were invited to Government House. Despite the recognition of a nonwhite middle class, white society, according to Powles, considered anyone who was admittedly mixed race as belonging to the "lower class."[6] Although the governor and his family formed part of the white elite ruling class, the governor was often critical of the local whites. Governor Ambrose Shea, for example, in commenting on the isolation of the Out Islands, criticized the poorly organized communication system, concluding that the Out Islanders were "slaves of the petty traders."[7] Governor Haynes-Smith also complained to the Colonial Office of the plight of the Out Islanders and the iniquitous truck system.[8] The governor, however, acted as a mediator between the official class, the local whites, the mixed-race, and blacks. Magistrate Powles thought he had Governor Henry Blake's support in the well-known Lightbourne case (discussed later), but when local whites brought specific charges against him, the governor yielded in order to keep the peace.[9]

British officials also formed part of the official white elite sector, including the colonial secretary, attorney general, receiver general, chief justice, stipendiary and circuit magistrates, commandant of police, resident surgeon, and surveyor general. Most of these posts were held by Britons, but occasionally white Bahamians also held high office. In 1897 Ormond D. Malcolm, for example, held concurrently the posts of attorney general, speaker of the House of Assembly, and acting head of the judiciary.[10] As already noted, some of the local elite regarded the British officials with contempt, as was common all over the British West Indies and perhaps elsewhere in the empire. Chief Justice Yelverton in a letter to the *Nassau Guardian* on 4 May 1892 charged that the health of Nassau was threatened by the storage of coal in the Board of Trade premises on Bay Street. He contended that the poisonous gases released by the coal would cause illnesses, among them yellow fever.[11] In reply to this warning, an anonymous writer signing himself "Colonist" sarcastically suggested in the same newspaper that offices for such English officials as Yelverton should be built over coal, and the resultant fever should be "regarded as Providence to clear the atmosphere of the civil service of some officials who are exhaled and emanate from Downing Street."[12] The chief justice regarded the letter as being in contempt of court. When the *Nassau Guardian* editor Alfred E. Moseley, son of its English-born founder, refused to reveal who the writer was, Yelverton fined him £65 and imprisoned him until the fine was paid.[13] The governor ordered Moseley's release after the editor had served thirty hours in jail, and it was reported that more than three thousand people accompanied Moseley from the prison to his home, some in carriages, others on foot. For two days business in the town was wholly suspended.[14]

Such antipathy toward Chief Justice Yelverton and other British officials did not negate the strong loyalty the local creole whites felt to Great Britain and the British Empire. In spite of the Bahamas' proximity to and commercial ties with the United States, the official life of Nassau tended to be more English than American. While newly arrived English people said "how *American* we are in custom, speech and dress," American visitors commented with even greater justice "how thoroughly *English* Nassau is."[15]

Bahamian society was miniscule, and according to outsiders such as Austen Chamberlain, an investor in sisal cultivation, "not very interesting."[16] An Anglican priest remarked, "It is a little kingdom of its own."[17] The leading citizens formed a close-knit group who controlled every aspect of Bahamian life. Everyone who mattered was known to everyone else, and snobbery was rife. Most male members of the elite were engaged in commerce—usually import and export business—or were lawyers, and many held political office, either officially appointed or elected.

One of the most prominent merchants was ardent Methodist R. H. Sawyer, CMG, who had gone into business with his brother-in-law Ramon Menendez in 1849 and had profited handsomely during the American Civil War. He was a founder of the Bank of Nassau and became its president and managing director. Besides being involved in the usual import and export business, he provided coal and water to visiting steamships and was agent for the major shipping lines between Nassau, New York, Cuba, and Miami and for the recently formed Inter-Insular Mail Line. His success in politics assisted him in his successful business enterprises. He entered the political arena in 1858 when he was elected representative for Harbour Island. Eight years later he was the winner of the seat for the town of Nassau and served in the House of Assembly for twenty-four years, gaining the confidence of members and influence over "matters affecting the welfare of the colony."[18] R. H. Sawyer was later appointed to the Executive Council (1869) and Legislative Council (1879).

Several other leading whites had qualified professionally as lawyers, physicians, or dentists or were local publishers, and the achievements of some were outstanding by any standard. The grandson of Michael Malcolm, founder of the Presbyterian Church in Nassau, and the son of Sir Ormond Malcolm, first Bahamian chief justice, Harcourt Malcolm read law at Lincoln's Inn and was called to the English Bar in 1899. Returning to Nassau, he was called to the local Bar and established a practice in Nassau.[19] Another individual who achieved local distinction was Joseph Baird Albury. Born in Harbour Island in 1876, he attended Queen's College high school in Nassau and Wycliff College in Gloucester, England, and qualified as a medical doctor at St. Mary's Hospital in 1902. On returning to Nassau he engaged in private practice and stood in for other doctors from time to time at the Nassau hospital.[20] Dr. J. B. Albury's father, the Hon. Joseph Benson Albury, was also a physician.

Other notable whites served as career civil servants, such as Percy William Duncombe Armbrister, who began as a clerk in the post office in 1878. By 1893 he was warehouse keeper and examining officer (comptroller of customs). He also became a resident justice and served in several districts during the last years of the nineteenth century. Returning to Nassau, he was appointed receiver general and treasurer in 1916 and also served as a member of the Legislative and Executive councils.[21] Among the white merchants was George B. Adderley who, besides exporting sponge, dye-woods, and salt and dealing wholesale in "provisions, breadstuffs, liquor, wines, lumber, shingles and cabinet woods," was agent for the Northern Fire and Life Assurance Company of London.[22]

The white elite maintained a firm grip over the economy and the political and administrative machinery. Further entrenching their power were their close family relationships. Methodist missionary T. Raspass commented that "white people here have intermarried for many generations past and are all related to each other in most instances in several ways."[23] Powles asserted that "the House of Assembly is little less than a family gathering of Nassau whites, nearly all of whom are related to each other, either by blood or marriage."[24] Among the leading white families interrelated by marriage were the Adderleys, Malcolms, Duncombes, and Armbristers. At least one member of each family held a political or administrative office in the late nineteenth and early twentieth centuries.

Members of the white elite of Nassau emulated the upper and middle classes of England. Extremely proud of their British traditions, they appeared somewhat proud, supercilious, and exclusive.[25] They regarded their titled members and those nominated for civic honors as belonging to "the nobility of the Empire."[26] Their society revolved around the official life of the mini-metropolis, various recreational clubs, and the Anglican, Methodist, or Presbyterian churches.[27] Social life for the upper class was a series of private visits, the occasional dinner party, picnics, dances, clubs, and participation in various sports, including cricket, rugby football, polo, and tennis. Powles was critical of the pretensions and style of Nassau's upper crust, the absurd ritual of leaving calling cards and signing the governor's book, the formality of their clothing in the hottest weather, their stuffy afternoon dinners, and the love of gossip. Favorite topics were dress, the "wicked coloured" servants and the "inferiority of the coloured race in general."[28] Neville Chamberlain, who was sent by his father to develop a sisal plantation in north Andros, was glad to escape Nassau's society, which he described as "this weariness."[29] Men of the white elite patronized the old and esteemed Club, where Neville Chamberlain played a game of whist with Chief Justice Yelverton in December 1890. The Club was said to date back to 1742.[30]

There were charitable societies, and the Temperance Movement resulted in various orders led by the Anglican and Presbyterian churches. The elite also administered several charitable trusts, including the Aaron Dixon Charity, which provided for the education of fatherless children.[31] Masonic lodges did some charitable work as well. At least two lodges existed for the elite. The more popular of the two, the Royal Victoria Lodge No. 443, established on

23 June 1837, was under the United Grand Lodge of the Ancient Free and Accepted Masons of England. It met in the Masonic Temple that had been built in 1885 on Bay Street.[32] Also meeting there was the Union Lodge No. 231, which was under the Grand Lodge of Scotland. Some fair-skinned mixed-race men, such as James Carmichael Smith and Elias Dupuch's mulatto sons Joseph and Gilbert Dupuch, were members of the Royal Victoria Lodge. Joseph Dupuch, a successful sponge merchant and building contractor, was architect and builder of the Masonic Temple.[33]

Churches played a significant role in the spiritual and secular lives of the white elite. Membership in the Anglican, Methodist, and Presbyterian churches afforded prestige and status and also supplied the sons and daughters of the elite with a decent, segregated education not offered by the Board of Education's government schools. Members of one of the three churches, the elite attended Christ Church Cathedral, Trinity Methodist Church, or St. Andrew's Kirk, the latter two being predominantly white. In spite of controversy about ritual, some still considered it particularly prestigious to attend Christ Church Cathedral, considered the "Mother Church" of the Bahamas and usually attended by the governor and his family. In 1892 it had seating for 1,200, which included 400 seats free of pew rent for the poor. It was by paying pew rents that whites commanded better seats in the church. Segregation was rigid. Blacks and those of mixed race were encouraged to worship at St. Mary's Chapel-of-Ease for Christ Church, established in 1868, on Virginia Street in Delancey Town, and St. Agnes in Grant's Town, the black section of Nassau.[34]

In line with the Victorian attitude, Edward Churton, fourth Bishop of Nassau, advised his clergy in 1888 on the need for "caution, tact, and discernment," warning them that "the two races cannot be treated as precisely on the same footing." He chided them to aim

> at promoting a better understanding between white and coloured: Denounce tyranny and contumely on the one hand: cheating, tale bearing, and detraction on the other. Yet do not force the two social elements into closed compact that they are not yet prepared for. Be content to see the White children at your school forming themselves into a group apart from the others. Let the coloured people generally for the present, yield the front sittings in their Church to the descendants of those to whom their fathers were slaves. "Liberty, fraternity, and equality" are not, I think, attained at one stroke by an Emancipation Act, not even in fifty years.[35]

Trinity Methodist Church's congregation was mostly white and included well-to-do whites described as "the best in the Colony." Ebenezer, the eastern Methodist Chapel, attracted a mixed congregation, while Wesley's in Grant's Town was almost entirely black.[36] The Presbyterian Kirk, however, remained a church largely for the descendents of the original Scottish founders and disgruntled Methodists, some of whom were among the white commercial elite. A few people of color were also members.

As noted in chapter 1, the Anglican and Methodist churches offered high school education. Some of the affluent families sent their sons to America and England to be educated. In England they attended reputable public schools.

Catering to upper-class girls was St. Francis Xavier's Academy, a fee-paying school established in 1890 by the recently arrived Roman Catholic Sisters of Charity of St. Vincent-on-Hudson, New York. Like St. Hilda's and Queen's College, this school was segregated by color. Very light-skinned girls from well-to-do and respectable mixed-race families might be admitted, but no really black child was acceptable. In the early 1900s a well-respected black West Indian physician, Dr. William Pitt, who had some leading white families among his patients, applied for admission of his two daughters to Queen's College. The trustees, embarrassed, hesitated and then reluctantly admitted them. *Tribune* editor Etienne Dupuch records, however, that "the children took care of the situation. They made it so uncomfortable for the girls that the doctor had to send them away to school."[37]

In the late nineteenth century, West Indian and Bahamian society suffered from the racist ideology common among the local and metropolitan whites. Some of the prejudices and views that whites had formed of the "Negro character" during slavery, although somewhat modified, persisted well into the twentieth century.[38] Moreover, the bias of social Darwinism and its offshoot "anthropo-sociology," which claimed to be based on scientific data, further influenced European and American ideas and caused the hardening of racist attitudes in the latter part of the nineteenth century.[39] Many whites believed that Africans and their descendants were subhuman, ignorant, and savages, and their culture was inferior. In fact the "linking of race and culture led to the wholesale condemnation of African tribes as racially inferior."[40] Travel writers and temporary residents visiting or living in the Bahamas in the latter part of the century echoed these Victorian attitudes. G.J.H. Northcroft, in many ways sympathetic toward non-whites, described them condescendingly: "With the smiling carelessness, the easy inconsequence, and the love of the Spectacular which characterize the 'junior race' they live and laugh, work And Play together—amusing or annoying by turns but always interesting to the Unprejudiced eye and the sympathetic ear."[41]

Local white opinion was evident by the elite's discriminatory policy toward nonwhites. Their mouthpiece, the *Nassau Guardian,* founded in 1844 and run by the Moseley family, was clearly aimed solely at the white population. As late as 1961, the *Nassau Guardian* emphasized in an advertisement in "Editor and Publisher" that it reached practically 100 percent of the *white* population of the Bahamas.[42]

Proximity to the United States, with its deteriorating race relations toward the end of the nineteenth century and its rigid color line, did not help matters. A person known to have "Negro" blood was socially a "Negro" in America. In Nassau, however, as in the West Indies generally, many light-skinned mixed-race people "passed" for white and were accepted by the elite. Writers Ives, Powles, and Stark pondered over the ambiguous color line. Ives considered the question tactfully:

> It is true that the blood of a portion of the "gentry" is said to be perfectly pure. But it is difficult in some cases of mixture to accurately draw the colour line. And it is wise to ignore it, and ask no questions of one's partner in the voluptuous waltz, which might result in banishing the inquisitor from high-toned society. It is at times injudicious to scrutinize closely hair that appears straight or nearly so.[43]

Powles was more direct:

> Although there is plenty of pure unspotted white blood scattered through-out the Bahamas, a good deal of the upper crust of Nassau Society is decidedly mixed . . . though the skins of most of them are fair enough to pass for pure white anywhere in Europe, their African blood would at once be detected by any southerner or West Indian.[44]

Indeed, Powles was bemused as to where the color line should be drawn. He parodied a well-known epigram:

> God bless the white folks one and all, though hark ye,
> I see no harm in blessing too the darky!
> But which is the darky and which the white!
> God bless us all! That is beyond me quite![45]

Within these lines, class remained strictly demarcated by color. A person might not be pure white, but that person's associates would always be "light" or lighter. Indeed, someone who was "passing" would not "associate with anyone a shade darker than themselves." A man who was admittedly mixed race could not even talk to a lady of a "so-called" white family.[46] The white elite or "Conchs,"[47] as white Bahamians came to be known, mostly ignored and had contempt for nonwhites except as domestics or laborers, although there were some notable exceptions. They disregarded almost completely the existence of the black masses.

Nassau's society was segregated in almost every aspect. Color separated the races in housing, secondary education, occupation, and social intercourse. Even boats like the *Dart,* which plied the waters between Nassau and Harbour Island, had sections for whites only. No nonwhites were allowed to enter the *Dart*'s cabin. The racial situation was perhaps not as harsh as in the southern United States with its inflexible and legislated color line, but on the other hand, it did not conform to the West Indian norm. As Northcroft observed: "It lacks the exclusiveness of the former and the equality of the latter."[48]

A few whites and nonwhites might meet on friendly terms for business, but they never entertained one another in their homes. Occasionally, light-skinned mixed-race men who held political or senior civil service positions would be invited to Government House. Marriage of an admittedly mixed-race person to a white was out of the question. It was not uncommon, however, for men of the white elite to have mixed-race or black mistresses or "sweethearts" by whom children might be born. These children, of course, would not be recognized by white society. Being mixed, they would automatically belong to the brown or lower class.

A special brand of justice seemed to exist for whites. Powles may have exaggerated slightly when he said that "even-handed justice between black and white is all but unknown in the Bahamas." But when, for assaulting a black girl, he sentenced the white man and Methodist James Lightbourne to one month's imprisonment without the option of a fine, he caused an uproar. There was a common saying at the time in Nassau that "no white man can go to prison in Nassau." Powles, a Roman Catholic, especially upset the white Methodists, many of whom were members of the House of Assembly. Accused by Governor Blake of stirring up racism, he was forced to resign. The House refused to pay his and his wife's passage back to England. Needless to say, the chief justice reversed Powles's decision against James Lightbourne.[49]

The affair did not go unnoticed by the brown and black population. Led by Alexander Bain, the black developer of Bain Town in Over-the-Hill, New

Providence, they petitioned the secretary of state for Powles's return, arguing that he had "fearlessly and impartially discharged his magisterial duties." They believed that Powles had left because of "a persecution organized against him by persons who do not wish to see justice equally administered towards all classes of the community."[50] Among the petitioners was George A. Bosfield, an educated mixed-race man who worked as a master tailor. When he had been summoned before magistrate Powles in 1887 for violating an act that compelled houses within the city limit to be built in a certain way and had filed information against seventeen of the leading whites for similar offenses, the House of Assembly immediately repealed the act.[51]

Powles could sometimes be tactless. After the Lightbourne trial, he had "indiscreetly" commented that he distrusted Methodists and would not "believe them under oath."[52] Moreover, he had encouraged James Carmichael Smith, a fair-skinned mixed-race politician and postmaster, to establish the *Freeman*, which strove to protect the laboring class while criticizing the white mercantile elite. The first issue denounced the Nassau merchants and accused them of imposing "modern slavery" on the Bahamian poor.[53] This of course infuriated the Methodists. Powles thought he was justified as he had sentenced three black men to prison for assaulting women. Apparently this was a common practice among Bahamian men.[54]

Governor Henry Blake, aware of the antagonism between Powles and the Methodists, commented to the secretary of state at the Colonial Office: "I confess I have received his resignation with satisfaction, and I have strained a point in the financial arrangements to facilitate his departure from the Colony; his continuation in which would have developed a colour question much to be deprecated."[55]

By the 1880s a mixed-race "middle class" had emerged. At that time the mixed-race community of Nassau comprised "a widely-graduated scale of hue and appearance, and a highly complex parentage."[56] The mixed-race sector was not a homogeneous group. Persons belonging to it ranged from black or off-black at the bottom to "light-brown" and "high-yaller" and near white at the top.[57] The lighter-skinned mixed-race persons considered black people inferior, and there was little interaction between them.[58] Some of the lighter-skinned browns sought to "adopt elitist values and attitudes to law and order and social institutions."[59] Oliver Cox stated that the mixed-race person derived prejudice from the "dominant prejudice of whites and strives to identify his racial sentiments with those of whites." He added that the white class is "envied, admired, and imitated religiously but they are never questioned."[60]

Notwithstanding the racist attitudes among the white elite, "a certain degree of co-option of the mixed race middle class was tolerated."[61] Mixed Bahamians might be granted favors, but it usually depended upon "shade"; that is, the lightness of their skin. This counted in West Indian societies and probably accounted for the acceptance of Thomas M. Mathews, a light-skinned mixed-race man who held several judicial posts in the Bahamas and was later appointed clerk of courts and keeper of records in British Honduras in 1871.[62] Similarly, W. E. Armbrister, who was colored, was accepted as "white" by the elite and socialized with them. Perhaps another reason for acceptance of some mixed-race persons was the general lack of wealth among most of the elite. Governor Blake wrote to the earl of Derby in the 1880s stating that the "there are no wealthy men here."[63] An anonymous writer informed L. D. Powles: "They have tastes, habits, airs and manners of rich people, when they are as poor as church mice"—an exaggeration, but apparently most of the mercantile elite were heavily in debt with their properties mortaged.[64] On the other hand, by the late nineteenth and early twentieth century, a fair number of brown and black men had become respectable citizens, successful businessmen, and men of substance. Most were craftsmen, tailors, minor civil servants, or teachers, but a few owned their own small businesses. These included owners and operators of boats and carriages, a livery stable, restaurants, importers of Out Island produce, and at least one sponge broker. Before the white mercantile elite had established a nearly absolute grip on the import and retail trades, there were a few nonwhite-owned groceries and dry goods and liquor stores, mainly in the less central sections of the city.

By the late nineteenth century William Parliament Adderley—born in Grant's Town, the son of Joseph R. Adderley and grandson of Alliday Adderley of Yoruba descent—was a building contractor and a grower, buyer, and exporter of fruits and vegetables. He also owned a dry goods store, the "Big Store" at the southwestern corner of George and King streets.[65] David Patton, described by Powles as "a full-blooded African" was also among the affluent nonwhites. He owned Union Livery Stables on Bay Street, renting carriages out "at all hours, day or night," and supplying drivers. Besides keeping stables, he owned a farm of a few acres and exported oranges.

At the turn of the century William B. North, son of English merchant James A. North and a black mother, owned a liquor business on Balliou Hill Road and was a grocery retailer. He was also involved in the sponge industry as an outfitter. Edward Adolphus Isaacs, born in 1871 of a Jewish father and black mother, opened several restaurants in the late 1890s located on East

Bay Street, Frederick Street, and Market Street, which catered to the brown middle class and poor whites.[66] Tailoring was another popular trade for nonwhite men. Hardly any clothes were ready-made during this time. The well-to-do therefore purchased cloth—a favorite fabric was doeskin—and employed a tailor. In 1901 fifteen tailors were listed in the Nassau directory, all nonwhites.[67] Included were Ernest L. Bowen, who operated his business on George Street, Robert M. Bailey located at Marlborough and West streets, and J. A. Bosfield, whose shop was on King Street, all very close to Bay Street. All "master tailors," these men apprenticed young boys to learn the trade.[68]

Also appealing to nonwhites was printing. Milton Bethel, a mixed-race man, became a printer in the late 1890s after serving an apprenticeship with Alfred E. Moseley, publisher and editor of the establishment paper, the *Nassau Guardian*, established in 1844. Leon Dupuch, father of Etienne Dupuch, was obliged to leave school at the age of nine and also indentured to Moseley. Starting off as a paper boy, he gradually rose to be foreman of the jobbing department. Later he became editor of the *Watchman,* a semi-weekly publication like the *Guardian*, but aimed at the "Outs." According to Etienne Dupuch, the Outs were *not* among the small number who were invited to Government House. Not satisfied with the policy of the *Watchman*, Leon Dupuch launched his own paper, the *Tribune,* in 1903. Choosing the motto "Being Bound to swear to the dogmas of no master," he aimed to run a "free, impartial newspaper aimed at the truth." It became the voice for the leaders of the nonwhite community.[69]

As mentioned, James Carmichael Smith, a light-skinned mixed-race man, also started an anti-establishment newspaper, the *Freeman,* in 1887. Smith served as postmaster general, a post usually reserved for whites. As Neville Chamberlain noted, his appointment to that position by Governor Shea "was much to the horror of the Old fogies."[70] Smith was not actively engaged in the day-to-day operation of the newspaper but was devoted to the struggle for "the complete emancipation of his race."[71] He recognized the inequalities in the society and was determined to be a voice in the fight for justice for the nonwhite and black population. Smith was not afraid to challenge whites. He wrote newspaper articles in the *Nassau Guardian* commenting on statements made by James Gardiner, an English scientist working on a government project. While agreeing with Gardiner that the "metayer system" retarded "improvement" and endorsing "peasant proprietary alongside larger-scale capitalist farming," he questioned Gardiner on the amount of capital available in the Bahamas. Smith also objected to Gardiner's comments on the "laziness and lack of energy of the black population, the standard Victorian Englishman's view of the African: lazy, unmotivated, needing guidance and protection."[72]

James Carmichael Smith was perhaps the most outstanding mixed-race Bahamian man in the late nineteenth century. His father had made money during the blockade-running era and ensured that James received a good elementary and secondary education. James attended the Boys Central School and the Nassau Anglican Grammar School. This was followed by four and a half years at sea, which included visits to Australia and China. The Anglican bishops, especially Edward Churton (1886–1900) took an interest in Smith. Apparently Smith could speak on any topic and was elected to the House of Assembly in 1882 and served until 1896.[73] In spite of the fact that he was a monarchist with loyalty to the British government, Smith was more "radical and outspoken" than previous nonwhites in the House of Assembly. Critical of the mercantile oligarchy's stranglehold on the Bahamas' socioeconomic and political machinery, Smith voted with his conscience, sometimes voting against the government for which he worked, and even if his views on an issue coincided with those of the Methodists, who were ardent supports of the white merchant class.[74]

Smith pushed for changes in the status quo relating to matters that he felt were unfair to the nonwhite majority. He introduced a successful bill in 1885 to regulate the payment of advances and shares to captains and seamen of boats engaged in the sponging industry.[75] A very active member of the House, he served on various committees and presented petitions for various groups, including licensed draymen, who needed a shed to protect their animals.[76] However, individual members could not often succeed in bringing radical change. After the election of 1889, when six nonwhite members were elected to the House, Governor Shea stated that the increase in the number of "colored" members "has little significance as the question of race or colour was scarcely heard of." He added that "those 'coloured' men in the Assembly will not be the cause of any inconvenience."[77]

Members of the mixed-race middle class were bound by their status and the church toward certain attitudes on morality. As in the British West Indies generally, monogamy was the ideal for all classes, but as Lowenthal demonstrated, "each [class] approaches it by a different route and to a different degree." Formal marriage was the norm for the upper class and the brown middle class, who emulated the mating and family patterns of the elite.[78] However, for mixed-race men, as for the white elite, a double standard existed. Provided that they cared for their families, it was not uncommon or overly frowned upon for mixed-race men to have "sweethearts" or mistresses, by whom they had several children. For middle-class mixed-race women, an affair outside marriage was scandalous. As among the white elite, illegitimacy carried a searing social stigma. If a girl of that class became pregnant and did not marry the father of the child, she was ostracized—a terrible fate in such a small community. Her parents, if they could afford it, sent her to the United States, where she remained either forever or at least until the scandal subsided. If she had the baby at home, she was permanently banished from the society of her peers.[79]

James Carmichael Smith was involved in an unfortunate "affair" that shook the city of Nassau in 1893. Stephen A. Dillet, the respectable mixed-race first mate of the lighthouse tender, discovered that his twenty-five-year-old daughter, Elizabeth, was pregnant by the respectable and esteemed James Carmichael Smith, postmaster of the Bahamas. Stephen Dillet insisted that an investigation be made, and this was duly held before the governor and the Executive Council.[80] The love letters implicated Smith, and he was probably the father, but he had no intention of marrying Elizabeth Dillet. It seems that he had hoped to keep her as a mistress and had been willing to settle £150 on her. He had arranged for her to go to New York to have the baby. When questioned by the council, however, Smith denied charges and tried to prove that Miss Dillet was a prostitute. The Executive Council suspended Smith from his position as postmaster and rejected his subsequent petition for reinstatement. Smith then appealed to the Colonial Office in London and was exonerated by the secretary of state, but when he returned to the Bahamas he seemed to have lost his energy and drive. We can speculate that he was sidelined for his views on race pride and his criticism of the white elite. He married in the same year a woman from Yorkshire, who was visiting Nassau at the time the scandal broke. Three years later, in December 1896, he was appointed assistant postmaster at Freetown, Sierra Leone, and was soon promoted to postmaster. Retiring in 1911, he and his wife settled in London, where he became an active member of a circle of Pan-Africanists and contributed numerous articles on a wide range of subjects. He also worked for the British Treasury and Ministry of Food during the First World War. Miss Dillet, on the other hand, was taken from New York, where her father found her in a "House of Refuge," to London. There she was placed in a special home. She vowed not to return to Nassau, as she refused to face the shame.[81] Elizabeth Dillet later married a Colton. She died in England on 19 February 1951 and was survived by a daughter, Elsie Colton.[82]

Among the black masses, such uproar would not have occurred. To the brown middle class, illegitimacy was immoral and irresponsible. To the black laboring population of the West Indies and the Bahamas, "illegitimacy and the mother-centered Home" were not "symptoms of social disorganization." They were "accepted features of folk life."[83] Monogamy was the norm for the black urban working class, but marriage did not necessarily precede the birth of children. Marriage might follow, but not until late in life. Marriage gave the urban working class an "established position in the community."[84] Very little stigma, however, was attached to separation and illegitimacy.

The majority of the black laboring class never became "men of means," but there were exceptions. Neglected and oppressed, members of the black majority were regarded as social outsiders, which paradoxically allowed exceptional blacks who made sufficient money to rise into the nonwhite middle class.[85] Among them, as already noted, were David Patton, Alliday Adderley, and his son, William Parliament Adderley. Others included Leon Walton Young, Thaddeus de Warsaw Toote, and his son, Thaddeus Augusta Toote. Young began as a ship and house carpenter. Later he became a building contractor and land developer. He immigrated to Key West in his twenties and on his return to Nassau he was hired by Charles E. Bethel, a prosperous white liquor merchant and property developer. Young soon earned a reputation as a successful contractor. He also became a land developer, owned a shop, and later became involved in politics and national affairs. Apparently Young tried not to buck the establishment, and some saw him as working with the white elite.[86]

"Sankey," whose real name was Thaddeus de Warsaw Toote, was described as a young man by Charles Ives and others as an entertainer, renowned for his comic duet and dance with his cousin "Moody." By the late 1880s he had almost given up the entertainment business and was engaged in odd jobs. At the turn of the century he owned his own store on the corner of Deveaux and Bay streets.[87] He and William P. Adderley were able to provide secondary and tertiary education for their sons, Thaddeus A. Toote and Alfred F. Adderley. Both studied law at the Inns of Court and at Cambridge University in England and became prominent in their profession and in politics.

As previously mentioned, the black laboring class lived mainly in Grant's Town, Bain Town, and Delancey Town as well as in liberated African villages. Blacks for the most part lived apart from the whites and from the mixed-race middle stratum, whom they distrusted and disliked, partly because of that group's aspirations to "white social norms" in the face of "insurmountable social barriers."[88]

Important secular organizations that were an integral part of African-Bahamian culture were the friendly societies and later the lodges, which were attuned both to African roots and to the sociopolitical aspirations of poor blacks. Some of the early friendly societies emerged within the black community with ethnic affiliations but were tolerated and even encouraged by the regime, which passed legislation to ensure official control. Friendly societies provided a form of insurance for members and their families in times of illness and death. The earliest, the Grant's Town Friendly Society and Eastern Friendly Society, had been established in 1835 to enable industrious persons to provide for themselves against sickness and to defray funeral expenses. By 1910 about seventy-four friendly societies and lodges existed in New Providence and about 160 in the Bahamas as a whole, with a membership of eight thousand. Howard Johnson argues that friendly societies gave African Bahamians an "extended political role" in "response to the formal political structures which were dominated by a small group of white Bahamians."[89]

The financial roles of the early black societies did not receive encouragement but rather opposition from Bay Street and government-oriented banks and the post office savings system. Rumors of mismanagement or malfeasance discrediting the black societies led to tighter controls curtailing their financial operations. Such actions led to the growth of a system of saving and sharing with African roots and an African name: it was known as *asue,* or *su su* in the British West Indies, meaning "partner," or "meet and turn." This system, largely organized by women, involved regular contributions by individuals—small in size but representing a large proportion of weekly wages—which were paid out in relatively large lump sums in strict rotation. The ramifications and sophistication of the system were beyond the understanding of most Bahamian whites.[90]

Essentially, African traditions were present not only in the black population's belief systems but also in their recreational activities. Native Baptists and members of the Pentecostal Church were almost all black and worshiped in "the traditional, evangelical and fundamentalist forms of Christianity with revivalism and spiritualism." Their God was more "accessible to direct persuasion and they believed both in salvation by faith and in the spirit world, where the dead possessed supernatural powers and mediated among the living."[91] Members of the "Shouter Chapel" and Native Baptists demanded active congregational participation, and characteristics of these churches included the "emotional sermon, rhythmic anthem singing traditionally accompanied by hand-clapping and the phenomenon of spirit possession."[92] Visitors to Nassau and the Bahamas who attended ceremonies at the Shouter Chapel in the early 1900s did not understand or appreciate that spirit possession, which appeared disorganized and hysterical, was "the supreme religious experience for the person of African origin." It was "not a haphazard public emotional display" and was not to be ridiculed. In fact, this phenomenon was not unique to the Bahamas black community but was also the custom in black communities throughout most of the Caribbean and in some areas of the United States.[93]

Similarly, most persons of European descent did not understand the beliefs in the practice of *obeah*, "a combination of superstition, medicine and worship."[94] Visiting writers such as Northcroft characterized the African features in their religion as "strange." Whites were fascinated, frightened, and confused by the persistence of belief in obeah. An Anglican priest saw obeah simply as mumbo-jumbo and accused some of the Baptists of being "semi-heathen people . . . living under obedience to their native elders, mixed with a superstitious dread of obeah and witchhcraft."[95] He failed to realize that "it was a complex science, which required the secret skills of special practitioners, obeahmen (or women), if possible native Africans, who consequently commanded great prestige and power in the community."[96] Governor Blake reported in 1886 that the reason for high mortality at the hospital was that people rarely applied for admission until they had "exhausted the means of cure known to the 'Bush' doctors or 'obeah men.' Many were almost dead when they arrived at the hospital."[97] Blacks used bush medicine for nearly every ill, especially in the Over-the-Hill areas and the liberated African settlements. In the Out Islands it was even more prevalent, as they were rarely visited by a physician. It can be conjectured that both white and black Out Islanders knew the medicinal value of particular plants in the remote settlements and used them "with great faith."[98]

African traditions in the belief systems and religious practices of Bahamian blacks and in their recreational activities were intertwined, with common features shared with black cultures of the United States and the West Indies. Music, derived from the ante-bellum slave songs of the United States, and the sacred songs in the early Wesleyan and Baptist hymnals, was very important in the lives of ordinary blacks, not only at church but at work and play and in traditional celebrations of rites of passage—above all, at funerals and wakes. African Bahamians also gathered at sunset on other occasions, such as the eve of Emancipation Day and Christmas, to sing all night. Whereas the wake music was sad, this music was predominantly merry and was called "setting up." After midnight, refreshments of coffee and bread were served. After this came the "anthems," or religious folksongs, not learned from a book but passed down from one generation to another.[99]

Also popular among the black laboring population was the telling of traditional folk tales. Storytelling around fires or on the floor of the huts followed the singing. Tales were divided into "old stories" and fairy tales with roots in Europe and Africa. Many came by way of the American South and the Caribbean proper and concerned animals and their thrilling adventures. The African-inspired B'Booky and B'Rabby stories, popularized in America by Joel Chandler Harris, were favorites. The introduction of the lion and elephant also were probably of African origin. The ultimate trickster B'Nansi or Anansi, the Spider (the name derived from the Twi or Ewe word for spider) was common to West Africa and the Americas. Very often stories and "sings," like West Indian calypsos, referred to recent events and familiar persons. Some were woven and shaped by Bahamian material, involving ships, wrecks, large hauls of fish, or various adventures, or misfortunes such as the cholera in the 1850s and the hurricane of 1866.[100]

The most popular form of entertainment, though, was music and dancing. Clement Bethel has demonstrated that while religious music in the Bahamas was heavily influenced by Africa, it came almost exclusively by way of the United States, whereas secular music, with its emphasis on drumming and dancing, emanated more directly from Africa. Bain Town was one of the prime areas in New Providence where many of the African-derived ring dances were frequently practiced.[101] However, they were also popular in liberated African settlements such as Fox Hill, Gambier, and Adelaide. Some whites, especially priests and missionaries, saw such dancing as un-Christian and sinful, probably objecting to the vigorous hip movements and coupling, which had sexual overtones. An Anglican minister wrote in the mid-1890s: "The black population find their chief delight in dancing of a disreputable character . . . in a dance called 'Gumbai' or jumping dance . . . a species of an African war dance."[102] In spite of moves by the Christian churches to suppress dancing, it remained a favorite form of recreation: ring dances, including the fire dance, described disparagingly by Powles as "no doubt, a relic of savage life," and the jumping dance and ring play, to the accompaniment of a goatskin drum and perhaps a concertina and two pieces of iron.[103]

These dances could be held at any time, and there were special days that called for special celebrations—notably Emancipation Day, as in all ex-slave colonies. This was celebrated throughout the Bahamas on 1 August in various ways in the different settlements. Powles observed that every August some of the Africans elected a queen whose will was law on certain matters.[104] Northcroft noted that "processions, dances and entertainment of various sorts are held and sometimes . . . proceedings are kept up for nearly a week."[105] Friendly societies in Nassau traditionally marched to Government House, the residence of the governor, on the eve of Emancipation Day to present grievances of the past year in hopes of redress. Some also met in downtown Nassau and marched in procession to various churches, including the elitist Trinity Chapel and Christ Church Cathedral, where a special sermon was preached by a Methodist minister or Anglican priest or bishop.[106] According to Cleveland Eneas, people gave thanks in their various churches and afterward gathered on the Fox Hill Parade or the green for speech making and "general merry-making."[107] The festivities included the European plaiting of the maypole and African-inspired dances and singing. Traditional African dishes such as *accara, moi-moi, agidi*, and *foo-foo* were on sale at stalls with other native foods.[108] Fox Hill Day was a spectacle as well as a celebration, drawing whites as well as nonwhites out of Nassau and blacks from Over-the-Hill settlements. People arrived by chartered steamers, in carriages, carts, and small boats, or on foot.[109]

Guy Fawkes night was celebrated on 5 November. This tradition originated in England, commemorating the foiled attempt on the part of Guy Fawkes to blow up the king and Parliament with gunpowder in 1605. Powles recorded that whether the people of Nassau knew its significance or not, every November an effigy of Guy Fawkes was "carried in procession with bands of music and torches, and solemnly hung on a gallows prepared for that purpose." It seems that the white elite participated freely along with the blacks and mixed-race middle class at the Guy Fawkes celebration and at the Christmas Junkanoo.[110]

Powles observed: "About Christmas time they seem to march about day and night with lanterns and bands of music, and they fire off crackers everywhere. This is a terrible nuisance, but the custom has the sanction of antiquity, though no doubt it would have been put down long ago if the white young gentlemen had not exhibited a taste for the same amusement."[111] Traditionally, however, John Canoe, as Junkanoo was originally known, was essentially a black festival of the oppressed, found also in Jamaica, other British West Indian islands, and even in North Carolina. Whites were mostly spectators. Three days' holiday had been given to the enslaved at Christmas, and they celebrated in their own way, usually ending with a "gran dance."[112] Scattered newspaper accounts confirm that the annual celebrations took place, especially in Nassau. By the 1880s the Junkanoo festivities were enthusiastically celebrated. The *Nassau Guardian* gave a vivid account of the December 1886 festivities. Bay Street was brightly decorated and lit, and shops remained open on Christmas Eve:

People were in the streets all night. At midnight brass bands were heard in several directions, while concertinas, banjos, drums, whistles and human voices heralded in the "joyful morn." There were less noisy crackers than usual, while . . . rockets and other fireworks took their place. At 3 a.m. the Market was "all alive oh!" while at six it was difficult to get along Bay Street in front of the Market in comfort. All Nassau seemed to have turned out! Morris dancers or some cousins of theirs had revel for an hour or two . . . and then got too tired . . . or too full of spirits . . . to prosecute their gyrations. . . . The majority of these dancers are graceful in their movements and picturesque in their dress, but others are vulgar and dirty.[113]

Such volatile behavior probably alarmed the elites, just as it dismayed the "respectable" churches, which often were critical of the deleterious effects of the festivities during what they considered a holy and sacred season. In 1890 an Anglican priest bemoaning the poor attendance at Christmas services wrote:

The coloured people have their own ways of holiday-making which certainly do not conduce to the religious observance of the festival. On Christmas Eve and throughout the succeeding night, there is an incessant letting off of crackers, beating of drums and blowing of penny whistles and trumpets, crowds are parading in the streets, and many wearing masks and dressing themselves up in fantastic costumes.[114]

The John Canoe festival was not only a way of letting off steam. It assumed new dimensions in the 1890s when it was used "as an agent of social change and a way of prodding the Government into action."[115] On Christmas Eve of 1890 the conservative *Nassau Guardian* stated that a "masked army" would proceed down Bay Street, to the grounds of the Royal Victoria Hotel, and as was customary, to Government House, "where they will deliver an address to His Excellency the Governor. The members of the army are young mechanics and cigar makers who are desirous of obtaining advice as to whether they shall go to Cuba or wait here for employment."[116]

Pressure from the churches and commercial sections led the government to keep tighter controls over the Christmas festivities. Concerned about the danger caused to the public from the throwing of firecrackers and other explosives, and the indiscriminate use of the horn, trumpet, and other instruments, the government passed the Street and Nuisance Prohibition Act in 1899. The act forbade the firing of crackers and the blowing of horns in public streets but waived the regulations from 6:00 to 10:00 p.m. on Christmas Eve and from 4:00 to 9:00 a.m. on New Year's morning, thus effectively leaving Christmas Day free for religious observances while transferring the main celebrations from Christmas Day to early on New Year's Day.[117] Undoubtedly the Act did much to dampen the spirit of John Canoe. According to the *Nassau Guardian* of 27 December 1899, Christmas Day that year "was ushered in with much less noise than had been customary hitherto."[118]

Town dwellers—that is, those who lived in Nassau, the political, commercial, and social capital—had the best chance of upward mobility. They could obtain middle-class status much more easily than could Out Islanders, although color and race made this difficult. The town offered better educational facilities, and education was a key mechanism for achieving status. Economic success was even more important. In Nassau it was easier to accumulate capital and purchase freehold property and to achieve political power. L. W. Young, for example, had received only a basic education, and yet he rose to become a real estate developer and member of the House of Assembly.[119] Political power and land ownership did not necessarily bring parity of status. Although respected, Young was never accepted by the elite as a social equal. Race and color still ultimately determined class status.

It was easier for whites who left their poverty-stricken Out Island communities to settle in Nassau and eventually to be accepted into white society. Such persons usually were from Abaco, Harbour Island, and Eleuthera. Their numbers were insignificant, and little has been recorded about their lives and subsequent entry into Nassau society. Without money they could not settle in the city center. A small number settled in the eastern suburbs, along with the brown middle class, between Victoria Avenue and the area known as the Pond.[120] Some of them made their homes farther east around Fowler Street, swelling the existent small seafaring village. This settlement of poor whites became the type of community known to some as "Conchy Joe Town." Originally Conch was what the loyalists called the "older inhabitants" of the Bahamas, but it seemed to have lost its earlier meaning. By the late nineteenth and early twentieth centuries, the term Conchy Joe came to mean "poor white."[121] Poor whites at first attended only public schools that were integrated. As time passed and they were able to acquire some capital, they sent their children to the segregated Queen's College high school and other private schools. Conchy Joes despised nonwhites and were in turn held in contempt by browns and blacks. Being white, however, made them acceptable to the white elite as shop assistants and minor civil servants. Some of the more talented individuals became teachers. Many of the men, however, were engaged in seafaring activities, including piloting, fishing, and boat building.[122] Some were tradesmen and craftsmen in other fields. A number of women, such as those from Current settlement, brought with them to Nassau the special art of shell jewelry.[123]

The Out Islands

In order to learn more about these people it is necessary to examine the settlements of the Out Islands. These communities can be divided into three basic types: first, those that were entirely white, such as Spanish Wells in North Eleuthera and Man-O-War Cay, Cherokee Sound, Guana Cay, and Hope Town, all in Abaco (a few black families lived in Hope Town, but whites were clearly dominant and there was no evidence of recent miscegenation); second, biracial communities, such as New Plymouth and Green Turtle Cay in Abaco, Dunmore Town in Harbour Island, and Governor's Harbour, Eleuthera; and third, the all-black ones, which were in the majority.

Divided by race in many cases, the Out Island settlements nevertheless had much in common. All were extremely poor in material terms. Isolation, poor communications, and sheer neglect by the Bay Street clique made for great hardships in the Out Islands. Beset often by droughts and occasionally by hurricanes, Out Islanders were not infrequently on the point of starvation.[124] Having little wealth, most Out Islanders lived at the same economic and social level. The majority of the adult population engaged in subsistence peasant farming. Even in the northern maritime communities, farming was the predominant occupation. Harbour Islanders and the fishermen of Spanish Wells farmed on the mainland in Eleuthera. In the latter island and on the more southerly islands such as Cat Island, Long Island, and San Salvador, some people walked miles to and from their fields. Farming required dedication and backbreaking labor. Crops usually included red and guinea corn (early corn), peas, beans, potatoes, onions, peanuts, tomatoes, cassava, pineapples, and watermelon. Most crops were harvested between January and April. Fishing for scale fish and diving for conch to supplement their diet was also practiced on a small scale by Out Islanders.

A small number of Out Islanders engaged in salt production, an old Bahamian industry. In communities at Inagua, Ragged Island, and Rum Cay, salt was the predominant industry. Salt raking, however, was practiced on a smaller scale at Exuma, Long Cay (also known as Fortune Island), and Long

Island, mainly for local consumption. Inagua's population had dramatically increased from 172 in 1847 to over 1,100 in 1871 because of the development of the salt industry, and increased further by 1882 because of the use of the island as the collecting point for stevedores on passing steamers or seasonal laborers serving Cuba, Panama, and other parts of Central America. Mathew Town, the only settlement in Inagua, was neatly laid out on a grid pattern and was populated by a small number of whites and near-white shop-keepers, who dominated the local trade and credit. The ordinary black Inaguan suffered under the iniquitous truck system. Inagua's salt trade began to suffer from protective American duties in the 1870s and came to an almost complete stop in 1884. Long Cay was the port from which "stevedores and deck hands were hired" originally and became the preferred port of call for the steamers for several years. Inagua's population, especially the ordinary black inhabitants, faced starvation, some subsisting on crabs, the supply of which was rapidly diminishing.[125]

When Powles visited Long Cay in 1886–87, he described it as "the most flourishing" of the Bahamian Out Islands because of the emigrant labor business, when Bahamian men from Long Cay and Inagua were employed by the Atlas Shipping Line and the Mexico Central Railway Company to work as stevedores, deck hands, and railway workers. At first, laborers collected from Long Cay were paid in cash, but as Howard Johnson notes, this practice soon changed and the 'steamship lines had reverted to the practice in truck."[126] While abroad the laborers received half their monthly wages, and on their return the other half was remitted to their agents at Long Cay and Inagua to be paid at the end of their contract.[127] Leading merchants or employers on Inagua and Long Cay had tight control over the laborers. One such man who lived on Long Cay was J. A. Farrington, known as "King John" since "he virtually owns the island and everybody upon it." He was a light-skinned mixed-race person and the blacks were in debt to him, "so that they are not only subjects of, but subject to the autocrat of Fortune Island."[128]

Although blacks were in the majority among the dependent labor force, Howard Johnson argues that the credit and truck systems were not primarily racial in orientation but were key elements in a "machinery of class slavery" in which merchants dominated both whites and blacks. The laboring class was exploited and impoverished, while the merchants were able to accumulate capital. Johnson concludes: "In the Bahamian context, the merchants had replaced slaves with a dependent laboring population susceptible to their economic and social control."[129]

Ship building was also a vital industry; boats were needed in everyday life and to sustain the farming, fishing, and salt industries, the trade with Nassau, and the sponge, turtle, and fishing industries based in Nassau. Boat building was carried on in many of the islands but especially by a small number of men, mainly white, located on the Abaco Cays and Harbour Island, and by a few blacks on Andros and Grand Bahama. Ship building and pilotage were operated on the truck system. Powles noted on a visit to Grand Bahama:

> Shipbuilding goes on here to a limited extent, but owing to the prevalence of the truck system the unhappy workman derives little benefit therefrom. Mr. Adderley (an African gentleman who is both magistrate and schoolmaster) brought to my notice a case in which men building a schooner for a Nassau merchant were being paid, at a low rate of wages, in flour instead of cash. We sampled the flour, which was invoiced to them at one pound sixteen shillings a barrel, and found them not fit for human food.[130]

Because of the credit and truck systems, money was generally scarce. Even in the large settlements such as Dunmore Town in Harbour Island, Governor's Harbour in Eleuthera, and New Plymouth in Green Turtle Cay, Abaco, there was little class distinction or occupational diversification. However, these towns, for the most part older and closer to Nassau, were distinguishable from the rest. All were bifurcated or biracial and had populations of more than a thousand.[131] Each was the educational, political, and commercial center of its district and the seat of the resident justice. The towns contained a post office, a small library, and a rudimentary road system. Dunmore Town and Governor's Harbour had medical doctors in 1897.[132]

Dunmore Town, Harbour Island, with a population of 1,472 in 1891, was the foremost Out Island settlement. Described as "a miniature Nassau," it was prettily laid out on the slopes of a ridge crowned by the commissioner's residence, the second oldest Anglican church, a spacious and imposing Methodist chapel, several churches and lodge halls, many two-storey houses, a good harbor crowded with sailing vessels, loaded wharfs, and warehouses, and a general air of commercial prosperity.[133] Dunmore Town's proximity to Nassau and its success at farming the commonage on the mainland of Eleuthera, gave it an advantage over many other settlements. It traded not only with Nassau, but also directly with ports in the United States. There were some industries as well. In the late 1880s, the Harbour Islanders established three small sugar mills in Dunmore Town to process their sugar cane for the inter-island trade and local consumption.

Dunmore Town exhibited residential and social segregation, perhaps as rigid as in Nassau, though whites and nonwhites were much more equally divided numerically and a higher proportion of nonwhites were of mixed ancestry. As in Nassau, the whites lived near the bay or on the hill overlooking it in houses similar to those in downtown Nassau. Most of the boat owners, substantial farmers, shippers, and shopkeepers were white.[134] The mixed-race and black people lived at the back of the hill or on the lower slopes to the south in small one-storey houses or simple wooden shacks raised on limestone rocks. Some owned small boats or were craftsmen or independent small farmers. The majority, however, were unemployed or were laborers or mariners working for white employers. Except for a small number of Baptists, the races shared worship in the settlement's Anglican and Methodist churches, although the seating in the latter was rigorously divided. Educationally, whites were better off than nonwhites. Public school education was nominally integrated, but in practice whites took advantage of the several private schools and were generally better educated than their nonwhite fellow "Brilanders."

Powles recorded a notorious event at Harbour Island in 1885. Five nonwhite men—Israel Lowe, John D. Lowe, David Tynes, William Alfred Johnson and Joseph Whylly—all of them faithful members of the Methodist "chapel" who had contributed both "money and manual labour to the construction of the chapel—quietly entered the white peoples" door and walked up the aisle. The service was discontinued and the men were prosecuted the next day before the resident justice, who fined them a pound each, with the option of imprisonment, for "brawling." The case was not appealed, and it was many years before the church was desegregated.[135] As already noted, segregation was also practiced on the Harbour Island–Nassau mail boat, the *Dart*.

Governor's Harbour, in the center of Eleuthera, had originally consisted of a huddle of poor cottages on Cupid's Cay, but after it was made the seat of the resident justice and the pineapple industry developed, the cay was joined to the mainland to form a double harbor. It was a biracial community and its inhabitants practiced racial segregation. The poorest blacks and some mixed-race people still lived on Cupid's Cay, but the richer inhabitants established themselves on the mainland. The houses of whites were scattered along a slope that rose about 150 feet above the harbor. Powles described it in 1887: "The houses on this hillside are white and clean, standing each of them in its own garden and the whole place . . . looks very like a pretty little English watering-place."[136] Governor's Harbour also had an Anglican Church and Methodist and Baptist chapels. Blacks attended the latter. In some ways Governor's Harbour could be considered the unofficial capital of Eleuthera, especially because of its successful agricultural industry in the last quarter of the nineteenth century.

New Plymouth on Green Turtle Cay, Abaco, with a population of more than fifteen hundred persons in 1885, was the second largest biracial township in the Bahamas. It flourished in the late nineteenth century during the heyday of pineapple cultivation. In 1890 nearly a million pineapples (as well as a consignment of oranges) were shipped from Green Turtle Cay to the United States, and in the same year the Munroe Company established a canning factory that shipped more than three thousand cases of pineapples a year to England.[137] Practically all the businesses, shops, and boats in New Plymouth were owned by whites, while nonwhites were ordinary mariners and agricultural laborers, many of them working at sea or on the mainland of Abaco for months at a time. The community in the 1880s had a generally prosperous air, despite disparities of wealth and power and rigid customary segregation.[138]

As in the other biracial settlements, the whites lived together in the best locations—beside the harbor in whitewashed or brightly painted stone or wooden buildings—while the black and mixed-race people lived on the fringes, including in the swampy and less healthy area at the head of the township creek, crowding into small, clean, but rudely constructed huts with insufficient rooms. The government school was integrated (and coeducational) and maintained relatively high standards, though it seems to have reached only a fraction of eligible children. All sections of the community worshiped at the same churches, but segregation by seating was as rigid as that practiced in Harbour Island. The Methodist Church was the largest church and was attended mostly by whites, with the nonwhites seated at the rear. The Anglican Church had a larger black and mixed-race membership, but the whites enjoyed the best pews at the front and on the north side.[139]

As a scholarly visitor, T. Wesley Mills, noted in an article published in 1887: "The two races co-operate in perfect harmony for general good; the Black accepting an inferior *status* in the society without a murmur."[140] Though Mills's assertion was no doubt exaggerated—the nonwhites were quiescent probably because of the greater polarization of the races and the socioeconomic supremacy of the whites, which was even less open to challenge than in Harbour Island and Nassau—there does seem to have been little overt racial tension in New Plymouth in the 1880s and 1890s. The only riot reported at Green Turtle Cay in the late nineteenth century was a general protest against the government following the seizure of a wrecking prize, the schooner *Pajaro* in July 1880, for a breach of the revenue laws. When the schooner was taken over by the local customs officer, a mixed crowd of blacks and whites went on board, removed the sails, "and committed other acts of lawlessness" in a vain attempt to prevent the vessel from being carried to Nassau for adjudication in the Court of Vice Admiralty.[141]

Racial prejudice and color awareness were strong everywhere in Eleuthera although considerable miscegenation had taken place in the past. Social stratification was based not only on race but also on social attitudes and associations. Light skin colour in Eleuthera was an important attribute, especially where marriage was concerned.[142] At the Current settlement, Stark described the people as near-whites, or "octoroons or quadroons."[143] Early in their history the people of Current settlement segregated themselves. Whites and light browns lived in the mainland settlement, while the blacks lived on Current Island. The two settlements were separated by a narrow but rough tidal channel.

In all-white settlements, such as Spanish Wells, Cherokee Sound, Man-O-War Cay, and Hope Town, separation of whites from nearby black settlements or visiting black fishermen or tradesmen was strictly observed. Governor Haynes-Smith noted that in these white settlements, the people could trace their ancestry back 150 years. In biracial settlements they refused even to be buried in the same burial ground with those of the black race.[144] Powles observed of the white Abaconians: "Their one idea has been to keep the stream of their white blood pure."[145] Stark felt that racial feelings in Spanish Wells and in other parts of North Eleuthera and in Abaco were perhaps as strong as those in the southern United States.[146] Long Island, which is more than sixty miles long, had a more mixed population. Once cotton had failed completely, many of the white planters were too poor to emigrate and remained in small hamlet-sized scattered settlements resembling family yards, named for themselves. After emancipation the former enslaved either stayed nearby, taking over their former owner's land and lifestyle when left on their own, or moved in their family units to another location on one of the island's deserted plantations. Long Island therefore developed as an island without real townships except for Clarence Town, formerly known as Great Harbour. The descendants of former masters and the former enslaved lived similar lifestyles: growing crops, raising animals including sheep and goats, raking salt, and building boats for fishing and carrying their provisions, salt, and stock to Nassau.

Generally there was an absence of a deep-rooted prejudice against mis-

cegenation, resulting in a myriad of complexions and complex family relationships. Dame Ivy Dumont recalled that both of her grandmothers were
"dark" with "crinkly hair, and both of them married men who were almost
white."[147] There were, however, small pockets of white settlers living at Mangrove Bush, Grays, and Salt Pond, who did not mix socially with brown and
black persons. Several settlements were mixed, such as Simms, Deadman's
Cay, and Clarence Town, while others remained all black, such as Seymour's
and Burnt Ground in the north, and Dunmore's and Hard Bargain in the
south.[148] The colour question was not a burning issue in all-black settlements, such as those on Long Cay, Rum Cay, Watlings Island (since 1926
known as San Salvador), Exuma, Cat Island, Andros, and Mayaguana. Most
people were laboring class, either farming or sponge fishing for a living. At
Mayaguana the population was entirely black and very poor, surviving on
"the barest means of subsistence." A few settlements, such as Albert Town,
Long Cay, had a white resident justice and his family and a white priest or
missionary. These figures were respected, almost revered, and were considered important whether white or of mixed race. The black Out Islanders,
nevertheless, were aware of color and would not graciously welcome a dark
mixed-race or black person as their commissioner.[149] These racial attitudes,
similar to those in Nassau, molded the Out Islanders' attitudes toward marriage and kinship ties. The family unit was an important facet of Bahamian
life in all three types of settlements. From the available evidence, it seems
that the most common household was the nuclear family type.

It was customary in all-white settlements, such as Man-O-War Cay and
Hope Town, for girls to marry very young, between fourteen and sixteen, but
sometimes as early as thirteen. In biracial settlements, it seems that whites
married a little older, usually in their late teens and early twenties.

The majority of whites were endogamous, marrying within the community to someone they had known all their lives. It was not uncommon for
the couple to be closely related. In fact first cousins often married in Hope
Town, Abaco, and second cousins were considered to be "distant family" in
Green Turtle Cay. An Anglican priest remarked of the marriage patterns of
Hope Town in 1897: They do "not go for the most part beyond the settlement as such names as Russell, Roberts, Albury and Malone occur again and
again."[150]

Dr. Clement Penrose, one of the Johns Hopkins University team who visited the Bahamas in 1903 on behalf of the Geographical Society of Baltimore,
attributed the "shocking condition of degeneracy of Hope Town" to the constant intermarrying of the white inhabitants. Penrose observed that in 1903,

Hope Town had about a thousand pure whites and twelve nonwhites. There was no evidence of racial intermarriage. Almost all the white inhabitants were closely related and descended from a loyalist widow, Wyannie Malone, who arrived in Hope Town in 1785 with her four children. New blood was brought in early by "Joe" John Albury of Harbour Island and Nathaniel Key of St. Augustine, Florida. Thereafter, their offspring intermarried so closely with the descendants of Wyannie Malone, that in a short time "the relationship between the three families was very close." By constructing a diagram of the Malone family tree with the assistance of older inhabitants and the clergy of the settlement, Dr. Penrose asserted that there was indeed an "enormous amount of intermarriage between the various members of the Malone, Russell, Albury and Key families in Hope Town." He concluded that "early in the history of the Malone family . . . indications of degeneracy were absent; but they began in the fourth generation and rapidly increased thereafter until they culminated by the presence of five 'idiots' in one family."[151] The position was not much better at Spanish Wells. Tenaciously retaining their racial integrity, the Spanish Wellians persistently intermarried, scorning the mainland blacks though themselves limited in number. In 1903 Dr. Penrose claimed that this close intermarriage had resulted in an unusually large number of locomotor-ataxia, cataracts, and other eye diseases. Dwarfism was also common. Penrose added: "We noted, also, that the mental acumen of many of the inhabitants of this place was rather low."[152]

In the light of modern scientific knowledge, Dr. Penrose may have exaggerated the effects of close intermarriage in Hope Town and Spanish Wells. Some diseases named, such as mental illness and dwarfism, were indeed hereditary. Leprosy, also found there, was infectious or contagious in origin, with a very long incubation period, not strictly genetic. Locomotor-ataxia, which caused an unsteady gait in children, could be due to hereditary ataxia but in adults was more likely the result of tertiary syphilis. Similarly, some eye diseases, such as cataracts, in young people could be hereditary but sometimes was also caused by syphilis.[153]

More for economic than cultural reasons, tightly knit family units based on the nuclear household with large numbers of children were the norm for Out Islanders. Blacks, who usually married later than whites, considered it taboo to marry a kinsman. Blacks rarely married relatives, and even then, such a marriage was more likely (in order to "marry up" to a person of lighter complexion) among mixed-race Bahamians than among blacks. It has been said that the Tynes, Hanna, and Heastie families, light-skinned mixed-race people at Pompey Bay, Acklins, intermarried for several generations in order to keep their color "up." The Honourable Arthur Hanna, descended from the Pompey Bay community, admitted that Pompey Bay people "held themselves as a community as the whites of Acklins, people acted white."[154]

Orry Sands revealed that her aunt, who was from Pompey Bay and was very light-skinned, married a Rolle, "a black fellow" who was in the grocery business. Despite this, her husband Rolle could not "stay in Pompey Bay," so she had to leave that settlement. William Aranha, surveyor general, reported in March 1933 that "many complaints were made about the high handed section of the Pompey Bay people . . . who have attempted to eject all persons not citizens of Pompey Bay." Father Knowles, rector of the District of Long Cay, which included Acklins and Crooked Island, suggested "that certain vacant crown land in the vicinity of Pompey Bay should be reserved to the exclusive use of the inhabitants of Pompey Bay." Knowles described the people of Pompey Bay "as being of a somewhat better class than the general run of the inhabitants of Acklins and Mr. Aranha who has made surveys in the locality is inclined to agree with that view."[155]

Courtship for white, mixed-race, and black people on the Out Islands was formal and not dissimilar to custom in Nassau. Once a suitor's parents approved of the match, he would write to the girl's parents, requesting visiting rights. If he was illiterate, he would employ a competent scribe for his formal missive as well as for any love letters he chose to send. Initially, virginity was highly valued; sexual relations were reserved for those at least betrothed. Marriage gave both the man and the woman a new status in the community. Children were proof of virility in the men and fertility in the women. Marriage was considered permanent and final except in extreme cases. Divorce, which was extremely difficult to obtain anywhere in the Bahamas, was virtually unknown in the Out Islands. Husbands often left wives temporarily or for long periods to go on a voyage or work projects, but even if men were gone for years, such separations were not considered a step toward divorce or a license for promiscuity. If a couple separated by mutual agreement and lived apart, they were still considered by their community to be married.[156] "Outside" (i.e., "illegitimate") children and unmarried mothers were more common in all-black and mixed communities than in all-white settlements but were nowhere as numerous as throughout the British colonies in the Caribbean proper and in the Bahamas itself in the mid-twentieth century.

Women with illegitimate children often had difficulty finding a husband, and if they married, the "outside" child might be raised by a woman's mother or another female relative. Illegitimate children were not usually brought to a new union, and some families therefore were headed by women.[157] Though no precise figures are obtainable for Bahamian consensual or common law marriages, such arrangements were uncommon, largely limited to those who could not marry or remarry formally. There were, though, a good many single mothers, especially in the black and mixed settlements (as in Nassau and the Caribbean generally), and the official figures disguised or hid a virtual double standard of sexual morality.[158] A young man was almost expected to have premarital sex, and many married men had extramarital love affairs, some even establishing an extra-residential union with a single, separated, or widowed woman.[159]

The formal commitment to monogamy, the predominance of marriage, and the stigma attached to illegitimacy were no doubt influenced by the churches. The Methodists successfully challenged the primacy of the formerly established Anglican Church in the all-white and mixed northeastern settlements, while in the black Out Island communities the Baptists were by far the most successful with their emphasis on congregational participation and practices with which people could identify. In Cat Island an Anglican priest reported in 1894 that the island "is a hotbed of Baptists whose 'leaders' are coloured and uninstructed."[160]

By the 1890s virtually all Out Islanders were nominally Christian in predominantly black and Baptist settlements. However, African-rooted traditions were still strong, especially on Cat Island and Andros. Powles noted on a visit to Cat Island in 1887: "The people here are very superstitious, and what is called 'obeahism' is very common among them. Anglican priest, Reverend F. Barrow Matthews, Rector of All Saints Parish on Andros in the 1890s, after visiting at least ten stations along the coast, commented that the people were very superstitious."[161] Bishop Henry Churton, visiting Andros in 1902, recorded that the year had been marked with "a bad outbreak of heathenish practices.... The old African superstitions die very hard."[162] Authentic obeah practices were also common in mixed settlements but not noted in all-white communities.

The use of bush medicine was common in all Out Island settlements and was vital because of the lack of doctors and formal medicine. The most vivid account was given in Amelia Defries's account of "Aunt Celia" of Eight Mile Rock, Grand Bahama, who picked her medicine in the bush, freshly boiled it for each patient, and boasted that "nobody never dies of my treatment."[163] Aunt Celia also acted as midwife, as did many of her black counterparts in the Bahamas and the Caribbean generally. In fact, much medical work was done by missionaries, clergy, or resident justices stationed in the settlements, as no clinics or hospitals existed in the Out Islands at this time.

Materially, the Out Island settlements were similar. Most adults farmed; some fished. Children attended primary schools, usually leaving at around the age of twelve or thirteen in order to assist their parents in the fields. Some learned a craft or trade. All shared a common language, although there were certain settlements where people spoke with peculiar pronunciations. Powles observed that the people of Hope Town spoke with a "pronounced Irish brogue."[164]

Some Out Island communities had peculiar and outstanding characteristics of their own. Duncan Town, Ragged Island, situated on an isolated three-square-mile cay over 200 miles from Nassau and only 60 miles north of Cuba, although extremely poor in monetary terms, was self-sufficient. Powles in 1886 found it a prosperous and industrious settlement of almost four hundred people, predominantly black and living under the easygoing leadership of the white descendants of their former owners, the Wilsons, and a white Welsh-born resident magistrate. Ragged Islanders farmed and ran stock on the neighboring cays, and the whole community made a modest profit from the export of salt from their excellent salina to the United States. Locally, they bartered salt and palmetto straw mats and baskets, for which their women were famous, with other Out Islands and New Providence. Ignored by the government, for the most part Ragged Islanders, intrepid mariners and pilots, were ideally located for salvaging the numerous wrecks along the ragged edges of the Crooked Island passage and the Old Bahama Channel. They also carried on an active smuggling trade with nearby Cuba.[165]

Other outstanding settlements were Port Howe in Cat Island and Tarpum Bay and Rock Sound in Eleuthera. Port Howe had a population of more than five hundred in 1888 and was described by an Anglican clergyman as a "prosperous settlement."[166] It was thriving and contained relatively well-to-do people owing to its fertile soil and enormous pineapple crops. Tarpum Bay and Rock Sound were sustained by agriculture, especially crops of pineapples and tomatoes. In addition, Rock Sound boasted a pineapple preserving factory and an excellent harbor. Both had small boat-building industries.

Environmental factors and limited economies led to similarities in important events and celebrations, including funerals, weddings, Christmas, New Year's Day, and Emancipation Day. None however, were as elaborate as in Nassau and its suburbs. Christmas in particular was a special time of merrymaking in nearly all the islands. The all-black and biracial settlements celebrated Christmas in a similar way to the Nassauvians. For Androsians, Christmas was one of the few occasions when most of the men and boys were at home. Just before Christmas whole families visited Nassau, accompanying the men at the conclusion of the last sponging voyages of the year. While the men disposed of their sponges, the Andros womenfolk did their modest Christmas shopping before returning home.[167]

On Christmas Day, 1893, Neville Chamberlain wrote to his sister Ida in England from his plantation near Mastic Point, Andros: "Great crowd in all their best clothes with banners flying and great noise of drums and fifes advance up the road from the creek. About half way up a shower soaked them. This did not dampen their enthusiasm." The crowd visited the Chamberlain estate, coming onto the piazza, the band playing until their host gave them three-penny and six-penny bits, which raised their enthusiasm to the highest pitch. They then brought the band closer still, whistling, stamping, and banging and did a slow march around the piazza, after which they danced. Chamberlain told his sister that a (traditional) "Rushing" meeting was being held by the blacks in another settlement at the nearby Mastic Creek on New Year's Eve.[168]

In other islands the Christmas and New Year's festivities varied slightly. In Eleuthera Junkanoo was held, but in some settlements the chief amusement was an entertainment given by the various lodges on Christmas Eve. In 1897, for instance, the Gregory Town Lodge of the Grand United Order of Odd Fellows, gave a program including "dialogues, recitations, addresses, songs and instrumental music before a large and attentive audience which included the Resident Justice and his wife."[169] In the biracial settlement of Green Turtle Cay, Abaco, New Year's Day was celebrated by the appearance of "Old Skin" or Bunce, who was carried in a wheelbarrow covered in canvas along the streets of the town, where persons of both races turned out. A hawker preceded the barrow, telling stories of how Bunce was caught. Money was collected, after which Bunce, who was clothed in a tatterdemalion (ragged and torn cloth) or ragamuffin costume of paper and rags, danced for donors. No one seems to know the origin of this curious character, but he seems to be an amalgam of masked and costumed figures found in West Africa and rural England.[170]

Not surprisingly, Emancipation Day on August 1 was not celebrated in the all-white settlements, but many black and biracial communities marked the day with celebrations similar to those in New Providence. In Cat Island in 1888, Rev. Barrow Matthews reported that harvested produce and fruit were used to decorate the church—seemingly combining the celebration of emancipation with the older cropover festival from Africa, along with the harvest festival tradition then being revived in the Church of England.[171] At Harbour Island in 1890 it seemed that the entire black population, smartly dressed and led by the Friendly Society and Lodge, congregated on the whites' harborside area of Dunmore Town to celebrate Emancipation Day.[172]

Despite the differences and cultural distinctiveness of the two ethnic groups, the majority of Out Islanders of both races shared similar lifestyles. Unsophisticated, conservative, and for the most part lacking in a good formal education, they mainly farmed and fished for a living. Notwithstanding their equality of poverty, the whites segregated themselves completely from blacks, not only by forming all-white settlements but also socially within biracial communities. The intense racial feeling and deep-set prejudice kept the two races separate. Their villages were stratified, the whites dominating every aspect of life, their ideas on race akin to those in Nassau, the social, commercial, and political capital of the Bahamas.

In Nassau the white mercantile class dominated and did little to assist either the white or black Out Islanders or the New Providence nonwhite population. Nevertheless, the brown middle class and some of the black laboring class, considered social outcasts, were gaining in wealth and position. Most of the population, however, including Out Island whites, suffered from endemic poverty, poor educational opportunities, and oppressive labor systems. While rapid industrialization and modernization were taking place in North America and Europe, a pre-industrial subsistence economy lifestyle lingered on in the Bahamas until well into the twentieth century.

3

GRADUAL CHANGES IN THE BAHAMAS, 1880–1914

During the latter part of the nineteenth century worldwide advances in scientific and technological research resulted in many changes that would transform twentieth-century life. Especially significant were the new developments in the fields of electricity, communication, and transportation. The electric light patented by Thomas A. Edison in 1880 heralded the new age of electricity. Bell's telephone in 1876 and Marconi's invention of the wireless in the 1890s, followed by his transmittal of messages across the Atlantic in 1901, began a new era in communications. The French Lumière brothers' development of the cinematograph in 1895 and the subsequent development of the motion picture would profoundly affect twentieth-century life. In the sphere of transportation, the internal combustion engine made the manufacturing of the automobile possible, while Wilbur and Orville Wright's successful flight in an airplane in 1903 spelled the beginning of revolutionary changes in transportation.

These new inventions and improvements were felt in the larger towns of Great Britain. As the head of an immense empire that covered about a quarter of the earth's land surface and included a quarter of humanity, England at the turn of the century still held center stage in the world's economy.[1] Its industrial production, trade and shipping, and immense investment overseas sustained its economic and financial power. Threatening England's supremacy were Germany and the United States, two countries that had industrialized rapidly and had capitalized on the technological advances. England, on the other hand, was slow in adapting to the new developments in technology and in the chemical and electrical industries.[2] Improvements were made in education, and the conditions of the poor were bettered. The Old Age Pension Act in 1908 and the National Insurance Act in 1911, introduced by the

Liberal Party elected in 1906, were steps toward raising the standard of the working class in England. Also significant during these years was the growth of socialism, the expansion of trade unionism, and the founding of the Labour Party in 1906.

Important changes were taking place within the empire as well. The death of Queen Victoria followed by the ending of the Boer War in 1902 concluded an era of "exuberant imperialism."[3] Still avidly loyal to Britain, the dominions in the early twentieth century, themselves witnessing increasing industrialization and urbanization, also experienced the growth of nationalism. Canadians, Australians, and New Zealanders were demanding more freedom in the development of their own national institutions but within the empire. During this period India advanced to representative but not responsible government, and between 1908 and 1910 the Union of South Africa was established. By 1914 the "greater colonies" had begun to work out a new relationship with Great Britain that would in time develop into the British Commonwealth.[4]

In contrast to these advances, the British West Indies lagged far behind both economically and constitutionally. The acceleration in industrialization reached the major towns and cities, but the growth of nationalism and democratic ideas for the most part was much more gradual.[5] The British Caribbean, suffering from a legacy of slavery and the indifference of the home government, entered the twentieth century in dire economic straits and still largely dependent on agriculture. Free trade had destroyed the privileged status of West Indian sugar on the world market, and by the turn of the century the West Indies had become a "forgotten derelict corner of the world."[6] The Bahamas, which never grew sugar commercially, was even worse off. Except for the occasional boom in its economy brought on by external events, such as the American Civil War, it depended on poorly managed agriculture and sponge fishing. It was one more colony of no particular importance.

The Economy

The traditional industries still sustained the Bahamian economy. Bahamian laborers, for the most part employed under the truck system until the end of World War I, lived in a society that had little money in circulation. Wage labor, however, was increasing. The stevedores who worked on the cargo steamers serving the West Indies and Central America were paid in cash. Similarly, men engaged in the lumbering industry at Wilson City, Abaco, and the emigrants who lived in Key West and Florida realized their earnings in money. The latter usually sent a portion of their pay home to relatives.

While the Bahamas was slowly becoming a cash economy, a few improvements were made in the communications system and the utility and health services of Nassau. However, these did not appreciably affect Out Island life and only slightly touched the lives of the majority of Nassauvians. Increasing numbers of Bahamians were exposed to West Indians and to the hardening discriminatory practices in the southern United States. The launching of the anti-establishment newspaper, the *Freeman*, and the Anglo-African League in 1887 revealed the growth of racial consciousness in the Bahamas, especially in Nassau. Several incidents during the 1880s demonstrated dissatisfaction with the status quo, if not protest, among the nonwhite middle class. The establishment of the Roman Catholic Church in the Bahamas, with a more enlightened view of segregation in its churches, did little to stimulate any appreciable change in the rigidly color-conscious Bahamian society.

In 1880 about 75 percent of the population lived on the Out Islands and were involved in sponge fishing and agriculture. The sponge industry flourished in the late nineteenth century, peaking between 1890 and 1910. A mainstay in many Out Island communities, sponging supported their fragile economies from 1850 to the 1930s. But it was desperately hard work even for the most fortunate fishermen, requiring long absences from their families and barely above a subsistence occupation even when the world market prices were relatively good. As noted in chapter 2, the sponging industry was operated on a credit and truck system. The governor, writing to the secretary of state for the colonies, described it thus: "but the whole community have been for many years tied and bound by a system of payment by truck that extends to every part of the colony and leaves the cultivator or sponger in a position of practical slavery."[7]

Until the great blight of 1938–39, the Bahamas sponge grounds were the most productive in the world, exporting over a million pounds a year by 1900, with a peak of almost 1.5 million pounds in 1905. Bahamian sponges had to compete in Europe with Mediterranean production and in the United States with the sponging grounds in American territorial waters off Florida, centered on Key West, Tampa, and Tarpon Springs. The wholesale price was driven down by competition among the all-black Bahamian sponge fishermen from different islands, who at the peak in 1900 constituted a third of the total male work force. This tendency to competitive overproduction was expertly managed by the Nassau broker-exporters. Some were Bay Street merchants, but most were Peloponnesian Greeks whose sponging and fishing traditions went back countless generations and who enjoyed family connections in the metropolitan trading houses.[8] As L. D. Powles disclosed in

1888, however, those who most cruelly exploited the ordinary sponge fisher-men were not the foreign-born brokers but the native sponge outfitters and boat owners (mainly white), who were "as gods, reaping where they have not sown" and who enforced the worst iniquities of the truck system on their poorest non-boat-owning black mariner compatriots.[9]

In the latter part of the nineteenth century the pineapple industry, also operated under the credit and truck system, flourished and peaked in 1892. In that year a total of 665,332 dozen pineapples were exported, valued at £56,061. Additionally, just over 100,000 dozen pineapple slips were exported to Hawaii, which had been acquired and developed by the United States. The development of the pineapple industry in Hawaii, bolstered by the protectionist McKinley Tariff of 1897, almost destroyed the export of fresh Bahamian pineapples. However, the pineapple magnates saved the day by setting up factories to process, preserve, and can the fruit for a wider and longer-term market. The pioneer in this field was J. S. Johnson, a member of the House of Assembly, who formed a company and set up a canning factory in Nassau. By 1900 the factory and its branch plants in Eleuthera were processing as many as seventy-five thousand cases of canned pine-apples in a season.[10] A successful factory was also established in Eleuthera by C. T. Sands.

Another industry was the growing of the sisal plant (*Agave rigida sisilana*) introduced by the colonial secretary C. R. Nesbitt in 1845. It was not, how-ever, until the governorship of the "progressive" Sir Ambrose Shea (1887–94) that sisal and hemp production was strongly promoted to take advantage of seemingly ever-rising world demand. Shea had implicit faith and optimism that he could transform the Bahamas' economy through developing the new industry. In 1889 he had legislation passed to encourage the cultivation of the fiber plant.[11] He persuaded the Out Islanders at several public meetings that sisal, which had been considered an "obnoxious weed," could become a commercial crop, and that it was a means of escape from the "thraldom of the credit and truck system."[12] At his urging, Crown lands were offered to 'poor settlers' (mainly black) in ten-acre lots at five shillings an acre: the land would become freehold property if it was developed in sisal within ten years. In contrast, huge acreages were either sold or leased on extremely generous terms to companies and individual investors (mainly white), including the secretary of state for the colonies, Joseph Chamberlain, whose son Neville Chamberlain, the future prime minister, managed the twenty-thousand-acre family estate near Mastic Point in Andros for several years.

By 1890 the sisal industry had become firmly established, and in the following year about 48,000 acres (excluding the 20,000 leased by Joseph Chamberlain) had been allotted for fiber cultivation, with more than 6,000 acres already planted. Machines had been imported to clean the fiber, although much was done by hand.[13] By 1893 some 70,000 acres of Crown land had been acquired for the industry, of which nearly 12,000 acres were already under cultivation. Sisal was growing nearly everywhere, and smallholders received small grants of land to participate in the boom.

In the spring of 1894 Shea visited the Chamberlain plantation, "previously a wilderness," in which £50,000 had been invested. He noted that 5,000 acres were already under cultivation. He opined that the "fine plantation" was "now a settlement of animated life and industry with a happy population."[14] Anglican priest Rev. F. B. Matthews was also enthused at the progress and the "new state of things" at Mastic Point. The developments included new houses, fine roads, a railway laid out from the coast for several miles into the forest, and a jetty. He stated that Chamberlain had managed to reduce excessive drinking and to close unlicensed grog shops and had opened a general store and a savings bank for the people. Matthews noticed a remarkable change in the demeanor of the people.[15]

Neville Chamberlain and his brother Austen held the usual views common to Europeans regarding nonwhites, especially the black laboring class. Neville Chamberlain called on James Carmichael Smith, the mixed-race postmaster, on 25 November 1891 and described him as "very pleasant and intelligent." However, he and his brother saw black-skinned people as "feckless, childlike," and "thriftless."[16] Austen Chamberlain, writing to his father Joseph in January 1891, stated: "The blacks are a noisy, light-hearted too often thievish and immoral race but are not dangerous unless drunk."[17] He added that the reputation of idleness "is much exaggerated as when we think that they are idle, they are working on their own lands." In fact, as in slavery, this was a part of their resistance and protest.

In the early days of developing the plantation in June 1891, twelve or thirteen black laborers "assembled for work and promptly struck for higher wages." Chamberlain raised their wages for the rest of the week but reverted to the usual wage the following week. When this was announced, only one man turned up for work and was "alarmed lest he should be discovered by the others. After clearing a quarter of an acre he left."[18] The strike continued for nearly two weeks. One or two laborers were willing to return to work but had a "fear of their companions." Neville Chamberlain subsequently brought in twenty-one men from New Providence to assist, while keeping on the Androsians, and engaged the newcomers under an agreement for wages of one pound and four shillings a month, rations every day, and conveyance between Nassau and Andros. They received an advance of twelve shillings.[19]

Besides Andros, sisal was also grown at Savannah Sound, Eleuthera, Long Island, Exuma, Rum Cay, Cat Island, Inagua, and Abaco. On Great Abaco there were three large plantations and several small farms owned by British and American companies. Little Abaco attracted a wealthy London company, which had acquired 10,000 acres and had planted nearly 2,000 acres. Shea noted that there was a steady decline in the truck system, since on the plantations the laborers were paid in cash.[20] Shea's expectations that sisal would revolutionize the Bahamian economy were not realized. By 1895 optimism had turned to despair. Neville Chamberlain wrote to advise his father that there was "practically nothing going on here—I confess I do not feel sanguine about the future." The next year he admitted defeat: "the plants don't grow and I am again feeling very low and despondent about the whole concern." He concluded, "I no longer see any chance of making the investment pay."[21]

Although this story of failure reverberated throughout the Bahamas, substantial exports of sisal were made between 1898 and 1902, boosted by the Spanish-American War. By 1912, though, all the large plantations in the Bahamas had failed and were abandoned. The sisal industry in the Philippines, boosted by American capital, was revived following the war, and prices fell. However, a considerable quantity of sisal was also grown on smallholdings in the Bahamas. Sisal produced in the Bahamas was beaten by hand in salt water, causing a decline in the quality, price, and production. Despite this sisal remained a vital part of the impoverished Bahamian economy until the end of the First World War, some islands depending solely on it for survival. Indeed, in 1915, 100,000 pounds of hand-cleaned sisal were shipped to Nassau from Nicoll's Town, Andros, and eight tons of machine-cleaned fiber came from the Estate of Berry Islands Limited, at Whale Cay.[22]

As noted in chapter 2, emigrant labor in the form of stevedoring was operated on the truck system, and it continued as late as 1897. Despite this, it brought prosperity to Inagua and Long Cay. By the beginning of the twentieth century, "another version of the truck system was used in Inagua in connection with labourers employed on one year contracts with American companies in Mexico, Panama, and countries on the South American mainland." The laborers signed on with a local agent who received a commission for every man he recruited. They were paid "one-half of their wages in cash in the country of their employment, and the other half was paid to them on their return to Inagua."[23]

The agents, however, found ways to keep the laborers indebted to them. Often the laborers signed on before the steamship arrived to convey them to their place of work, and they were obliged to use credit for food and drink. Additionally, while the laborers were away, their families were maintained by being "paid in truck at 'exorbitant rates.'" On their return to Inagua, the agent "deliberately delayed settling the accounts" of the laborers. The *Watchman* newspaper, a semi-weekly publication established by Leon E. H. Dupuch in November 1901, promised impartiality, strove to be watchful about the welfare and interest of the colony, and was critical of "the iniquitous system of contract labour." The newspaper stated: "The labourers who were shipped from Inagua to Bluefields or to Tampico are not only unprotected in their rights, but were mercilessly mulcted [swindled]." Abuse of laborers by the agents included the issuance of worthless bank drafts, lack of protection in Mexico, unwholesome food, and being required to pay for medical treatment, contrary to contracts ensuring free healthcare. The *Watchman*, aimed at the "Outs" (i.e., "coloureds") lasted until 1906. Leon Dupuch by then had launched his own newspaper, the *Tribune*, in 1903.[24]

Governor Grey-Wilson visited Inagua in mid-1907 and, upon noting the injustices meted out to the emigrant laborers, had a bill drafted to protect them. "After a very perilous progress through the House of Assembly," an act "For the Protection of Workmen in the Colony" was passed in 1907.[25] It did little to stamp out the truck system, which remained intact as late as 1919.[26]

The Growth of Racial Consciousness

The *Freeman* newspaper, established by James Carmichael Smith in March 1887 "as the organ . . . truly representing the working classes—the African race in the Bahamas," was also highly critical of the truck system. On 5 April 1887 the *Freeman* described the truck system as "modern slavery" and gave a detailed account of its pervasiveness in the agricultural, sponging, and turtling industries. It was particularly critical of the outfitters: "verily Outfitters are as gods reaping where they have not sown, and gathering and controlling exclusively where they have strewn jointly." It did partly blame the "Fisherman and other employees . . . for their present condition," but noted that their wastefulness, although "deplorable" was the result of the "influence of the truck system under which they and their ancestors have been living for the past 50 years."[27]

As elsewhere in the Caribbean, black and mixed race Bahamians in the late nineteenth century expressed a sense of racial pride and identity.[28] Paul

Adderley argued that by 1880 a small group of nonwhite Bahamians organized a black nationalist movement and identified with Pan-Africanism. They "openly advocated an awakening of racial consciousness, a promotion of African awareness linking Africa with all the diaspora."[29] Manifestations of this growing consciousness were evident in the objectives of the friendly societies, many of which were ethnically constituted, predominantly comprising liberated Africans and their descendants.[30] Friendly societies provided funeral and sickness benefits as well as support "for matters of importance to the black community." They operated as proto-political institutions.[31]

James Carmichael Smith made a telling speech to the combined friendly societies in 1887: "Let us Endeavour to become more and more united, let the children of Africa throughout the Western Hemisphere remember FA-THERLAND or MOTHERLAND, let them remember AFRICA which is sometimes called the Dark Continent, but which to us in the West, [is] the land of the Rising Sun."[32]

Smith was a member and probably among the founders of the Anglo-African League, which was established in 1887 "on the initiative of the president of the Bahamas Friendly Society," Samuel Bosfield. A printer and treasurer of the Freeman Printing Company, Bosfield attempted to bring unity among the friendly societies. The Anglo-American League was obviously the political arm of the Bahamas Friendly Society, the president of which believed that collectively, the groups would have a "greater impact in pursuing various public issues for their mutual benefit." The league utilized the *Freeman* newspaper to publish reports lobbying the "local and colonial governments for electoral, economic, and social reforms" that they were convinced would benefit the black and mixed-race Bahamian people who were in the majority. Rosanne Adderley further commented:

> These reports provided a level of detail more akin to secretarial minutes than to a journalistic account of a particular event. One might almost speculate that *The Freeman* served as a kind of unofficial chronicle for this organization, notwithstanding the fact that the articles concerning Anglo-African League meetings appeared under the byline "From our Reporter."[33]

Adderley suggests that the *Freeman* "believed that the majority of its readers were members of the League" and that its membership "included a substantial numbers of liberated Africans and their descendants."[34] At an enthusiastic meeting of the Anglo-African League on 21 February 1888, eight organizations were present. These groups sent delegates to the meeting but did not represent all the friendly societies that had membership in the league. In its editorial of 21 February 1888 the *Freeman* reported that "all the various Friendly and Benevolent Societies in New Providence, with two exceptions, and all those on the Out Islands, have entered the Union. . . . Today the Anglo-African League is an Association of twenty-two societies, with an aggregate male membership of about four thousand."[35]

Early in 1888 the Anglo-African League petitioned members of the Legislative Council and the colonial secretary in London to establish the ballot box system at elections "instead of 'naming' as was then 'in vogue.'" Their request was not heeded. The league also sent a delegation to call on the powerful white merchant and politician R. H. Sawyer to introduce the bill to vote by secret ballot. Sawyer shrugged it off, stating that it was "premature," and he thought "that the people were not educated to its use, and the ignorant voter would be in a more defenseless position than under the present system."[36] "Citizen," writing to the *Freeman,* displayed his disgust: "He thought the Vote by Ballot premature seven years ago and . . . judging by his political character . . . he will think so seven times seven years hence."

The *Freeman* was critical of the inadequacies in the education system. In certain of the Out Islands, usually where there were few whites "and the coloureds were in the immense majority," settlements and even entire islands lacked public schools. Teachers were for the most part untrained, and demands were made for the establishment of a Normal School or Training College to train and qualify teachers. The league also addressed the economic sector. It suggested an alternative to the government's plan to subsidize the booming sisal industry by paying large premiums to sisal exporters, who were mainly members of the white mercantile elite. The Anglo-African League opined that instead, smaller premiums should be given to individual sisal growers, who were mainly black.[37]

At a March 1888 meeting of the Anglo-African League the subject of a bill "To Amend the Election Act, 1885" was hotly discussed. The *Freeman*'s editorial for 13 March 1888 thundered, "A Revolution in the Franchise!" "200 Pounds or Imprisonment," "The Next? A Star-Chamber!" If the amendment passed, the candidate would have to swear before a justice of the peace that he was qualified to stand, having £200 in assets. If he made a false declaration, he would not only be prevented from taking his seat but would be convicted of perjury and sentenced to prison for a term not exceeding four years' hard labor. Members of the Anglo-African League were incensed, especially Corresponding Secretary Louis N. Duty, who made a fiery speech at a league meeting held in the Grant's Town Friendly Society Hall on 12 March. His arguments were reported in the *Freeman* on 20 March, stating that the amendment "strikes a blow at the Constitution" and was an attempt to subvert it in order to "restrict the political rights and privileges of the voters." In the *Freeman* of the same date the letter writer "Bahamian" was indignant and saw the amendment, if it became law, as "a legal instrument of intimidation" that would "be used most stringently to arrest the march of progress which is being made towards equality in this Colony."[38] The pro-establishment Nassau *Guardian,* on the other hand, in its editorial of 14 April, saw it as an issue

> scarcely important enough to merit much debate or evoke much warmth of feeling. It was an independent measure on which the members of government differed from one another. It can do no harm, for practically it will have little effect and cannot in any way restrain the freedoms of popular elections. As its nature has become known, the angry feelings excited have died away, and outside of the smallest circles, no one regards it with any concern, or as of any importance.[39]

The amended bill passed, but with the harsh penalty reduced to one month's imprisonment. The nonwhite members of the House of Assembly, including James Carmichael Smith and G. A. Macgregor, voted against it, along with some government members.[40]

The Anglo-African League lasted only about two years. It can be suggested that there was disunity among the various friendly societies, some of which consisted mainly of creole blacks and mixed-race persons, not liberated Africans. While creole blacks probably identified with the Bahamian society, liberated Africans, especially those who had arrived in 1860, according to Rosanne Adderley, did indeed "remember powerfully" the homelands from which they had come and obviously felt a strong connection "for the communities and cultures they had left behind." Indeed, a group of African members of the Congo No. 1 Society attempted unsuccessfully to return to the kingdom of Kongo, "lands besides the Great River in Central Africa," which had been annexed by Belgium. Reverend Daniel Wilshire, superintendent of the missionary Baptist church in the Bahamas, assisted the Africans in sending a petition through the British government to the Belgian government. The government of the Congo was quite disposed to facilitate the return of the Africans, but as Rosanne Adderley suggests, "the proposed return seems to have fallen apart in the face of logistical questions from both the Belgian authorities and the British Colonial Office."[41] Adderley concluded that "the very real" Kongo petition "illustrated the depth of the connection displaced Africans felt for the communities and cultures they had left behind. . . . This 1888 group negotiated at least a dual identity as Kongo people with a past they wished to reclaim as integrated immigrants in an African-Bahamian world."[42]

In practical terms the numerous ethnically based friendly societies, lodges, and the like obviously led to some rivalry and discord. Dr. Cleveland Eneas, in his account of Bain Town, recognized the reason for so many friendly societies, lodges and burial societies: "There was sufficient heterogeneity among African and black Bahamians to warrant separate social classes. The social segregation, which manifests itself in different lodges and churches, was practiced with a bit of seriousness." He continued: "No N'Ongo (Yoruba) man would associate with a Congo under any circumstance. He regarded him as someone to be shunned and segregation was rife."[43] Friendly societies in the Bahamas represented ethnic groups including the Yoruba, Egba, Congo, and Nangobar.

Social Control by the West India Regiment and Police

The maintenance of law and order, as Howard Johnson has demonstrated, was important for the white mercantile elite that dominated the socioeconomic and political machinery. The white elite, including the Bahamian merchant class and the colonial officials, dominated law-making and "coercive agencies like the police." "Social control" was important in order to protect the economic interests of the small elite and to suppress disorder that "might threaten the lives of the dominant class." Reminiscent of enslavement, tight control ensured the preservation of the class system and "hierarchical relationships."[44]

A small police force that was parochially based, with churchwardens and vestries appointing honorary constables from 1789, came under the overall authority of a colonial provost marshal. An 1833 act set up a formal constabulary for the first time by authorizing the police magistrate to appoint six "able bodied men" as salaried policemen for New Providence and enabled the Out Island justices of the peace to add up to a further dozen for the other islands. The police force was expanded by the 1850s, and complaints of police brutality began to be heard. The Bahamas Friendly Society just before Christmas 1858 wrote a letter to the *Bahama Herald* newspaper complaining of the treatment toward "the coloured and black man; if they are detected in a fault and cast into prison before the week is ended, you see them chained hand and foot, and driven around the town like savage beasts . . . but, Sir, we ask, where is the white man when he does a crime? Is he chained? No."[45]

The 1860s saw a marked increase in crime and unrest, which accelerated during the American Civil War when blockade runners and easy money flooded into Nassau. The police force was reorganized and expanded during the period 1860–65. Police salaries from the inspector downward were increased, and police officers were put on the same footing as other public servants. The garrison troops of the West India Regiment remained in Nassau, however, as a backup for the forces of law and order. Rarely used and often mistrusted by the whites, the African troops were in fact more than willing to act against local disturbances.[46]

In 1881 a royal commission recommended that the scattered detachments of the West India Regiment stationed in the Bahamas, British Honduras, Barbados, Trinidad, and British Guiana be more strategically and economically concentrated in Jamaica and St. Lucia.[47]

This suggestion was vigorously opposed by Governor Charles Lees in December 1882. "The population of the Bahamas is docile and law-abiding," he wrote to the colonial secretary, Lord Kimberley, "but your Lordship is aware that it is almost entirely composed of a race easily excited, and when under the influence of passion, capable of but little self control."[48] Howard Johnson argues that official attitudes toward the withdrawal of troops in the 1880s "were largely shaped by the views of the white mercantile elite which had controlled the economic and political levers of power in the Bahamas since the period of slavery." Johnson stressed the close family relationships and "homogeneous interests" of the elite that the regiment was intended to protect.[49] Similar exaggerated fear of the removal of British troops was also experienced generally in the British West Indies.

When the decision to withdraw the garrison was announced in 1885, the House of Assembly sent a memorial to Governor Henry Blake asking for reconsideration. "Such a step as this we cannot but regard as one which will be absolutely fatal to the future progress of the Colony," they proclaimed: "Its good government will be placed in jeopardy, and insecurity to life and property will, under these circumstances universally prevail."[50] Blake agreed that there was a danger but attributed it less to the volatility of the blacks than to the discord between blacks and whites. "While I cannot speak too highly of the general conduct of the population," he wrote in August 1885, "the fact remains that there is a strong feeling on the part of the black and coloured peoples against the white population of Nassau. I have heard this from too many sources to have any doubt on the subject."[51] The governor's feelings were apparently underlined by the wave of antagonism against whites expressed by black Nassauvians when a black policeman was shot to death in 1886 by a white man named Sands, said to be deranged, and who was acquitted for that reason. L. D. Powles reported: "A member of the New York Yacht Club, who knows the Bahamas thoroughly, once said to me, 'was there the day Sands was arrested, and I never shall forget it as long as I live! No one who saw that crowd could doubt there was an undercurrent of race-hatred with which the White Conchs will have to reckon sooner or later.'" Powles also commented that "the way the whites talked of this [murder] habitually was . . . that the man was only a nigger, and it was a pity a few more were not shot."[52]

Governor Ambrose Shea "did not share the exaggerated racial fears" of the white elite but was concerned about maintaining "a stable business environment" in order to attract British capital to invest in the production of sisal. In 1888 the colonial secretary recommended that the removal of the troops be offset by a substantial increase in the size and strength of the local police force. Shea replied that he thought public security might be weakened rather than strengthened by such a measure. He suggested that the British government station a gunboat to protect the colony. The Colonial Office was not impressed and expressed the view that "imperial defense considerations took precedence over the domestic concerns of individual colonies." Colonial Undersecretary Edward Winfield observed caustically in a minute of 19 December 1888, "It seems to be generally agreed that there is a strong antipathy of the black population to the small handful of whites in the Bahamas which does not exist in anything like the same degree in any other Colony—but they cannot expect the Imperial Govt. to maintain troops there merely to preserve internal order."[53]

Ultimately, a solution was found to the problem along lines followed in many other parts of the empire. The formulation was largely the work of Colonial Secretary of the Bahamas Captain H. M. Jackson, who had previously served in Sierra Leone and the Gold Coast, where police were drawn from foreign parts and combined civil with quasi-military functions. Jackson's plan was to double the Bahamian police force by creating a separate unit, recruited from outside the Bahamas, trained like soldiers, and housed in barracks rather than living at home. In due course the new paramilitary police would supplant the original force through natural attrition. Governor Shea favored the recruitment of policemen from the "warlike tribes" of India, but such distant recruiting proved impractical. The Colonial Office informed

Shea in 1889 that the withdrawal of the West India Regiment was certain and that the members of the new police force might be recruited from the West Indian colonies "to prevent any feeling of local sympathy between [the] Police and the inhabitants of the Bahamas."[54] Captain Jackson preferred Barbadian blacks, who had impressed him by their reliability as soldiers in the West India forces during the Ashanti War and who were already serving as police replacements for the troops withdrawn from British Honduras.

The Police Act of 1891 stipulated that the new constabulary force was to consist of a commandant, inspector, sub-inspector, sergeant, two corporals, and forty constables, later increased to seventy-five. The new force would be recruited from abroad and would be "quite distinct" from the existing force, which would be gradually phased out.[55] The conditions and pay scales for the new constabulary were "made deliberately unattractive" so as to discourage local recruitment and hasten the reduction of the Bahamian component in the police, which was soon demoralized by being treated as an inferior arm. The new police force, consisting almost entirely of Barbadians, was established well before the last soldiers of the West India Regiment left Nassau at the end of 1891. Barbadians also formed the backbone of the Trinidad Police Force by the 1890s.[56]

Even early on, the "foreign" accents and style and supposed officiousness and superior attitudes of the new policemen often provoked resentment and resistance, such as the riot that erupted in Grant's Town in April 1893. On 15 April a number of blacks stoned and destroyed the Grant's Town Police Station, guarded by three of the constabulary, and rescued a prisoner confined there. The rioters then smashed the public lamps, and when the inspector of police was sent, they assaulted him. Three policemen were sent to Grant's Town the following day. They too were compelled to leave because of the violence of the "mob." Tense days followed. When the commandant's orderly returned to the barracks seriously wounded, and the rumor circulated that some officers on solitary beats had been murdered, the police were so enraged that they broke barracks. Grant's Town was "ablaze," and there was much stone throwing. Fortunately, the constabulary was ordered back to the barracks before anyone was hurt.[57]

The main spark of the riot seemed to be the hostility of some Over-the-Hill people, especially Bain Towners, against the Barbadian policemen, considered "interlopers" by the local people. Those who were particularly hostile and were labeled ring-leaders of the riot were Francis Bain, Louis Duty, a black merchant, and a man referred to simply as Brown. Francis Bain had apparently led the rioters to the barracks gate and taunted and threatened the policemen, alleging that they had taken his cutlass, which he needed for farming.[58]

Mr. Halkett, the commandant of the constabulary, testified that the troublemakers were "a small minority" and that trouble emanated from Louis Duty's rum shop. Grant's Town and Bain Town both had many rum shops, licensed and unlicensed, and drink could be had at all hours. However, there is no evidence that the rioting crowd was drunk. The governor deemed Louis Duty "the chief foment of the disturbance." Apparently Duty had written a letter to the *Nassau Times* against the constabulary.[59]

The people of Grant's Town and Bain Town were embittered by the abrupt manner of the constabulary. Others complained that they performed their duty roughly, and the Methodist minister Reverend Willerup observed that some of the constabulary took advantage of the seedier side of Grant's Town life. He observed some policemen in the "house of a loose woman drinking and playing cards." He admitted that Grant's Town on a Saturday night was "a most difficult place."[60]

The government's reaction was quick and decisive. Action was taken against the rioters. Two of the seven were tried and convicted, including Francis Bain. He was sentenced to six months' imprisonment, but on appeal his sentence was reduced to a fine of one pound for assaulting two constables. Immediately after the disturbances the authorities called in the gunboat *Partridge*, which arrived after the trouble had subsided. Following a stay of six weeks offshore the gunboat departed on 1 June 1893. The government also appointed a committee to make recommendations concerning the reorganization of the police force. This committee recommended that the force be restructured by the formation of two divisions within it. One made up of Bahamians would patrol the eastern district, Grant's Town (and presumably Bain Town), and the Out Islands, and the other division, mainly made up of Barbadians, would patrol the city district. It was felt that the Bahamian force could control those areas where it was most likely for "collisions to occur, and more importantly for the government." The new arrangement would also protect the properties of the elite from the rioters. Howard Johnson commented that the white elite in the late nineteenth century was "not embarrassed to admit direct links between property interests and the formation of the new Constabulary."[61] As Johnson further noted, the "propertied classes came to repose confidence in the Constabulary." The reorganization of the police force had more than "local significance"—it demonstrated "techniques of control used by the Colonial authorities" on behalf of the dominant elite, "at the periphery of the British Empire."[62]

Modernity Comes to Nassau

Improvements in communications, electricity, and transportation between 1892 and 1914 primarily benefited the white elite. Cable communication established in 1892 between Nassau and Jupiter, Florida, was obsolete by 1913. Its use had not dramatically affected the lives of ordinary citizens, but its installation had made possible direct messages to the United States and England. It had put the governor and well-off businessmen, usually white, in touch with the outside world. When the disturbances of April 1893 occurred in Grant's Town, Governor Shea sent a telegram to Joseph Chamberlain, secretary of state for the colonies, on 18 April, which he received the next day. A gunboat requested by the governor arrived in Nassau on 24 April. Before cable communication, it would have taken weeks to make similar contacts and perhaps months before action was taken. The cable had also made more outside news available in the local press. The *Tribune* in the early 1900s included many articles on racial issues in America and South Africa, the situation in Cuba and Haiti, and the pros and cons of the Bahamas confederating with Canada.[63] In 1913 the introduction of the more modern wireless telegraph supplied an efficient service between Nassau, Miami, and England and brought even more up-to-date world news. At the outbreak of the First World War in 1914, news of the British declaration of war on 4 August reached Nassau a day later.[64]

More of a luxury were the first telephones, installed after the passing of a special act in 1906. The initial 150 subscribers, mostly the elite living and working on central Bay Street or nearby and many on party lines, were connected through a central switchboard serviced by six operators. Five of them were women, and all were white except one, who was a light-skinned mixed-race woman. The system expanded slowly into the eastern and western suburbs until an automatic exchange was introduced and set up in Vendue House at the foot of George Street in 1916. This exchange had a capacity of 600 lines, but as late as 1918 there were only 400 subscribers in Nassau with 412 telephones, and the average number of calls a day was a mere 1,866.[65] The majority of subscribers were white, but some of the better-off mixed-race persons also obtained telephones.

Electricity became available at much the same time as the telephone and spread a little faster. The Electric Light Act was passed in 1907, but it was not until 1909 that a gas generator was installed in Vendue House, producing a weak direct current. The ceremonial illumination of Christ Church Cathedral, St. Andrews Presbyterian Church, Trinity Methodist Church, the Colonial Hotel, the Club, and a few dozen street lights on 16 June 1909 created quite a stir, but as late as 1916 there were only 443 subscribers and 276 street lights, mostly on Bay and Shirley streets. Because of the slow spread of the service, some of the wealthiest residents had to wait until a major expansion and reorganization in 1922 before they enjoyed electric power. For average Nassauvians, black, white, and of mixed race, it was too expensive even to wire the house in order to install the new service, much less to pay the rates. Many of the mixed-race middle class did not get electricity until the mid-to-late twenties, with the black majority having to wait even longer, continuing to depend on kerosene lamps.[66]

The introduction of electricity, however, made possible at least two other important innovations: the local manufacture of ice and the advent of the cinema. For more than half a century, under a system controlled and subsidized by the government, bulk ice had been imported from Maine during the winter and stored in a thick-walled ice house located on central Bay Street between the Fish Market and the Sponge Exchange. The contract to obtain, store, and distribute the ice was granted by the government to a single Bay Street merchant because only a monopoly (with a government guarantee) was thought to make the business worthwhile. But by 1913 ice was being produced in Nassau and immediately outdated the traditional system. Ten years later the government, which wished to control a commodity as vital as ice, passed "An Act to Provide for the Control of the Ice House and to regulate the supply and sale of ice."[67] Until the 1940s government continued to grant a monopoly contract to favored Bay Street merchants on the pretext of guaranteeing supply and preventing profiteering. Ice moved from being a luxury to being almost a necessity. Except for the laborers at Wilson City, Abaco, and perhaps some Harbour Islanders and some inhabitants of Inagua and Long Cay, most Out Islanders did not receive ice. Wealthy elites and some mixed-race middle-class Nassauvians had iceboxes; ice was delivered by dray or collected by servants.

Government also became concerned, for different reasons, about the control of the newly introduced moving pictures. The first movies were shown in Nassau in 1911. In the following year the Cinematograph Act was passed and a license was required from the police commandant for the public exhibition of films. It also stipulated the type of movie that could be shown and gave the governor power to make rules—suggesting that the concern to censor socially dangerous content was more important than a desire to control a potentially valuable commercial asset. By 1913 Nassau had two motion picture theaters, though only a minority had the money to patronize them.[68]

The person centrally responsible for introducing the wonders of electricity to Nassau was an American. Patrick H. Burns was born in Cleveland, Ohio, in 1869 and had worked for Western Union as a telegraph messenger, clerk, and telegrapher from 1883 until he was sent to oversee the installation of the telegraph cable from Jupiter to Nassau in 1892. He was appointed official superintendent of telegraphs the same year, responsible for the installation and management of telephones, electric power, and the wireless telegraphy link. When they were amalgamated in 1913, Governor George Haddon-Smith appointed him superintendent of all three services. Burns lived the rest of his life in Nassau. He was the father of Helen (Nellie) Burns Higgs, who became a well-known horticulturist.[69]

Before 1905 and for many years afterward, when people took quiet walks, early morning strolls, or carriage rides to the Nassau Market, they encountered pedestrians, carriages, drays and bicycles. It was not until after 1905 or 1906 that they saw a car. The very first car in Nassau was a tiller-steered three-horsepower Oldsmobile imported by the U.S. consul Henry Mostyn in 1905. Every time it passed on the street people ran out to stare. By 1908 there were perhaps six cars in the Bahamas, of which Governor William Grey-Wilson's Rochet-Schneider was by far the grandest—an open four-seater landau, redolent of upholstered leather, purple paint, and polished brass.[70]

No licenses were required until the Motor Car Act of 1908, which decreed a car license fee of £5, a driving license fee of £1, and a minimum age of seventeen for drivers. No driver's test was stipulated. The maximum speed allowed was twenty miles an hour, or ten miles an hour in town. Cars were required to have a light attached that would signal their approach during the hours of darkness and would also illuminate the license plate. By 1911 cars had become more numerous, and notices appeared in the *Tribune* advertising automobiles for hire and tires for sale. The year before World War I broke out there were 36 licensed automobiles throughout the Bahamas, most being in Nassau, compared to 276 horse-drawn carriages.[71] The majority of cars were owned by the white elite.

Advances in Health and Sanitation

The early years of the new century saw small advances in health and sanitation services. It was customary for many untrained or unqualified persons to practice medicine. There were also "quacks" promising marvelous cures. In view of this, the Medical Act passed in 1906, "For the Registration of Medical Practitioners."[72] It sought to improve the quality of medicine by stipulating who could be registered as a medical practitioner. It was illegal to practice without a license. In order to be registered one had to hold a medical degree or diploma from a university or accredited institution in the United Kingdom or in any other British territory. Any non-British degree had to be recognized by the governor-in-council and was subject to limitations and conditions specified on the certificate or license. Because of the shortage of doctors and the widely scattered nature of the islands in the archipelago, unqualified practitioners, some with training in science but without medical credentials, were licensed to practice. Although useful, and sometimes indispensable in isolated island communities, unqualified practitioners could at any time have their licenses revoked. In 1912 only three Out Island medical officers were employed by the hospital system. They were Dr. Bate stationed at Inagua, a stevedoring port; Dr. Johnson based at Harbour Island, servicing Spanish Wells and some mainland settlements; and Dr. Mackintosh at Abaco, presumably based at Green Turtle Cay. Most Out Islanders had no doctor. Of the 42,000 persons living in the Out Islands, only 5,000 lived in the three districts where medical officers were stationed. The majority either came to Nassau for treatment or depended on the unqualified practitioners.[73]

Commissioners, ministers of religion, and school teachers, who had frequently had some exposure to healthcare issues, often served in that capacity. Conditions were difficult, and supplies of medicine were scarce, as the chief medical officer noted in 1913 on a trip to the Out Islands.[74] He promptly prepared a list of concentrated mixtures and tablets with a small pamphlet of instruction in the use of medicine for simple ailments. The Pharmacy Act of 1913 gave permission for a limited number of unqualified persons to sell drugs in the Out Islands.[75] The system of unqualified practitioners and untrained pharmacists continued largely unchanged into the 1940s and 1950s, especially in the islands to windward, as portrayed in the fascinating memoirs of "Doctor" Evans W. Cottman.[76]

Qualified medical personnel varied in dedication and skill. Resident Surgeon Dr. Culmer was described by Governor Allardyce as "hopeless," a poor administrator whose methods were old-fashioned, although he was "not a bad surgeon." The governor felt Culmer had served in the position too long and preferred dinner parties and bridge to the practice of medicine.[77] But although some physicians in private practice had little interest in their profession, doctors were generally highly respected. Dr. William Pitt, a black West Indian who acted as chief medical officer in 1916, had a good reputation among his white and nonwhite patients as fine doctor.[78]

Because of its origin as a poorhouse (founded in 1809), its cumbersome management, and the dubious quality of its services, the hospital in Nassau entered the twentieth century with the reputation of being a place of last resort for persons from the poorest (mainly black) sectors of society. It was divided into four sections, one each for the sick, the indigent, lepers, and the insane, though the total number of beds was only 167. In the sick wards there was insufficient differentiation between the sexes, the young and old, and between surgical, obstetric, chronic, and infectious cases. The insane asylum had no accommodation for private patients, and acute and mild cases were often not segregated. Consequently those who could afford it arranged for treatment at home, even for leprosy and insanity. In fact the lunatic asylum was referred to by Governor Grey-Wilson in 1912 as "accommodation of the poorest class of negroes."[79]

The Medical Department Act of 1911 and the Public Health Act in 1914 were attempts at modernization, though they were limited by a meager budget and the persistence of old attitudes.[80] Under the 1911 act the hospital was placed under a superintendent and a board of seven commissioners (including four members from the House of Assembly) appointed annually by the governor. The medical supervision of all hospital services was made the responsibility of a chief medical officer. Minimum qualifications were required for a resident surgeon, other doctors, a matron, nurses, and midwives. All midwives practicing in the colony were supposed to be examined by the resident surgeon before being licensed, and student nurses were required to serve a three-year apprenticeship before receiving certification. Such measures were positive but had little immediate success because the majority of doctors and matrons continued to be expatriates (predominantly white and few of them highly qualified) until the 1950s.

The strengthened Board of Health also sought to improve health and sanitary conditions on New Providence. A rigorous system of quarantine for incoming ships using Athol Island had been in place for decades and was likely the reason for cessation of cholera, yellow fever, and smallpox epidemics. But occasional typhoid outbreaks, dysentery, tetanus, and worm infestations defied attempts to improve sanitation, and the increase in other serious diseases reflected ignorance and inefficiency as well as a deficient diet. Additionally, there was no public water supply, and the precious commodity was still obtained largely from public or privately owned wells. The water was often brackish. Some of the white and mixed-race elite had rainwater storage tanks underneath their homes, as did the hospital, but they were unprotected from mosquitoes and other insects. Sewerage arrangements were primitive, and the few persons who had water-closets had them installed to drain into uncemented cesspools. The privy pit closets, the commonest form of sanitary convenience in Nassau in the early 1900s, were perhaps less of a health hazard.[81]

The Public Health Act of 1914 attempted to reinforce preventative measures. The Board of Health was charged with advising the governor on everything pertaining to the health of the colony and was given the power not only to inspect houses and yards but to oversee the cleaning of streets, drains, latrines, and the public market—duties previously assigned to the Board of Works. The Board of Health was also to inspect food and condemn any unfit for human consumption and to impose fines for infractions, including the sale of adulterated milk. The 1914 act also included regulations against the spread of infectious diseases. If infectious patients could not be effectively isolated at home, they were to be removed to the hospital. Those with chronic infections were forbidden to practice as bakers, barbers, boatmen, stevedores, bookmakers, butchers, cooks, dairymen, domestic servants, fishmongers, carriage drivers, straw vendors, nurses, tailors, dressmakers, or washerwomen—almost the entire gamut of service occupations practiced mainly by blacks and mixed-race persons. People contravening the law were liable to a fine of £10 or a month's imprisonment.[82] Children with infectious diseases were banned from school, and infected persons were forbidden to use the public library. Potentially more disruptive was the prohibition of holding a wake over an "infected" corpse.

Perhaps because of the social stigma attached to the most dangerous diseases, they were not listed as notifiable under the 1914 act. Official inquiries at the beginning of World War I helped to expose the startling extent of serious health problems among the black and mixed-race population, particularly the scourges of tuberculosis (TB) and venereal disease (VD). Many people suffering from TB—which flourished in slums and conditions of poor nutrition but was regarded with shame—were neither hospitalized nor segregated. But 12 percent of persons admitted to hospital in 1912 and 1913 were suffering from TB, and more than half died because they had applied for admission in the advanced stages of the disease.[83]

The situation concerning VD was equally serious. Syphilis was more prevalent than the less dangerous gonorrhea, and cases were steadily increasing in the first two decades of the century. The figures given in the 1912 Health Report for both VD and TB were so shocking that the House of Assembly refused to print them for fear of the damage it would cause to tourism. Once again only severe cases reached the hospital, but 27 percent of all patients hospitalized in 1913 (i.e., 146 persons) were suffering from VD. In 1916 the acting chief medical officer, Dr. William Pitt, told Governor William Allardyce that he believed 90 percent of Bahamian "coloureds" were affected "in one way or another by this terrible curse." Though this was an obvious exaggeration, Dr. Pitt's successor reported: "So widespread are the ravages of venereal disease that I am afraid the wage-earning capacity of the labouring classes [obviously meaning nonwhites] is likely to be seriously impaired."[84]

The governor and the white members of the House of Assembly were not unduly concerned about the health of nonwhites in general, but a perceived threat to the viability of the labor force probably encouraged them to act. In December 1917 Governor Allardyce appointed the Commission on Venereal Disease to investigate the growth of VD over the previous two decades. Recommending the appointment of a government bacteriologist to conduct detection tests and take advantage of the latest advances in medicine, the commission looked for scapegoats (including black Bahamians) for the epidemic. It blamed returning migrants who had contracted the disease in Florida, foreign workmen who had come to Nassau during the building of the Colonial Hotel, and also the waiters who worked in the hotel during the tourist season. Most important, though, was the spread of the disease through prostitution, which was found to be prevalent in Nassau despite the passage of the Immoral Traffic Act in 1914. The dance halls, where liquor was sold and "vulgarity prevailed," were claimed to be "principally places of assignation and centres for the dissemination of venereal disease."[85] So great was the stigma attached to this terrible social disease that people kept it as secret as they could and sought cures from bush doctors and quacks rather than regular practitioners. In examining the volunteers for the Bahamas contingent for the British West India Regiment, the hospital doctors found an appallingly large number of VD cases.[86] A contributing cause was the temporary migration of laborers to Wilson City, Abaco, and to Florida in the United States, where some contracted the disease and returned home to infect others.

Labor and Migration

Wilson City was a lumber town named after Governor Grey-Wilson (1904–12), who had arranged the timber license. The town grew up out of the timber business established in 1906 on Spenser's Point near the south end of Great Abaco. An American firm based in Minneapolis and registered as the Bahamas Timber Company obtained a hundred-year timber license for the Crown pine forests of Abaco, Andros, and Grand Bahama.[87] Described by

Steve Dodge as "a marvel in its time," the company boasted a ship channel dredged to a three-hundred-foot dock, with a huge loading derrick and conveyor beltways serving a mill that produced up to 18 million board feet of timber a year for markets in the United States, Cuba, and the rest of the Bahamas. Light railway lines radiated into the hinterland to feed the mill, and the steam engines fueled by pinewood waste drove generators that provided electric light in 1908 (before electrical services were introduced in Nassau) and produced over a thousand twenty-five-pound blocks of ice a day in advance of Nassau. By 1912 Wilson City was employing an average of 540 persons a day, pumping between £21,000 and £28,000 a year into the Bahamian economy.[88]

Wage labor at Wilson City attracted a majority of Abaconians, mostly black, many of whom came with their families, and a large number of single men from other Bahamian islands as well as Turks and Caicos.[89] Though the company ran its own stores, it provided a welcome market for Abaconian farmers and fishermen, especially the whites on the offshore cays who did not care to work alongside blacks. Cheap board lumber raised the quality of local housing. Wilson City also created a boom among the white boat builders of Hope Town, Man-O-War Cay, New Plymouth, and Harbour Island because the cut timber was mainly shipped off in large schooners (up to two hundred feet in length) rather than in steam freighters.

Not all the effects of Wilson City were beneficial, and the operation lasted barely a decade. Accidents were common among the largely inexperienced laborers, especially in the mill, in logging, and on the railway. The commissioner at Cherokee Sound, commenting on the unexpected number of deaths in his district in 1912 (thirty-one, against only thirteen births), blamed the poor medical facilities as well as the laborers' ignorance of first aid methods. More insidious was the importation of Jim Crow–type segregation from the United States. The managerial staff—five families of white Americans—lived in well-built white bungalows on a hill overlooking Spenser's Bight, the Sea of Abaco, and the Atlantic Ocean beyond Lynyard Cay. They enjoyed their own white-painted Methodist church, a private school, electricity and piped water in their homes, and even a tennis court—Abaco's first recreational amenity. A few white Bahamians lived in these homes, but most were occupied by white foreign managers. White skilled and semi-skilled workers lived on a street near the base of the hill. About four hundred black workers lived in a "cluster of 120 houses in four rows" located in a swampy hollow near the dock and painted red. They had the use of a red church, where segregated services were held. The black section was called Jericho, apparently because it was surrounded by a wall. Methodist ministers ran a day school for the children of the white American administrators and a night school for the black Bahamians, the latter being held in the red church. Overcrowding, the predominance of male workers, and the constant migration led to social tensions and moral and health problems including "social diseases."[90]

Growing frustration among the laborers culminated in a very tense situation just before Christmas in 1913. The Bahamas Timber Company was experiencing financial difficulties and had not paid the laborers for two weeks. They announced that there was no money on hand to meet the payroll, and the workers became mutinous and threatened riot and arson. The problem was beyond the competence of the few local constables, and the general manager appealed to Nassau for assistance. Governor Grey-Wilson arranged for an emergency loan from the Royal Bank of Canada and dispatched the money to Wilson City along with the police commandant and twenty-two policemen. All was quiet and orderly by Christmas when the policemen returned to Nassau, with the thanks of the company officials for protecting company property from "threatened overt acts" and preventing a "disaster."[91]

Even more than the growing dissatisfaction with the traditional truck and credit systems, including the methods used in the sponge and salt industries, the labor troubles at Wilson City were a portent of what could happen in a modern industrial setting, especially when coupled with American-style racialist employment practices. The scattered nature of the Bahamian working population, its lack of sophistication in labor organization, and its desperate need for cash wages as well as the general lack of industrialization probably prevented more frequent and serious disturbances.

The Wilson City operation was perhaps premature. Because it was located at a fixed site, it soon depleted its hinterland, and returns diminished. By 1916 the Bahamas Timber Company was employing 375 men and making so little money that management decided to pull out. The mill was closed and the machinery and equipment, including some of the rail lines and even some of the houses, were dismantled and shipped off. Wilson City became a ghost town, completely uninhabited. Several years later, however, more mobile and temporary timber operations were begun by the Abaco Lumber Company, which inherited the logging leases. It was based first at Norman's Castle in northern Abaco, between 1926 and 1936, and then at Cornwall and Cross Harbour south of Wilson City in the early 1940s, before transferring to Grand Bahama in 1944, with much more lasting if indirect consequences.[92]

Between the 1880s and 1920 increasing numbers of Bahamians—the majority of them Out Island males between the ages of fifteen and sixty-four

who were fleeing oppressive conditions and impoverished settlements—
were attracted by wage labor and migrated to the southern United States,
especially Miami and other parts of Florida.[93] The migration occurred in
several phases, and in fact Bahamians were among the pioneer developers
of south Florida. The United States had acquired Florida in 1819, and by
1845 it had achieved statehood. During its early development it had better
communication with the Bahama Islands than with the rest of the United
States. This would change with the completion of the north-south railroad, which reached Miami in 1896 and Key West in 1912. The subsequent
peopling of the southern counties of Florida with Americans led to the
tightening of immigration restrictions, culminating in the Johnson-Reed
Act of 1924.

As early as 1847 Bahamian "Conchs" (whites), mainly from the northern
settlements, were among the first settlers of Key West, Florida, where they
continued to engage in boat building, fishing, turtling, sponging, and wrecking and traded with Cuba in the Gulf of Mexico. Driven by the poverty of
the Bahamas and the dissatisfaction resulting from having to compete with
the newly emancipated blacks, they were attracted by the fact that Florida
was a slaveholding state resolutely adhering to "Southern values," where they
could "gratify their contemptuous dislike without stint and without reprisals." This connection was sustained and intermittently reinforced for at least
fifty years, a migration largely peopled by white families with relatives in the
Abaco Cays and northern Eleuthera who were living in similar houses and
with lifestyles to those found in Hopetown, New Plymouth, and Dunmore
Town.[94]

Key West, although it remained a bastion of white racialist supremacy,
later became a mixed community when many Bahamians, attracted by wider
opportunities and better wages, migrated there after American slavery ended
in 1865. Similarly, in the 1880s, political turmoil in Cuba and U.S. restrictions
led to the transfer of Cuban cigar manufacturing to Key West, which spurred
a second wave of black Bahamian migrants. Governor Blake reported in 1885
that black Bahamians had begun to migrate to Key West periodically or permanently, adding that "the expansion of cigar manufacture for the American
market has raised it from a village to a comparatively wealthy town."[95] By
1892 the population of Key West reached twenty-four thousand, including at
least eight thousand persons of Bahamian origin.[96] Much racial tension existed, stemming from the desire of the white Methodists to have segregated
churches. The district chairman of the Methodist Church expressed concern
for the Bahamians, "both white and coloured," commenting in 1892: "The

Methodist Episcopal Church South does not welcome the Blacks; and it is a very rare thing for a Coloured person to enter one of their churches. You can form no idea of how sharply the colour line is drawn." He added though, "But our Bahamians are really in a different category from the newly-freed Negroes of the Southern States. They have received from us perfect recognition and equal church privileges." However, despite the chairman's words that Bahamian blacks were welcomed to attend the Methodist Church in Key West, in June 1893 a missionary stationed there stated that "during the last Synod, a considerable number of White people petitioned for a White church." He upheld the Methodist position there, commenting that "it was not accepted of course."[97]

The United States' virtual acquisition of Cuba led to Key West's decline as a migrant destination. Bahamians, however, took advantage of the opportunities made possible by the opening up of southern Florida with the extension of Henry M. Flagler's Florida East Coast Railroad, making possible the establishment of farmlands, the building of resort hotels, and the Colonial Hotel in Nassau between 1899 and 1900. The fertile tracts of southern Dade County opened up once the railroad reached Florida City in 1905. Bahamian blacks readily migrated, eager to fill a labor shortage that guaranteed them between $1.25 and $1.50 a day, the equivalent of 5 to 6 shillings a day, compared with the going rate in New Providence of 1 shilling and sixpence to 2 shillings a day for whatever wage labor was available.[98]

Much of the emigration was only temporary, as the prevailing need was for manual labor to clear bush and build drainage channels and for agricultural workers to plant and reap. The majority of the migrants were males, most of whom stayed in Florida for less than a year at a time. But once the rapidly expanding Miami and other towns developed, more Bahamians came as families and stayed permanently. Bahamian fishermen, carpenters, masons, domestics, and even members of the nonwhite middle class joined the flood that became known as "the Miami Craze."[99] The peak of the Miami migration came in 1911 as Bahamian economic conditions worsened. In April of that year the British ambassador in Washington reported that there was seemingly an insatiable demand for Bahamian workers in southern Florida and that the migration was assuming "such propitiations as to cause anxiety to the Government and inconvenience to sponge outfitters and employers of labour" in the Bahamas. In the previous three months alone, 875 Bahamian males and 221 females had landed, and only 210 males and 87 females traveled in the opposite direction. So many Bahamians had settled in Miami that the ambassador recommended the appointment of a British vice-consul there to look after their interests and relieve the governor of "a considerable amount of work and anxiety."[100]

Governor Grey-Wilson, who was proposing that Canada annex the economically depressed Bahamas, was concerned about the loss of Bahamian labor but at the same time saw the migration as a safety valve and a source of valuable cash remittances. Most of the money was remitted in registered letters (rather than in postal orders, as for example from Panama to Barbados and Jamaica), so totals were difficult to assess. But the amount sent by registered mail and postal orders and carried by returning migrants may have totaled U.S. $100,000 a year by 1920, when the commissioner in Exuma estimated remittances of $15,000 to that island alone. The commissioner at the Bight, Cat Island, commenting on the introduction of American currency into the community, stated that it had "made many a heart glad. It is a common occurrence for registered letters to contain $40 and $50 coming to wives from their husbands and to parents from children."[101] Howard Johnson, however, stated that remittances, although they provided "financial support" for members of the family who stayed at home, were often used "primarily to satisfy consumption needs rather than productive investment." Remittances "formed a major source of income" and were used to build new houses but were also sent to Nassau to purchase clothing and imported foods. "The Out Islands became 'remittance societies.'"[102]

Though exact numbers are difficult to calculate because of the mixture of temporary and permanent migration, probably 5,000 black Bahamians were permanently settled in Florida by 1914. In 1910 the United States Census recorded that within the black population of 5,000 there were 3,500 British subjects, most of whom would have been Bahamians.[103] Bahamians congregated in two main areas: Coconut Grove on the south Miami waterfront, and northeast of the railroad tracks downtown in what was then called "Coloured Town" but was later known as Overtown (representing an area reduced by the more or less enforced migration of blacks to Liberty City in the late 1930s and almost erased by the building of Interstate 95 in the 1960s).[104] Outside Miami smaller segregated Bahamian communities were found in Florida City and Homestead to the south and northward in Dania, Fort Lauderdale, West Palm Beach, Fort Pierce, and even as far away as Daytona Beach—all places connected with Miami by the Florida East Coast Railroad.

Bahamians were welcomed for their skills, their willingness to work for comparatively low wages, and their general cheerfulness and because they caused less trouble than the American blacks. Their long experience of coexistence with Bahamian whites in harsh conditions enabled them to steer the delicate line between independence and accommodation and to turn "knowing their own place" to their own advantage. Several incidents of white mob or police brutality between 1907 and 1927 involved the British ambassador in Washington and almost threatened international incidents. Surprisingly, even the system of Jim Crow segregation had some advantages for Florida Bahamians. It provided the sense of community, effective integration between permanently settled and more temporary migrants, and extensive networking already found in Over-the-Hill, Nassau. Although attempts by the Anglicans and Methodists to establish missions to black Bahamians in Miami had limited success because of white opposition and lack of suitable black pastors, migrants enthusiastically formed their own churches as well as friendly societies, lodges, and, after 1917, branches of the Universal Negro Improvement Association (UNIA).[105] Bahamians living in Miami were deeply affected by the severe discrimination suffered in Miami and by Marcus Garvey's ideas (discussed in chapter 4), which were reaching the Bahamas.[106]

Bahamians brought their culture to their respective settlements, including their distinctive style of housing—"two story wooden frame houses, with wide, two tiered balustrade porches designed to take advantage of the ocean breezes"—and their festivals and dances. Modest Junkanoo parades were held at Christmas and New Year; celebrations marked Emancipation Day and Queen Victoria's birthday each August; and in 1911 migrant workers in West Palm Beach combined these celebrations with a parade and dance in honor of the coronation of George V. The famous black anthropologist Zora Neale Hurston commented later on the pervasive musical folkways brought to much of the east coast of Florida "by the flood of Negro workers from the Bahamas." She stated that Bahamian music "is more dynamic and compelling than that of the American Negro and the dance movements are more arresting: perhaps because the Bahamian offerings are more savage. . . . Nightly in Palm Beach, Fort Pierce, Miami, Key West and other cities of the Florida east coast, the hot drum heads throb and the African-Bahamian folk arts seep into the soil of America."[107]

In Florida many mostly menial jobs were reserved for blacks, but because of strict customary segregation, craftsmen and specialists such as tailors, cobblers, hairdressers, and morticians found a relatively prosperous clientele among people of their own color. Though Bahamian migrants were mostly poor and unskilled, a minority came from the middle classes and had accumulated some capital. Some such persons became shopkeepers and also found that they had a reservoir of customers without competition from the privileged white merchants in Miami like those they would have experienced in Nassau.[108]

Ironically, another benefit of Jim Crow segregation for Bahamians was mentioned in an official report from central Eleuthera in 1909: "In Miami the black man has to be extremely careful as to how he conducts himself, otherwise his liberty and even his life are endangered, and for this reason alone he abstains from liquor, saves his money and remits to his people at home."[109] Additionally, the advantage of living in a segregated area, like "Colored Town" in Miami, was that it gave Bahamians a foothold in the United States, along with experience that after World War I might encourage them to migrate to the modern and industrialized cities of the northern United States. A few black Bahamians, along with other West Indian migrants, had already settled in New York some time before the Harlem Renaissance of the 1920s. They included Nat and Julian "Cannon Ball" Adderley and T. A. Toote's brother, Frederick Augustus Toote, who became leader of the Philadelphia division of the UNIA in the 1920s and an ardent supporter of the great radical black activist, Jamaican-born Marcus Mossiah Garvey.[110]

As Howard Johnson has pointed out, though, the Florida migration also had short- and long-term disadvantages. It speeded up the depopulation of the Out Islands, leaving many with hardly any able-bodied men and most with a disproportion of women, old people, and the very young. As a "remittance society," the Bahamas became a context where external money raised aspirations and increased the taste for foreign goods while weakening the indigenous economic structure and actually widening class divisions. Similar to the returnees sporting their Panama money in Bridgetown, Barbados, or Kingston, Jamaica, the symbol of Florida wealth was the black "dude from Dade" in outlandish clothes (said to be changed twice a day, three times on Sundays), strutting a style in ironic contrast to the industrious sobriety practiced abroad. Their success was a model for other blacks to emulate, but their imported behavior and ideas were probably disturbing to local whites. The most prosperous of the returnees might hanker to build new homes and retire to the Out Island of their birth, but few if any were willing to return to farming for a living or be satisfied with Bahamian wage levels.[111]

Perhaps the most serious consequence of all, prolonged migration produced social dislocation and distress. Women deserted by their husbands sometimes took up with other men for support or comfort, and children lacked parental discipline. The absentee men themselves—despite their reputation for hard work, frugality, and sobriety—also formed liaisons and had more temporary sexual encounters (at the work camps and the seedier edges of Miami and Nassau), resulting in unprecedented levels of venereal disease.

While many Bahamians migrated to Florida in the late nineteenth and early twentieth centuries, small numbers of Chinese, Greeks, Lebanese, and Jews entered the Bahamas, fleeing from their homes because of political changes, religious persecution, population pressure, and poor economic conditions. The Chinese first arrived in the Bahamas as early as 1879, when a migrant from Cuba, Pan Yuong, opened a small restaurant on East Bay Street, and the *Nassau Guardian* noted: "It is astonishing how the Chinese settlers are thriving in our midst. We now have about a dozen Celestials who are patterns of industry, ingenuity and perseverance."[112] Others, including the Cheas and the Wongs, who came in the early 1920s and established businesses, are discussed later.

The first group of Greeks arrived in December 1887 to engage in the sponge trade. Originally sponsored by the Vouvalis Company, which had established a packing and exporting firm in London in 1882, many of the original Greek immigrants to the Bahamas eventually established their own sponge businesses after accumulating some savings. One of the earliest independent buyers was George Damianos, who established his business in 1890. Fearing that the Greeks were encroaching on the local sponge industry, Bahamians had protested as early as the late nineteenth century, but the "large scale invasion" into sponge outfitting by the Greeks never materialized. They concentrated on the buying, packing, and export of sponge.[113]

Also arriving in the Bahamas in the late nineteenth century was a small number of Lebanese. As Howard Johnson has explained, "They were a part of a significant exodus of Christian minorities escaping from Turkish misrule in Syria, which then belonged to the Ottoman Empire." Estimates are that between 1870 and 1900 approximately a million people emigrated from that territory. The last two decades of the nineteenth century experienced "a formidable movement" of Lebanese into the Americas.[114] Among the earliest Lebanese to arrive was J. K. Amoury (formerly Herbase) in about 1891 and the Bakers (formerly Ouwade) in 1894. On arrival, having little capital, the Lebanese began as "itinerant peddlers," catering to the lower end of the market. Later, after accumulating some capital, they retailed goods at fixed locations. Jewish immigration to the Bahamas was small but significant. But Jewish traders were virtually unknown in the Bahamas before 1923.[115]

Establishment of the Roman Catholic Church in the Bahamas

Entering the Bahamas in the late nineteenth century was the Roman Catholic Church. There were earlier ties, but no resident priest arrived until 1885. From January 1837 the Bahama Islands were included in the Vicariate of Jamaica, one of three in the West Indies, created by Pope Gregory XVI. In August 1845 Reverend Arthur Le Mercier Duquesnay, on his way from Jamaica to Louisiana, stopped in Nassau and offered mass in a private house. Another visit shortly after was made by the vicar general of Jamaica, who estimated that there were about sixty Catholics, mostly non-Bahamian, residing in Nassau. Patricia Glinton-Meicholas noted that they included "consular agents and merchants from Cuba, Haiti, the Southern United States, Greece and Spain, and a few English or Irish Catholics, who came mainly as civil servants."[116]

In 1858 the Bahamas was transferred from the Vicariate of Jamaica to the Diocese of Charleston, South Carolina. Reverend William Hayes Neligan was appointed vicar general of the Bahamas in 1866 and visited regularly until 1873. He estimated that there were two hundred Catholics in New Providence at that time. During the American Civil War (1861–65), many Roman Catholics were among the southerners who "flocked" to Nassau. Masses for such visitors were celebrated at the Royal Victoria Hotel, which had been built at the beginning of the war. Dr. Kirkley Sands states that the economic slump following the end of the American Civil War, the devastating 1866 hurricane, and the disestablishment and disendowment of the Anglican Church contributed to the transference of the Roman Catholic Church from the "financially embarrassed Diocese of Charleston" to the "more affluent" Archbishopric of New York.[117]

Two governors, John Pope-Hennessy (1873–74) and Sir Ambrose Shea (1887–95), were Catholics and probably assisted in the efforts to persuade the Catholics to have a more permanent presence in the Bahamas. Glinton-Meicholas asserts that Surgeon-Major F. G. Ayde-Curran of the British West India Regiment and his wife Lady Georgiana were instrumental in assisting with the establishment of the Catholic mission in the Bahamas.[118] Their petition for the appointment of a resident priest in the early 1880s was finally heeded in 1885, when Reverend Charles George O'Keefe was sent to Nassau. In July that year the Bahamas was transferred from the Diocese of Charleston to the Archdiocese of New York. Later, on 25 August 1885, the cornerstone of St. Francis Xavier Church (later Cathedral) was laid, and a mass was held in a completed St. Francis on 13 February 1887.

The Catholic mission came to be dominated by American Benedictine monks, probably as a result of the arrival in 1891 (and a decision to stay until his death in 1928) of a dynamic American priest of German extraction, Father Chrysostom Schreiner, OSB, sent by his abbot from St. John's Abbey, Collegeville, Minnesota, to recover from tuberculosis. Chrysostom Schreiner was the first permanent Catholic priest in the Bahamas. Endowed with a powerful intellect and dogged determination, Father Chrysostom divided his time between New Providence and San Salvador, which he claimed to have proven was the landfall of Christopher Columbus in the Bahamas, resulting in the name change from Watlings Island to San Salvador.[119] With the assistance of other priests from St. John's Abbey he accomplished much in developing, expanding, and educating the membership in the Roman Catholic Church in the Bahamas.

The Sisters of Charity from New York at St. Vincent on the Hudson, the first permanent missionaries, arrived in 1889 and lived at a former residence purchased by Bishop Corrigan and converted into a convent on West Hill Street, very near to St. Francis Church. The nuns established St. Francis Xavier, the first parish school, as a free school for poor (mostly black) children. During the following year, the Sisters of Charity established St. Francis Xavier Academy (later Xavier's College), originally attended by upper-class white girls but later integrated to accept middle-class nonwhites. By 1906 there were three Benedictine fathers, nine Sisters of Charity, one academy, and three free schools, catering to about 470 children. An act to incorporate the Roman Catholic mission in the Bahamas, vesting the title to the property then owned by the Catholic Church, was passed by the Bahamian legislature on 3 May 1911.[120] Before World War I, Chrysostom Schreiner set the pattern and tone of the expansion of Catholicism in the Bahamas. Roman Catholic priests, aided from the beginning by the nuns, offered their converts attractive churches, agreeable rituals, opportunities for participation, and a general absence of segregation within the churches. In due course nonwhite Bahamian females as well as males were attracted into Catholic orders.

The gradual pace of modernization evident since 1880, and the upheaval of World War I, led to limited changes in the Bahamas. The passage of the Volstead Act by the United States Congress in December 1919 was perhaps more important to the Bahamas than the events of 1914–18.

4

WORLD WAR I AND PROHIBITION

News of Britain's declaration of war on Germany on 4 August 1914 was received the same day in Nassau and Inagua and two weeks later in some of the more remote islands. The response in the Bahamas was extremely patriotic, as it was in most parts of the empire. As soon as news of the war reached Nassau, the legislature quickly met to declare its unswerving loyalty and devotion to the throne and the empire. Offering any help that was needed, it passed a Proclamation Act and Emergency Relief Act giving the governor and governor-in-council unlimited powers for defense purposes.[1] Usually parsimonious, the House of Assembly quickly voted £10,000 from public funds for the war effort, which was augmented to nearly £50,000 by the end of the war.[2]

Governor Haddon-Smith held a public meeting in Rawson Square, where he made a speech announcing the news and assuring the people that they were in no direct danger; he encouraged them to increase food production in case imports were restricted. A more formal patriotic meeting was held in St. Andrew's Hall presided over by the governor. An unusually wide spectrum of Nassauvians was present. Predictably, the center seats were reserved for the all-white Imperial Order of Daughters of the Empire (IODE), clergy, and public officials, while the representatives of the various mixed-race and black friendly societies and lodges and the general public were seated at the sides and back of the hall.[3] Two committees were appointed: the Recruiting Committee and the War Relief Committee. The Recruiting Committee represented a cross section of Nassau society. Headed by the commandant of police, Englishman R. H. Crawford, it was made up of G. M. Cole (white), S. A. Dillet (mixed race), L. W. Young (black), and D.S.D. Moseley (white).[4] A subcommittee of the War Relief Committee, in which whites predominated, was appointed for raising funds and war material.

In the initial drive nearly all Bahamians contributed money, some beyond their meager means—such as the people of Mangrove Cay, Andros, who raised more than £17, mostly in pennies and coppers.[5] Governor Haddon-Smith described the Bahamas' financial contribution as munificent; he boasted that although the majority of Bahamians were poor, they had "not only denied themselves luxuries, but in many cases, the necessaries of life. . . . There have been seamstresses and market women earning a few shillings a week insisting on giving either three or two shillings."[6] Patriotic orders and societies such as the IODE and the Bahamian Red Cross, headed by the white elite, were tireless in raising funds and making and shipping garments and other supplies. The energetic and gifted white proprietress and editor of the *Nassau Guardian* and the mixed-race owner-editor of the *Tribune,* Gilbert Dupuch, competed in raising funds for the West India Regiment. However, not everyone favored Bahamian generosity. A letter writer to the *Tribune* in October 1914 complained that the £10,000 voted for the war could be better used to repair roads, especially on the Out Islands, where poor people were suffering. Gilbert Dupuch himself, though loyal to the cause, commented in November that Out Islanders were being forced to give.[7]

The Recruiting Committee was aided by the eagerness of all Bahamians to join up. Among the volunteers were stevedores unemployed after the sudden ending of visits by ships of the Hamburg-American Line and sailors and farmers affected by the temporary slump in the prices of sponge and sisal. Most, however, were simply adventurous or idealistic, like fifteen-year-old Etienne Dupuch, who "thought this was an answer to my dream of carving my name in glory by giving my life for a just and glorious cause."[8]

But for the first year of the war, the Bahamians ready to serve were thwarted by the unwillingness of the British government to accept nonwhite colonials. The intensification of fighting revised this policy, forcing the War Office to raise mixed-race and black troops from the West Indies. Stipulations nevertheless barred nonwhites from being appointed as commissioned officers. Moreover, they were unable to be promoted beyond the rank of sergeant until toward the end of the war.[9]

On the first anniversary of the outbreak of war the new Governor, William Allardyce, made a renewed appeal for recruits. Well aware of the delicate color situation, he tactfully guided a resolution through a public meeting at St. Andrew's Hall providing for the raising of a small contingent in the colony, whose expenses would be defrayed by public subscription, to accompany their West India Regiment from Jamaica to England. Those men of purely European descent who wished to volunteer would make their way to Canada to join Canadian forces.[10]

At the beginning of the official recruiting program in August, only thirty persons were selected. The first man to volunteer was William F. Albury, one of the few whites to join the British West India Regiment; he signed up with ten others and was later placed in charge of the first contingent until their arrival in Jamaica. Some were medically unfit; others were too young and had falsified their age, like Etienne Dupuch, the light-skinned son of the ambitiously middle-class owner of the *Nassau Tribune*. He wrote: "The age for volunteers was 18, but this did not deter my ambitions to be among the first volunteers to leave the Bahamas on this adventure. The first contingent bore the honorable name of the Gallant Thirty. I wanted to be one of these gallant men. I was rejected for two reasons: too young and too small."[11]

The Gallant Thirty represented a wide cross section of the Bahamian population both professionally and racially and included civil servants, tradesmen, mechanics, farmers, and fishermen.[12] The official photograph taken at the time suggests that six of them were Bahamian whites. After a rudimentary drilling, the first contingent was given a splendid send-off. Two days before they left, impressive ceremonies took place on the Eastern Parade Ground and Rawson Square, which, along with downtown Nassau, was colorfully decorated. Nearly the entire population turned out to hear the governor speak and present instructions to Private William F. Albury. Bands played and cheers were raised as the contingent left on the specially leased schooner *Varuna* to join the British West India Regiment at its depot in Jamaica. On the day before their departure Lady Allardyce hosted them to a reception at Government House, usually out of bounds to nonwhites. Gifts were provided, mainly cigarettes and tobacco. The second Bahamas Contingent followed in November 1915, made up of 105 men, and the third in May 1916, consisting of 87 men. These were augmented by five further drafts of 78, 53, 51, 50, and 32 between August 1916 and September 1917.[13] In total, 1,800 men offered themselves for service. Approximately 700 Bahamians served overseas. Besides those who joined up in the Bahamas, 53 Bahamians living in England, the United States, and British Honduras enlisted, along with 50 Bahamian laborers from Panama. With few exceptions, those who served in the West India contingent were mixed race and black. The small number of white Bahamians volunteering for the war included about 36 old scholars from Queen's College high school, who joined the Canadian forces. A few whites also joined the United States Army. Of those enlisted in the Bahamas, 6 were killed in action, 3 died from wounds, and 28 died from other causes.[14]

The initial enthusiasm for the war among ordinary Bahamians soon disappeared. This was evident from the steadily declining numbers of recruits for the armed forces. After the first adverse effects, however, the Bahamian economy made a modest revival as wartime conditions raised sponge and sisal prices and the internal market for foodstuffs improved. While the United States remained neutral, the tourist trade in Nassau was hardly affected, and in fact the numbers for the 1915 winter season exceeded twenty-six hundred who came in 1914.[15]

It was America's entry into the war, rather than the lighting restrictions imposed in 1916, that signaled the collapse of the tourist season in 1917. Changes in transportation to and from Nassau curtailed food imports, especially flour. On the outbreak of hostilities, the German steamers of the Hamburg-American Line that had called two or three times a week at Inagua and Long Cay ceased their operations. Perhaps the hardest hit in the early stages were the stevedore laborers. A floating population of about 400 to 500 men lost their jobs and their livelihood. Governor Allardyce remarked in April 1916 that many were stranded and penniless at Mathew Town, Inagua, and the War Relief Committee came to their assistance to avert starvation.

But some islands, such as Long Cay, experienced positive effects. A black school teacher in Acklins named Bullard wrote in January 1917: "Death has stared the Long Cay people in the face, and in awful fright they started to cut down land, light fires, and put in corn, potatoes and peas, and they are rejoicing in the prospect of the best harvest in the history of the island." The Crooked Island district generally increased its food production under the able direction of Commissioner Cleare, who reported at the end of December 1917 that "never in the history of the islands has there been such a turning to the soil as in the year 1917."[16]

Most of the Bahamas, however, suffered food shortages. Governor Allardyce visited Washington to negotiate for food supplies and urged the House of Assembly (consisting mainly of white merchants) to organize judicious distribution of imported food, to suppress profiteering, and to encourage less consumption. The legislators had informed Governor Allardyce that in spite of their pledge under the War Contingent Act of 1916 to provide two hundred fresh recruits a year to serve in the British West India Regiment, the Assembly was no longer willing to pay all the costs of kitting and shipping the recruits and their separation allowances.[17]

This was one of the reasons why fewer black Bahamians were volunteering for service. Another was the opportunity beginning in 1918 for three thousand Bahamians to work as laborers for three to six months on the port facilities at Charleston, South Carolina, to provide for the provisioning and maintenance of the American army in France. In work organized by the Mason and Hangar Construction Company for the U.S. War Department and Labor Department, laborers could earn $3.30 (or 13 shillings and 7 pence) per ten-hour shift, at least four times what could be earned in Nassau.[18]

A more deeply seated reason, however, was privately conveyed by Governor Allardyce to the British government some months before the South Carolina project materialized. He was almost certain that news of the conditions in the fighting zones, including pernicious racial discrimination, had filtered back to the Bahamas. Following a tour of the Out Islands in July 1917, the governor informed the British minister in charge of recruiting that he found some of the people "unpatriotic, not to say disloyal." Mixed-race and black people saw the war as "a white man's war." Those in the biracial settlements of Governors Harbour and Rock Sound, Eleuthera, were particularly hostile, while most in the black settlements in Andros and Cat Island appeared indifferent to the war and adamantly opposed to enlisting. Overall there was a "general desire on the part of the coloured generation in the colony to escape from military service."[19]

The adventures, discomforts, and horrors of war are graphically conveyed in an autobiography of Sir Etienne Dupuch, *A Salute to Friend and Foe* (1982), the only published firsthand account, by one of the last survivors of the 1915–17 Bahamian contingents.[20] Like the other men who had volunteered, Dupuch experienced discomforts and distasteful episodes. However, he also had the opportunity to mix on close terms with ordinary Bahamians and to meet West Indians and Europeans for the first time in their own countries. He made lifelong friendships with many of his black fellow draftees and encountered educated West Indians with liberal ideas, including a few white officers, such as the Trinidadian Captain Andrew Cipriani and the Anglican chaplain J. C. Wippel, future principal of Codrington College. Dupuch and other Bahamian nonwhites experienced kindness from white civilians, especially French women, who were relatively unprejudiced racially. Some soldiers developed brief friendships with European girls, which would have been impossible in the color-conscious Bahamas.[21]

Other experiences were more shocking and cumulatively traumatic. Enrolled in the Fifth Reserve Battalion of the British West India Regiment consigned to Alexandria, Egypt, Dupuch and the others endured appalling conditions on the transport SS *Magdalena*. A fire on board almost got out of control, the food was disgusting, sleeping quarters were squalid, and the ship carried no proper medicines. Unaccustomed to such cold weather, some soldiers from the tropics succumbed to pneumonia, and one morning Dupuch woke up next to a corpse. Additionally, the extremes of hot and cold in the desert, along with poor food and inadequate medical attention, killed many West Indians, including some Bahamians.

Throughout his military service Dupuch remained a private in rank, subject to discipline that was often petty and callous. He also endured the casual brutality and pointless inefficiencies inseparable from life in the ranks; some dangers; and a great number of racial indignities. Painfully aware of the prejudice that existed in the Bahamas, soldiers including Dupuch were nevertheless shocked and humiliated at the treatment they received. As loyal British soldiers fighting for king and country and for freedom, they constantly met signs stating "Out of bounds to native troops."[22] Through conversations with senior Indian non-commissioned officers, they learned of the nationalistic feelings festering in India against the British, and how Indians felt about holding "inferior positions in their own country." Dupuch admitted, "It was then for the first time that I realized that the lowest, dirtiest, scrubbiest Englishman was considered superior to the finest Indian."[23] Like hundreds of other West Indians, Bahamians returned home with a different outlook on the world. Dupuch confessed: "I was a changed person when I returned to my island home at the age of 20 after seeing the peoples of Europe wallowing in a cesspit of human degradation. I was a very bitter man and swore never again would I lift a finger, certainly not risk my life, in defense of King and country, or anything removed from my limited sphere of activities"—an attitude he later changed.[24]

With new knowledge and a broader outlook, Dupuch took a greater interest in the affairs of his country. From his experience in the army he was determined to be "instrumental in helping to break down racial barriers in the Bahamas."[25] Indeed, throughout his life, Dupuch was adamantly opposed to racial discrimination among Bahamians and was always critical of racialist attitudes that stemmed either from British officials or from the local white elite. He saw it as his "clear duty to try to mend the breach among the races so that we could all go into the future together as a united Bahamian people." This concern led him in subsequent years to oppose actions by the Bay Street oligarchy that might provoke dangerous political reaction among blacks; to attempt (with limited success) to establish a multiracial middle party; and to oppose black power politics so adamantly that he ended up supporting Bay Street once it was in opposition. He proudly reiterated the claim in his later editorials that he had broken down racial discrimination in the landmark resolution passed by the legislature in 1956.

However, as the years passed, Dupuch grew increasingly conservative and became more aware of class distinctions that eventually made more of the Dupuches to identify with their white European rather than their black African antecedents. Dupuch also changed his views on imperialism, developing a highly personalized ideal of the British Empire and Crown and a craving for the symbols of rank.[26]

Discrimination, Identity, and Marcus Garvey

Race Relations

Race relations in the Bahamas were not simply polarized, as outsiders have often presumed, but were complex, often ambiguous, and influenced by racial tensions in the United States. One example followed the scandal attached to the collapse of the Bank of Nassau in 1916 as a result of dishonesty on the part of the bank's directors and auditors—all members of the Bay Street oligarchy and powerful members of the legislature, whom Governor Allardyce was reluctant to prosecute, pointing out to London that since "whites have not the respect or the standing with the dark population," he feared massive resignations, making the administration of the country "very difficult or impossible." Allardyce's fears proved exaggerated. In fact the bank's cashier, Robert Wheately Turtle, a white Bahamian, was charged with and convicted of larceny and six counts of falsification of accounts. He was sentenced to seven years' imprisonment, and a nolle prosequi was entered on other charges against him. Because of the prominent positions of the other officers of the bank, the attorney general and the governor tried to protect them, relenting only when the secretary of state for the colonies persisted. They were all tried; they pleaded guilty and were convicted. However, they were treated leniently, merely paying fines.[27]

Yet in commenting on the case, Gilbert Dupuch's Nassau Tribune, proud to be known as "the organ of the coloured population," extended sympathy toward the "honourable gentlemen" convicted and chided the judge for his "harsh and scathing" comments on the incompetence of the auditors. The governor responded by explaining that one of the directors prosecuted, W.C.B. Johnson, deputy speaker of the House of Assembly, had considerable influence over the editor of the Tribune and was a close political friend of the black member of the House, Leon Walton Young.[28]

Some Bahamians were particularly sensitive to race and class issues, and letters and editorials on the topic were common. A letter to the *Tribune* in February 1911 claimed that "coloureds" were being discriminated against at the sponge exchange and separated from whites at church meetings.[29] In November 1917, in response to letters in the American press regarding suggestions that the Bahamas (like the Danish Virgin Islands) might be annexed to the United States, a strongly anti-American letter was printed in the ultra-conservative *Nassau Guardian*. The letter writer retorted that the Bahamas did not wish such a relationship since "the United States on the whole cannot be considered a civilized country" because of the discriminatory policy that compelled black people to "submit by law to residential segregation," and to "'Jim Crow' travel." Additionally, American blacks had "an inferior franchise, labor limitations, and insecurity of property," compared with those in the Bahamas and suffered from "insecurity of life" because of the threat of lynchings. When another letter appeared in the same newspaper on 7 November in support of the first, the American consul, Mr. Doty, protested, charging that the first communication was libelous. D. S. Moseley, editor of the *Nassau Guardian*, apologized and closed the subject, stating that his journal did not endorse the opinions in the letters and that the United States was held in high esteem by his newspaper.[30] Presumably the letter writers feared that strife might come from greater polarization under influence of the American South.

Indeed, this was no idle threat, as witnessed by the experiences of Bahamians in Florida and South Carolina during World War I and shortly afterward, when growing bigotry and intolerance, fanned by the rebirth of the Ku Klux Klan in 1915, increased racial tensions and racial consciousness among Bahamians living in America as well as some Bahamians recruited as laborers by the Mason and Hangar Construction Company at Charleston, South Carolina.[31] Edward (Ned) Isaacs, son of mixed-race restaurateur Edward Adolphus Isaacs, on returning to Nassau from Charleston was much more intolerant of whites as a result.[32]

Garveyism

Violent incidents, such as the near lynching of the Irish Archdeacon Irwin, priest of the all-black St. Agnes Bahamian Anglican Church in Miami, was countered by the rapid spread of Marcus Garvey's Universal Negro Improvement Association after its formation in 1914. Bahamians were not implicated in the fierce race riots in the "Red Summer" of 1919 in America. Few Bahamians were active participants, but Johnny Demeritte, a Bahamian who had been severely wounded during the war, was an exception. He participated in a race riot in Liverpool, England, before leaving for the Bahamas.[33] A number of Bahamians, especially those who migrated to Florida and some northern cities in the United States, were attracted by what the UNIA offered and became involved with the movement. The most notable of these were Frederick Toote and Captain Joshua Cockburn. The son of black Nassau merchant Thaddeus "Sanky" Toote (and the brother of lawyer and politician Thaddeus Augusta Toote), Frederick Toote became Garvey's chief organizer in Philadelphia. Captain Joshua Cockburn was an enterprising Bahamian who had gained his master's certificate as a pilot on the West African coast and was commander of the ill-fated SS *Yarmouth* of the Black Star Line in 1919 and 1920. Hundreds of émigré Bahamians joined the twelve UNIA chapters in southern Florida. There were perhaps as many as three chapters located in the Bahamas.[34]

Most Bahamian migrants moved frequently between Miami and Nassau at least until 1924 when the John Reed Act was passed, virtually excluding Bahamians from the Florida labor market. They no doubt discussed Garvey's ideas of race pride, self-reliance, and nationhood and his plans for linking blacks everywhere into a vast network of production, trade, political cooperation, and eventual independence. Cockburn, then living in New York, visited Nassau in May 1920, where he was welcomed by a large and enthusiastic crowd at a meeting in the Good Samaritan Lodge Hall.[35]

Bahamians, both men and women, dominated the Universal Negro Improvement Association branches in southern Florida. FBI agent Leon E. Howe stated in a report of June 1921 that more than 95 percent of the members and officers of the UNIA in Miami, Coconut Grove, Homestead, and vicinity "are aliens, mainly Bahamian Negroes and hence *British citizens*." He added that of the approximately 10,000 Negroes in Miami, more than 7,000 were alien.[36] Bahamian members in the Miami branch included Samuel C. McPherson, third vice president, and Oscar E. Johnson, financial secretary, both tailors by profession, and Percy A. Styles, assistant secretary and a trustee. McPherson also sat on the advisory board. Leaders of the ladies' division of the Miami UNIA included Lily Farrington as president, Emma Rolle as secretary, and Alicia Johnson, treasurer. Among the returning Garveyites to Nassau were Samuel McPherson, Oscar Johnson, and Rev. Richard Higgs.

The latter gentleman had suffered violent and frightening experiences. He claimed that he had been kidnapped, handcuffed, gagged, and severely beaten because of his alleged doctrines of racial equality. After living in the United States for twenty-three years he was ordered to leave Miami. Shortly after his arrival in New Providence, Higgs told his story in a sermon at the Metropolitan Baptist Church in Grant's Town, Over-the-Hill. Police Commandant Whebell, who had used surveillance to obtain the information, reported to the colonial secretary that Higgs had "aroused considerable feeling among coloured folk here and I believe he intends holding a series of meetings which I am endeavoring to have covered. . . . I find feelings and opinions are very bitter against Americans and it is quite probable that there may be clashes between the two races whenever they meet."[37] Higgs no doubt preached at other Baptist churches, which played an important part in maintaining solidarity within the black community, as did the Grant's Town Wesley Methodist congregation and the friendly societies and lodges.

The UNIA movement caused perturbation at home and abroad. In May 1921 the white Methodist minister in Miami reported that he was being forced to close the mission to migrant Bahamians due to the lack of a black pastor. He wrote that the most distressing aspect was that it revealed "the tendency of a strong section of the Colored people to throw off friendship of the whites." This, he claimed, was the result of agitation by the UNIA and the influence of Marcus Garvey, who had recently visited Miami and Key West.[38] Two months later a Methodist minister in Nassau, commenting to the Wesleyan Methodist Missionary Society in London on the "undercurrent flowing into this colony, coming from America, via Miami," stated that a magazine in the vestry of Wesley Methodist Church, Grant's Town, contained the following statement on race turmoil in the West: "the Negro must look upon every white man as his *potential* enemy." The minister was not certain how widely the article was circulated but opined that "the attitude of the Negro is very different indeed from the attitude when I first came here in 1905. This is undoubtedly due to the emigration to Florida and the vile treatment the Negroes have received there."[39]

Although the record is silent on female participation in the Bahamas' UNIA, it can be surmised that there was female membership as there was in Miami. There Bahamian women dominated the ladies' division—Lily Farrington, president; Emma Rolle, secretary; Olga Minus, assistant secretary; and Alicia Johnson, treasurer. Justina Gunta, a native of Jamaica, was described as the "Lady President" of the UNIA in the Bahamas. The organization had a branch in Nassau and one in Gambier, established in the early 1920s.[40]

Among the male members of the Bahamian branch of the UNIA in 1928 were officers S. W. Johnson, president; S. J. Gibbs, treasurer; and Charles E. Duncan, secretary. Membership also included Samuel McPherson and

Oscar Johnson, Garveyite returnees from Miami; Leon Walton Young, a Fox Hill carpenter who had lived in Key West for a few years and later became a property developer; and Dr. Charles Knight, a physician from Jamaica, who was among the several West Indians to settle in Nassau in the early twentieth century and who had some influence on the black and mixed-race middle class. Also members were tailor Reuben Bethel—nicknamed the "Honourable Marcus Garvey"—and Captain Stephen Albert Dillet, writer, orator, politician, and senior public servant in the Imperial Lighthouse service.

It appears that Dr. Claudius R. Walker, physician, educator, and politician, and Bert Cambridge, musician and politician, were Garveyites. Admirers of Garvey included Alfred F. Adderley and Thaddeus A. Toote, both lawyers and politicians, and R. M. Bailey, a Barbadian by birth, who was a political activist though never elected to the House of Assembly. As in other West Indian colonies, the UNIA weekly paper the *Negro World*, which was widely distributed in the area, was received by Garveyites and other interested Bahamians. British governors banned it in many places and passed ordinances against seditious publications. In 1919 the Bahamas legislature passed the Seditious Publications Act, which remained in force for five years.[41]

However, quite a large number of Bahamians continued to receive the *Negro World*, usually sent by post in plain envelopes from New York. One intercepted copy was directed to Nassau's leading black lawyer, Alfred F. Adderley. On opening it, mixed-race postmaster Charles O. Anderson, in respect for Adderley, commented that it may not have been a seditious publication within the meaning of the Seditious Publications Act, "yet its circulation in a mixed community may have a mischievous effect by fostering a spirit of unrest and discontent." Others receiving the banned publication included C. C. Smith, a mixed-race merchant, Dr. Knight, Samuel R. P. Barnswell, Richard A. Benner, and J. Gibbs.[42]

Garvey-Related Black Organizations

Bahamian Garveyites, like their counterparts in British Caribbean colonies, seem to have been involved in and indeed dominated a number of organizations with objectives similar to those of the UNIA. Perhaps UNIA members in New Providence—because of the close scrutiny of the colonial authorities, the increasing power of the white mercantile elite, and their own loyalty to the British monarchy—feared victimization if they blatantly revealed their beliefs and association. Reuben Bethel, a Garveyite and lodge member, admitted that he and other members had tried to form a union for some time but dropped the idea, being "intimidated by the white race."[43]

Among organizations established in the early part of the twentieth century were the Union Mercantile Association, the Rejuvenation League, and the Citizens' Union. The Union Mercantile Association was headquartered in the Elks Lodge Hall on Blue Hill Road, Nassau. Similar to the Black Star Line, its objective was to purchase a motor boat large enough to run between Nassau and Miami for the use of "the colored people of the Bahamas." Its prospectus stated that it would provide "comfortable transportation for passengers travelling between the Bahamas and Florida regardless of creed or color." At the same time it insisted that "no person other than a person who is wholly or partly of African origin shall be eligible to be a director or hold any office whatsoever in the company." The organization hoped to raise £8,000. Shares of one pound each could be paid in three installments. Nearly three hundred shares were sold on the evening of 29 May 1920. Subscribers included A. C. Huyler, William A. Mather, Samuel Henry Tinker, W. J. Gibson, Thomas William Lunn, Bruce Alfred Huyler, and William Augustus Patton.[44] Directors were mainly upwardly mobile members of the lower strata.[45]

Lawyer Adderley acted for the association. Speaking at the meeting on 29 May 1920, he stated that "this was a movement to enable Coloured People of the Colony to be independent of the Whites," and their intention was to import goods at a lower rate than those supplied by white merchants. Reuben Bethel added that if this proved successful, this was only the "forerunner of other movements to make the Colored People more independent."[46] Meetings were held in June, July, and early August, and then the record is silent. At least 2,000 shares were sold and over £800 were collected by 2 July 1920. Dr. Knight, at a meeting on that date, attempted to assuage fears that the directors were going to "rob them of their money." He stressed unity and assured the gathering that the association would not only buy boats but would be involved in commercial trading. During the August meeting A. F. Adderley expressed his pride in his African heritage: "I don't think it is necessary to apologize to anyone and we should not be ashamed to call ourselves Africans. . . . We are not after Racial Antagonism but if we are asked by anyone why we are making such a move we will tell them to make you honor us."[47]

The UNIA, in addition to advocating black pride and self-reliance, sought to develop among blacks the idea of cultural self-improvement. It aimed to establish educational and training colleges to further the education of blacks. Black Bahamians who had migrated to or were living temporarily in New York were keenly aware of this and developed closer links with Garvey's supporters, both in the Bahamas and in the United States. Dr. Claudius R.

Walker, who attended City College in New York and later studied medicine at Howard and Meharry University, along with other Bahamians who supported Garvey, founded the Bahamas Rejuvenation League in New York and Nassau.

Aiming to improve education for black Bahamians, the league offered three-year scholarships at either the Hampton Institute or Tuskegee. Some scholarships were awarded, and plans were made to present trophies on an annual basis to pupils in public schools for the best student and essay; the plans were sanctioned by the Board of Education.[48] Frederick Toote, H. A. Tynes, B. G. Johnson, and Theo Farquharson were members of the Rejuvenation League. Farquharson, born in Acklins, migrated to Inagua and then to the United States, where he lived for fifteen years; he would organize a labor union in Inagua in 1934. Records on the Rejuvenation League are scanty, but the *Nassau Guardian* reported in May 1921 that a branch of the league was established and that the first meeting was held at the Metropolitan Baptist Church.[49] A ladies' committee of the Rejuvenation League in Nassau held a garden party in July that year in aid of the league's scholarship fund. Among the guests were members of the white and nonwhite elite who gave the league "respectability": the Anglican Bishop, Shedden; his sister Mary Moseley, editor of the *Nassau Guardian;* and Leon W. Young and A. F. Adderley.[50]

The third organization that seemed to have been influenced by Garvey was the Citizens' Union, established in 1926 by Charles O. Anderson, mixed-race postmaster of the Bahamas. He had served as a member of the House of Assembly between 1895 and 1925, and although he was part of the establishment, "he always identified with black causes." Thaddeus A. Toote was its second president.[51] The main objective of the Citizens' Union was to foster economic independence and to "inculcate the spirit of self-reliance and cooperation among the black masses." A related financial institution, the Citizens' Union, incorporated with an authorized capital of £10,000 with power to engage in a restricted form of banking, among other activities, was criticized by Etienne Dupuch, editor of the *Tribune.* Although commending the efforts of the union, Dupuch feared its competition with the Royal Bank of Canada, which had established a presence in 1908. C. O. Anderson, in a strong letter to Dupuch, whom he accused of being inconsistent in his attitude, retorted that the Citizens' Union would fill the gap between the Royal Bank of Canada "and the ubiquitous sharing societies in which thousands of pounds are placed yearly and loaned to those who are unable to obtain accommodation at the Bank because of the exorbitant rates of interest."[52]

Garvey's Visit to Nassau

By the early 1920s Claudius R. Walker, from Over-the-Hill, had already experienced higher education and, along with other black Bahamians, supported Marcus Garvey. The UNIA survived in the Bahamas at least until 1930. Justina Gunta, a "Garveyite to the core," probably helped reorganize the Nassau branch in 1927; like its parent body, the branch seems to have declined during Garvey's imprisonment (1925–27). However, by November of the next year, it had a full slate of Bahamian officers, including S. W. Johnson as president.[53] Also assisting in strengthening the branch in Nassau was the executive secretary of the UNIA division in Detroit, Michigan, J. A. Craigen, who later became estranged from Garvey. He visited the Bahamas in April 1927 under close surveillance by the police in preparation for Garvey's visit during the following year.

While in Nassau Craigen met with Etienne and Gilbert Dupuch, Leon Walton Young, and Sankey and Thaddeus Toote. He spoke on the same platform with S. C. McPherson and Young at the People's Theatre on Blue Hill Road, which catered to the black population. He also spoke in the African Methodist Episcopal Church and at open air meetings in Fox Hill. He opined that "the masses of Negroes of the Bahamas are anxiously hoping that a better day may come, especially economically; because of this soul-longing they are in a very receptive mood to grasp the principles of the UNIA." On the other hand, he was critical of the "many outstanding Negroes of Nassau [who remained] aloof from the association because of the belief that their licenses to practice law and medicine would be taken away from them." Also evident was segregation, and he perceptively commented on the "old game of playing off light-complexioned Negroes against blacks—while all are despised by whites."[54] Marcus Garvey made a brief visit to Nassau on 19 November 1928 and was watched by top-ranking police officers in uniform and plain clothes. Met by local members of the UNIA and supported by a large crowd estimated at "a couple thousand people," Garvey was given a warm welcome. A standard bearer displayed a shield with the royal coat of arms of "His Excellency," while a specially decorated car at the dock transported him to the residence of Leon W. Young and his wife, where Garvey spent the night.

That afternoon UNIA members took him on a sight-seeing tour around the island and at 7:30 p.m. to Liberty Hall on Lewis Street in Over-the-Hill. In spite of rain, a crowd estimated at 2,500 gathered at the nearby Southern Recreation Grounds; Etienne Dupuch estimated the crowd as the "largest audience that had ever gathered in that spot."[55] Black West Indian physician Dr. C. H. Knight chaired the meeting. Speakers included Captain Stephen A. Dillet, Marcus Garvey, and Leon W. Young. Garvey captivated his audience, speaking for over an hour, delivering one of the "best and most forceful speeches" ever "made on a platform in the Bahamas." His remarks were moderate and diplomatic. While thanking the government of the Bahamas for its courtesy, he condemned the government of Bermuda, which had banned his visit. Typically, Garvey pointed out the weaknesses of black people but showed his confidence in their progress:

> At one moment he extolled the merits of the white man and condemned the Negro as a lazy good-for-nothing specimen. At the next moment, he declared that the same lazy good-for-nothing man had reached the point where he was capable of managing his own affairs, and his white brother, who fathered him all the way to the present moment, should be relieved of the burden.[56]

Effects of World War I, Emigration, and the Garvey Movement

The First World War, emigration, and the Garvey movement all impacted the Bahamas significantly, resulting in hardened racial attitudes and upheaval in social life. Anglican priests often complained about the "dearth of religious life" and the increase in the drinking of intoxicating liquors, which were more accessible owing to the reduction of duty on cheap spirits. Family life also suffered because of the dislocation brought by war and emigration. Many males had emigrated, and females outnumbered males by 5,451 in the overall 1921 population of 53,031. Women, who had traditionally been the backbone of the Bahamian family, particularly in the area of farming, took on even greater responsibilities and more diverse occupations, especially in Nassau. Although the majority remained housewives, an increasing number of women worked outside the home, especially black women undertaking work in the domestic field. Some women in the white elite and a few mixed-race women joined the civil service as clerks and wireless operators. A small number of white women owned dry good shops, while others were employed as shop assistants, caterers, fancy shell workers, publishers (e.g., Mary Moseley), librarians, and private school teachers. Mixed-race women and a few black women found occupations as nurses, dressmakers, stenographers, music teachers, and public school teachers.[57]

Rowena Eldon, for example, after spending six years at St. Hilda's High School, later worked for an insurance company and afterward in a wholesale and retail business owned by T.H.G. Lofthouse, a wealthy white merchant. She was one of the first mixed-race women to work in a Bay Street store in downtown Nassau.[58] Governor Allardyce commented in 1918 that "with few exceptions the local youth is past praying for. The young women have a much higher sense of responsibility."[59] Between 1914 and 1915, more girls than boys were receiving a secondary education in private schools.[60]

Discrimination

Despite the growing disparities among whites, they united to maintain their racial purity and were vigilant in protecting their interests against immigrant minorities in the 1920s. American influence exerted by hotel and shipping tycoon Frank C. Munson of the Munson Steamship Line was partly responsible for the hardening of racial barriers. Munson's discriminatory policies reinforced the already deeply prejudiced feelings of whites against brown and black Bahamians. By barring all nonwhites from the Colonial Hotel, he upset a few near-white men, such as the excellent photographer Fred Armbrister, who had moved among white society in Nassau in spite of his mixed-race pedigree. Armbrister found this hotel ban a most disturbing experience, which, as Benson McDermott stated, was "to haunt him for the rest of his life." Armbrister died a tragic death in the Nassau asylum in the mid-1950s.[61]

Sporting and recreational activities were still segregated. The Wasps and Albion teams that competed in the football season were all white. Blacks who played tennis were banned from the hotel courts and from the prestigious and strictly segregated Nassau Lawn Tennis Club. They were compelled to play on the inferior courts in the Roman Catholic grounds and the recently built Gym Tennis Club in the Pond area. Mixed-race and black tourists who visited Nassau stayed at private homes or guest houses such as that of the Worrells on East Bay Street or at the Magnolia Apartment Hotel. Even needlework guilds for young ladies at Government House were segregated; the Queen Mary Needlework Guild had only whites, while respectable mixed-race ladies, including the Hills, Molly Albury, and the Blacks, Bosfields, and Isaacs, most of whom were fair-skinned, attended the "Needleworkers."[62] Boy Scout and Girl Guide companies were strictly segregated. Anglican Bishop Shedden stated in 1927 that no nonwhite Girl Guide group existed. There were two white groups, the Greens attached to Queen's College and the Reds of St. Hilda's. Plans by a Miss Thompson, a member of the church executive at Wesley, to start a nonwhite troop of guides were squashed by the assistant commissioner of the guides, despite the existence of a black

Boy Scout group attached to Wesley. When Lord and Lady Baden-Powell, chief scout and chief guide, visited the Bahamas in early 1930, they were appalled to find that the two races in the guides were segregated, even in their "turn-out" parades. While the whites congregated at Government House, the mixed-race and black guides turned out at Addington House at the grounds of the Anglican bishop's residence. Lord Baden-Powell, when making inquiries about the absence of nonwhites, was told that they had not been included in the celebrations because their uniforms had been blown away in a recent hurricane. Lady Baden-Powell was reportedly so annoyed that she disbanded the Girl Guides at least temporarily; they still exist in the Bahamas today.[63]

The impact of World War I, Prohibition, and Garvey's movement probably influenced nonwhites to become more involved in politics during the 1920s. Entering the House of Assembly for the first time was the young and talented lawyer Alfred F. Adderley, son of William Parliament, and grandnephew of Campbell Adderley. It was the second time that a father and son were "actively involved in politics," the first pair having been T. A. Toote and his father Thaddeus "Sankey" Toote. In 1923 A. F. Adderley was elected to a seat in Eleuthera, previously a stronghold of the white merchant class. He served for two years but for some reason did not seek reelection in 1925 when additional black members were elected, including Samuel C. McPherson, Leon W. Young, and Wilfred Cash (New Providence), Thaddeus Toote (Cat Island), Robert J. Bowe (Exuma), James Bismark Williams (Crooked Island), Thaddeus Augustus Toote (Watlings Island and Rum Cay), A. Etienne J. Dupuch (Inagua), and Wilfred P. Adderley (Andros Island). At the end of 1925 there were eight nonwhites in the House of Assembly; nine if the light-skinned R. T. Symonette elected for Harbour Island is included.[64] Robert J. Bowe was also very light-skinned and may have been passing for white.

Politically, nonwhites seemed more united, at least temporarily. During the middle part of the decade, a group of mixed-race and black men supported the same issues as some whites. The black and mixed-race men included Robert M. Bailey, T. A. Toote, A. F. Adderley, W. P. Adderley, L. W. Young, S. C. McPherson, Etienne and Leon Dupuch, Stephen Albert Dillet, L. L. Young, W.E.S. Callender, Bert Cambridge, and Inagua-born L. W. Duvalier. More enlightened whites were C. C. Sweeting and W.C.B. Johnson. Two black women, Lillian Weir and Gladys Bailey, were also involved and sat on the platform at the first meeting of the group. They met for the first time on 20 September 1924 at the People's Theatre, advocating gradual constitutional and social reforms, especially "on behalf of the lower classes," which included adequate public schooling, improvements in the civil service, better sanitation, and deepening of the harbor. Race was not emphasized at this juncture. The *Tribune* reported that the meeting was attended by "a large and enthusiastic number of citizens" despite the inclement weather.[65] Their joint platform climaxed in their unification to support the introduction of the secret ballot. The organization became known as the Ballot Box Party.

Corruption was blatant in the elections following the Ballot Box Party's establishment. The *Tribune,* for instance, reported on 28 July 1928 that "corruption would seem to be so widespread that it is difficult to resist the conclusion that the constitution, which so many are so anxious to preserve, is nothing but an illegal plutocracy masquerading as a democracy."[66] It opined that arguments against voting by ballot in the Bahamas were absurd: "The masses in this colony are at the present time trained to use the ballot in the hundreds of friendly societies which exist in all parts of these islands." The *Tribune* also cited "the brazen and reckless manner in which the election was carried out in the Fox Hill section of the eastern district." It warned that "corruption at elections must be checked" and the ballot system must be introduced.[67] The pro-establishment *Nassau Guardian,* surprisingly, published a letter critical of the election: "The open method of voting seems to have many obvious evils and is open to every conceivable form of corruption and intimidation. . . . The presence of a howling mob surging up and down the polling booth would not be tolerated in England and it cannot be approved here."[68] Acting Governor A. C. Burns commented to the secretary of state for the colonies that "the *Tribune* is consistently anti-Government and anti-white, yet the irregularities of which it complains resulted in the defeat of a white candidate and the election of two Negroes. It is true however, that the two successful candidates, Messrs. Leon W. Young and Wilfred G. Cash, had the support of the prominent white politicians including two unofficial members of the Executive Council."[69]

A note at the Colonial Office between Freeston and Grindle on 24 July of the same year revealed that while the Colonial Office viewed the "present system" as "theoretically indefensible . . . to abolish it would result in return of the black or coloured members for nearly every constituency in the islands. Steps would be resisted vehemently by the white population whose political ascendancy rests to no small degree upon influence which they are liable to exercise over present arrangements. . . . Even if the secret ballot could be constitutionally introduced, the resulting fear of the black and colored ascendancy could lead to an immediate demand for Crown Colony Government." The Governor of the Bahamas, Sir Charles Orr, refused to take any action regarding the introduction of the ballot. Freeston closed the discussion with the comment that the matter "lies with the present legislature and nothing that might be said by the Secretary of State would do much to alter their attitudes."[70]

The number of nonwhites increased to ten after the 1928 elections.[71] Despite these gains, the House of Assembly remained dominated by white merchants, a minority of whom, as noted, offered support to nonwhite candidates.

National Identity and Resentment of the Outsider

Bahamians of both races had mutual feelings on certain issues. As Howard Johnson has demonstrated in his excellent essay "National Identity and Bahamian Culture,"[72] Bahamian "homogeneity" existed and was in part "a response to incursions of immigrants from the rest of the British Caribbean (attracted by the relative prosperity of the Bahamas) and from Haiti." The "animus against West Indians was the continuation of a long-established tradition." Despite the racial, class, and color divisions, "resentment of the outsider provided the cohesion which transcended those divisions." William Wylly commented as early as 1812 that Bahamians did not consider themselves West Indians. This view was repeated by Sir Allan Burns more than a century later.[73] Bahamians vigorously argued that geographically they were not part of the Caribbean and took measures to control immigration. One means was through general acts of the legislature and the more subtle and flexible orders in council, applying to particular cases and short-term situations. From 1920 the principle had been established that anyone coming to settle or work in the Bahamas had to have the approval of the governor-in-council. This proviso was relaxed, though, in times of need, most notably when the Purdy and Henderson Company was allowed to bring in hundreds of Cubans and other West Indians and artisans among the workforce of eighteen hundred used to reconstruct the British Colonial Hotel in 1922 as the New Colonial Hotel. Quite a number of West Indians employed at the time stayed and settled in Nassau, including Clement T. Maynard, a Barbadian with experience in France, Brazil, Panama, and Cuba whose son became the deputy prime minister and was the father of a future Bahamian cabinet minister; and Lionel Leach, a Trinidadian who helped in the reconstruction of Kingston, Jamaica, after the 1907 earthquake.[74]

This attitude toward West Indians was expanded to include other foreigners, especially if they posed an economic threat. Secretary of State for the Colonies Amery concluded that although the majority of Bahamian legislators saw the necessity of hiring outsiders for most of the senior posts in the civil service, "this is all part of the chronic hostility which prevails in the Bahamas against imported officials, or foreigners as they are impudently called in the colony."[75]

Similarly, intense local feeling among whites and nonwhites was aroused in early 1922, when Englishman Major Edgar E. Turner, commissioner of police since 1919, on the advice of another imported official, the acting stipendiary and circuit magistrate J. M. St. John Yates, had two local men arrested without the attorney general's knowledge. William F. Albury, who was white and had served with distinction in the First World War, was arrested on the serious charge of sodomy, and William Polhemus, a nonwhite, was charged with stealing liquor from the club at which he worked. Both cases were subsequently dismissed owing to the lack of satisfactory evidence. In Albury's case the acting attorney general, A. Kenneth Solomon, felt "that no reasonable man in the community" would convict the accused. The House of Assembly demanded that an inquiry be made into the police force.[76]

Members of the House of Assembly seemed to have had a vendetta against the two officers. Accusations of collusion were hurled at the commissioner of police and the magistrate. Local feelings ran high, fanned by "a mass of gossip."[77] Etienne Dupuch, who took the side of the officials, recalled the hearings at which Solomon presided:

> The Speaker of the House, a lawyer (Mr. H. Malcolm), was appointed to represent the House. He pressed the case against the officials in the commission, and the room—Legislative Council Chamber—where the investigations were held daily crowded with hostile members of the House who made audible remarks during the hearings. It all reminded one of the "lynch" court in the Southern United States.[78]

Yates and Turner were exonerated but were sent to posts in other parts of the empire. Dupuch stated that his decision to battle on the side of the officials caused the town to jump on his neck "like a ton of bricks." He claimed that he stood alone and paid a high price for his stance.[79]

Bahamians also reacted when their livelihood was threatened. Feelings of jealousy between Bahamian black laborers and the Cuban workers imported to work on the site of the New Colonial Hotel ended in a disturbance that resulted in fifty-five Cubans being returned to Havana. Little information is available on the actual incident. Apparently a Bahamian was attacked by a Cuban and a fight ensued, after which some Cubans went on strike.[80]

Perhaps the greatest resentment demonstrated against foreigners was focused on squashing competition from the minority immigrant groups including the Chinese, Greeks, Lebanese and Jews. Though the numbers entering the Bahamas were extremely small, their arrival by the mid-1920s and subsequent active participation in the Bahamian economy was enough to cause concern among some native merchants. One who was uneasy was Robert J. Bowe, a near-white Nassau businessman and member of the House of Assembly representing Exuma. In late April he made efforts in the legislature to have immigration entry restricted, especially for the Chinese, Syrians, Turks, Arabs, Romanis, Hindus, and Egyptians. Arguing that Lebanese and Chinese competition was threatening native businessmen in Jamaica, he predicted that if Bahamians were not careful, these "middle-man minorities" would also pose a threat to the Bahamian merchant.[81]

Bowe's efforts in 1925 were not enthusiastically received by his fellow legislators or the society at large. Leon W. Young, who seconded Bowe's motion for the appointment of a Select Committee on Immigration, was more concerned with keeping out such people as "gypsies, who came here and practiced art among the people" rather than with safeguarding Bahamian businesses against minorities, whereas Roland T. Symonette saw economic competition as a "natural consequence of the free enterprise system." When the bill restricting immigration was eventually drafted and presented to the House of Assembly for a second reading, a motion was adopted postponing discussion of it for six months.[82]

It was not until 1928 that the matter was discussed again. By that time white merchants who were also members of the House of Assembly expressed concern about the undesirable business methods of foreigners, believing, as did A. Kenneth Solomon, that the immigrants were posing a threat to the entrenched Nassau merchant class. Attempts were made to limit entry to Chinese immigrants, as evidenced in the minutes of the Executive Council between 1927 and 1933, revealing that members of the council delayed granting naturalization to Chinese merchants who had settled in the colony.[83] A series of acts between 1928 and 1931 restricting immigration to the Bahamas also limited the participation of the trading minorities to certain businesses as well as restricting entry to West Indian artisans who were attracted by Nassau's 1920s economic boom. These discriminatory legislative measures clearly showed the hostility of the Nassau merchant class and their determination to suppress economic competition, especially when the economy began to contract.[84]

The Bahamas at the End of World War I

The signing of the Armistice by Germany on 11 November 1918 was met by wild enthusiasm in Nassau and the Out Islands, although news took some time to reach many of the Out Islands. Bells were rung, bunting put up, and market women danced in the streets for joy. Queen's College scholars, proud of their thirty-six "Old Boys" who had taken part in the war, paraded to Government House and 13 November was declared a public holiday. To add to the excitement, in January 1919 Nassauvians caught their first sight of an aircraft when two American naval seaplanes visited the city from Miami.[85]

Troops returned sporadically in 1919, heroes for a day. They were feted by various organizations, including the Imperial Order of Daughters of the Empire. Casualties among them were remarkably light, and few received decorations for war efforts. Only one Bahamian (identity unknown) earned a Distinguished Service medal, while four civilians were awarded British honors: Harcourt Malcolm, speaker of the House of Assembly, O.B.E.; Elizabeth A. Lofthouse, president of the IODE, M.B.E.; Agnes A. Johnson, secretary of the Red Cross Guild, M.B.E.; and Mary Moseley, Secretary of the Ladies' Committee for the British West India Regiment, M.B.E.[86]

Men of the Bahamas' war contingents returned home to an environment little changed. Poverty still characterized the colony, which depended almost totally on sponge fishing and farming. Seasonal tourism helped keep the economy afloat and to stimulate true wage labor, which was replacing the truck and bartering systems. Education had not seen any dramatic changes. It remained handicapped by the perennial problems of poor accommodation, shortage of supplies, lack of trained teachers, and over-dependence on the monitorial system, and a public secondary school system was still nonexistent. Nassau's communication and transportation systems had not expanded appreciably, and what little there was benefited only Nassauvians. Out Islanders remained socially the same, upholding their ideas of racial purity in the biracial and white settlements, most of which suffered from diminishing populations due to emigration.

In terms of the world and the empire, Nassau, the metropolis of the Bahamas, was "a small backwoods community of an inconspicuous island of the western hemisphere."[87] For the most part restiveness against colonialism and the wave of democratic sentiment that the war stimulated in other colonies bypassed the Bahamas, where few echoes were heard and no leader emerged to advance the struggle for equality. Etienne Dupuch and others who had been exposed to the new egalitarian and socialist ideas were powerless to fight the Nassau establishment, and the Bahamian population remained mostly apathetic and politically unaware. The passing of the Volstead Act by the United States Congress in December 1919 was to be more important to the Bahamas in its effects than the events of 1914–18.

Prohibition and Its Effects

In January 1919 the Eighteenth Amendment to the United States Constitution was ratified. The Volstead Act, passed in December of that year, introduced national prohibition to take effect in 1920, outlawing the manufacture, sale, importation, or transportation of "intoxicating liquors." While Congress agreed to an act banning the liquor trade, it did not provide sufficient funds for enforcement. This oversight led to the emergence of a lucrative trade in bootleg liquor by a thriving underworld.

The Bahamas, because of its proximity, became an important center for the trans-shipment of liquor into the United States.[88] Prohibition was a mixed blessing. On the one hand, it caused an unprecedented boom in the Bahamas' poor economy, which led to improvements in public works and social services, and coupled with the spillover of the land boom from Miami, the infusion of new wealth was used to boost the nascent tourist industry. On the other hand, while Nassau prospered, the Out Islands were neglected, and with them agriculture and sponge fishing.

Because of new United States immigration restrictions, Out Islanders were unable to emigrate there easily. To add to their economic woes, several severe hurricanes hit the Bahamas in the late 1920s, and many people drifted into Nassau. The decade of the '20s, which saw much progress in the laying of the material foundations of Nassau, also witnessed the growth of many social ills marked by the widening gap between the "haves" and "have nots." The white elite and nouveau riche merchants began to experience economic competition from the small trading minorities like the Greeks, Chinese, and Lebanese who had migrated to the Bahamas since the 1880s. Moreover, and owing to American influence, the color line was hardening.

The year after the end of the Great War was one of virtual depression in the Bahamas. Exports of the two main staples, sponge and sisal, declined after a temporary wartime boom, and remittances dried up as servicemen and migrant workers returned to swell the labor market. Tourism did not recover quickly due to the disruption of shipping and an unfavorable currency exchange rate between sterling and the dollar, the effect of which was especially felt because of the dependency on imports. These setbacks were further exacerbated by natural disasters. A prolonged drought hampered food production, and a hurricane in September 1919, although missing Nassau, affected most of the Out Islands, destroying crops and seriously damaging the sponge fisheries.[89]

The effects of Prohibition changed this gloomy picture, at least in Nassau.[90] The decade of the 1920s witnessed an unprecedented increase in trade, a vast movement of alcoholic beverages from the Bahama Islands to the U.S. mainland. A high Bahamian import duty on the liquor entering this trade produced a sharp rise in revenue.[91] As early as March 1920 the *Times* of London reported that Prohibition had "transformed the Bahamas Government's financial position as if by magic from a deficit to a comparatively huge surplus, provided labor for large numbers of unemployed Bahamians and put more money in circulation in this little British colony than has been the case for many years."[92]

Nassau with its excellent harbor facilities was ideal for the movement of liquor, including West Indian rum, English gin, and Scotch whisky. It was filtered through the northern islands—mainly Bimini and West End, Grand Bahama, which are in close proximity to the American coast. Even before the Volstead Act came into force, Nassau harbor was swarming with ships unloading thousands of barrels of liquor from English and Scottish liquor merchants. The wharves and some streets were crowded with cases of liquor. Men, women, and even children were employed, the men as stevedores, with the women and children assisting them by rolling the barrels off Bay Street to nearby warehouses, which quickly multiplied.

By February 1921 Governor Harry Cordeaux wrote that there were thirty-one bonded warehouses, needed to store 13,700 barrels and 37,400 cases imported so far. Revenues soared from £81,049 in 1919 to £204,296 in 1920 and £1,065,899 in 1923. Despite the reduction in duties, the increased vigilance of U.S. agents, and Bahamian customs evasion, according to Philip Cash, "at no time before 1930, did the value fall below £500,000."[93] Cash further observed: "The whisky trade therefore remained of prime importance throughout the decade, declining more noticeably after 1930 and returning to its pre-Prohibition levels by 1935."[94]

Internationally, much to Mary Moseley's chagrin, the Bahamas soon earned notoriety as a bootlegging haven. Its role in rum-running also received increasing attention and criticism from the American government and came to be regarded at the Foreign office as a threat to Anglo-American relations. Miss Moseley was incensed at the English and American newspapers, which accused Bahamians of collusion with the bootleggers. The Americans on several occasions accused Bahamian officials at West End, Grand Bahama, Bimini, and Nassau of issuing two sets of clearance papers to American ships involved in illicit smuggling and also of illegally transferring the ships' registries.[95]

There was more than a hint of corruption. A federal Prohibition agent declared that a certain customs officer at Nassau explained to him how two sets of clearance papers could be obtained. The customs officer did not say there would be money required outside the regular fees but "intimated that he and the boys expected to be taken care of."[96] Such claims of irregularities were strongly denied by Bahamian officials. Governor Cordeaux assured the Colonial Office that the part the colony played in the "gigantic" smuggling of liquor into the United States was infinitesimal. He argued that the bulk of the profits went to Americans who bore the risk of landing it undetected on the American coast.[97] It is clear, however, that Bahamians did nothing to discourage bootleggers but aided and abetted them.

Finding it too risky actually to run the liquor, most Bahamians involved in the trade confined their activities to the legitimate occupation and safer business of selling it wholesale to foreign bootleggers within the limits of the colony, either from liquor stores in Nassau or from floating depots on hulks at sea.[98] As Major H. M. Bell recorded in his fascinating book, *Bahamas: Isles of June,*

> It was not the business of the dealer who possessed liquor to inquire wither it was bound; that was the business of the Customs and the Buyer. The men who made the greatest fortunes in Nassau never sailed a ship nor sold to any person in the United States a pint of booze. They did not have to go far; buyers flooded their offices, took the liquor direct to chartered ships and sailed away.

Bootlegging activities brought riotous times to the usually quiet streets of Nassau. But as Bell emphasized, "There was no roughness to speak of, and no killings, though guns were out time and again when rival gangs met."[99]

American authorities soon focused their attention on Bimini, Gun Cay, and West End, Grand Bahama, which were becoming notorious as ports of entry and centers of the liquor smuggling trade. As early as February 1920 permission was granted for the consignment to Bimini of an amount of liquor greatly in excess of local needs. The owner of the liquor, Charles Vincenti, an American of dubious character, was virtually kidnapped by U.S. federal agents and taken to Miami for trial on smuggling charges. Following protests by the Bimini commissioner and the Bahamian government, Vincenti was released, and the federal agents were accused of illegal arrest. The incident, however, signaled the emergence of Bimini's involvement in the bootlegging business.[100]

Bimini became a well-known "wet" spot for Americans, who came by boat and airplane as often as twice a week to drink and make merry. By 1927 there were at least three bars and liquor businesses within a distance of a half mile on the main street of the small island of North Bimini.[101] Similarly, West End became the resort not only of international smugglers but also of trippers eager to enjoy the delights of drinking in a raffish atmosphere. Activities at Gun Cay and Cat Cay, just south of Bimini, were even more flagrant. As a report from the United States Treasury Department revealed in 1927, Bahamian schooners owned by licensed liquor dealers in Nassau were anchored almost permanently inside the cays. From such vessels, whisky and other alcoholic beverages were sold, and schooners and power boats from Nassau constantly replenished the stock.[102] One notorious vessel, the hundred-foot barge *Dreamland*, lay permanently at anchor behind North Cat Cay, without sails or power. It held thousands of cases of liquor and was visited frequently by unlighted American motor boats, which took on hundreds of sacks of liquor. Besides one of its owners and three other whites, it had a crew of seven black Bahamians. Their main task, like that of many Nassauvian men and women, was to sew the special triangular-shaped conveniently portable, floatable burlap sacks, each designed to contain six bottles.[103]

Bahamians, mostly white, were involved as liquor merchants. Some nonwhites, such as William B. North, also sold liquor but on a smaller scale. A few Bahamians were directly implicated in rum-running. Most notable was Captain Roland T. Symonette, a poor young light-skinned mixed-race man from Current, Eleuthera. His adventures during Prohibition laid the basis of one of the largest Bahamian fortunes, earning him entry into the Bay Street oligarchy and its eventual leadership. Symonette was listed in a confidential memorandum in 1922 as one of the most active Bahamian ship captains engaged in smuggling, and in the following year his first wife, Nellie, testified that he had made a million dollars in three years, mainly by running liquor between Nassau and the American mainland.[104]

A handful of opportunistic Britons and Canadians were also involved in rum-running, but the more dangerous aspects of the trade were dominated by Americans. Most notorious of these was William McCoy, whose bootleg whisky had such an excellent reputation that it was called "the Real McCoy." With the help of a legally registered company, the British Transportation and

Trading Company, registered in November 1921 in Nassau, he embarked on a lucrative bootlegging career. He claimed to have run over 175,000 cases of liquor from the Bahamas to the American mainland. McCoy's chief supplier was an Irish American named George Murphy who headed the Bahamas Island Import and Export Company, the largest bootlegging firm in Nassau.

When Prohibition ended, McCoy returned to the United States, but Murphy remained in Nassau and became a prominent member of the Bay Street clique.[105] He later developed Shirley Slope and Tower Heights, launched horse racing at the Hobby Horse Hall Track, and became manager of the Fort Montagu Hotel. Representing Exuma in the House of Assembly from 1935 to 1946, he ended his career in the Legislative Council.[106]

By 1921 the atmosphere of Nassau had changed. Bootlegging activities had intensified, and Bill McCoy was joined by many other colorful but shady characters who were in Nassau to buy liquor and to prevent any fraudulent sales to organizations that employed them. In McCoy's words, Nassau was

> well launched on her third and most prosperous era of activity. . . . The big money clan rushed in upon her. Adventurers, businessmen, soldiers including a renegade officer or so, sailors, loafers and at least one minister, they thought to make their fortunes by keeping America wet. Bay Street . . . was no longer a sun drenched idle avenue where traffic in sponges and sisal progressed torpidly. It was filled with slit-eyed, hunch-shouldered strangers, with a bluster of Manhattan in their voices and a wary truculence of manners.[107]

The Lucerne Hotel on Frederick Street was the unofficial headquarters of the bootleggers. It included among its clientele Chief Justice Sir Daniel Tudor and other British officials. Letters to the *Tribune* attested that much drinking, dancing, and noisy partying took place at the Lucerne and at the nearby Hotel Allan and Bucket of Blood nightclub. Editor Etienne Dupuch wrote disapprovingly of the incursions of the "flapper" generation, of the "orgy at the Lucerne," and of the crowd of excursionists dancing all night and every night, who had introduced to Nassau a new "dance abomination" called the Charleston.[108] The climax of the partying was the Bootlegger's Ball held in late July. Attracting mainly foreigners, it began on a Saturday afternoon and ended late on Sunday, to the disproval of many locals. According to H. M. Bell, the owner-manager kept relative peace in the Lucerne with the assistance of Tom Lavelle, an Irishman who carried guns in his hip pockets.[109]

Though the editors of the *Tribune* and *Nassau Guardian* bemoaned Nassau's growing materialism and neglect of the traditional industries, the Bahamas' newly acquired wealth was expended mainly in financing public works, improving communications, and making the Bahamas, especially Nassau, more attractive to tourists and wealthy investors. Before the end of the decade the city of Nassau had a modern pipe-borne water supply and sewerage system, although it served only a limited area north of the ridge, and city water was available in Over-the-Hill only from standpipes. Similarly, electricity supplies were expanded with the installation of a new power plant in 1922.[110] These developments and the much improved cold storage facilities mainly benefited the white elite and well-to-do mixed-race middle class.

Infrastructural Improvements

Following some public debate, dredging began in Nassau Harbour to make it suitable for deep draft vessels such as passenger liners. Previously, such ships had had to anchor outside the bar and discharge their cargoes by lighters and their passengers by tenders. In rough weather ships had to anchor off Clifton in southwestern New Providence, and everything had to be transported about sixteen miles over very bad roads. In order to accommodate the ships, a concrete dock six hundred feet long and a hundred feet wide was constructed. It was connected to Rawson Square by a steel bridge. Completed in 1928, the wharf was named the Prince George's Wharf in honor of a visit by Prince George, Duke of York (later George VI), who landed at Nassau on 1 October 1928.[111]

The increase in the number of motor vehicles in New Providence was a reflection of the new prosperity. Ownership of a car soon became a status symbol, and the Sunday drive became the favorite pastime of the white elite and well-off brown middle class. Whereas only six cars had been imported in 1918, 297 were brought into Nassau in 1922, and by the end of the decade nearly a thousand were registered throughout the colony. The rapid growth in the numbers of cars, speeding and reckless driving, and the rise in traffic accidents stimulated public criticism and the need for more traffic regulations, which were instituted early in 1927.[112]

In 1922 New Providence boasted thirty three and a half miles of roads within the city limits and suburbs, and sixty-five miles outside, many of which had been tarred by the end of the decade. By contrast, such improvements did not extend to the Out Islands, with the exception of certain major settlements such as Harbour Island and Governor's Harbour and a good "earth" road about seventy miles long in Eleuthera, completed in 1930 to assist in developing the island agriculturally.[113] Communications were also improved during the decade of the 1920s. While the telephone system was being extended in New Providence, most of the Out Islands were without lines or had only their main settlements linked by telephone, as in like Eleuthera, Cat Island, and Long Island.[114] By 1925 rudimentary wireless telegraphy stations were installed at Harbour Island; Governor's Harbour, Eleuthera; Hope Town and Norman's Castle, Abaco; Mathew Town, Inagua; and for obvious reasons, Bimini and West End, Grand Bahama.[115] For the majority of islands, communication was still difficult. Haziel Albury, a teacher from the settlement of Man-O-War Cay, Abaco, related that anyone wishing to send a telegram had to travel by sailboat to Hope Town at the whim of the wind, while those receiving a telegram via Hope Town had to pay an extra four shillings (the equivalent of a dollar) for its delivery by boat. Ordinary mail of course took far longer, though Abaco was served by a motor mail boat as early as 1924.

By 1929, in most islands, sailboats had been replaced by government-subsidized motor and mail boat services.[116] Through the Development Board, which was authorized in 1914 and activated in 1920, the Bahamas government introduced many other improvements. Under the energetic chairmanship of R. H. Curry, a member of the Executive Council and the chief Bahamian steamship agent, obviously with a vested interest, and then H. G. Christie, a member of the House of Assembly and the most successful real estate agent, the Development Board spent thousands of pounds on advertising to attract wealthy Americans and Canadians to travel to the Bahamas as visitors or settlers. Both chairmen encouraged government and individuals to improve social and material conditions in order to keep incomers comfortable and happy.

Tourism

By 1929 Nassau was well established as a resort, owing to its unrivaled winter climate, fine bathing beaches, and its "old world atmosphere." Advertising by the Development Board also stressed elite sporting activities such as yachting, duck and pigeon shooting, and tennis on grass courts at the all-white Nassau Lawn Tennis Club or hotels, which had the same racial policy. Golf was also available at Fort Charlotte and at the recently completed (and racially exclusive) Bahamas Country Club at Cable Beach. Algernon Aspinall's *Pocket Guide to the West Indies* (1923) also mentioned the Nassau Club and the luxurious Porcupine Club on Hog Island, which extended hospitality "to visitors suitably introduced." All of the charter members of the latter group were wealthy white Americans who were charged a subscription of fifteen dollars for two weeks and twenty-five pounds for the season.[117] Similar island retreats were the Bimini Rod and Gun Club, built by the American investor Thomas J. Peters at a cost of $1 million and opened in 1920, and the members-only Cat Cay Club, set up on Crown land of South Cat Cay in the late 1920s by another wealthy and enterprising American, C. J. Martin. On New Providence, American and Canadian residents and visitors could dine in luxury and play roulette and poker at the Bahamian Club, the first establishment to be granted a gaming license, owned by yet another American, C. F. Reed.

Though many white elite Bahamians were honorary members of the Bahamian Club, few chose to patronize it. They preferred the Nassau City Club, well liked for its Saturday night turtle dinners, and the Royal Nassau Sailing Club, located just beyond the Fort Montagu Hotel and catering mainly to white officials and the leading local elites, augmented by visitors "suitably introduced." Nouveaux riches, however, were not entirely welcome, especially if they were not of unimpeachable white provenance. Legend has it that the young and successful Roland Symonette established his Nassau Yacht Club in 1931 because his color and poor background meant he was blackballed from joining the exclusive whites-only Royal Nassau Sailing Club.[118]

The government was also concerned about improving hotel accommodation. A contract with the Munson Steamship Line guaranteed Nassau weekly direct passenger and freight service during the season and a fortnightly service during the summer, compared to the monthly freight service from England via Bermuda. Additionally, a service was established to connect Nassau with Halifax in Canada and with Bermuda, Jamaica, and British Honduras, the best that could be negotiated with the Canadian National Steamship Line. There were also frequent sailings from Miami to Nassau, a voyage of fifteen hours. Perhaps the most important innovation was the introduction of a daily twenty-four-passenger seaplane service during the winter months from Miami by Pan American Airways, which began on 2 January 1929.[119]

Guests were ensured accommodation at the major hotels: the large and modernized New Colonial Hotel; the Fort Montagu, completed in 1926 (later called the Montagu Beach Hotel or often simply the Montagu); and the more traditional Royal Victoria. The New Colonial was rebuilt within six months after a 1922 fire and following swift negotiations by the government and the Development Board in a new lease with the Munson Steamship Line, which advanced a loan of £430,000 at a low interest rate with incentives for early completion. There were also smaller hotels, such as the notorious Lucerne and Allen. Some visitors lived in boarding houses or with private families as paying guests.

The tourist industry, which should have created many new jobs and training skills for Bahamian laborers, failed to do so because of the discriminatory policy of its management. Most of the New Colonial's employees were imported, and as the editor of the *Tribune* argued, far from creating jobs, the Colonial gave rise instead to competition. Etienne Dupuch, in a later editorial, described Frank Munson as "a viciously prejudiced man. In his office in New York he employed only white elevator operators. At the time this was one of the jobs given to black men." It was only after much protest from cab drivers and boatmen that hotel-sponsored transportation for guests ceased and locals were hired, and it was not until 1925 that hotel management agreed to employ Bahamians as bellboys.[120] Nonwhites were employed in the other Nassau hotels, but in the 1920s, 1930s, and even beyond, the few nonwhite tourists were forced to find accommodation in the limited range of black- and mixed-race-owned boarding houses.

Land Development

In the 1920s and 1930s it seemed as though the Bahamas was becoming an exotic extension of Florida, with American investors buying estates and cays, building homes, and laying out developments on Hog Island and the New Providence mainland. With land changing hands at an unprecedented rate, its value increased enormously, especially in New Providence.[121] Before the 1920s land was not a very valuable commodity, at least monetarily. Extensive Crown lands, amounting to 2,427,744 acres, were ungranted in 1922. Despite improvements in the surveyor general's office, many tenants were in arrears with their rentals, and although many paid for land, they neglected to collect the grant or lease document. Stricter policies were instituted in the early 1900s, whereby Crown land was no longer sold unless the plot of land was required for immediate building purposes or the tenant undertook permanent improvements on it.[122]

American speculation and development raised the value of land. Large tracts of Crown land that had lain dormant for centuries were purchased by Americans and local speculators.[123] Speaking of the "tremendous boom" in real estate and the numerous applications to acquire vacant land, Governor Cordeaux expressed fear of Americanization and his reluctance to sell or lease so much Crown land: "I don't like the idea of parting, though it's difficult to refuse genuine development schemes. Americans are buying every available inch of private land in New Providence and paying enormous prices for it—and there will soon be nothing British left except the Flag!"[124]

This boom, which would reach its peak in the 1960s, worked to the advantage of local white entrepreneurs, mostly merchants, who added real estate to their traditional business and who benefited from the liquor trade. Perhaps the most successful realtor was Harold Christie. Like Roland Symonette, he started as a poor, near-white outsider, but he was destined to become almost synonymous with Bahamian real estate. Christie began operations in 1922 on a shoe-string and opened proper offices on Bay Street in 1926, advertising "the best residential locations that Nassau and the outer Islands afford . . . water front properties . . . small islands." He believed that foreign investment in land meant prosperity for all Bahamians. No doubt he also saw it as "a natural resource of tremendous potential for personal wealth and power."[125]

Some land transactions never materialized. In Grand Bahama, for example, an Anglo-American corporation called the Grand Bahama Development Company leased a large area of Crown land, about 430 square miles, in order to construct a harbor at the west end of the island, which planted the seed for the later development of the Hawksbill Creek area and the creation of Freeport in the 1950s.[126]

Several cays in the Abacos were leased but remained largely undeveloped. Certain conditions were laid down to the lessees and buyers, such as the agreement prohibiting the use of the cays for the illegal export of liquor into the United States. Though eager to safeguard its reputation, the government did not protect the mostly black local farmers. A clause in the agreement stipulated that purchasers or lessees were entitled to evict native inhabitants who were annual tenants of the Crown and farmed but did not live on the cays. Some protection was given to farmers by a clause stipulating that small cultivators be given two years' notice, rent free, or compensation if immediately removed.[127]

The failure and hardship of traditional agriculture, the local farmers' ignorance of the value to others of their beachfront lands, the muddled and tenuous titles, and the inefficient surveyor general's office and land registry all worked in favor of the realtors and investors. Over the years Bahamian realtors built up a sizable bank of properties bought at very low prices. Obtaining specialized knowledge of land tenures, registration, sales, and covenants, they were able to offer any tracts or islands desired by a buyer. Colonial administrators, ambivalent toward them and the value of their activities, fought a long battle to retain command of at least 2.5 million acres of yet ungranted Crown lands.[128] It was ironic, however, that Governor Cordeaux himself was responsible for leasing several cays in the Abacos, including Murray Cay, to Charles J. Alexander and the much larger Grand Cay to Dr. Charles S. Dolley, a longtime American resident in the Bahamas. Cordeaux also negotiated the huge lease to an Anglo-American corporation called the Grand Bahama Development Company.

Most of the successful 1920s land sales were of private land, and the majority of these were in the most populous and partially modernized island of New Providence. The most notable transaction was the sale of extensive pineapple and sisal fields owned by the J. S. Johnson Company and skirting some of the island's best beaches to the west of Nassau. This development became known as Westward Villas, with lots 60 feet wide and 130 feet deep selling for £100. Those with houses built and furnished sold for between £2,700 and £4,000. By 1926 many lots had been purchased by American and local speculators, but owing to the slump in real estate in Florida, no houses had been built.[129]

A similar development was Vista Marina about a mile west of Fort Charlotte. Situated on the fertile estate known as the Grove in the 1920s and once owned by one of the colony's largest slave owners, James Moss, this became the property of an expatriate Englishman, G. R. Baxter, who engaged Harold Christie as the exclusive sales agent. Targeting wealthy Americans and the local elite, the Vista Marina advertisements read: "Nassau's Ideal Residential Section, adjoining the Country Club and Golf Course, with half-a-mile of Bathing Beach, this beautiful suburb, with its hills sloping towards the sea, affords every advantage to home builders that the city affords." Even if mixed-race or blacks could afford to purchase lots, they were barred by restrictive covenants. Confidential conveyance documents ordained: "no lot or any part thereof or any interest therein in the Vista Marine Subdivision of the GROVE Estate shall be sold, leased or otherwise conveyed to any person other than a full-blooded member of the Caucasian race."[130]

In the far west of New Providence, the Miami firm of Nelson and Bullock purchased extensive estates of Clifton, Old Fort, and adjacent properties. Only one or two houses were built during the 1920s, including the impressive concrete Old Fort and Carmacoup mansions. Within forty years Lyford Cay, which was included in this area, was to outshine even Cable Beach as the enclave of millionaires.[131]

On the eastward and westward extensions of Nassau's north-facing ridge, buildings were already extensive. Just east of the town, George Murphy's Shirley Slope was advertised in March 1923 as "Nassau's first restrictive Realty Development." Nearby, another American migrant, Edward Toote, began a similar development called Buen Retiro. In 1926 a house that had originally been built for about $4,900 sold for £10,000.[132] A mile or so farther east the first fine houses were built on Village Road near the Montagu Beach Hotel, and Allan Kelly, who had profited from bootlegging, constructed three houses near the entrance to Sans Souci, which gave its name to the new development.[133]

This inflow of American people, money, and ideas reinforced and extended Nassau's pattern of residential segregation. However, there was a trickle-down effect in both money and ways of making it, which helped to divide the relatively fortunate nonwhites from the impoverished black majority. Mixed-race and some upwardly mobile black businessmen made significant if modest advances and were also involved to a degree in property developments. Sections of Over-the-Hill were expanding by immigration of Out Islanders and West Indians, the remigration of black Bahamians from Florida, and the general growth of the black population, all of which offered opportunities for more modest developers.

Among the outstanding local black entrepreneurs was Leon Walton Young, who developed Walton Ville in the southern district and Kemp's Addition in Grant's Town, south of Young Street, both opened in 1923. Mason's Addition was another subdivision developed primarily for nonwhite Out Islanders, by less well known Origen Mason. Lots 50 by 100 feet sold for £25, on which wooden houses could be built for £100 each. H. N. Chipman developed Rainbow Village, later called Chippingham, which became the home of immigrants from Long Island, Inagua, Barbados, and Jamaica. Besides those white Americans and the Bahamians W.C.B. Johnson and Roland Symonette, there was at least one white American, Captain J. S. Engler, who developed a black residential area: south of Wulff Road, on the Grant's Town southern boundary, it was named Englerston. Offering "homes on easy terms," Englerston was dubbed "Nassau's Master Suburb." The area adjacent to this became known as Coconut Grove (or simply the Grove), probably accommodating Bahamians who had returned from Miami. The Grove later caused confusion with "the White Grove" on the waterfront three miles to the northwest.[134]

Government High School and Queen's College

Small amounts of the revenue resulting from Prohibition were invested in expanding and improving educational and health services. The latter part of the 1920s saw some improvements in education.[135] In 1925 the first teachers' conference was held in Nassau, attended by nearly fifty teachers, mainly from the Out Islands, and by nearly fifty monitors. The monitorial system ceased to be used in Nassau, but because of the extreme shortage of teachers it continued in the Out Islands for another forty years.[136]

Establishment of a government secondary school was the major educational innovation in this era. The Government High School was founded after some public pressure, including from black middle-class politicians like Thaddeus A. Toote and R. M. Bailey. The idea for the institution originated with the Board of Education, which intended that the school be used to train teachers for the government's primary schools. It was established in the premises of the recently closed Boys Central School in Nassau Court, opening its doors competitively to children of all classes and sexes. It began with a staff of one—headmaster Albert Woods, an Englishman—and an enrollment of five, including three teachers-in-training from the Boys Central School. By mid-1926 there were thirty-nine pupils but the school still had only one teacher until two additional staff members were recruited the following year. Its academic curriculum enabled its students to enter for the external Cambridge exams and in 1932 for the Cambridge Overseas School Certificate. Although the school's policy was to admit all racial groups, an annual fee of ten guineas or £10.10 was unaffordable for most nonwhite parents.[137] It nevertheless soon became apparent that mixed-race and black children would predominate. Some white children attended, including the young Stafford Sands, who would later become a powerful politician. As Reverend Dyer, observed, however, "very few white children attended schools where colored children predominate."[138]

The 1926 Secondary Education Act to encourage and assist secondary education in the Bahamas raised the statutory education grant and, as noted, made sure that Queen's College benefited the most. As Governor Clifford admitted in 1934:

> Secondary education has been built in the Bahamas on a political basis, the principal object is not so much to provide secondary education for those fitted for it, as to secure subsidies for private schools so that children who do not wish to attend Government primary schools, can secure a state aided education in schools where there is some degree of social and racial discrimination.[139]

The upturn in the economy brought on by Prohibition meant that they had more money at their disposal to obtain this. The only other secondary schools in the early 1920s were provided by the Anglican, Methodist, and Roman Catholic churches. The Anglicans operated the Nassau Grammar

School for boys until 1922 and St. Hilda's High School for girls, which closed in 1924. Both schools, as previously noted, were attended predominantly by whites. Colman Barry, a Roman Catholic priest, professor of history, and author of *Upon These Rocks*, admitted that because St. Francis Xavier Academy was a private school charging tuition, and because of the prevailing discrimination against blacks, "it was an all-white school for many years" as "few blacks at this time could afford tuition."[140]

The admissions policy of Queen's College warrants discussion. Class, color, and economics played a large part in having one's child accepted into Queen's College, both from the standpoint of the parents' means and for the sake of the school's financial position. Historically, Queen's College affairs were intertwined with those of the Methodist Church in the Bahamas District, and the headmaster of the school made annual reports at the Methodist Synod, which was dominated by the white elite. Victoria Hall, which housed the original school, was built with funds from local Methodist and Presbyterian guarantors, who were representative of the leading white families. The hall was settled upon a Trust separate from the Nassau Circuit affairs and incurred a debt that took some years to be paid off. The business operation of the institution, however, was "entrusted to a Board of Managers" comprising circuit stewards, Methodists in New Providence, and six gentlemen, including Methodists and Presbyterians chosen annually by the district meeting. The Methodist Missionary Society in London, while it had welcomed the establishment of Queen's College, saw the school's role as providing a good education for the "general populace." Queen's College did not satisfy that expectation, as it catered mainly to the white minority.[141]

Income from fees at Queen's College was never enough to meet the expenses of the school, which was dependent on an annual grant from the Methodist Missionary Society in London and "generous gifts" from the guarantors. Reverend Richard Dyer, on his appointment as headmaster of Queen's College in September 1925, reported that the school was experiencing "extreme difficulties" due to the "unavoidable depletion of staff." According to Colbert Williams, Dyer persuaded the Legislative Council to reverse their 1847 decision not to offer grant-in-aid funds to church schools. He assisted in the drafting of the Secondary Education Bill of 1926, which was quickly passed and provided subventions to non-state institutions. Queen's College was the only non-government school to qualify under the act prior to 1945. The grant did much to alleviate the financial burden of the school and to increase enrollment.[142]

Several mixed-race, middle-class, and highly respected families, such as the Norths and DeGregorys, had their children admitted in the early 1900s to the originally segregated Queen's College, thus demonstrating an ambiguous admission policy. The children of these families were usually light-skinned but not always. The School Committee would usually accept darker children in spite of their color, provided they were not too dark. For example, William B. North's four daughters were admitted in the early 1900s and his youngest son in 1925. Three daughters were fair-skinned, but the youngest daughter was darker and had kinky hair. Some nonwhites were given places, while others were denied them.

In 1927 Dr. Gascoigne S. Worrell, a well-established and respected mixed-race Barbadian physician who had made his home in the Bahamas since 1914 along with his American wife and children, applied to have his eight-year-old daughter Thelma admitted. When the School Committee refused to accept her, Dr. Worrell wrote to headmaster Dyer to inquire into the reason for the rejection. Within a week Dyer replied: "I have to inform you that the Committee of Queen's College is anxious to retain the use of the College for white children only."[143] Two years before, Missionary Minister Rev. Richards and Dyer had observed that the whites wanting that the "purity of their race be preserved" would not send their children to Queen's College if it was allowed to become a mixed institution. Richards concluded that he and Dyer had "no intention of trying to alter the status quo ante."[144] Yet several mixed-race girls were among the top scholars.[145]

The School Committee and Dyer upheld the ambiguous admission policy. Colbert Williams argued that "unquestionably the majority of the School Committee . . . was against the admittance of black children." They argued that Queen's College was established by whites to educate their children.[146] A number of black members at Wesley Chapel, led by the Weir family, also requested the Methodists to provide secondary education for their children. This caused a dilemma among local Methodists and their British ministers. They realized the urgent need for a high school for nonwhites, but to integrate Queen's College was anathema. Dyer offered to resign as headmaster of Queen's College in 1929 to serve as minister of the all-black Wesley Church and head the experimental secondary school for nonwhites. This was denied him, and the high school soon closed.[147] A similar policy existed at the Anglican St. Hilda's school, which discriminated against browns and blacks but accepted a small number, such as Rowena Eldon and Mary Doris Smith, who excelled.

Improvements in Public Health and Medical Services

Advances were also made in public health and the medical service during the 1920s. Major improvements, including the provision of a potable water supply and the sewerage scheme, mainly benefited the white elite and some mixed-race families. These two schemes covered the entire city area from the Montagu Hotel in the east to Fort Charlotte in the west—but not Grant's Town or Bain Town in the south. Most blacks lived outside the range of the new system, and the nonwhites who were included were rarely able to afford to have their houses piped to benefit from the new facilities. For the most part they had to be satisfied with standpipes or public faucets.[148]

Sanitary conditions for the majority of the population were dismal. The House of Assembly at first refused to vote monies needed to pay a sanitary expert from England. But when a number of American visitors became ill with typhoid fever in 1925 and 1926, the legislators were eager to maintain the Bahamas' reputation as a health resort and agreed to contract Sir Wilfred Beveridge in 1927 to examine Nassau's sanitary conditions. His report revealed the extremely unhygienic conditions existing, particularly in the eastern district, Grant's Town, and Bain Town, all primarily nonwhite areas.[149] Beveridge noted in the eastern and southern districts the extreme congestion and appallingly unsanitary cesspit latrines, unsanitary pigsties close to dwellings, unprotected and often contaminated wells, roaming animals, and uncollected garbage. Moreover, poorer residents in these areas often lived in structurally defective and dilapidated wooden shacks. Some products of overcrowding, ignorance, poor nutrition, and lack of hygiene were health problems that mainly affected residents: namely, tuberculosis, venereal disease, pellagra, worms, and neonatal tetanus. In addition, typhoid fever was rampant, with eighty-one cases reported between February and September 1927.[150]

Medical conditions revealed a grim picture. Lepers and tubercular patients were not yet segregated, and the isolation ward of the lunatic asylum consisted of dark, bare rooms in a dilapidated building, devoid of hospital equipment, offering no comfort for patients, who were often left unattended. Corpses were often left for long periods before being moved to the mortuary.[151]

Recognition of sanitary and medical problems demonstrated that a new consciousness about health conditions was developing among the elite, stimulated by the tourist industry, the influx of a large number of laborers including West Indians and Cubans, and pressure from the Colonial Office.[152]

Improvements began to be realized with the appointment of a bacteriologist in 1923, which helped in diagnosis of VD and also to change attitudes of the inhabitants. Legislation was passed in 1928 for the establishment of a leper colony, and a new Midwives Act passed in January 1927 required that all practitioners be examined and registered. Other innovations in health included the establishment of a dental clinic and X-ray department in 1924, the posting of additional medical officers to the Out Islands in 1925, and the voluntary establishment of an infant welfare center in December 1925. Organized by a committee of elite women, it employed an experienced health visitor from Canada and received an annual sum of £300 from the legislature. Clinics were opened in the St. Agnes School in the southern district, at the Victoria School in the east, and at Quarry Mission in the southwest. Established primarily to serve the mixed-race and black population, the centers aimed to control the high infant mortality rate.[153] Providing their services free of charge were two foreign doctors, the English bacteriologist Dr. Greaves and Dr. Worrell, a mixed-race general practitioner from Barbados.

Unequal Development on the Out Islands

While some improvements and expansion were taking place in New Providence, the Out Islands lagged behind and remained almost forgotten; migration to Nassau continued. This trend put more pressure on the already unsatisfactory state of public amenities in Nassau, intensifying social problems in the capital despite the improvements.

The 1920s saw a general decline in the traditional agricultural pursuits and in sponge fishing. Influenced by large revenues accumulated from bootlegging and the investment brought by the land boom, the House of Assembly concentrated its efforts on developing tourist amenities in Nassau while adopting an indifferent attitude to planning a constructive agricultural policy to assist the majority of the population still living on the Out Islands. Slight improvements were achieved by the establishment of self-help associations, notably the Cat Island People's Association in 1924 begun under the leadership of English priest E. E. Smith, who was criticized for "stirring up" class or race hatred in a questionnaire circulated to the People's Association.[154]

Out Island Migration into Nassau

Tightened United States immigration restrictions also brought increasing numbers of Out Islanders to Nassau. The result of this internal migration and the effects of bootlegging on the capital were unemployment and underemployment, crime, juvenile delinquency, and the growth of prostitution and illegitimacy. Between 1921 and 1931 New Providence's population increased by 6,781, or 52.3 percent. Whereas less than a quarter of the total population lived in New Providence in 1921, ten years later the proportion had risen to a third, with most persons coming from Cat Island, Inagua, Long Island, Harbour Island, Crooked Island, the Berry Islands, and Rum Cay. Nassau received most of the migrants, but other settlements that were involved in the liquor traffic, including Bimini and Grand Bahama, also showed significant increases in population.[155]

The steady influx of Out Islanders into the capital created new social problems. Jobs became scarcer, wages were reduced, and the cost of living remained high in New Providence. Colonial officials and Wesleyan missionaries found it difficult to maintain a satisfactory standard of living in Nassau. It was much worse for the ordinary working person and the migrants.[156]

Increasing Social Problems and Restlessness

Increasing poverty among migrants and residents living in a seemingly prosperous and carefree city led to rising incidence of crime, including stealing, housebreaking and burglary, and juvenile offences. The bootlegging trade had also led to the dissemination of firearms and an atmosphere of illegality. Violent crime, almost unknown in Nassau, began to be noted.[157]

The increase in crime led to overcrowding of the prison, where two serious incidents occurred in 1928, causing a riot and the temporary takeover of the prison. One of the prisoners rushed an officer with an axe and was killed.[158]

A commission of inquiry on the riots discovered much slackness at the prison. Prisoners mixed freely both inside the prison and on work gangs. Despite the overcrowding and failure to segregate the more and less dangerous prisoners, a white prisoner, one Captain Reeves, was given preferential treatment. The chief jailer, a Barbadian named Clarke, used prisoners to perform personal and domestic services. He and his family lived within the prison compound, and the main gate was not locked until the last member of the family was in, which could be after 9:00 p.m. With the increase in criminal activity and violent crime, the commissioners recommended that steps be taken to tighten discipline and security, by introducing a more rigorous form of solitary confinement and ensuring that prisoners not be allowed to retain any unauthorized articles in their possession. It was also suggested that they be provided with more useful work.[159]

The steady rise in juvenile crime was a vexing social problem, though the regime was slow to recognize and address it. Juvenile offenders brought before the courts were charged with larceny and breaches of the vagrancy act. A letter to the *Nassau Guardian* in September 1922 commented on the problem of drinking among juveniles and women. Drunkenness, vandalism, and prostitution were on the increase as growing numbers of unsupervised young boys and girls from the Out Islands made their home in Nassau.[160]

The interrelated causes and effects of bootlegging were an increase in poverty and illegitimacy and a lack of parental control. The rate of illegitimacy in 1922 for the whole colony was about 30 percent, which compared favorably with some other Caribbean colonies, such as Jamaica, where it was about 75 percent during the same period. While the Bahamas' rate was not excessive, in the Over-the-Hill mainly black area, illegitimacy was nearly 72 per cent. Fathers of "outside children" were not compelled by law to contribute toward their maintenance. Mothers were therefore forced to work, and while so engaged, had little control over their children, who wandered about the streets half-starved, frequently getting into trouble. Truancy was common in both Nassau and the Out Islands. Of 1,600 registered pupils in New Providence in 1922, only about 600 were regular attendees.[161] As early as 1921 a reformatory for juveniles was proposed, and A. F. Adderley, a black lawyer and member of the House of Assembly, even advocated an institution that was not a prison but one where "love and tender care reigns."[162] The majority of House of Assembly members thought the reformatory school was a waste of money. On the other hand, Cleveland H. Reeves, an exceptionally civic-minded mixed-race Nassauvian who was relieving officer at the General Hospital, blamed worsening social conditions in Nassau on the liquor traffic. He claimed that besides those Out Islanders who had flocked to Nassau for work, many of the opportunistic migrants were idlers who slept in people's backyards, got into fights, overcrowded the hospital, and caused a nuisance by begging for money and food. He advocated the establishment of a reformatory school.[163]

However, it was not until 1928 that the government established the Boys Industrial School, "a euphemism for the reformatory for juvenile offenders." During the following year, of the 289 cases brought before the courts, 31 of the offenders were whipped, while 14 were sent to the recently established institution.[164]

Bootlegging affected the Bahamas profoundly, changing social values, widening the gap between the classes, and creating a white nouveau riche group. As Gordon Lewis stated, Prohibition provided the "financial foundation of their status as the social and political ruling class of the island."[165] Although some of the nouveau riche group were resented at first, they joined and reinforced the power of the Bay Street elite. The advent of a strong American influence ensured the hardening of the color line. Economically, the new moneyed whites grew stronger, and their intolerance of foreign competition was evident in their efforts to impose controls over immigrant competitors. Several mixed-race and black middle-class men, some of whom had businesses on Bay Street, also benefited from the temporary boom in the economy. Those who gained least were the black laboring class.

The Rise of a Nouveau Riche Class

The traditional white elite headed by the Malcolms, Duncombes, Adderleys, and Moseleys, who dominated every aspect of Bahamian life, observed the growth of the new wealthy class during the 1920s. Initially they were reluctant to accept men like Roland T. Symonette, a seaman from Current settlement, who was not even pure white. Frank and Harold Christie, from just as poor a background, and Walter K. Moore all had to fight for a place among the elite. Their rise to positions of wealth and power, however, was phenomenal. Roland Symonette had actively participated in bootlegging and in 1922 had bought an interest in a Nassau wholesale liquor business known as Rost-Symonette (the predecessor of Robertson and Symonette). He soon used his profits to establish a boatyard on Hog Island. In 1929 he built the Rozelda Hotel, later known as the Carlton House. As far as color was concerned, he associated only with whites and considered himself as such. Money "whitened"! To consolidate his position and wealth, he entered politics in 1925 and was elected to the House of Assembly in that year. In less than a generation he and his family were accepted by the white community.[166]

Similarly, Harold Christie in 1926 moved his successful four-year-old real estate business into the more prestigious and expensive Bay Street, and in 1928 he was elected to the House of Assembly for Abaco. Walter K. Moore established himself as a leading commission merchant and was elected to the House of Assembly in 1925 for Grand Bahama.[167] The new class of "money barons" built or renovated large conspicuous and stately mansions to complement their new status. Symonette's home was situated on East Bay Street and W. K. Moore's, called "Villa Doyle," was on West Hill and West streets. Ralph G. Collins, an American resident of the Bahamas and a beneficiary of Prohibition, built a mansion on his extensive estate "Centreville" shortly after 1929.[168]

Widening the disparity between the whites, the possession of wealth also encouraged a "fever for money-making" to the exclusion of more traditional pursuits. The white society already had a small cadre of professionals and civil servants, including the lawyer Harcourt Malcolm, later speaker of the House, and Harbour Island–born A. K. Solomon, also a lawyer and politician, who married into the powerful Lofthouse family; his father-in-law, H. C. Lofthouse, was a prominent merchant and member of the legislature. Within this category of professionals were dentists C. C. Sweeting and G. H. Johnson, teachers Wilton Albury and T. A. Thompson, and P.W.D. Armbrister, a career civil servant.[169]

Immediately following Prohibition, not many young and ambitious white Bahamians were tempted to qualify professionally and emulate these people, except in the legal field. Commercial prosperity and high wages lured school leavers into shop keeping and other commercial enterprises. Bay Street firms were constantly on the lookout for intelligent young people, who could thus anticipate bright prospects.[170] Indeed, the prosperity saw the opening and improvement of numerous businesses, including City Lumber Yard in 1926, managed by George W. K. Roberts, and Nassau Garage on Union Street (later named Elizabeth Avenue), owned by Joseph Taylor of New York and Rupert Perpall of Nassau. Asa Pritchard's Standard Supply Company, predecessor of the still extant wholesale business, was also begun in the early 1920s.[171]

Non-Whites Benefit from Prohibition

Mixed-race and black people in Nassau also benefited from Prohibition. Quite a number had businesses on or near Bay Street. Mixed-race merchant Christopher C. Smith bought Johnson House on the corner of Bay and Union streets and operated a large grocery business there, in conjunction with the Magnolia Apartment Hotel on the corner. The hotel had accommodation for about twenty guests and was built especially for wealthy nonwhite tourists who were barred from the white-owned hotels.[172] Similarly, mixed-race Joseph Whitfield and Edward A. ("Durham") Isaacs operated restaurants on the corner of Deveaux and Bay streets and Bay and Market streets respectively.[173] Percy Hanna recalled that such restaurants were patronized by mixed-race and black taxi drivers, who were barred from the Greek-owned Grand Central, which was segregated.[174] Louis Isaacs, Durham's brother, operated an ice cream parlor on Bay Street, while mixed-race Harry S. Black owned and managed the more exclusive Black's Candy Kitchen. Though it catered to all races, darker mixed-race and black clients were served in the front section, while fairer nonwhites and whites could be served in the sit-down back section of the establishment.[175] By the 1920s William B. North had moved his liquor business from Balliou Hill Road to the Market Range, just off Bay Street. The DeGregory brothers expanded and improved their meat business by installing refrigeration. They also built an elaborate new residence on Virginia Street to reflect their newfound wealth and status.[176]

Diversity was the hallmark of mixed-race and black involvement in business. Willie Weeks, for example, had the franchise for Rudge and Raleigh cycles, operating two bicycle shops on Bay Street. Jim Bowe Gardiner operated three tobacco shops, and Sankey Toote, the member of the House of Assembly for Cat Island, established a number of stores on Bay Street west of Deveaux Street. William Parliament Adderley still owned and operated the "Big Store" on King Street, which dealt in dry goods, candy, fruit, and vegetables. Near his shop were numerous tailor establishments. The leading tailors in the 1920s included Arthur Lunn, R. M. Bailey, R. I. Bartlett, E. A. Bowen, Oscar Johnson, and Reuben Bethel.[177]

The black laboring class benefited less from the brief prosperity but profited from higher wages, the increased money in circulation, and the greater availability of jobs. By the mid-1920s some of the Over-the-Hill blacks also owned small shops, among them Robert Thompson, Joe Adderley, and the Neelys, who were accumulating savings to educate their children.[178]

Mixed-race Nassauvians and more mobile blacks were becoming more aware, as were their counterparts in the Caribbean generally, of the benefits of higher education and the advancement it offered. Educated men like British-trained lawyers Alfred F. Adderley and Thaddeus A. Toote were held in awe and at the same time acted as models and inspiration for the middle-class nonwhites and aspiring blacks. One was William B. North's son Terry North, who attended Ellesmere College in Shropshire and the University of London, where he trained as a medical doctor. Several girls studied nursing in New York, including Terry's sister Yvonne North, his cousin Carmita De-Gregory, and a friend, Alice Hill.[179]

Some mixed-race and black men, including Cecil Bethel and Milton Cooper, were sponsored by the Anglican Church and sent to Codrington College to study for the priesthood. While Milton Cooper was ordained and became a highly respected priest, Cecil Bethel had a change of conviction and never took orders. Instead, on his return to Nassau he resumed his former profession of tailoring. In the early 1930s he opened a school, St. Cyprian's, but it closed during the depression years. In 1941 he began a long and distinguished teaching career at the Government High School, ending up as headmaster in 1968.[180]

Others received higher education in the United States. Bertram Cambridge, from Grant's Town, studied the organ in New York in 1919–22, returning home to lead an orchestra that played at private parties and later at night clubs. His orchestra, along with other local groups, played in hotels from the early 1950s. During the '20s, '30s, and '40s hotels usually imported white bands from the United States.[181]

Conclusion

Prohibition had pervasive effects on Bahamian society. Before the 1920s the entrenched mercantile elite had little real capital. Their color, more than their wealth, separated them from nonwhites. Bootlegging profits created a new moneyed class that was mostly white. Nouveaux riches soon consolidated their wealth in successful businesses and sought seats in the legislature. Values were subtly changing. The newly rich liquor families might not have been accepted easily by the established elite, but as Major H. M. Bell stated in 1934, "money ruled. Mammon was king—those who did not pay him reverence were too few to matter."[182] Social distinctions among whites widened, as class was now distinguishable by wealth as well as color.

Similarly, the color line grew more rigid. American investment brought more than just money to the Bahamas. With the arrival of Americans such as Frank Munson came the Jim Crow attitudes and system of segregation practiced in the hotels and the exclusive clubs. Because of the growing importance of the tourist industry and the dependence on American investment, the white elite, who needed few lessons in racism, did little to stop the increasingly blatant discrimination against brown and black people in public places and educational establishments.

The brief prosperity of the Prohibition years was marked by the consolidation of commercial enterprise and the improvement and modernization of public facilities and communication in Nassau. Concentrating on the expansion of the tourist industry, the legislators greatly neglected agriculture and took on an indifferent attitude to the faltering sponge fishing industry. The brief bonanza not only set the economic pattern but also delayed political and constitutional progress in the Bahamas. When the Wall Street crash came in 1929, many Bahamians were already experiencing desperate poverty once again.

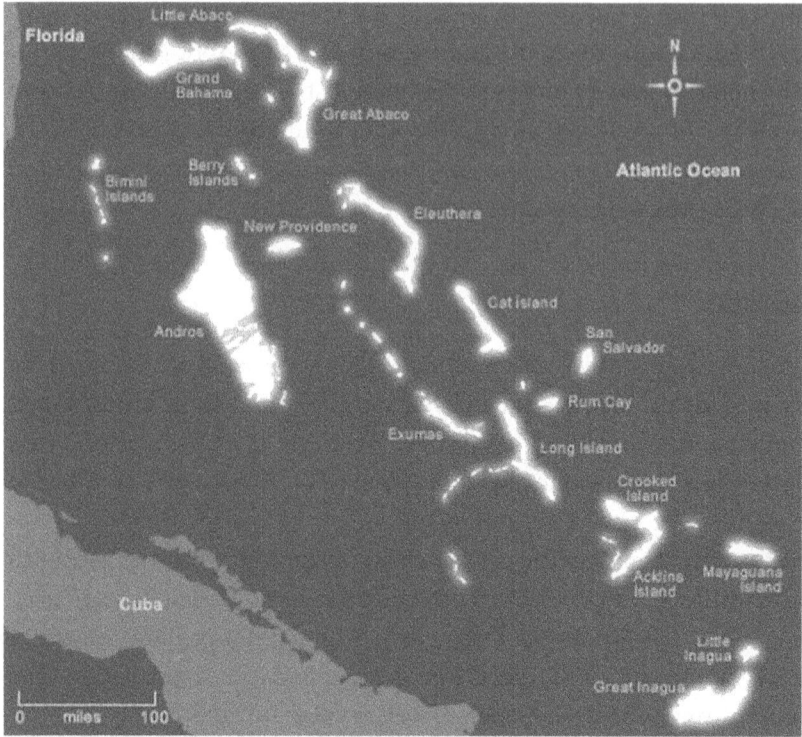

Map of the Bahamas. Courtesy of the Department of Lands and Surveys, Nassau, Bahamas.

The Duke and Duchess of Windsor at the airport. The Duke of Windsor served as governor of the Bahamas between 1940 and 1945. Courtesy of the Department of Archives, Nassau, Bahamas.

The Duke and Duchess of Windsor at Clifford Park. Photograph by Stanley Toogood. Courtesy of the Department of Archives, Nassau, Bahamas.

Charlotte Street, one of Nassau's oldest streets, circa 1877. Photograph by Jacob Frank Coonley. Permission of the National Art Gallery of the Bahamas.

On the Shore Road, East of Nassau. Photograph by Jacob Frank Coonley, 1877–1904. Permission of the National Art Gallery of the Bahamas. From the Mary Moseley Collection, donated by Rev. David Jennings to the Nassau Public Library and later transferred to the Bahamas Archives. Courtesy of the Department of Archives, Nassau, Bahamas.

Cumberland Street, 1901–6. Photograph by William Henry Jackson. Permission of the National Art Gallery of the Bahamas.

The sponge boats with the Colonial Hotel in the background between 1904 and 1922. Sponging was a Bahamian industry from about 1841 until 1938. A fungus hit the sponge beds in 1938, devastating the industry; it would never fully recover. Henry Flagler built the hotel in 1899–1900, and it was destroyed by fire in March 1922. It was rebuilt in 1922–23 and later renamed the British Colonial Hotel. Permission of the National Art Gallery of the Bahamas.

George Street in the 1920s, looking south to Government House on the hill. Photograph by James "Doc" Sands. Permission of the National Art Gallery of the Bahamas.

Market Delivery. Northward view on Market Street toward Gregory Arch, 1901. Photograph by William Henry Jackson. Permission of the National Art Gallery of the Bahamas.

Bay Street in the 1950s. Courtesy of the Department of Archives, Nassau, Bahamas.

Bay Street, circa 1957 to the 1960s. Courtesy of the Department of Archives, Nassau, Bahamas.

MONDAY, OCTOBER 1, 1956

P. L. P. Crusade Delegates

MR. H. M. TAYLOR   MR. L. O. PINDLING   MR. MILO BUTLER

The *Nassau Herald* "Crusade for Freedom" delegation, 1 October 1956. *Left to right*: H. M. Taylor, L. O. Pindling, Milo Butler. Courtesy of the Department of Archives, Nassau, Bahamas.

The "Magnificent Six": six members of the PLP elected to the House of Assembly in 1956. *Left to right, standing*: L. O. Pindling (South), Milo Butler (West), and Samuel Isaacs (East); *left to right, seated*: Sir Randol Fawkes (South), Cyril Stevenson (Andros), and Clarence Bain (Andros). Courtesy of the Department of Archives, Nassau, Bahamas.

Reverend H. W. Brown, former pastor, Bethel Baptist Church. Portrait from "Baptist Preachers Helped Build a Nation," by Tosheena Robinson Blair. Courtesy of the Brown family and the Department of Archives, Nassau, Bahamas.

Sir Etienne Dupuch, aged seventeen and in full battle dress, mounts guard in the Sahara desert of Egypt during World War I. Dupuch was later knighted for his service to the Bahamas. Courtesy of Eileen Carron and the Department of Archives, Nassau, Bahamas.

Sir Randol Fawkes. Courtesy of the Department of Archives, Nassau, Bahamas.

"Suffragettes Call on Governor," *Nassau Daily Tribune*, 20 January 1959. *Front, left to right*: Dr. Doris Johnson, Mrs. Mary Ingraham, Georgiana K. Symonette, and Eugenia Lockhart. *Rear, left to right*: Mrs. Mildred Donaldson, Mrs. Shirley Sands, Madam Willamae Saunders, and Mrs. Marion Stuart. Courtesy of the Department of Archives, Nassau, Bahamas.

The "Gallant Thirty": the first Bahamian contingent to enter World War I, photographed before departure for Jamaica on the sloop *Varuna*, 9 September 1915. Courtesy of Rev. David Jennings, the Nassau Public Library, and the Department of Lands and Surveys. From the Mary Moseley Collection, donated by Rev. David Jennings to the Nassau Public Library and later transferred to the Bahamas Archives. Courtesy of the Department of Archives, Nassau, Bahamas.

William Cartwright, House of Assembly member for Cat Island, 1949–50, and a founding member of the Progressive Liberal Party in 1953. Courtesy of the Department of Archives, Nassau, Bahamas.

Women carrying cases and barrels of whisky on the dock of Nassau Harbour, 1920. Courtesy of the Department of Archives, Nassau, Bahamas.

Workmen employed by Sir Harry Oakes line up for their pay, circa 1930. Courtesy of the Department of Archives, Nassau, Bahamas.

Rawson Square in downtown Nassau in the late 1950s or early 1960s. Courtesy of the Department of Archives, Nassau, Bahamas.

Sponge fleet, Nassau Harbour. Photograph by J. F. Cooley. Courtesy of the Department of Archives, Nassau, Bahamas.

James Carmichael Smith (*third from right*), a mixed-race Bahamian, established the pro-black newspaper the *Freeman* in Nassau during 1887. A founding member of the Anglo-African League established in the same year, Smith also served as postmaster of the Bahamas (1889–96), the second nonwhite person to hold that post. He was elected to the House of Assembly in 1882 for the western district of New Providence, which he represented until 1896. In December 1896 he was appointed assistant postmaster at Freetown, Sierra Leone, where this photograph was taken. Courtesy of the University of Cambridge Library, Cambridge, United Kingdom.

5

THE 1930S AND THE DEPRESSION

Tourism and Restlessness

The Wall Street Crash on 29 October 1929 precipitated the worst economic decline to that date in American history. Not only did it wreak havoc on American industrial production, the construction industry, and the banking system, causing massive unemployment, but it also induced a worldwide economic depression. President Franklin D. Roosevelt's New Deal policy was an attempt to cope with the Depression and to ensure national survival. One of the most far-reaching measures was the devaluation of the U.S. dollar, which was taken off the gold standard.[1]

Britain and Europe were affected by the financial distress in America. Unemployment soared in the United Kingdom, and in August 1931 the Labour government fell and was replaced by a "national" or coalition government under the leadership of Ramsay MacDonald. The British also abandoned the gold standard, and this led to a revolutionary change in the international financial system. Its immediate effect was the devaluation of the pound. A more permanent result was the creation of the "sterling area," which consisted of the British Empire (excluding Canada and South Africa) and included Portugal and the Scandinavian countries, which exported heavily to Britain.[2] The economic crisis brought about a new order in the financial system that necessitated change in the general economic policy, resulting in the establishment of a system of preferential trade within the empire. As a result, an increased proportion of British imports were drawn from the empire, and the proportion of British exports to the empire rose appreciably. The empire, however, did not achieve economic self-sufficiency, as then Chancellor of the Exchequer Neville Chamberlain had hoped it would.

Despite Britain's dominant role in the empire, ever since the nineteenth century the "white settler" territories of Canada, Australia, New Zealand,

South Africa, and Ireland had been moving toward autonomy. As codified by the Statute of Westminster, passed in 1931, the dominions gained independence from the fetters of the Colonial Laws Validity Act of 1865, which had prevented the passage of legislation repugnant to British law. The statute also ensured that no British law applied to a dominion without its consent. While these developments were ushering in a new era of Commonwealth relationships between the dominions and Britain, change came more slowly in the non-self-governing segments of the empire, including the distant colonies in the British West Indies.[3]

British Caribbean society in the 1930s was still ruled by an alliance of the Colonial Office, a small minority of whites, and a few influential nonwhites. The black and Indian laboring population lived little above subsistence level, trapped in an inflexible economy based predominantly on sugar and with restricted possibilities of emigration. Moreover, the depression of the 1930s fostered the growth of the trade union movement and coincided with the rise of the party system and growth of national consciousness. Economic distress, poverty, and discontent caused an explosion of strikes and riots throughout the British West Indies during the mid- and late thirties. In search of leadership, the black laboring classes found a new breed of West Indian politician, one who was charismatic, in some cases a demagogue, and who appealed to them directly.[4] The labor strikes and riots of the later 1930s shocked the imperial government but caused it to focus with new urgency on the dreadful plight of the West Indian masses.

However, the Royal Commission on the West Indies, appointed in 1938 under the chairmanship of Lord Moyne to investigate social and economic conditions, did not visit the Bahamas. The latter colony's economy, based more on commerce than agriculture, had been boosted during Prohibition, and although the Bahamas saw poverty, economic distress, and some unrest, especially in the Out Islands, neither the scale of the disturbance nor the state of economic conditions was thought to warrant an investigation by the commissioners. Whereas the riots and strikes in the British West Indies were a catalyst for gradual social and political change, in the Bahamas the unrest was more isolated and not serious enough to cause alarm. As a result, change in the Bahamas was even slower in coming. Yet Bahamian society, especially on the Out Islands, suffered severely from depression and poverty in the late twenties and early thirties. As previously mentioned, neglect of and indifference to the plight of Out Islanders by the House of Assembly, compounded by a series of severe hurricanes in the late 1920s and early 1930s, accelerated migration from the outlying islands to Nassau. In turn, the capital suffered from increasing social problems, especially vagrancy and crime.[5] Nonetheless, the decade of the 1930s witnessed the growth and development of tourism and foreign investment in Nassau, as outlined in this chapter. Progress was also made in elaborating on the amenities needed to serve these industries. Bahamian society was gradually being Americanized.

The increasing importance of tourism, while boosting a number of nineteenth-century Bay Street businesses, primarily benefited the white nouveau riche mercantile and professional class in Nassau. By the end of the decade this class had firm control of the House of Assembly and dominated most aspects of Bahamian life. As the gap between rich and poor in Nassau grew wider, discriminating policies grew more severe, causing an increase in racial tensions and consciousness. The white mercantile clique seized a firmer grip on the economy, and black businesses on Bay Street became fewer. Barred from working in most Bay Street establishments, the mixed-race middle class and some of the more mobile blacks were limited to the lower echelons of the civil service and to the equally poorly paid teaching profession. With the advent of the Government High School, nonwhites increasingly sought a higher education for their children. The majority of the black laboring population, however, suffering from many hardships and from growing unemployment, became increasingly restless. Two isolated incidents, one in New Providence and the other at Inagua, demonstrated that discontent was far from uncommon in the Bahamas.

Depression

The Bahama Islands in late 1920s were still recovering from the effects of a series of hurricanes in 1926 and 1928 when the severe hurricane of 24 September 1929 "slammed into New Providence" the following day and "squatted" there for three days and nights.[6] By 1930 the optimistic mood of the twenties had changed. The government realized that the "boom" years were over and that "excessive" income and "eager" spending had come to an end. Colonial Secretary Charles Dundas, later to be appointed governor, had expressed fear about the decline in the revenue as early as July 1929. Urging a policy that would reduce the construction of public works, he advised caution, but saw no cause for alarm.[7] By 1930, however, the effects of the Depression began to be felt. From that year the revenue of the colony steadily declined and would continue to do so for the next five years. Between 1929 and 1935 the revenue dropped from £556,799 to £277,544 and the expenditure from £578,584 to £276,961.[8]

The economic outlook for the Bahamas had worsened considerably by 1931. Pre-Prohibition industries had all failed or were fading. The pineapple and citrus businesses were extinct, and sisal production was negligible. Agriculture in the early 1930s was in a desperate state due to the problems of poor soil, the use of archaic methods, poor marketing techniques, and general neglect. The attitude of the House of Assembly was one of indifference. Sponge fishing, still the leading industry in the early 1930s, suffered from hurricane destruction and ruthless overfishing. Little was done to increase diminishing supplies through artificial sponge culture. By 1932 sponge fishermen were finding it difficult to make a living, and vessel owners and outfitters sometimes lost money. It was not until 1936 that the imperial government, alarmed at gloomy reports, sent a scientific team to inquire into the industry and promote conservation and productivity. By then it was almost too late. Complete disaster struck the industry in late 1938. A mysterious fungal disease, appearing in November and December of that year, had within two months wiped out 99 percent of the sponge beds in the Bahamas.[9]

Government revenue fell from a high of £1.5 million in the middle 1920s to less than a third of this in 1929 and to a sixth by 1935, and the decline was accompanied by progressive cutbacks in public works, in services including education and health, and in salaries, wages, and employment. Concurrently, even stiffer U.S. immigration and tariff policies almost cut off the outflow of Bahamian migrants and the inflow of migrants' wages and remittances, while choking off traditional exports. Public servants in the lower echelons of the public service, comprising mainly whites and mixed-race high school graduates, barely survived on their meager salaries. But those suffering most were unskilled black laborers, subsisting on extremely low wages or no income at all. Some middle-class white and nonwhite women, because of increasing economic constraints, began working out of the home. Many whites and some middle-class light-skinned mixed-race women worked as clerks in the civil service, as teachers, and in private businesses as stenographers. Others became seamstresses, operating usually out of their homes. Black women generally worked as laborers in sponge clipping, cutting quarry stones, and weeding, and as domestics, farmers, and petty shopkeepers. Many black women made their living through marketing, which traditionally played a significant part in their lives and those of their slave and liberated African forebears. Most grew vegetables in their own garden plots or yards, to be sold from door to door, or in roughly made stalls in the streets, often in front of their homes, or in the Nassau market.[10]

In the early 1930s wages were as low as one shilling a day, making it difficult for the laboring classes to make ends meet. Many were willing to work for extremely low wages rather than no wages at all. Employers of scores of such laborers were bootlegging millionaire Ralph G. Collins and later Sir Harry Oakes. Collins was considered a philanthropist when he employed hundreds of laborers, most of them poor nonwhite Out Island migrants, for a shilling a day plus a hot midday meal. They were hired to construct a ten-foot wall around the perimeter of his huge property close to downtown Nassau, stretching from Shirley Street in the north almost to Wulff Road in the south. Collins's motives were not necessarily racist, but property separated from the black section in the west and south appreciated in value. Collins also created a physical boundary between himself and the nonwhites who lived to the west, south, and east of his property. The northern periphery of the property was enclosed with a black cast-iron fence with spikes and barbed wire in places. It could be argued that Collins's extensive orchard was susceptible to poaching and encroachment on the "far outskirts of his property."[11] When the property was later subdivided, the northern section was sold to whites, the middle to mixed-race middle-class families, and the southern section to upwardly mobile blacks—delineating visible class and ethnic barriers. In later years the wall was to assume great symbolic importance.[12]

Harry Oakes, originally from Maine in the United States, after fourteen years of prospecting, had finally explored the Kirkland Lake region of Ontario, where he was convinced there was a rich vein of gold. Oakes's hunch was right. His company, Lake Shore Mines, eventually produced an estimated $250 million, the second largest strike in Canada. Oakes became a Canadian citizen, involving himself in numerous projects in the Niagara region, but resented the heavy taxes levied on his fortune by the Canadian government. It was at this stage (in 1934) that he met Harold Christie, who lured him to the Bahamas.

Soon after his arrival in Nassau, Oakes, through Harold Christie, bought thousands of acres of land in the western part of New Providence. This property included most of the area now known as Oakes Field and Stapledon as well as a 3,000-acre stretch running from Cable Beach across Lake Cunningham to Lake Killarney. At one stage Oakes owned nearly 10,000 acres of New Providence, in addition to numerous residences, including "Westbourne" on Cable Beach and "The Caves," his first family home in Nassau on West Bay Street.

Oakes started a farming project at the Caves, growing strawberries and planting thousands of imported coconut trees and citrus plants. Later he laid water mains from Westbourne to pipe fresh water downtown to the New Colonial Hotel, which he bought from the government in 1940, renaming it the British Colonial Hotel. Among the many other projects were the contribution of £15,000 to build a new wing on the Bahamas General Hospital; the construction of a polo field, Five Stones Park, in the middle of what is now known as Westward Villas; and the importation of sheep from Cuba to improve the local stock. Perhaps Oakes's most significant legacy, though, was the laying out in 1939 and 1940 of the first major air strip, which would later become the Oakes Airfield.[13] Important too was Oakes's assistance to the poor of the Bahamas during the Depression years. In all his various projects, he hired local black laborers. There were usually hundreds of workers on his payroll at one time, sometimes as many as 1,500. In the mid-1930s and early 1940s, times of high unemployment and low wages, Harry Oakes paid his laborers five shillings a day, one shilling more than the minimum wage laid down in 1936.[14] He also provided his workers with gloves, fed them hot meals at the job site, and bought a bus to transport them back and forth between his properties and the town.[15]

Not all recent Out Island migrants and resident Nassauvians were fortunate enough to be employed, however. Jobs were scarce, and unemployment in the early 1930s was "painfully high." In May 1933 the House of Assembly, alarmed at the rise in the number of beggars and amount of crime, increasingly accompanied by violence, passed a resolution to relieve unemployment. The resolution proposed a scheme whereby employers would hire people on a part-time basis and also suggested the repatriation of Out Islanders, designating £2,000 to assist returning migrants.[16]

The majority refused to return and, unable to find jobs, many took to begging and loitering in the streets of Nassau. Not only did they become a menace to residents; they were also a source of annoyance to visitors, which was not to be tolerated. Becoming increasingly belligerent, some wharf loiterers were challenged by policemen one evening in August 1937, and they attacked the police with knives and razors.[17]

Some vagrants turned to crime, and during the early and mid-1930s, housebreaking and theft became notoriously common. *Tribune* editor Etienne Dupuch commented early in the decade that "one hears of a robbery almost every day."[18] The rise in lawlessness consisted mainly of acts against property but occasionally included an attack against an individual and even the use of firearms. Indicative of the uncommon violence were several armed robberies that took place within days of one another in the spring of 1935.[19] Following a brutal attack on J. P. Simms of Village Road and the infliction of serious injury on his relative, who was robbed and faced threats to kill her dying mother, several members of the House of Assembly and merchants called on the governor, resulting in the appointment of a Crime Commission.[20] Colonial Secretary J. H. Jarrett, who headed the commission, blamed the escalating crime wave on unemployment, the cessation of the liquor trade, and the return of laborers from the United States. The commission also observed that the influx of Out Islanders to New Providence in search of work had contributed significantly to the growth of violent crime. Over a period of ten years the New Providence population, mostly resident in Nassau, had increased by 52.2 percent, from 12,975 in 1921 to 19,756 in 1931. Four years later it numbered 20,100, representing 33 percent of the total Bahamian population.[21]

The government, although aware of this serious migration problem, was unable to find a satisfactory solution, and Out Islanders continued to pour into the capital. Governor Clifford's tour of the Out Islands in early 1932 revealed the desperate straits in which many Out Islanders found themselves. He was particularly distressed by conditions at San Salvador and Inagua, the two most southerly and least accessible islands. Circumstances at Inagua were especially depressing. With a reduced demand for stevedores and the collapse of the salt industry, Inagua's population had declined dramatically from 907 to 607 people, a drop of 28.8 percent between 1921 and 1931.[22] The people of Inagua found it difficult to feed and clothe themselves, and the other islands hardly fared better.

To this already gloomy situation came the two hurricanes in 1932. On 5 September a severe one swept the colony, especially affecting Abaco. Fourteen people were killed, five of whom drowned in a tidal wave, and between sixty and seventy were injured. Green Turtle Cay and Hope Town suffered extensive damage, with many people losing not only their homes but also their possessions.[23] In November the same year, after the storm season had officially ended, a hurricane that did immense damage to Cuba and Jamaica hit Long Island, Rum Cay, San Salvador, Crooked Island, and Acklins Island, killing at least nine persons and totally destroying crops on those islands. Several other islands in the Bahamas chain were affected but to a lesser extent.[24]

Sir Bede Clifford, on being appointed governor of the Bahamas in 1932, noted that with few exceptions, attempts to establish co-operative societies and farmers' unions had been unsuccessful. Farmers' associations were active in many villages in Exuma, and Clifford wasted no time in putting a proposal to the House of Assembly to establish a Produce Exchange in Nassau in order to market agricultural produce and to finance farmers. Encountering the usual apathy displayed by the House on matters relating to agriculture, the bill was deferred, and it was not until 1936 that the exchange became a reality.[25]

Tourism

The economic outlook worsened in the early '30s and Clifford was pessimistic about finding an immediate solution to the problem of agricultural underdevelopment and the increasing "drift" of population from the Out Islands due to the collapse of the sisal industry and the decline of sponging. Like most expatriate officials, he was at first skeptical about making tourism the mainstay of the Bahamian economy.[26] As the Depression worsened, however, he realized that there was no alternative but to develop tourism. He recalled in his memoirs that he advised his Executive council: "Well gentlemen, it amounts to this—if we can't take the liquor to the Americans we must bring the Americans to the liquor."[27] Clifford saw it as a choice between the tourist industry and bankruptcy. He realized that tourism could be further developed quickly enough to bolster the flagging economy and to replace the revenue lost with cessation of abnormal liquor exports.[28] Etienne Dupuch wrote later:

> Sir Bede was not satisfied to rule through his Council and the chosen few who were acceptable to Government House. He wanted more direct rule. And so he started inviting all the white members of the House to dinner at Government House. After each dinner party he published their names in the newspaper. This flattered and pleased them enormously. He ignored the coloured members of the House and this produced a deeper sense of cleavage among the races.

Dupuch added that Sir Bede felt "the tourist business called for an 'all-white' policy," thus supporting the system of segregation upheld by the local white elite. "Although he succeeded in stemming the downward economic trend . . . he did not realize the serious blow he had dealt to human relations in the colony."[29]

Governor Clifford and the Development Board worked closely and enthusiastically on a policy to encourage tourists, preferably wealthier ones. Transportation, communications, accommodations, and entertainment for tourists were improved. New contracts were negotiated for more frequent steamship services for smaller subsidies; a weekly Cunard sailing from New

York was added to the fortnightly Munson service, and larger and more luxurious ships made the Miami run. A pier for liners was constructed at Clifton, better facilities for seaplanes were built, and a direct telephone link was arranged between Nassau, New York, and Canada. A tighter contract was made with the Munson company, which had let the New Colonial Hotel fall into disrepair, enabling the government to take over if the Munson company did not fulfill its obligations. In fact the government did in due course repossess the hotel, golf course, and Paradise Beach, sub-leasing them to American hotel entrepreneur H. L. Doherty, who undertook extensive repairs on the hotel. By 1935 Clifford reported that the New Colonial and Montagu Beach hotels were full to capacity.[30] Funds were allocated to establish a "bathing beach" on Crown land opposite the New Colonial Hotel. Fort Charlotte was restored and its grounds were cleared of bush for sightseeing. Guides outfitted in period costumes gave tours, and visitors could buy the booklet *Historic Forts of the Bahamas*, written by Harcourt Malcolm, local historian and speaker of the House of Assembly.[31]

Governor Clifford, a sports enthusiast as well as a surveyor, personally supervised the layout of polo and cricket grounds beside Fort Charlotte, sponsored international tennis and golf tournaments under the aegis of what is now called the British Colonial Hotel, and encouraged George Murphy to develop horse racing at Hobby Horse Hall, an improvement on the original Montagu Park course in that area. The first race on the improved track was held in 1934, initiating a sport that was to become increasingly popular among ordinary Bahamians as well as well-heeled tourists.[32] Spectators were accommodated in segregated areas. The covered and well-equipped Grand Stand area had amenities lacking in the open air black and mixed-race section. An offshoot of this development was horseback riding for leisure among the elite.

Mainly through the efforts of Roland T. Symonette, commodore of the Nassau Yacht Club, which he founded in 1931, the Miami–Nassau ocean race and the spring championship races of the international star class yacht racing association were inaugurated in Nassau during 1934. These events attracted a number of outstanding yachtsmen to the colony and resulting in the development of friendships between them and the local elite. The government also supported John E. Williamson, a pioneer of undersea photography, in developing his Seafloor Post Office, which provided a useful service and a unique experience.[33] The number of tourist visitors, still limited to the winter season, rose from 10,295 in 1932–33 to 25,000 between December 1934 and March 1935. Perhaps more gratifying was the quality of the visitors: at the upper end of the international social scale, they included a mix of important celebrities of the stage, politics, and literature and represented American money and British titles. In April 1935 Nassau was referred to as "the social centre of the south," where "the society set of Palm Beach and other Florida resorts mingled with the fashionable colony here in a gay whirl of parties prompted by the visit of Their Royal Highnesses the Duke and Duchess of Kent."[34]

A number of the transients—including Sir Herbert and Lady Holt of Montreal and Sir Frederick and Lady Williams Taylor, also originally from that city but recently settled in London, England—built substantial homes on newly developed Prospect Ridge, Cable Beach, or the Eastern Bay, and a few of the more reclusive bought their own Out Islands, including Betty Carstairs, the developer of Whale Cay in the Berry Islands, and Mr. and Mrs. Louis Wasey of Cat Cay. Celebrated author Ernest Hemingway first visited Bimini in 1935, returning practically every year to fish and relax. His book *Islands in the Stream*, published posthumously in 1970 though written in the 1940s, was largely set in Bimini. Fishing enthusiast Michael Lerner of New York, in conjunction with the Museum of Natural History, established the Lerner Laboratory at Alice Town, Bimini, to promote research into marine life. Dunmore Town, Harbour Island, which boasted "the Little Boarding House," was just beginning to attract tourists.[35]

Besides beaches and sports, historical attractions, and a range of attractive shops, visitors to Nassau were offered local entertainment and indigenous crafts. Catering to visitors and locals alike, the nightclubs, which became popular in the 1930s, also encouraged social drinking and prostitution. Two outstanding nightclubs, the Silver Slipper and the Zanzibar, were built in the 1930s in Grant's Town, Over-the-Hill. The former was foreign owned, while the Zanzibar was co-owned by black entrepreneurs Milo Butler, Bert Gibson, Preston Moss, and Felix Johnson. Both catered to a varied clientele. Patrons attended in parties, usually fraternizing only with those at their own tables and thus segregating themselves. Local black orchestras usually played at the clubs, and "native" floorshows were performed to please the white tourists, who could brag that they had mixed with "picturesque natives." On the dance floor one was likely to rub shoulders with almost anyone. At the Zanzibar one night, leading black middle-class lawyer and politician A. F. Adderley recognized the black drayman who had called him "Boss," whip raised in greeting, in H. G. Christie's office the previous day. Adderley recognized the irony of the situation: "In the day gotta tip the whip, but in the night you rub shoulders."[36]

The new nightclubs, as this incident demonstrated, were important social crossing places, not just for tourists but for different levels of local society, where authentic music and dance were usually sustained and developed.[37] The best known orchestras at the time were led by black and mixed-race musicians, such as Bert Cambridge (also a politician), Rudy Williams, Noel Maellet, and Leonard White. In the 1930s bands usually included violins as well as the more usual instruments like the saxophones, trumpets, drums, and bass. Members of the orchestras were obliged to read music they had learned from visiting musicians or those in the Police force.[38] American bands were hired by the hotels and the elite clubs during the tourist season in Nassau. If nonwhite musicians—such as mixed-race Maxwell Thompson, who played saxophone and clarinet in the Cambridge Orchestra—wished to hear a foreign orchestra, they had to seek special permission to enter the outside premises and were allowed to listen at the windows. The Bert Cambridge Orchestra, renowned for its "high class music for high class people," played periodically in the off-season at the exclusive Porcupine Club and at some hotels. Thompson also revealed that in some settings, such as the Jungle Club at the Montagu Beach Hotel, certain poor whites were not allowed in as patrons.[39]

Several musicians in the 1930s entertained the tourists, some gaining popularity in Nassau and the United States. Included among these were Charles L. Lofthouse, A. Blake Higgs, and George Symonette. Lofthouse, a member of the white elite class, popularized goombay—that is, Bahamian secular music—writing such songs as "Bahama Mama," "Goombay Papa Beat the Drum Again," and "Moonlight Nights in Nassau."[40] Black song writers and musicians, such as Blake Higgs and George Symonette, also gained recognition, sometimes playing in the street and later at the Imperial Hotel and club, owned by Alexander Maillis of Greek descent. Blake's songs often reflected the major happenings of the day, and he popularized many traditional songs, such as "Brown Skin Gal, "Pretty Boy," and "John B. Sail." George Symonette was renowned for his piano playing and singing.[41]

Other less well known black entertainers were Philip Brice from Fox Hill, "Cowboy," and "Shorty the Serenader," who sang and played for American visitors. Although such entertainers sang songs about freedom and hard work, they were tempted to cater to tourists, who regarded them as "picturesque." Art historian Krista Thompson argued that the white mercantile elite's maintenance of Nassau's image as picturesque "led to social control of space," including who was to occupy the "tourist oriented landscape." The white elite also controlled behavior. Responding to changes in metropolitan tastes, the elite allowed some black native performers in elite clubs in the late 1920s and 1930s. Nassau's black majority was used when necessary to boost tourism, depending on the time and tastes. Krista Thompson states: "Whether black Bahamians were touristically 'in fashion' or not, their presence was constantly being mitigated and controlled in the name of the tourist industry." Blacks were rendered in particular ways and their "picturesque qualities went from being a pictorial ideal to a social policy." Visitors to the islands were "naturalized as parts of the landscape," while the black majority was "simultaneously disempowered and dispossessed."[42]

The traditional Junkanoo celebrations at Christmas and New Year's Day, dating back to enslavement and representative of indigenous African culture, were a time of merriment and drinking. During the 1920s the masqueraders had become more flamboyant, wearing more elaborate headdresses and costumes and singing as they "rushed." The Depression years witnessed drunkenness among the masqueraders, and in 1932 and 1933 there were complaints of disorderly and drunken behavior. In addition many of the paraders failed to wear costumes. During the following year, the Junkanoo on Boxing Day (the day after Christmas) was stopped on account of drunkenness, and for the next few years Junkanoo was banned altogether.[43] A voluntary committee was formed in the early '30s, its members representing a wide cross section of civic-minded Bahamians, to raise funds and offer prizes for the best costumes in various categories. There was still drunkenness, but parades were generally more orderly, especially those on New Year's Day. In 1938 Boxing Day was for the first time declared a public holiday, and the Junkanoo parade shifted from Christmas Day to the morning following.[44] The event was increasingly regarded as a tourist attraction.

While local elites benefited from "the plums" of tourism, mingling with traveling elites, the black majority struggled to make ends meet in the increasingly segregated resort city of "white Nassau." The gap between rich and poor, and white and nonwhite, widened in Nassau. "The merchants of Bay Street . . . saw to it that everything should be done to attract visitors who would spend money in their shops."[45] As a result they not only restricted nonwhite participation in some businesses but also, as we have noted, legislatively controlled the immigrant minorities of Lebanese, Jews, Chinese, and Greeks.[46] In the mid- to late 1930s foreigners wishing to invest usually first approached lawyer K. Solomon and, after 1935, his brash and brilliant nephew Stafford L. Sands. Harold Christie then provided suitable land, and Roland T. Symonette, who headed businesses in ship building and general construction, helped them to develop it. This small group also benefited from their interest in other lucrative enterprises, such as the grocery, wholesale, and liquor businesses. They, along with the white Bethell, Kelly, and Roberts families, controlled the socioeconomic and political life of the colony.[47]

Some Bahamians were critical of the ruling elite's concentration on tourists and moneymaking to the detriment of the locals. An anonymous writer complained to the *Tribune* in 1938:

> I can only come to the conclusion that we really need a thorough change among our so-called leaders today. They have sold Sunday for the almighty dollar; they have sold themselves for a mess of pottage and now they are trying to sell the last and only privilege that Bahamians have and pride, our walks along the waterfront. I wonder sometimes they don't ask ourselves to lock up ourselves in our homes at certain hours of the day so that tourists can have the rights and privileges of the tourists for themselves. Mr. Editor, I think this is absurd that the people in whom we have put our trust and confidence to take care of our interests and welfare betray us so often. . . . I think it is time that our people stir up themselves and say what we would have and what we will not have.[48]

As in the Caribbean generally, the tourist industry made the racial situation worse. In the Bahamas racial discrimination was more severe (except in Bermuda) than in the other Caribbean colonies. The substantial white presence, representing about 10 percent of the population, and long historical ties with the southern United States led to antagonistic race relations. As noted, whites separated themselves socially from the black and mixed-race population, seeking to educate their children separately, segregating themselves in seating patterns in church and in some cases Sunday schools and being buried in separate graveyards.[49]

Frank Taylor argued that racism was "historically a built in feature of West Indian tradition of hospitality." The development of tourism during the twenties and thirties hardened the already existing color line in the Bahamas. Like Jamaicans and Barbadians, the majority of Bahamians suffered from discrimination in most tourist related facilities, "a reflection of practices current within the society as a whole."[50] Tourism in the Bahamas, as Taylor stated for Jamaica, "served noticeably to strengthen the 'aristocracy of skin' . . . and to sharpen the contrast in life styles between the various sections of the community."[51] In the Bahamas, racial discrimination worsened as the cleavage between whites and nonwhites widened. The new wealth among elite whites, the American influence, and tourism all widened the gap between the classes.

Wealthy Bahamians were usually white, although some nonwhites were well off. Skin color and race were also significant. Nonwhites often had an ingrained self-hatred and inferiority complex. As in the Caribbean generally, the divisive element within the mixed-race and black middle class tended more to "perpetuate than to eliminate color prejudice."[52] Regarding post-emancipation Trinidad, Bridget Brereton stated: "Racism was directed against blacks and coloureds and there developed a preoccupation with 'colour and shade.'" She continued: "Caribbean societies were based on racism and sensitivity to colour and shade, even though no formal apartheid system existed and in law all were equal."[53] In the Bahamas, until at least the passing of the 1956 Resolution against Racial Discrimination, segregation was rife in some residential areas, schools, churches, and clubs.

Tourism, which stimulated much cultural development in Trinidad during the 1940s, also had a profound effect on the development of straw work, an ancient craft, and on Bahamian culture generally. The straw market proper started in the mid-1930s, behind Prince George's Wharf. Dressed in large straw hats and brightly colored head kerchiefs, the women who made shell jewelry and carved coconuts often sang as they worked, presenting a picturesque spectacle to tourists; a few men worked there too. In his book *Bahamian Lore,* Robert Curry, son of the Development Board chairman, condescendingly commended the vendors for being "amiable women" and the "coloured folk" for being "unceasingly interesting."[54]

Tourists and winter residents, with stereotyped ideas about the "docility . . . manners, superstitions, idiosyncrasies, and modes of thought" among the "natives," visited black settlements and watched indigenous African-inspired dances; they witnessed the "Holy Rollers" at their prayer meetings, "rolling more enthusiastically at the thought of the collection they would take up from the rich visitors."[55] Similarly, young black boys dived from the docks for coins, at great risk to themselves but much to the amusement of tourists.[56]

In trying to please tourists, "using language to make them feel important and respected" and giving salutations such as "boss," Bahamians and West Indians in general degraded themselves.[57] Furthermore, as Rex Nettleford argued, commercializing the indigenous culture to entertain tourists caused "psychic confusion," and a "dichotomy as to how West Indians see themselves, the industry and the people coming in as tourist/visitors." He further stated that the tourist industry depicted a "paradise of happy go-lucky people as if they were without history, personality or religion"—that is, perpetuating the stereotype of Quashie characteristics; tourism had encouraged West Indians to satisfy foreign audiences "in search of instant or passing titillation" rather than "coming to grips with awesome challenges of cultural definitions."[58] At the time some colonial officials, despite some positive cultural developments, held reservations about the effects of the tourist industry. Allan Burns, colonial secretary in the Bahamas during the mid- to late twenties, expressed some skepticism: "It was a glorious playground, but a very expensive place. The tourists poured money into the colony, but the people, both white and coloured, gave a great deal of their character in exchange for it."[59]

Tourism and foreign investment especially affected the white elite Nassauvians, although the middle-class whites and nonwhites also subtly became Americanized. Frank Taylor's comment on the Jamaican situation was also true for the Bahamas: "Along with the American tourist there had also come the American film, Hollywood values, and apparently Hollywood's vulgarity." A letter writer to the *Tribune* in March 1930 complained about the loudness, drinking, and vulgar dancing by some staff members of the New Colonial Hotel who were waiting to embark on the SS *Munargo*. The writer was shocked: "What an example for our girls to see stocking-less, painted, half drunken dissipated young men and women displaying to all around how far they have fallen into a state of utter depravity and disgrace."[60] A 1933 letter to the *Tribune* claimed Nassau was going mad under the influence of American culture. The writer said young people were frivolous, "dancing, drinking and living a sporting life, in and out of season."[61]

As Nassau's reputation grew internationally, the influence and wealth of the white mercantile clique increased, while that of the mixed-race and black middle class diminished in relative terms. Politically, nonwhites lost ground in the House of Assembly after 1935. The growing strength of the nouveau riche politicians, united with the influential older elite and benefiting from openly corrupt election practices, made it increasingly difficult for nonwhites to win seats. Governor Dundas admitted in 1938 that "the corrupt practices of electioneering in this colony are notorious and not disputed by anyone."[62] Race was not always the issue, as illustrated when the black tailor turned politician Samuel C. McPherson withdrew from the southern district election in 1935, unable to compete with influential and wealthy Kenneth Solomon or the popular black physician Claudius R. Walker. Etienne Dupuch summed up the position succinctly: "Money mattered. While S. C. McPherson was too poor to buy votes, A. K. Solomon bought toys in England to be given to the children in the Southern District."[63] Walker was well known and highly respected. Whereas in the 1928 elections nine nonwhites had been elected to the House of Assembly, constituting about a third of its members, in 1935 only four were returned.[64]

Benefiting from the economic expansion brought by tourism and foreign investment, the white mercantile elite consolidated its power, controlling the political machinery and the economic enterprises. In addition to Solomon, Sands, and Christie, there were the Bethell brothers, sons of long established liquor merchant Charles E. Bethell, who were co-owners of the large liquor firm Bethell-Robertson. Dominating the hardware business through their respective firms were Herbert McKinney of the John S. George company, Gurth Duncombe of the Ironmongery, J. Burnside of General Hardware, C. J. Kelly of Kelly's Hardware, and W.H.H. Maura of the Bahamas Cuba Company, later renamed Maura Lumber Company. George Roberts, founder of the City Lumber Yard in 1930, seeing a need for more efficient service to the Out Islands, also acquired a fleet of boats.[65]

While this elite group was gaining in power and wealth, a small white middle class was also developing, including teachers, civil servants, and shop assistants. Members of this group, among them such families as the Lightbourns, Johnsons, Sweetings, Frenches, Alburys, and Coles, usually sent their children to Queen's College. Not many of the young and ambitious white Bahamians wished to pursue higher education and qualify professionally, except in the legal field. Commercial prosperity lured them into shop keeping, other commercial enterprises, and the civil service. There were notable exceptions, such as William H. Sweeting, son of Dr. C. C. Sweeting who was a career civil servant, and Leonard J. Knowles, who read law at King's College, London University, obtaining an LLB with honors in 1937. While wealth was beginning to create division among the Nassau whites, their race and small numbers united them as a social group. Although the wealthy and the middle class did not usually socialize, they assisted each other by finding positions in business or civil service jobs for white youngsters. Under the system of patronage that had developed by the late thirties, it was not surprising that the Bahamas Country Club in 1937 employed a local white for the post of bookkeeper, passing over the application by a mixed-race Queen's College graduate with better qualifications.[66]

Mixed-race and black businessmen on or near Bay Street, many of whom had benefited from Prohibition, were pitted against wealthy white competition and were pushed off Bay Street in the 1930s. Having little money, many were forced to sell to the white elite. Those whose businesses survived the

Depression underwent little expansion. Some mixed-race and black merchants managed to keep their businesses going, such as the DeGregorys and Out Islanders who had migrated to Nassau, including Herbert and Eugene Heastie, Edgar Bain, and Ulric Mortimer. Many black merchants established businesses Over-the-Hill, including Willis Russell, J.A.C. Royal, W. W. Allen, William A. Carey, Arnold F. Pindling, Inspector Nottage, William Neilly, and Charles Rhodriquez.[67]

Education and Social and Cultural Awareness

The increasing white domination of the economic and political life of the Bahamas and a new awareness, stimulated to some extent by West Indian residents who were generally better educated than the majority of Bahamians, had encouraged enlightened mixed-race and black families to seek a better education for their children. Such highly educated men as A. F. Adderley, T. A. Toote, and C. R. Walker were held in high esteem. Adderley and Toote were successful lawyers, and Dr. Walker, who settled in Grant's Town, practiced medicine there, ran a night school for young people, and had the most contact with ordinary people.

It was still relatively rare, however, for any Bahamians to pursue secondary education, partly because of the expense and the attitudes of the day. The Government High School, which became a means of upward mobility in Nassau, was out of reach for most, costing £10 a year. Beyond the matter of fees, some parents saw little justification in providing secondary education for their children, particularly the girls. There was unease that secondary education would "create a class of persons" who could not "be absorbed into the community." Governor Clifford, like some of his colleagues, secretly feared that such people would "ultimately form a variety of socialistic Intelligentsia whose activities will probably be directed towards fostering of racial animosities in the hope that they will create for themselves amongst the coloured populace a status which will provide them with a vicarious livelihood."[68]

Such attitudes were slowly changing, however. The Government High School in 1935 was in its tenth year of operation and had established a fine academic reputation. In spite of challenges—scarcity of funds, a small and poorly paid staff, poor facilities, and until 1935 having only one teacher, the headmaster Albert Woods—the school excelled in the Overseas Cambridge Examinations. With an average of 37 children between the years 1927 and 1935, the Government High School boasted 23 Cambridge school certificates and 48 Junior Cambridge successes. Over the same period Queen's College, a much larger school, obtained 17 senior school certificates and 39 junior passes. Therefore, when it was suggested by the governor and some members of the legislature in the early thirties that the Government High School be closed, there was a public outcry among nonwhites.[69]

In fact, the threat of retrenchment in the education grant in 1934, and the possibility of closing either the Government High School or Queen's College, prompted Secretary E. W. Thompson at Methodist Missionary Society headquarters in London to question Reverend E. V. Paget, chairman of the Bahamas District, about whether the white Methodists in the Bahamas "could be induced" to open Queen's College to mixed-race and black children whose parents could afford it. He concluded that it would strengthen the Methodist Church's strong position and influence, removing "what every Missionary feels to be a scandal and reproach to our Christianity." Paget confidentially replied that the present Queen's College Committee "would strenuously be opposed to opening doors to all classes of the community." He added that he had heard one of the strongest members of the Committee say: "I have no wish to prevent children of coloured parents getting secondary education, but I know as a matter of fact if we opened our doors to such children, it would mean the end of Queen's College."[70]

Government High graduates increasingly took advantage of available opportunities. Some were absorbed as teachers in the government school system, and a few went to England or North America, studied law as articled students at home, or entered the clerical grades of the civil service.[71] Among the outstanding graduates of the Government High School to enter the teaching profession in the 1930s were Miriam Cash and Kenneth Huyler, who were posted at Western Senior School. They joined other talented mixed-race and black teachers, usually with a less academic background. Included among these were Louise Bailey (R. M. Bailey's daughter), Eunice Taylor (later Weir), Donald Davis, E. P. Roberts, T. Gibson, C. I. Gibson, Molly Albury, and Thelma Gibson. Some, like Molly Albury, profited from summer school at the Booker T. Washington Institute in Tuskegee, Alabama. Others attended night school offered at Western Senior School between 1938 and 1939.[72] Another Government High School graduate, Gerald Cash, Miriam Cash's brother, articled as a law student in the chambers of A. F. Adderley, the first Government High School student to do so. Serving a pupilage of five years and successfully passing his examinations, he was called to the local Bar in 1940. He later read law at Middle Temple and was called to the English Bar in 1948.[73] Among those studying abroad were Anatol Reeves (later

Rodgers), Cleveland Eneas, and Kenneth Rodgers. Reeves and Eneas studied in the United States at Spelman College, Atlanta, Georgia, and at Tuskegee, respectively. Reeves was appointed assistant teacher at GHS in 1941 and later married Kenneth Rodgers, one of the first nonwhites to study medicine at Edinburgh University. Other nonwhites who had studied medicine in the United Kingdom included Terry North and Ricardo DeGregory.

Corresponding to the craving for education was a new social and cultural awareness among mixed-race and black people. Additional exposure gained abroad and increasing means caused nonwhites, especially women, to feel a duty to assist the poor. Frances Butler, affectionately known as "Mother Butler," was the mother of Milo Butler and had lived in Miami for some years in the early part of the century. Returning to Nassau a week after the 1929 hurricane, she founded the Mother's Club with the chief purpose of collecting used clothing and furniture for distribution to the poor, aged, and needy. As the years passed the Mother's Club became a predominantly black and Over-the-Hill institution. A special committee was set up to promote a Christmas treat for the aged. In 1940 the Mother's Club built their own club house in Gaol Alley off East Street.[74]

Among the nonwhite upper-middle-class persons who were involved in charitable work in the thirties was fair-skinned Clarita Toote, wife of lawyer and politician Thaddeus Toote. Having leisure time at their disposal, she and Ethel Adderley (also light-skinned), wife of the esteemed A. F. Adderley, formed a Ladies Committee that spearheaded relief work in collecting money and clothing for the hurricane victims of Bimini and Grand Bahama in 1935.[75] The Adderleys and Tootes were leaders in the nonwhite middle stratum. Carrie Lunn, who was interviewed by Dr. Olga C. Jenkins in the 1980s and 1990s, commented on the fact that "The 'dark' (elite) men seemed to marry women who were lighter than they." She continued: "Now Mrs. Toote was a very nice-looking person with pretty brown skin. Mr. Toote was a dark man. But they were styled (classified) like the upper class of coloured people. . . . They also palled around with the fair-skinned Knowles . . . and would socialize in certain things." Carrie Lunn, who was sister-in-law to Ethel Adderley, stated: "In my day, you would hardly find a white woman marrying a coloured man. No, you'd hardly find that. Maybe somebody from away. A dark man might come here with a white wife, but not the Bahamians. Now today, they marry, white marry black."[76]

Despite this practice, there was still an ambiguous color line among the nonwhite community. Generally, there was a strong distinction between black and "colored." A. F. Adderley and T. A. Toote, who were both black, were esteemed members of the mixed-race middle class because of their outstanding intellectual and educational achievements and professional standing. As noted, some mixed-race children attended Queen's College, and several boys, including Basil North, were even members of the predominantly white Boy Scout troop. In the Bahamas, white and mixed-race scouts camped and "turned out" together. There seemed to be no racial problems among that scout troop in Nassau. However, five mixed-race scouts, a part of the delegation attending the 1937 international scout jamboree in Washington, D.C., encountered discrimination in Miami, where they spent the night. On arriving in Miami, the five mixed-race scouts, including Basil North, were separated from the white members of the group. While the mixed-race boys stayed in a private home, the white scouts stayed in a hotel that discriminated against nonwhites. This experience deeply affected one of the mixed-race boys, who committed suicide shortly after his return to Nassau. Scout Basil North, according to his Key West–born mother, Leonora Terry North, had been asked by the scout leader to look after this boy in Washington, as he seemed to be acting strangely. North had spoken to him before leaving the Bahamas, making him aware of discriminatory policy in the segregationist United States. He blamed the parents: "Some of these people did a disservice by their children, bringing them up to think they were white."[77]

Paradoxically, during the decade of the thirties, mixed-race and black people were exposed to a new kind of cultural awareness through the talented and unconventional musician and composer Meta Davis Cumberbatch. Born in Trinidad to middle-class black parents, she studied music at the Royal Academy of Music in London. There she married a young Trinidadian doctor, Roland Cumberbatch, who obtained a job in the Bahamas. Moving to Nassau in 1927, Dr. Cumberbatch was immediately posted to the underdeveloped and predominantly black Cat Island. Undaunted, wearing her hair in a natural "Afro," Meta Cumberbatch, her Bleuthner piano in tow, soon revived the Cat Island Association, teaching music, singing, and needlework under great hardships. Later, during the early and mid-thirties, Meta Cumberbatch was to give piano recitals in London at such places as Wigmore Hall as well as in Nassau. At one recital she attracted the patronage of Lady Clifford, the governor's wife. Combining classical works with African-inspired folk songs, she created a new feeling of black pride, especially among her pupils, as she continued to foster the growth of the arts in all forms.[78]

Restlessness

The new consciousness evident during the Great Depression in the thirties was not restricted to mixed-race and black people. There was evidence of a developing attitude among an enlightened minority of whites (or near whites), some of whom were from the Out Islands, that was sympathetic to the underdog in the society. Recognizing the injustices in the society, including discrimination that also sometimes affected them, they began to vocalize their feelings. Included in the group were such individuals as Henry M. Taylor, Cyril Stevenson, Jack Stanley Lowe, and Holly Brown. Taylor was a Long Islander who taught and worked as a clerk in the civil service, the Nassau-born Stevenson was a reporter with the *Nassau Guardian*, and Lowe was from Eleuthera, a school teacher and journalist with the small newspaper *Bahamas News*. They began writing letters to the *Tribune*, addressing problems of unemployment, low wages, aliens, police inefficiency, and the secret ballot.[79] Because of their jobs and their shaky financial standing, they had to be careful. Brown, although not much better off, was more independent.

Born in Nassau in 1898, Brown had a Grenadian father and a light-skinned Bahamian mother. After serving as a member of the Gallant Thirty in the First World War, he returned to Nassau. His small salary as a wireless telegraphist motivated him to migrate to Canada in 1929, where for nearly eight years he operated a garbage collection agency, returning to Nassau in early 1937. His exposure to Canadian society and to the devastating Depression, when economics and politics were of primary concern, had convinced him that the Bahamas needed a newspaper fighting for the underdog. Along with Lowe he founded the *Herald*, the first issue appearing on 1 May 1937.[80] Published weekly for the rest of the 1930s, the *Herald*, more than the *Tribune*, became the "champion of the working man."[81]

Outspoken in its criticism of high public officials, the *Herald* particularly identified with the local labor situation. In view of the lucrative tourist business, the paper was critical of the minimum wage set for unskilled labor in 1936.[82] The minimum wage for unskilled labor was set at four shillings a day for men and two shillings a day for women. Incensed by the lack of consideration shown by the legislature toward the community at large, Brown advocated an equitable income tax. For this he was called a Communist. Brown admitted to spreading the rumor.[83] Whether this rumor was believed or not, the white elite did not appreciate the opinions in the *Herald*. Within a year of its establishment, the House of Assembly passed the Newspaper Security Act, which required newspapers to provide a security bond in the sum of

£100 and one or more sureties before being allowed to operate. Holly Brown was convinced that the act was directed against the *Herald,* which he ran on a "shoe-string." He resigned on principle, stating that he would not be the editor of a "shackled" newspaper. He turned it over to Lowe, who operated it until his death in 1953.[84]

Governor Charles Dundas, who was colonial secretary when the Depression first hit, was well aware of the desperate state of the Out Islands and the explosive potential of New Providence. He was extremely concerned that the colony in his charge not follow the lead of the British West Indies in generating "social discord." The signs were significant, and according to a report from Commander Langston Jones, inspector of the Imperial Lighthouse Service in the Bahamas, because of "conditions of unrest prevailing amongst the coloured residents of the Bahamas," a Defence Corps had been "secretly formed." He further reported that the government was "in possession of machine guns and 'mob' gas, and that steel gates are being fitted to the local gaol to replace the former wooden ones."[85]

In July 1935, when Roland Symonette was building the Prince George Hotel, between three and four hundred men turned up looking for employment, and as soon as it was evident that most were to be disappointed, a near riot broke out, accompanied by stone throwing. Later in the year, eight hundred unemployed men turned out for forty advertised jobs at Fort Charlotte. Unable to find work, many took to begging or loitering and a few took to crime, including arson as well as theft. Within two weeks in the late summer of 1937 both the Nassau Theatre and the Montagu Theatre (which practiced seating segregation for those who could afford to patronize them) mysteriously burned down. By July 1937 Governor Dundas reckoned that there was a "Nassau mob of about 1000 persons" consisting of "young loafers, criminals and riff raff of that type." Dundas believed they were "potential hooligans" and if excited could become mischief makers.[86]

Not all Bay Street politicians were unsympathetic toward the poor and the plight of unskilled labor. Percy Christie, brother of Harold Christie, identified to some extent with the black laboring masses. A shoe merchant and member of the House of Assembly for the western district, Christie attracted a large body of support in Nassau by fighting for the minimum wage of four shillings a day, which as noted was introduced in 1936. The Labour Union he established had a membership of eight hundred within a year, many of them unskilled laborers. Christie tried also to enroll skilled artisans but with little success. Two years later the government, aware of developments and restlessness among labor, appointed a Labour Bureau and a part-time labor officer, Welsh-born John A. Hughes, an expatriate resident of the Bahamas, who also held the post of senior Out Island commissioner.[87]

But Christie proved no equivalent of the white labor leader Captain Cipriani in Trinidad. And the Mexican-born black merchant Charles Rhodriquez, who ousted Percy Christie as head of the Bahamas Labour Union in 1938, largely on grounds of his color, likewise lacked the charisma of Jamaica's Alexander Bustamante or of Trinidad's Uriah "Buzz" Butler, who similarly "eclipsed" Cipriani. Craftsmen and the permanently employed shunned the union, and for unemployed laborers even the dues of a shilling on joining and a penny a week proved too much. The union was thus hampered not only by the lack of finance but also by an absence of labor legislation.[88]

An even less effectual union movement was begun in Inagua in 1934 by Theodore Farquharson, an Acklins Islander who had returned from the United States in 1928 after a stay of fifteen years to manage a family store at its main settlement, Mathew Town. Described as "an orator of the Hyde Park tub thumper type, with somewhat more education than the rest of his coloured brethren in Inagua," Farquharson was perhaps instrumental in causing several work stoppages, but he and his followers were not the instigators of the violent incidents that occurred at Inagua in 1937.[89] Though, as Nigel Bolland argues, "some of the same factors that produced labour rebellions throughout the British Caribbean were present," the incidents in Inagua were exaggerated in the international press.[90]

Inagua, located in close proximity to Cuba and Haiti, is the third largest island of the Bahamas, lying 370 miles south of Nassau. Being in the dry belt of the Bahamian archipelago, Inagua naturally produced salt, which soon became the island's staple product. By the early 1900s the successful salt industry had collapsed, and the economy in the late nineteenth and early twentieth centuries was sustained by the steamship labor business, which provided work for the male population. By 1882 Mathew Town had outstripped its main rival, Albert Town on Long Cay, having become the "main centre of labour recruitment" in the Bahamas. At this time most laborers were paid in truck, allowing them credit advances in food and drink. As we have seen, this exploitative practice continued well into the twentieth century.[91] With the outbreak of World War I, shipping was interrupted and steamship companies ceased calling at Inagua. By the early 1930s, Inagua, like most of the Out Islands in the Bahamas, suffered from acute depression. Migration, mainly to Nassau and the United States, resulted in a sizable decline in population—from 1,343 to 667 between 1911 and 1931.[92]

By the mid-1930s Inagua's stevedoring traffic and salt industry had been revived to a limited extent. Arthur Symonette, a local mixed-race merchant who was also a justice of the peace, spearheaded both operations. Evidence suggests that he employed the truck system, whereby he kept men indebted to him at his store. Labor unrest erupted in December 1936 and early 1937 when the Inagua-based stevedores held several strikes for higher wages. These actions were directed at Symonette for the way he operated the truck and credit system. However, aware of Symonette's power and influence, a number of Inaguan men united against him, calling themselves the "Rulers" or "Rock" of Inagua and forcing him to cooperate with them. It was into this atmosphere that the Ericksons, a New England family headed by Josiah Erickson, who in the previous year had purchased some Crown land, established the West India Chemical Company, employing fifty men and a few women to revitalize the salt industry.[93]

The Ericksons, however, soon encountered hostility from the local people. Some prominent Inaguans, including Symonette, felt threatened by the new wave of economic activity, which brought prosperity and new jobs. Hostility toward the Ericksons intensified when they imported unskilled laborers from Acklins, Long Cay, and Mayaguana, breaking the strike, and took over the steamship agency from Symonette. The influential group of men called the "Rulers," although they had little respect for Symonette, had an uneasy alliance with him. Symonette considered them his supporters against the intruders. As Nigel Bolland stated: "There was also an element of racial tension involved, as some Inaguans who had experienced discrimination in the United States resented white Americans taking superior positions in their own country." Resentment against the Ericksons increased after they threatened the acting colonial secretary that they would "import a number of ex-Marines to the island and run it as it ought to be run." They also upset some Inaguans by using an armor-plated car on the island.[94] Shortly after the strike in December 1936, a fight over a trivial incident occurred between Charles Kaddy, a white American truck driver for the Ericksons, and a local black stevedore, George Duvalier. He and his brother Willis had lived in the United States and were supporters of Symonette. They were believed to be among the so-called Band of Inagua Terrors, a group of reckless young men who had been in trouble with the law. When Kaddy drove his truck into the side of Symonette's store the fight quickly developed into a brawl involving Duvalier's supporters, including his brother Willis, against almost the entire white staff of the West Indian Chemical Company. All appeared before Commissioner Fields, a mixed-race Trinidadian physician, who had been stationed at Inagua since 1926 and was well liked by the Ericksons. Fields fined the combatants on each side two pounds each, but it appeared that the Duvalier brothers continued to harbor a grudge against the Ericksons.[95]

In June 1937 Reginald Alexander, leader of the Band of Inagua Terrors, was fined five pounds for using obscene language to Euphemia Henderson, whose daughter he had courted. Toward the end of June after an altercation with that family, the Henderson house was destroyed by fire. The arsonist, Arthur Ferguson, admitted that he had set the house on fire on the instruction of Alexander. Fields ordered both Ferguson and Alexander to stand trial in Nassau.

The next day George Duvalier, a friend of both of the accused, was arrested for assaulting a witness, the last to give evidence in the arson case, but he escaped from the courtroom. A policeman gave chase and received a minor wound after being attacked with a knife by Willis Duvalier. Commissioner Fields, while attempting to leave his office, was also attacked by Willis Duvalier and escaped injury only by sheer luck. George Duvalier, however, acquired a gun and shot and wounded Fields, who had gone to the wireless station to telegraph Nassau for help. George then ran to the Ericksons' store and fired at Josiah Erickson, but the gun misfired. Josiah and his younger brother escaped to their home. Arming themselves, the Ericksons proceeded to the wireless station accompanied by two American employees, including Kaddy. On leaving the station with Fields, they were attacked by Willis Duvalier. Both Ericksons and their employee Kaddy received minor injuries. In fear of their lives, the Erickson party and the commissioner spent the night at the Erickson household. Meanwhile, the Duvaliers had sought out and killed an employee of the West Indian Chemical Company, John Munroe. They also set fire to the commissioner's residence, the wireless station, the Erickson store, and the company's salt house.[96]

The next morning the Ericksons fled Inagua in their motor boat, along with three of their employees, Fields, and the wounded policeman. Developing engine trouble, they drifted southward and landed in Cuba. Having no means of identification, they were promptly arrested for possession of arms.[97] The Duvaliers, left in control of Mathew Town, terrorized the inhabitants for two days, though causing little further harm. Neither the Band of Inagua Terrors nor the rest of the inhabitants made an effort to stop their rampage. On Sunday 22 August, after commanding the town for the weekend, the Duvaliers left Inagua in a sailing boat. They were later arrested in Haiti and brought to Nassau for trial. Found guilty of murder in the Nassau Supreme Court on 3 November 1937, they were executed less than three weeks later.[98]

Before a detailed investigation was made and a report compiled, the incident at Inagua in 1937 was blown out of proportion by the press inside and outside the Bahamas. The British press, cognizant of the unrest in the West Indies, elevated the events to an importance on par with the riots in Trinidad and Barbados.[99] Locally, Etienne Dupuch, editor of the *Tribune*, gave the disturbance some importance and referred to it as a "riot," comparing it to similar outbreaks in parts of the British West Indies. Robert Bailey, a black tailor and political activist, wrote a letter to the editor of the *Tribune* alluding to the seething unrest in the colony and specifically to the violence in New Providence, the "burglary at Bimini," and the rioting and murder at Inagua. Bailey asked: "Can we believe that the Commissioner and fourteen heavily armed men including five white Americans with large financial interests in the island, left . . . only to try to get in communication with the capital, their wireless station being out of commission—burnt down—and there was no riot at Inagua?"[100]

The incident in Inagua was not a riot or a labor rebellion on the scale of those in the Caribbean, but as Bolland has argued, "to dismiss it as merely a 'local brawl,' as did a report in the West Indian Department of the Colonial Office, misses its significance." Bolland further states: "There is little doubt that conditions similar to those that caused the labour rebellions in the rest of the British Caribbean gave rise to this incident as there was 'a state of unrest' in Inagua, according to the commissioner, that was provoked both by labour and racial issues. The continuation of the truck system and the Ericksons' use of strike-breakers created resentment among Inagua's workers."[101] Discrimination toward blacks and browns was rife in class-conscious Nassau, but was not as marked in the predominantly nonwhite Out Island settlements. Inagua was a mainly black community but had quite a number of white and mixed-race families. Some Inaguans however, including the Duvaliers as noted, had spent time in the United States and had experienced blatant prejudice and Jim Crow policies.

While there is no evidence of racial discrimination practiced by the Ericksons, it is likely that the Inaguans encountered attitudes of white superiority displayed by the Americans. Commissioner Fields mentioned in a report the anti-American feelings harbored by some Inaguans. In fact, during the years 1935 and 1936, cases of unlawful and disorderly behavior increased.[102] Fields concluded: "While the rest of the inhabitants exhibited no willingness to help the Duvaliers, they equally made no effort and signified no willingness to stop them."[103] The disturbance at Inagua was not merely a clash of personalities but, as Bolland argues, can best be understood "as a microcosm of social change and social tensions . . . the conflict broke out between these particular people because they embodied these tensions." There was no mass uprising because of Inagua's isolation and "also because the feelings of resentment against the Ericksons . . . were not universal, even on Inagua."[104]

When chief commissioner John A. Hughes visited Mathew Town early in 1938, he found no signs of unrest. The mixed-race West Indian Fields had been replaced by a white Abaconian, Japheth Malone. Though the Ericksons did not like the new commissioner, calling him arrogant and racially prejudiced, Hughes claimed that Malone had won the "respect and affection" of the population. The settlement was calm, no trace of the truck system remained, the salt operations were back to normal, and many of the inhabitants had quietly returned to the business of smuggling with Cuba.[105] The disturbance in Inagua occurred in a potentially explosive atmosphere but failed to develop into a political or labor riot. Such a riot would occur, however, in Nassau in 1942.

A much more significant event, though unnoticed in the overseas press, was the disturbance in Nassau associated with the by-election in July 1938. This event was occasioned by the vacancy of one of the two seats for the western district of New Providence brought about by the elevation to the Legislative Council of the distinguished and quintessentially moderate black lawyer, A. F. Adderley. The seat, which traditionally went to a nonwhite, was contested by Milo B. Butler, described by the governor as a black merchant of "small means and little standing," and millionaire Harry Oakes. It was rumored that Adderley's appointment was to make room for Oakes.[106]

Oakes was visiting England at the time of the election. The campaign was managed by his agents, mainly white members of the legislature, led by his attorney Kenneth Solomon, who was leader of government in the House of Assembly. Behind the scenes Butler's credit was stopped at the Royal Bank of Canada under Bay Street pressure, while at the polls the Oakes party openly distributed money and liquor, under the eyes of the police stationed to prevent disturbance. When it was clear that Butler had been so decisively beaten that he would lose his deposit, he announced that he would lodge a protest against the glaring bribery. A drunken and unruly mob attacked the police when they closed the polling station, slightly injuring two white officers with missiles. Among those arrested were two of Butler's most ardent supporters, who were convicted and imprisoned for six months.[107]

The day following the by-election, Butler led about forty supporters downtown to the colonial secretary's office, where he excitedly voiced his grievances. Rumors began circulating that there was to be a serious riot to coincide with Emancipation Day on 1 August. The colonial secretary ordered an investigation into the matter. While the investigation was being undertaken, Butler was formulating a petition. Presenting it to the governor, he called for the secret ballot, the establishment of an election court of appeal, and a fairer representation of blacks on public boards and in the civil service. The Emancipation Day demonstration, however, was orderly and peaceful. Between seven and eight hundred people paraded the city streets with banners calling for the secret ballot. After hearing several speeches at the Southern Recreation Ground, they dispersed without marching on Government House, the usual place to deliver protests and complaints.[108]

Governor Dundas, though, believed that conditions remained explosive "and might with slight provocation have become critical." He became convinced that the secret ballot was the minimum now necessary to defuse the situation. At this time a black deputation from Grant's Town presented a resolution to the governor on the "burning question on the long overdue Electoral Reforms as it related to the institution of the Secret Ballot." Announcing his intention to dissolve the House of Assembly, the governor threatened to make the secret ballot the issue of a general election. Apprehensive that an election centered on the ballot question would become a racial issue, some legislators began to adopt a less hardline attitude. Dundas saw it as a compromise. But some of the political elite were critical of his dictatorial methods, accusing him of overstepping his constitutional boundaries. Even the proposer and seconder of the motion in the House of Assembly, Alvin Braynen and G. W. Higgs, lashed out at Dundas, declaring that the House was already dealing with the Ballot Bill.[109]

On the other hand, Oscar E. Johnson, a former officer of the UNIA of Miami and a leader of that body in Nassau, which was still meeting in the 1930s, led a march on 2 May 1939 from "Grant's Town up through the city, through a portion of the eastern district headed by a band and bearing a banner demanding the Ballot Box reform." Etienne Dupuch, editor of the *Tribune,* who was becoming more conservative, was critical of the demonstration, arguing that it "will only provoke hostility and aggravate difficulty at this time. Wise and judicious approach to the problem will produce the deserved results pleasantly." Johnson answered Dupuch, who assured him that his views differed only "in his methods of approach."[110]

On 6 June 1939, a Bill for the Secret Ballot in New Providence for a five-year provisional period passed its third reading in the House of Assembly, limiting it to New Providence.[111] The secret ballot was declared permanent in New Providence in 1942. For the Out Islands, which returned two thirds of the members, with Bay Street remaining paramount, the secret ballot was delayed until 1949. Johnson, called the non-extension of the ballot to the Out Islands "unthinkable," argued that "we . . . want fair treatment and better representation in all breeds of the Colony's situation."[112] Local Bahamian historian Hartley C. Saunders praised Johnson, stating: "Not since the departure of James Carmichael Smith did a writer clearly stipulate his concerns directly." He added: "This degree of confrontation was never heard of in the Bahamas before."[113]

Conclusion

The imperial government considered the Bahamas so different from the other West Indian colonies and its economic, social, and political problems so much less serious that it did not include the colony on the itinerary of the Moyne Commission, which surveyed conditions throughout the British West Indies in 1938–39. In May 1939 a Colonial Office report published in Nassau painted a dismal picture of backwardness and neglect in the development of agriculture in the Bahamas, as reviewed by E. A. McCallan, who had been director of agriculture in Barbados from 1920 to 1934. Bahamas Governor Dundas had appointed a general Out Island committee before World War II broke out, under the chairmanship of George Murphy, and initiated other committees to improve agriculture generally. The creation of a proper agricultural department and other proposals had to wait until after the war. Dundas's vision for the creation of a "true Bahamian black peasantry" was expressed in a confidential report that he made just before being replaced by the Duke of Windsor in 1940. Dundas concluded pessimistically that black Bahamians are "by nature and inclination essentially employees and that they are little fitted to be independent producers." Acknowledging that there were exceptions, he opined that "they will do far better as agricultural labourers than as producers."[114]

During the early years of the Depression, the majority of the Bahamas' population on the Out Islands suffered severe hardship and poverty. The failure of traditional industries and the unusual succession of hurricanes that hit the archipelago between 1929 and 1932 accelerated the flow of migration from the Out Islands into the capital. Despite the prosperity brought by Prohibition, the rapid growth of Nassau's population led to increased social problems. While job opportunities increased, especially during the winter months, wages remained dangerously low, and the majority of the population found it difficult to make ends meet. Unemployment, vagrancy, and crime were on the increase, especially in the summer or off-season. Even so, the thirties were formative years in the development of Nassau as a first class tourist resort and pioneer tax haven. As the Out Islands became poorer, Nassau gained fame internationally for the amenities it offered not only the tourist but also the financier and land developer. Many wealthy British and North American visitors made winter homes in Nassau, some taking up residence, such as Harry Oakes. The closer interaction between North Americans and Bahamians, through personal contact and the media, profoundly affected life in the capital, for evil as well as good.

The Nassau white mercantile class benefited from controlling the major commercial interests and political machinery, while mixed-race and black people became less influential. Individually, blacks, mixed-race persons, and a small number of whites, through the *Tribune* and *Herald,* were becoming more critical of the growing injustices in Bahamian society. However, their failure to unite assisted the white mercantile clique in consolidating its power. Finding it difficult to compete on Bay Street, many blacks including entertainers looked southward, establishing businesses in the Over-the-Hill district, a trend that entrenched the socioeconomic split.

As color consciousness grew among nonwhite Bahamians, if possible they turned increasingly to education for salvation. A minority gained a sound education at the Government High School and some light-skinned browns at Queen's College. Government High was fast becoming the intellectual training ground for the mixed-race and black middle classes. A small number pursued higher education abroad in England, the United States, and Jamaica. Education for blacks became the vehicle of upward mobility and a way of achieving greater economic independence, if not yet providing a heightened sociopolitical consciousness.

In spite of the growing restlessness among the black population, as demonstrated in the Inagua incident and the 1938 Nassau by-election, no national leader emerged to take command. Actions remained localized and ineffectual. Politically, the Bahamian population remained largely apathetic. Achieving a national movement was difficult because of the distances between islands and settlements as well as between classes. The disturbances during the thirties in the British Caribbean signaled a new type of leadership there and led to an investigation that paved the way for eventual political and social change. These upheavals, however, had little impact on the Bahamas. It was not until the effects of World War II were felt that the Bahama Islands were to experience a serious degree of unrest and the forces of change began to mobilize.

6

World War II and the 1942 Nassau Riot

Following the turbulent 1930s the British West Indian colonies saw growing militancy in union-based and other political parties, nurtured by a sense of nationalism, anti-colonial sentiment, and the teachings of Marcus Garvey. Many West Indian professionals and veterans—including a few Bahamians, some of whom had been influenced by progressive movements in London— had returned after the First World War with new democratic ideas. They had seen whites performing menial tasks, which assisted in undermining the myth of white superiority and the rigid class structure. Matters of race and class relations began to take on new meaning.

The demise of the sponge industry in the Bahamas had more impact on Bahamian society than did Britain's declaration of war on Nazi Germany on 3 September 1939. It was not until after the Japanese attack on Pearl Harbour and the subsequent entry of the United States into the war in late 1941 that substantial change occurred in the Bahamian way of life. American tourism continued to flourish between 1939 and 1941, augmented by the arrival of well-heeled refugees from Europe, led by the former King Edward VIII, now Duke of Windsor, and his American duchess, formerly Wallis Simpson.

Between 1942 and 1945 the Bahamas assumed considerable strategic importance as an antisubmarine and aircraft staging base, and New Providence became an important training ground for aircrews at the base site or Operational Training Unit, under the joint auspices of the British and United States governments. Pressing unemployment problems were solved, at least temporarily, when in 1943 the Duke of Windsor negotiated a contract with the United States government for Bahamian unskilled laborers to be hired on American farms depleted of labor by the war effort. The accord became known as "the Project" or "the Contract." As many as five thousand Bahamian laborers were engaged annually until the early to mid-1960s.[1]

The sponge industry had closed down in 1939 due to a fungus and though reopened in October 1946, it never fully recovered.[2] The collapse of this industry especially affected Andros and to a lesser degree Abaco and Acklins. Androsians who did not migrate to Nassau were forced to return to overworked soils and scale fishing.[3] Cases of starvation occurred, and destitution was so general that the hard-pressed colonial budget set aside £15,000 in 1939 for Andros relief.

For the less unfortunate in New Providence, chances for employment in the tourist industry improved until the end of 1941, and in addition to those working for expatriate settlers, a few hundred people found laboring jobs on the small U.S. Navy installations set up in Exuma and New Providence as a result of the Churchill-Roosevelt bases-for-destroyers deal in August 1940. Such benefits, however, were offset by inflation in prices caused by the dependence on imports and by shipping difficulties as well as opportunistic profiteering. Some essential commodities tripled in price between 1939 and 1942 while wages remained static.[4]

Tourism saw a marginal increase in "stopover" visitors and winter residents. As Philip Cash has stated, "this trend continued throughout the 1941 season so that winter residents were able to provide a source of revenue and employment." Stopover visitors increased from 12,905 to 13,656 between 1939 and 1940 and rose to 14,741 for the war-shortened winter season of 1941 (when the total number of visitors was up from 21,328 to 28,219, before falling to 6,054 in 1942 and 3,652 in 1943).[5]

Nassau, however, benefited from the presence of the international part-time residents, including the William Taylors, the Herbert Holts, and the Sigrist and Oakes families, who were joined by others, including the wealthy Swedish engineer-industrialist Axel Wenner-Gren. Founder of the Electrolux company in 1919, he made a fortune in the 1920s from the worldwide sale of two successful domestic inventions: the electric vacuum-cleaner and the solid-state refrigerator. Wenner-Gren soon became master of a large industrial empire, based in Sweden but with major interests in other parts of the world, especially the United States. His attempt to persuade the Nazis to make their odious internal and foreign policies more "acceptable" to other powers, and his offer to act as a diplomatic intermediary to help avert disaster aroused suspicion among the Americans and British, who believed he was pro-German.[6]

Attracted to the Bahamas by the absence of income tax and the proximity of America, Wenner-Gren acquired a residence on Hog Island and named it "Shangri-La." Besides establishing seafood and fishing businesses at West End, Grand Bahama, he developed most of the seven hundred acres of barren land that he had acquired on Hog Island. Excavating a network of shallow canals, Wenner-Gren connected Hog Island with the ocean to the north and the harbor to the south. Additionally, he constructed a "hurricane hole" (safe harbor), employing hundreds of laborers and sometimes as many as a thousand. Rumors circulated in Nassau that the canals and the government-sponsored hurricane hole were in reality intended for a fleet of German submarines and would be used as a Nazi U-Boat base. In 1942 the U.S. State Department, for other but undisclosed reasons, placed Wenner-Gren on the "Proclaimed List of Blocked Nationals." A few weeks later the British government followed suit, also blacklisting him. Wenner-Gren, forced to wind up his enterprises in the Bahamas, was banned from returning during the war. Making his home in Mexico, he retained close business connections with his white associates in the Bahamas, not least with Governor Windsor, whom Michael Pye scandalously implicates in a conspiracy to evade British taxation and launder money through Mexico.[7]

Such speculations were consonant with the almost surreal atmosphere in Nassau during the early war years. Wenner-Gren hosted celebrities such as Greta Garbo. Other visitors to the Bahamas included Lorenz Hart, who with Richard Rodgers had earned fame for the recent Broadway hit musical *Pal Joey*; Mary Martin, then billed in *The Great Victor Herbert*; and Mrs. Arthur McGrath, a travel writer and social correspondent who used the pen name Rosita Forbes. Forbes was a wealthy and restless world traveler who was persuaded to visit and perhaps settle in the Bahamas by Charles Dundas, whom she had met in 1937 in Lusaka, Northern Rhodesia. They were both old-fashioned British imperialists who shared the ideals of Cecil Rhodes and naively regarded the Bahamas Out Islands as little different from the "White Highlands" of British East Africa: beautiful farmlands undeveloped by their picturesque "primitive" native inhabitants.[8]

After her first visit to Nassau in the winter season of 1938–39 on the invitation of Governor Dundas and the Development Board, Forbes rewarded her hosts with the promotional book A *Unicorn in the Bahamas*, published in London and New York in the early summer of 1939.[9] Ten years later she published her more candid memoir *Appointment with Destiny*, revealing her love for the Out Islands, which she saw as "the real Bahamas, carrying the main population with unlimited space to cultivate." She chided the local regime for failing "to break down the growth of centuries and put back into cultivation land which in the days of slavery and the Loyalists settlers bore good crops. . . . With few exceptions," she claimed, "Nassovian [*sic*] interests are concerned with shop keeping and land values. Agriculture means nothing to the merchants of Bay Street. They would rather import canned goods from America than encourage difficult local production."[10]

Indeed, more than half of the Bahamian population still lived on the Out Islands, eking out a peasant life mainly from farming and maritime activities. Reginald and Evelyn Poitier and their family lived in the virtually all-black Cat Island until the late 1930s, farming tomatoes and other crops including string beans, sweet potatoes, yams, and corn. By chance their son Sidney Poitier, the first successful black film star, was born in Miami, where his father and pregnant mother had sailed to sell a hundred cases of tomatoes at the Miami Produce Exchange.

Harsh conditions forced many Out Islanders to migrate to Nassau, including the Poitiers in 1937. But jobs were difficult to find, and although the new migrants experienced electricity and other modern developments, they had to live in cramped wooden rented houses in Over-the-Hill. Reginald Poitier, aware of the distractions, crowded conditions, and the erosion of Out Island morals, noted that Nassau was not a good place "for raising tomatoes and children."[11] Just before his sixteenth birthday, Sidney, taking advantage of his American birth, was sent to join his older brother Cyril in Miami.[12]

For the wealthy, however, Nassau was attractive. The usual social and sporting activities continued unabated. When not attending cocktail or dinner parties, playing golf or tennis, or sailing, winter residents and tourists alike could shop in downtown Nassau for such luxury items as perfumes, doeskins, tweeds, linens, cashmere and camel hair coats and sweaters, and British chinaware. Indigenous products, such as straw hats, sisal bags, shell ornaments, cameos cut from conch shells, and conch pearls could also be purchased.[13]

The Second World War

As noted, the atmosphere of Nassau and the Bahamas did not immediately reflect the beginning of the Second World War. Many visitors were ambivalent about the war, American tourists were disinterested, and the ordinary people were too desperately poor to feel much of the patriotic loyalty evoked by World War I. Pressured by the Colonial Office into assisting with the war effort, the Bahamas government's contribution was generous. The House of Assembly imposed a war relief tax of 1 percent duty on all imports. Realizing that this would seriously affect the mass of people already suffering from inflation, the House removed tax from twenty-one articles, most of them articles of consumption, and raised tax on the remainder. With a reinforced treasury the Bahamas government gave a gift of £20,000 and lent the imperial government £500,000 free of interest for the duration of the war. It also contributed £35,000 from the sale of War Savings Certificates and stamps and gave £47,000 toward imperial defense.[14]

In addition to these officially sponsored contributions, money and material were obtained for the war effort by voluntary organizations. Etienne Dupuch, owner and editor of the *Tribune,* with views that had dramatically changed from those he had held on his return from the First World War, now "loved England" and was eager to help. It was on Dupuch's own initiative, the governor having turned down his plan, that the War Materials Committee was established in June 1940 (a month after the Dunkirk evacuation). The objective of the committee was to send war materials, especially metals, to Britain. Out Islanders were recruited to assist in the enterprise. Organizing expeditions, members of the committee took crews through tangled bushes searching for cannons of ancient fortifications, rusting engines, and iron rails "that were relics of the cotton, salt and sisal industries."[15] Old cars and other vehicles were dismantled, and the committee even collected gold jewelry. Hundreds of laborers were employed in collecting, sorting, and grading metal so that it went straight to the smelters. The War Materials Committee also made the second largest gift of food within the empire, exceeded only by that of Rhodesia. W.C.B. Johnson, retired speaker of the House, placed a canning factory that canned tomatoes, pineapples, and guavas at the disposal of the committee. It also bottled marmalade and honey, the latter especially for submarine crews.[16]

Several members of the War Materials Committee served as well on the Bahamas War Committee, which was appointed by Governor Dundas in July 1940. It was chaired by the speaker of the House of Assembly, Kenneth Solomon, found by the Duke of Windsor to be "a reactionary die-hard and blindly adverse to change in principle."[17] The Committee consisted of a majority of whites, including Chief Justice Sir Oscar Daly, Assistant Colonial Secretary Charles P. Bethell, Dr. "Joe" Baird Albury, and three members of the Executive Council, as well as two nonwhite members, Thaddeus A. Toote and Etienne Dupuch.[18]

Initially the committee was charged with raising funds to buy airplanes. At an early meeting members were asked to set an example. Etienne Dupuch, who considered himself the only "poor Joe" on the committee, surprised members by putting up £100, the same amount pledged by some richer members. When the list of donations was published, Dupuch noted that one of the amounts originally promised was greatly increased. He explained the discrepancy: "I heard later that the wife of the member concerned told him that he would lose face with the public if he did not substantially top my figure." Dupuch admitted that he "didn't have a sixpence in the bank," but that week he had paid off the *Tribune*'s last debt. It was the first time that the paper had been debt free for twenty-five years. Dupuch went to the Royal Bank of Canada the next day, borrowed £100 from his Canadian friend H. C. McLean, the manager, and "gave it to the fund as a thanks offering."[19] No member of that committee, white or black, would be outdone by an upstart journalist, especially one of color.

A variety of other war funds committees existed with predominantly white membership. One of the most popular was the King George's Fund for Sailors, which succeeded in raising £20,000. Herbert McKinney, who was a member of both major committees, was its chairman. The ultra-loyal Mary Moseley chaired the St. Dunstan's Fund for the War Blinded. She was also an active member of the Bahamas Central Branch of the British Red Cross Society, founded in 1939.

The Windsors in the Bahamas

Bahamians, with a few exceptions, were generally pleased to welcome the former king-emperor Edward, Duke of Windsor, in August 1940 to govern the Bahamas. Quietly ignoring the British government's real motivation to banish the duke to a post of such minimal importance, the local elite and socialite refugees were gratified by the arrival of one of the world's most glamorous figures. They were fascinated by Windsor's American duchess, and the couple's presence was seen as a boost to Bahamian tourism. Undoubtedly some in the narrow reactionary white community disapproved of the duke for having abdicated and resented the duchess for having been "the cause of it." Most, however, were willing to forgive him since their arrival had created much interest in the United States. Journalists, newsreel producers, and photographers from illustrated magazines had descended on Nassau to greet the duke and duchess.[20] In an undated typed draft, the duke expressed his feelings to Prime Minister Winston Churchill:

> Local interests have already quite naturally begun to use both the Duchess and myself to boost the American trade for the coming winter season. I will not go so far as to say that they have as yet done so in an undignified manner, and as Governor I have a certain amount of control.[21]

The black and mixed-race population was generally awestruck to have as their new governor the great-grandson of Queen Victoria, whom they regarded as having freed the slaves. They expressed their feelings enthusiastically in a separate welcome by nonwhites on 23 August at Clifford Park.[22] Black musician Alphonso "Blind Blake" Higgs, in writing a hugely popular calypso he recorded on his first album in 1951, was said to have been inspired by the duke's devotion to his wife:

> It was love, love alone
> Cause King Edward to lose de trone . . .
> I know King Edward was noble and great
> But it was love that cause him to ablicate [*sic*]
> It was love . . . [23]

Generally nonwhites respected the Duke of Windsor and, as Michael Bloch noted, optimistically hoped for "great things" from the royal governor. Nonwhites, though, were largely excluded from public life in the colony. Dominated by Bay Street merchants, lawyers, and politicians who "consistently refused to vote" adequate funding for public secondary education, mixed-race and black Bahamians were disadvantaged, much more than their counterparts in such British colonies of the Caribbean as Trinidad and Jamaica, in attaining greater economic and social positions in the society.

Whites and nonwhites did not mix. Most visitors were American and expected "rigid" segregation. As Michael Bloch wrote: "A man like Adderley (Alfred Francis) might thus sit on Leg Co and have excellent relations with white lawyers, clients and officials, but would never be seen in a white house or admitted to any of the major hotels."[24]

Bloch opined, "With Bay Street dominating the economic and political life of the Colony, the Governor and his officials had no choice in the short term but to accept the social system."[25] The Colonial Office's policy, in the long term, was to introduce gradually "social and economic reform" that would improve the condition of nonwhites. The Duke of Windsor, in spite of his weaknesses, could not discard the deeply imbued lessons of duty and correct behavior. He expressed concern for the welfare of the people under his governance. Shortly after his arrival, he announced a policy for developing the Out Islands and relieving unemployment and seemed genuinely concerned to improve the lives of the nonwhite population. In emergencies he was capable of acting decisively (if not always wisely), and following the example of his father, King George V, he was the first Bahamian governor to use the radio as a means of projecting a firm and agreeable image of the ruler to the ruled.[26] Radio broadcasting had been initiated at the time of Governor Clifford in 1932, being organized as Station ZNS in 1936–37.

Bloch argued that the Duke of Windsor was one of the few to recognize the dangers of keeping nonwhites "in poverty and subjection." Not having worked with them before, however, he "did not always feel at ease with them as individuals; the colored politicians in particular he often found petulant and aggressive. But it would be absurd to say that the Duke was what one would now call a 'racist'":

> By the standards of colonial governors of the time his personal treat-
> ment of "non Europeans" was perfectly acceptable and normal, and he
> was considerably more enlightened in his attitudes than the majority of
> Bahamian whites, or either of his predecessors, Clifford and Dundas.
> He had an excellent relationship with such Negroes as jazz musician
> Bert Cambridge (whose election to the House of Assembly in 1942 de-
> lighted him), and he took away from the Bahamas a young coloured
> valet, Sydney Johnson, whom he kept to the end of his life and loved
> as a son.[27]

Tribune proprietor and editor Etienne Dupuch disagreed. From childhood he recalled an occasion when the Duke of Windsor was on a world tour and made a statement in Australia: "The Press quoted him as commending the Australian people for maintaining an all-white policy." As an adult, he concluded: "All in all, the Duke was a likeable man but I considered him a very prejudiced man, and because of his lack of tact and restraint he was to reveal also the undesirable side of his character." Dupuch was convinced after his brother Eugene Dupuch, then a talented journalist with the *Tribune*, was passed over by the Duke of Windsor for an assignment to write articles in Britain about the Commonwealth's war effort. The duke chose the *Nassau Guardian's* nominee, Raymond Moss, a white Canadian bank clerk with no experience as a writer but who had married the niece of the influential *Guardian* editor and publisher Mary Moseley.[28]

Dupuch criticized the Duke of Windsor in the *Tribune* from the beginning of his term as governor. Dupuch made it known that he disagreed with Edward VIII's abdication. As a Roman Catholic, he also opposed divorce, and according to Michael Bloch, he regarded the Duchess of Windsor as a "low woman." When summoned to government house and told by the duke that members of the royal family were not criticized by the press in England, Dupuch told him that "he was not here as a member of the Royal Family but as head of a government in which he was chief executive officer, and as such he was accountable directly to the Bahamian people for his administration of their affairs. If a member of the Royal Family was above criticism, then he had no right to be Governor of the Bahamas."[29]

The Duchess of Windsor, who was born in the southern United States, "saw nothing strange in Nassau's color bar." In order to govern effectively, the duke had to cooperate with the "local ruling class." Indeed, in public both the duke and duchess managed to control their feelings about the Bahamas and its people. Although hiding their dismay behind smiles and their natural charm, they were "appalled by Nassau" and suffered severe depression and acute discomfort. The duchess expressed her feelings to her Aunt Bessie soon after arriving in Nassau in 1940:

> [16 September:] The heat is awful I long for some air that isn't caused by electric fans . . . I hate this place more each day.
> [7 October:] Where did you stay when you came to this dump and why did you come here?
> [21 November:] We both hate it and the natives are petty-minded, the visitors common and uninteresting.[30]

Of course there were certain exceptions. The Windsors soon made friends with the Sigrists and Oakeses, who made their homes in Prospect Ridge and Westbourne at Cable Beach available to the royal couple. The royal couple "put up" with Government House for just one week before accepting these offers of alternate quarters while the official residence was renovated and redecorated. When the professionals, well-known New York decorator Mrs. Winthrop Bradley and American architect Sidney Neil, were finished and Government House had been made more livable, the legislature was appalled by the cost. Having previously voted a mere £2,000, it grudgingly raised this to £5,000.[31]

The Bahamas Red Cross, IODE, and the War Effort

Despite their feelings the Windsors were adept at keeping up appearances. On his arrival the duke consented to be patron of the Bahamas Central Branch of the British Red Cross Society, founded in 1939, and the duchess was appointed as its president, replacing Lady Dundas. A prestigious and patriotic institution, the Bahamas Red Cross soon attracted a large membership. Its 189 life and 300 regular members were mainly upper-class white women who met at the Red Cross Centre in George Street in downtown Nassau. Mrs. Kenneth Solomon served as the first senior deputy president of the branch, while Mary Moseley was elected deputy chairman of the council. Ethel Adderley, wife of A. F. Adderley, was the only nonwhite regular member in the early days of the organization. Mixed-race and black people were included among the nearly 500 associate and working members enrolled not only from New Providence but also from nearly every Out Island in the Bahamas. Numerous private individuals assisted, both in New Providence and in the Out Islands, especially in sewing and knitting. Nearly a third of the knitted and sewn garments sent to England were made in the Out Islands.[32]

The influx of Allied servicemen into Nassau after 1942 created pleasurable work for the Red Cross and the exclusively white Imperial Order of Daughters of the Empire.[33] Most of the men were non-commissioned officers who could not afford hotel prices and were not usually invited to the parties of the social elite.[34] In March 1942 the IODE rectified this problem by opening a permanent canteen for members of the fighting forces on the first floor of the Masonic Building on Bay Street, lent to them for the purpose by members of the Royal Victoria Lodge of Free Masons. Airmen and soldiers could relax there, join games of cards, table tennis, and billiards, and enjoy light meals and refreshments at cost price in the company of "respectable" females. Cigarettes could be purchased by servicemen but not alcohol—only soft drinks, tea, and coffee were available at the IODE canteen.[35]

As more and more Royal Air Force airmen arrived, adding to the number of regular troops, which included the Cameron Highlanders and the U.S. Engineers and Marines, the Duchess of Windsor wished to set up a canteen for the men. She wanted to cooperate with the IODE, but many of the Bay Street matrons "violently" objected to the duchess's proposal to serve beer. Therefore in late 1942 the duchess opened a rival canteen, called the United Services Canteen. Situated on West Bay Street in the premises of the Bahamian Club, which had once catered to wealthy winter tourists and was owned by Frederick Sigrist, it boasted a restaurant, three reading rooms, a large bar and entrance hall, and showers and dressing rooms for swimmers. The duchess personally worked hard to make the canteen a success. She had the advantage of being able to obtain privileged supplies from the mainland through the duke's Washington connections.[36]

Both canteens were segregated, not only in clientele but also in volunteer staff. The mixed-race and black middle class, not to be outdone and also wishing to serve, established its own canteen to cater to black servicemen, most of them local. Headed by Ethel Adderley, Clarita Toote, and Rowena Eldon, the nonwhite group organized the Bahamas Defence Force Company Canteen on Queen Street, near the British Colonial Hotel. Its reputation, especially in the culinary arts, soon spread. Indeed, many white soldiers frequented the nonwhite canteen. Besides its day-to-day catering, it also sponsored special suppers and dances in order to raise funds to help the war effort.[37]

Bahamians generally were eager to become involved in the war effort, some wishing to serve in a more direct way. There was no conscription and little real encouragement or incentive for Bahamians to join the forces at the beginning of World War II, especially if they were of mixed race or black. The events during the first two years of the war did not make it imperative for the British to employ nonwhite troops from the British West Indies.[38] On the outbreak of war, however, a predominantly nonwhite local Bahamas Volunteer Force, headed by Canadian Colonel John Wanklyn, was raised by the imperial government for local defense. It later became known as the Bahamas Home Guard.[39]

Also financed by the colonial government was a full-time racially mixed local force designated the Bahamas Defence Force. Formed in 1942, it was later renamed the Bahamas Battalion and commenced training a contingent for overseas service as a part of the North American force, established in July 1943.[40] After completing their training in Jamaica in 1944, a nonwhite contingent of the Bahamas Battalion under the command of mixed-race officer Lieutenant Wenzel Granger saw active service in Italy and Egypt. The contingent returned to Nassau in January 1946.[41]

From the commencement of hostilities, however, individual Bahamians had been going overseas to join the forces in Canada as well as England. Several joined the American army, including George Roberts, Philip Worrell, Edward (Ned) Isaacs, Kenneth Sands, and Arthur Blakely.[42] Some of the volunteers were white, many of them old scholars of Queen's College. Leonard Knowles, Lester Brown, and Philip Farrington, for example, joined the Royal Air Force in England, as did nonwhite Basil L. Johnson, who distinguished himself. Other Bahamian whites, including Nassauvians Harold Adderley and Roy Solomon (Kenneth Solomon's nephew) and Abaconians Leonard and Hartis Thompson, joined the Royal Canadian Air Force. White women, including Rosemary Kelly and Ann Wanklyn, joined the Women's Auxiliary Air Force and other branches of the forces.[43]

A number of black middle-class women also volunteered, including Vernell Albury, Pearl Grant, Sybil Lightbourn, Shirley Wright, and Zoe Cumberbatch. Joining the Auxiliary Technical Service, a branch of the North Caribbean Force stationed in Jamaica, they undertook duties ranging from clerical work to the manning of British anti-aircraft defenses.

Other Bahamians who contributed toward the war effort included a small body of black Bahamian troops—the Bahamas Air Service Squadron—raised to act as auxiliaries to the Royal Air Force. Additionally, seventeen Bahamian workers, predominantly black, went to England in the summer of 1942 to serve as munitions workers. Overall, the total number of Bahamians employed in the forces exceeded a thousand, including civilian personnel attached to the U.S. Engineers and the RAF. About 300 of them served overseas, fifteen losing their lives.[44]

While Bahamians sought service abroad, their home, particularly New Providence, received a variety of visitors from overseas. During the early years of the war Nassau was chosen as a safe haven for English evacuees, including wives and children of British officers who could afford to send and maintain their families abroad. Among the refugees were the children of Belmont (Preparatory) School, which was normally based in Sussex.[45]

The Burma Road Riot, 1942

The entry of the United States into the Second World War in late 1941 brought mixed blessings for the Bahamas. On the one hand, it caused the collapse of the tourist industry and building construction, which exacerbated the already serious unemployment problem. On the other, the Bahamas benefited because of its strategic position in the Atlantic. Under the destroyer-bases deal between the American and British governments, agreed in September of the previous year, the United States established a naval air base on the island of Great Exuma, about 159 miles south of New Providence. A small detachment of troops was stationed at the base, located on a site of fifty-eight and a half acres northwest of George Town, the island's leading settlement. Although the base provided sorely needed employment to about 350 Exumians, there was resentment over the low wages paid. Unskilled laborers were hired at the Bahamas' minimum wage rate of four shillings (about one dollar) a day. According to Nassau building contractor Richard J. A. Farrington, this caused "a strong feeling against all white men in Nassau," whom they saw as preventing them from earning the two dollars a day that the Americans were willing to pay.[46]

Of much greater impact on the Bahamas was the operation to expand Oakes Field, a small landing field developed and donated to the government by Sir Harry Oakes, to construct Windsor Field. New Providence was chosen as the site of an Operational Training Unit under the auspices of the imperial and United States governments. The installation that had to be built was supervised by the U.S. Army engineering department and an American firm called the Pleasantville Company. Work began on 20 May 1942 on both sites. The Oakes Field site, known as the Main Field, was located just south of Grant's Town and Bain Town, the predominantly black section of Nassau. The other, Satellite Field, was located in the Pine Barren near the western end of New Providence. Collectively, they were known to Bahamians as "the Project." The operation employed nearly 2,500 men, many of them Out Islanders who had migrated to Nassau during the previous two decades seeking jobs. The Project not only provided work for Bahamians but also attracted an influx of many white American workers, who were brought in as foremen and accommodated at the British Colonial Hotel. Arriving at the same time, in early 1942, was a detachment of a British Army regiment, the Cameron Highlanders, which had been at Dunkirk. The fifty officers and 130 of other ranks were accommodated at Montagu Hotel.[47]

Black laborers worked mainly at unskilled jobs, but a few artisans such as carpenters, mechanics, and masons were also employed. Skilled white Bahamians, including two contractors, Morton Turtle and Karl Claridge, were hired as supervisors of unskilled labor. Because of the discrepancy in rates of pay for Bahamians, it was felt that there should be a liaison officer to deal with Bahamian labor. Legislative Council member the Honorable Sidney Farrington nominated Harry Glinton, a well-respected nonwhite building contractor. According to Etienne Dupuch, the governor, the Duke of Windsor, declared: "We can't have a colored man for this job. . . . We must have a white man." Dupuch wrote that the members of the committee looked in his direction "but the Duke seemed completely oblivious to his indiscretion. The job was given to Karl Claridge, and soon after this Nassau had its first riot." Dupuch believed that if Harry Glinton had been hired for the position, the riot would not have occurred.[48]

One of Claridge's first jobs was to build a road near the Satellite Field, which was completed in about two weeks, during which time he dismissed a number of laborers accused of laziness, on instruction from an American superintendent. Claridge was aware that the laborers were dissatisfied with their wages.[49]

A secret agreement had been made by the United States and British governments that wages for labor on the Project should be paid at the local rates, fixed by the minimum wage act in 1936.[50] Unskilled Bahamian laborers received four shillings (about one dollar) for an eight-hour day on building construction. However, they were expected to do more skilled work at the same rate of pay.[51] It was almost impossible to live decently on this wage because the cost of living had soared by about 40 percent, with the prices of food and clothing doubling and even trebling. Most black families, which generally comprised four or more persons, were forced to live below the poverty line.[52]

The Project was regarded as "an almost unhoped for blessing" among Bahamian laborers. Many had worked in the United States and at the base in Exuma for higher wages—as much as three dollars a day (twelve shillings sterling), so expectations were high. It was also rumored among the American employees that the Pleasantville Company was willing to pay much higher wages to Bahamians but was prevented from doing so by the Bahamas government. White American employees were earning much more for doing identical work, and this caused dissatisfaction among the Bahamian laborers.[53]

There were no political parties, and the Bahamas had no modern legislation dealing with trade unions or labor federations. However, a "growing sentiment" led to the establishment of a Labor Union in 1936, headed by white Bahamian Percy Christie and catering mainly to unskilled laborers. In May 1942 skilled workers formed a new organization, the Federation of Labor, and at the time of the riot, both the 800-strong Labor Union and the Federation of Labor were headed by Charles Rhodriquez, a mixed-race dry goods merchant in Grant's Town.

On 20 May the laborers complained to Rhodriquez about their low wages. He in turn outlined their grievances to the labor officer, John Hughes, who asked him to put the request in writing. Two days later, Rhodriquez called a meeting of skilled and unskilled laborers to discuss the Project wages issue, and a new scale of wages was unanimously adopted. A week later, on 29 May, a letter drafted with the assistance of A. F. Adderley, requesting wages of eight shillings per day for unskilled laborers, was delivered to John Hughes. Convinced of the complacent nature of the Bahamian population, Hughes chided Bert Cambridge when he expressed reservations: "Go on, Mr. Cambridge, you will never have any trouble in the Bahamas."[54]

Refusing to recognize the urgency of the situation, the government did not immediately make a decision on the matter, focusing instead on election preparations for the middle of June. The Duke of Windsor had left the Bahamas for Washington on 28 May and Acting Governor Leslie Heape promised that an advisory board would be appointed to consider the new wage scale. This was communicated on 30 May to the Federation of Labor, the leaders of which were unaware of any possible unrest.

The government's delaying tactics in response to labor demands did not sit well with the laborers. Many believed that Karl Claridge and Morton Turtle, both white, had prevented them from getting higher wages. In mid-afternoon on 31 May a group of laborers near Satellite Field went on strike. Claridge, their supervisor, persuaded them to return to work, with the exception of Leonard Storr Green, a young migrant from Andros and a newcomer to the Project, along with a few others. When Green and his allies tried to stop the others working, he was taken by the American supervisor to the Pleasantville office at the Main Field. Claridge followed in his bus.[55]

Green was interrogated, and when asked why he refused to work, he stated that it was impossible to live on four shillings a day, especially in light of current high prices. While Green was being questioned, a crowd of about four hundred laborers gathered outside the office and were talking loudly. Some, including Green, were shouting, "We want more money." Although unorganized, the laborers were able to register two complaints: that they had not been paid when prevented from working due to rain, and that they wanted higher wages. Hughes, who identified Green as the leader, addressed the crowd, promising to deal with the matter as soon as possible, and asked them to disperse. Some did, but a number of the younger men remained.[56]

By this time, the superintendent of the Nassau Police, Captain Edward Sears, had appeared on the scene along with a detachment of three or four policemen and tried to get the crowd to disperse. Green had a slight cut above his eye, and when the crowd saw Green's wound, they assumed that the white "Conchie Joe" Sears had caused it. Thinking Green had been arrested, the laborers began jumping on the fenders of the cars owned by the American foremen. Claridge attempted to leave in his bus but was surrounded by the crowd, who overturned his vehicle. When the crowd surrounded Sears he drew his revolver and fired in the air, and the laborers quickly scattered.

Although Hughes did not anticipate further trouble, as a precaution he called a meeting of "Representatives of Labor," including Rhodriquez, Dr. Claudius R. Walker (then a candidate for the southern district), and Alfred F. Adderley, counsel for the Labor Union. None of the three was clear about what had happened at the Main Field, but they nevertheless agreed to speak to the laborers.[57]

Early on the Monday morning of 1 June Adderley and Rhodriquez went to the Guns, an ancient fortification on West Bay Street where the men gathered to be transported to work. Adderley gave a brief speech, hoping to persuade them to resume work, in order to "preserve harmony." The men refused to move.[58] Adderley and Rhodriquez then drove separately to the Main Field, where Dr. Walker had made his address to a crowd of about a thousand who had gathered and were refusing to clock in for work. The men "appeared restive and sullen" and shouted, "No work today." Convinced that a solution would soon be reached, Adderley, Rhodriquez, and Walker left to prepare themselves for their day's work.[59]

At about 8:00 a.m. the laborers, now numbering about 2,000, assembled at the Main Field. Armed with sticks, clubs, and machetes, they marched through the southern district to town, singing patriotic songs including "We'll Never Let the Old Flag Fall." One of the rioters, Napoleon McPhee, insists that they sang "Burma Road Declare War on the Conchie Joe, Do Nigger Don't You Lick Nobody, Don't Lick Nobody." Perhaps they shouted these words, as the music was composed later. The laborers, wishing to put their plea to someone in authority, assembled at the colonial secretary's office where at 9:00 a.m. they were addressed from the steps by Attorney General Eric Hallinan, who urged them to choose a representative and send him to the colonial secretary's or governor's office. Hallinan promised that their grievances would receive immediate attention and added that the American authorities had been reluctant to use Bahamian labor on the Project, and had it not been for the intervention of the Duke of Windsor, they might not have any jobs at all. He appealed to the crowd not to spoil the good impression they had made. The excited and angry crowd received the wrong impression and interpreted his remarks as a warning—that if they did not return to work, the government would replace them with American laborers. Within minutes the enraged crowd released their fury by rioting up and down Bay Street, smashing windows and looting stores. A parked Coca-Cola truck provided a supply of missiles. It seemed that the rioters included a wide cross section of the laboring class of skilled and unskilled workers, some of whom had criminal records. Many were young and probably migrants from the Out Islands. Randol Fawkes believed that there were West Indians among the crowd.[60] (Women also participated in the rioting, at least on the next day, Tuesday 2 June, when the crowd attacked a business and a black policeman.)[61] Leonard Storr Green was also among the directionless crowd. He claimed that he was not a ringleader. Seeing him on Bay Street, Captain Sears threatened to send Green back to Turks Island. Green quickly retorted: "If you send me back to Turks Island, I'll send you back to Abaco." Sears then arrested Green, but as the crowd closed in and started throwing missiles at the police, Sears let him go.[62] Another rioter, Alfred Stubbs, alias "Sweet Potato," burned the royal family in effigy, while Napoleon McPhee, a stone mason, destroyed the Union Jack. When questioned about his behavior, McPhee swore: "I willing to fight under the flag. I willing to die under the flag. But I ain't gwine starve under the flag."[63]

By noon Bay Street, the center of white Nassau, lay in shambles. Nearly every establishment suffered damage and extensive looting. Hundreds of persons were seen leaving the city with armfuls of stolen goods. The crowd, angry and out for vengeance, had been pushed back Over-the-Hill, through a combination of force and persuasion, by the ill-prepared police force, led by Colonel Erskine-Lindop with the assistance of the Camerons, the various labor leaders, and other concerned citizens.[64]

In Over-the-Hill the turbulent crowd became quite unmanageable. Not pacified by the black leaders, including A. F. Adderley, Bert Cambridge, and Milo Butler, the rioters left the Southern Recreation Grounds, attacking and looting bars, especially those owned by white Bay Street merchants such as the Bethell brothers. By 12:15 p.m. the Riot Act was read, but in attempting to disperse the crowd in Grant's Town, the police and soldiers were stoned and hit by bottles. Shots were fired and one man, Roy Johnson, was killed. Another, David Smith, was wounded and died later that day in hospital. Five more Grant's Town men were seriously wounded and forty rioters were treated for minor injuries. In all three people were killed as a result of the riots and curfew, and two subsequently died from wounds.[65]

At about 12:30 p.m. when the police and military withdrew from Grant's Town, leaving four junior black officers at the southern police station, the Over-the-Hill area seemed relatively quiet. Trouble soon broke out again, however, when the hostile crowd, incensed by the killing, attacked the police station and set the fire engine alight. The rioters completely destroyed an ambulance parked near the station and broke into the Grant's Town public library and the post office. There followed general looting throughout the southern district.[66]

Milo Butler and Percy Christie, the only white men other than police and military authorities to venture into Grant's Town, urged that all clubs and liquor shops remain closed. It was not until 8:00 p.m. on 1 June—when a curfew was instituted and pickets were established in all streets leading to town—that calm returned to the Over-the-Hill area. A. F. Adderley drove through the district with his wife just before midnight and gave a similar report.

Further violence, however, broke out the next day. Shortly after the curfew ended at 6:00 a.m., a crowd of laborers and other troublemakers marched miles from Grant's Town to the Shirley Street pharmacy of George Cole, a white merchant, attacking and looting the business until the military intervened. Returning to the southern district, the rioters continued their rampage. Shortly after 10:00 a.m. they attacked a grocery shop owned by Richard

Holbert, a black merchant, and the East Street home of a black policeman, Corporal Bernard J. Nottage, whom they assaulted.[67]

At the time of the attack Holbert's shop was manned by his son Richard. Warning the crowd not to proceed, he shot and killed Donald Johnson, one of the rioters, who was threatening him with a hammer. Nottage and his brother-in-law Samuel Johnson were painting Nottage's newly constructed home when three men whom they knew appeared, grabbed the brushes, and upset three gallons of paint. When challenged by Johnson, the men began stoning the house. By that time a crowd of between 300 and 400 had gathered around with knives, cutlasses, and sticks, and they too joined in the assault, threatening Nottage's life. No reason has come to light as to why the rioting crowd attacked either Holbert or Nottage. Both were black; however they seemed fairly well off and Nottage, who was a well-respected policeman, could possibly have been identified with the white establishment.[68]

The Duke of Windsor was informed of the Nassau riot while visiting Washington, D.C., and he returned to Nassau on 2 June, preceded by a detachment of seventy-five U.S. Marines disguised as military police, ostensibly to protect the American military installations but available to support local forces. Eager to prevent further trouble and suppress alarming news, the duke censored the press, confirmed the curfew, and forbade meetings in any streets or public places except with the permission of the police.[69]

After consultations with his officials, the duke met with several black leaders including Dr. Claudius Walker on Wednesday afternoon, 3 June. Walker delivered an eloquent speech articulating the sentiments of the black laboring class, most of whom regarded the duke as their savior. Stressing the many problems that plagued the majority of Bahamians, mainly black, he informed the duke of a series of issues: their poor housing and education; their inadequate diet; how land, an important component of wealth, was "often snatched" by foreigners; the corrupt electoral system, which excluded women, who constituted more than half the population; the domination by the mercantile elite of political, economic, and social life; and the fact that African culture was denigrated by whites, who robbed the black masses of their dignity and self-respect. He stated that nonwhites generally were "forced to tolerate the racist ideologies of their white countrymen in order to survive," and to compound these injustices, members of the black majority were paid such meager wages that many found it difficult to make ends meet. He added that "the scales have been peeled off the eyes of the laborers." Dr. Walker ended with a personal message to the duke himself:

Two years ago when the radio waves brought the news of Your Royal Highness' appointment as Governor of The Bahamas, the deaf heard, and the dumb spoke, the blind saw and the crippled leapt for joy. Your reputation as a humanitarian and King preceded you. "Surely," we said to ourselves, "the Duke of Windsor will not allow us to continue to live amidst social inequities that sap our self-respect and prevent us from attaining our full status as first class citizens." Fifty-four Governors have preceded Your Excellency, but not one ever brought a ray of hope to the poor and oppressed. We believe that you are not just another Governor for one class of people but the Governor for all colors and classes of people. In faith believing, I ask on behalf of all my brothers and sisters, "Art thou He that cometh or look we for another?"[70]

That evening the Duke of Windsor personally made a broadcast to the colony, urging the laborers to return to work so that discussions could begin on the wage question.[71] The next day more than half of the laborers reported for work at the Project. Within a week the duke had personally negotiated a free midday meal and also obtained a shilling a day increase for the laborers. By 8 June, when order had been completely restored, the duke again broadcast to the community, announcing that the curfew was being lifted. The ban on public assemblies, however, continued until after the general elections between 19 and 22 June, which were held without incident.[72] Heading the commission of inquiry appointed by the duke were Sir Alison Russell, former chief justice of Tanganyika, and two well-respected white merchants, Herbert A. McKinney and Herbert Brown, who were not directly involved in politics although sympathetic toward Bay Street. Regarding the duke and his two nominees as too broadminded, the majority in the Assembly voted for setting up their own Select Committee. Though it included pro-trade-union Percy Christie and black lawyer T. A. Toote as token liberals, this committee was dominated by hardline Bay Street figures: Asa Pritchard, Roland Symonette, and the rising ultra-conservative lawyer Stafford Sands. At the same time the Assembly voted to compensate (indemnify) all those who had suffered damages in the riots.

Racial tension was an underlying cause of the riot, despite the Russell Commission's conclusion to the contrary and the Select Committee's silence on the issue. Bahamians suffered severe discrimination at home, as Dr. C. R. Walker testified before the Russell Commission. He stated: "The colored man makes all the concessions. I challenge any man in the Colony to say that I am wrong in that. The colored man is discriminated against in the churches, in the theatres, in the private schools."[73] Indeed until the late 1950s nonwhites were barred from hotels, were not allowed in some restaurants and movie houses, and were only allowed to enter some churches by the rear door. Certain schools did not accept nonwhite children, and many businesses were closed to nonwhites as places of employment.[74]

During the riot blacks were vociferous in their feelings against whites. English magistrate Frank Field, who had lived in Nassau since 1941, said that on questioning the crowd in East Street on 1 June, he was told the "Conchie Joes" had had it coming to them for a long time. Veteran journalist Mary Moseley, who on the day of the riots bravely ventured down Bay Street before taking refuge in the segregated Grand Central Restaurant on Charlotte Street, said that she overheard a man shouting, "The Americans are our friends and the Conchs our enemies," to which he added, "I am prepared to die like a hero." Trinidad-born black physician Dr. Roland Cumberbatch, who himself had been discriminated against, testified that on 1 June when he had almost reached downtown Nassau, he met a crowd, some of whom remarked: "No white man passing here today." John Damianos, a grocery merchant of Greek descent, stated: "My impression was that when they saw a white face they were particularly infuriated and I think it had reached a point which was largely motivated by some racial feelings. I have never seen anything like this before."[75]

The damage was not totally indiscriminate; shops owned by the speaker of the House of Assembly and the wife of one of the Project supervisors were severely damaged, but the shoe store owned by the white former Labor Union president Percy Christie was left untouched. White-owned liquor shops, the stocks of which fueled the aggression of some of the crowd, were particular targets.[76]

The reaction of the white administrators and Bay Street merchants was a mixture of belligerence and panic, while the brown and black middle class expressed shock and disowned the actions of the mob. One of the white supervisors from the Project, Karl Claridge, anticipating trouble, had stayed at home; the other, Morton Turtle, went fishing for several days. Some parents (including a few nonwhites) hurried into town to "rescue" their children from Queens College. A "Delegation of Citizens," about eight in number and including Roland Symonette, Speaker Asa Pritchard and Stafford Sands, whose car had been badly damaged, went to Government House demanding more forceful action. The colonial secretary, Eric Hallinan, testified to the Russell Commission that one of the delegation asked why machine guns had not been turned on the crowd. On hearing shots fired in Grant's Town, one of the merchants said: "That's the stuff to give them." No one remembers who had spoken.[77]

English and American officials also believed that race was a strong factor in causing the riot. The duke was convinced that the riot had resulted because of "strong racial feeling on both sides." Despite the order to the Russell Commission to leave the issue of race alone, the duke admitted in a private dispatch that personally he believed that the "Bahamas wage rate was only an excuse to make a vigorous and noisy protest against the white population." He continued that he regretted that "the flame of local race antagonism is still fanned by certain sections of Bay Street on one hand as an excuse for the continuation of reactionary policy and by the negro agitators on the other." The duke opined that if there had not been a strong military force on the island, the rioting might have continued on a "larger and better organized scale."[78]

Both the Russell Commission and the Select Committee recognized that the Bahamian laborers were dissatisfied with the discriminatory wages. House of Assembly members, most of whom blamed the riots on the government's negligence and attached no blame to their narrow policies for the events, criticized the government for not giving sufficient information on the wages. The Select Committee contended that labor leaders agitated in order to make political mileage and also accused the Pleasantville employees of spreading false propaganda among workers regarding the rates of pay.[79]

Significance of the Riot of 1942

Lawyer and historian Colin Hughes stated that the riots of the 1930s in the West Indies "triggered off a process of political and constitutional change when demands that had previously been the preserve of a handful of middle-class politicians, answerable to restricted electorates, and of a few trade union leaders, heading small and ill-organized labor movements, were transmuted into mass political movements." With regard to the 1942 Nassau riot, Hughes argued that the reluctance of the Colonial Office to intervene, and the failure of the black politicians of the time "to convert the momentary outburst of raw energy into a political movement, had no such immediate consequence." It would take another twenty-five years for blacks to take control of the legislature.[80]

Dame Doris Johnson, revered Bahamian politician, writing in the early 1970s, argued that the 1942 riot represented "the first awakening of a new political awareness . . . in the hearts of the black people, who were 80 per cent of the population. Time, and the remarkable foresight, courage, and initiative of a few dedicated members of that majority, were all required to crystallize this awareness into a mighty political force." Dame Doris described the riot as a significant milestone in the Bahamas' political revolution. She wrote:

> Did the band of disgruntled laborers—Bahamian laborers—realize that their actions virtually constituted a declaration of war against the white minority in power—the Conchy Joes as they were scurrilously called? Did they foresee that this vigorous revolt against one of many practices of inequality would cause stirrings in the hearts of the poor and not-so-poor Bahamian, in the young and not so young Bahamian—in the people who were destined to change the course of the Colony's history? Could they know, as they protested that particular discrimination, that they had taken hold of power—the power of political awareness—which would eventually enable them to shape their own destinies?[81]

Trade Union leader Sir Randol Fawkes, in a speech he delivered thirteen years after the riot, began it with: "Remember the first of June, 1942." Similarly, when the first Bahamian prime minister, Sir Lynden Pindling, was delivering a speech in the 1990s on the path to self-determination, he began it with the Burma Road riot: "When the great heroes of our struggle . . . stood on Burma Road, they did not stand alone. When they stood in the General Strike . . . against the property vote . . . for the women's vote . . . with the trade unionists . . . (and) for majority rule, they did not stand alone."[82]

Nona P. Martin and Virgil H. Storr published an article in 2007 that was critical of the interpretation of the 1942 riot by Hughes and this author. They did not agree that the riot was: "a short-lived spontaneous outburst by a group of disgruntled laborers," occurring against a background of narrow socioeconomic and political policies and not leading immediately to a mass political movement. I further argued that the leaders of the colored and black middle class in 1942 did not represent a united bloc in support of the black laboring class against Bay Street. Black leadership took a long time to emerge and organize itself politically. Demand for change was more than a decade in coming." Martin and Storr, however, saw the riot as the beginning of the movement that would ultimately lead to majority rule and independence.[83]

The riot could be characterized as "the first awakenings of a new political awareness," as there were more than "disgruntled laborers" in the crowd— they were joined by other black men and women demonstrating their anger against the Bay Street oligarchy and the acute discrimination of the time.

One of the most important recommendations of the Russell Commission and the Select Committee, following the major recommendation of the Moyne Commission Report, was the passing of labor legislation dealing with trade unions, workmen's compensation, and other related matters.[84] It was the first time that a House committee had recommended the establishment of labor policy through legislation.[85] The Russell Commission also recommended the establishment of a permanent Labor Advisory Board to advise the governor on the minimum wage to be paid to unskilled laborers throughout the colony. Its members agreed that legislation should be passed to make the Voting by Secret Ballot Act permanent in New Providence and that it should be extended as soon as possible to the Out Islands.[86]

Two days later the *Tribune* reported that shortly before the riot, the undersecretary of state for the colonies had visited New Providence and noted the need for certain reforms.[87] Early in 1943, about six months after the riots, the stevedores, threatening to strike, persuaded ship owners to raise their pay from 9 pence to one shilling a day. At the same time it was reported that the truck drivers and laborers at the Board of Works went on strike.[88] Hartley Saunders commented: "The actions of the stevedores, the truck drivers and the laborers of the Board of Works caused the Government to become concerned with the situation. This was the first time that such action had occurred in the Bahamas."[89] The Executive Council convened two special meetings and the recently appointed Labor Board also met. Further strikes by laborers and semiskilled workers at the Telecommunications Department occurred while these matters were being considered.[90]

The passage of the Trade Union Act and Workmen's Compensation Act in 1943 represented an "advance on the road of reform." Hartley Saunders hailed it as "the most complete victory in any camp. This was the first time that the Bay Street Boys retreated to the cries of the masses and the masses were beginning to realize that Bay Street was not invincible."[91] The strikes continued for most of the 1940s, and unions "mushroomed" in New Providence.[92] Besides the Bahamas Trade Union and the Federation of Labor already mentioned, these included the Bahamas Taxi Cab Union, Bahamas Plumbers Union, the Typographical Union with membership of 261, and the Bahamas Musicians Union with membership of 22.[93]

Despite these gains, the House of Assembly's reactionary behavior did not essentially change. The legislation was defective and severely restricted membership in a union. While the Trade Union Act made provision for the registration of trade unions and the legality of strikes, the latter were deemed illegal if they were aimed at coercing the government or if they inflicted hardship on the community. Moreover, civil servants, domestic servants, and hotel and agricultural workers were barred from joining a union. As the Duke of Windsor noted in chastising the legislature in late 1943, the two acts fell short of modern labor standards.[94]

Although the Secret Ballot Act was passed in 1944, attempts to extend it to the Out Islands—conducted by Etienne Dupuch and a number of black and mixed-race politicians who believed that if "handled sensibly," the secret ballot "would be a constructive force in the life of the community"—were vetoed by the Bay Street majority in the House of Assembly.[95] Stafford Sands summed up the Bay Street view shared by the *Nassau Guardian* by stating that "the people of the Bahamas had not reached the state of political development to warrant the ballot system."[96] T. A. Toote, Bertram Cambridge, and Milo Butler made impassioned speeches on the subject in the House of Assembly. Toote stated that to refuse to extend the ballot to the Out Islands "would be a gross insult and unpardonable sin against those Out Islanders who now vote under the open system." Toote labeled the system "iniquitous" and alluded to the emancipation from slavery, which he asserted was "only of body not of the mind." Disagreeing with the Bay Street view that the population was "not dissatisfied with the system of voting," Toote reminded the Assembly that many Bahamians had experienced secret voting as members of lodges and burial societies and that during the three elections held in New Providence since the passage of the Ballot Act, only a small percentage of the ballots had been spoiled.[97]

Cambridge and Butler agreed that it was "a gross insult that people on the Out Islands were considered too illiterate to use the secret ballot." Cambridge revealed that opposed to the Out Island ballot were the election chiefs, "who had the bag of cash on election day, and not the people, who only get a pittance." He reminded members of the "fear" that some had, that "the House of Assembly would be crowded with colored people" if the ballot was introduced. Cambridge disagreed with this view and alluded to the "charitableness which existed between the people of the colony."[98]

The secret ballot issue aroused "considerable feeling locally," so much so that a "mass meeting" was called by the nonwhite members of the House of Assembly after the Bay Street majority had refused the governor's invitation to recommend the act's extension to the Out Islands. The duke informed the Colonial Office that while the meeting was orderly, "the speakers were all of the racial agitator group" and were led by the Honorable A. F. Adderley, usually conservative, "a Negro, formerly a member of the House and now a member of the Legislative Council." He stated that the large majority of the white population was solidly against the extension, and on 3 July "a full house turned out to register their sentiments (some members who had been ill made a special effort)." Despite the impassioned speeches by the black members, the measure was soundly rejected by a vote of 17 for and 8 against (three government members and five nonwhites).[99]

Predictably, the Acting Governor D. G. Stewart and the Colonial Office were convinced that the "interest aroused in the colored section of the community who have now inspired to take it up as a racial 'cause' and a 'cause' which would have lain dormant much longer but for the attitude adopted by the House of Assembly." The Duke of Windsor also felt the matter might "result in a racial issue" that "might lead to serious trouble." Colonial officer P. Rogers felt that the *Tribune* "is trying to whip up opinion locally . . . and we know privately . . . that this has now been made a color issue in the Colony and that racial feeling is aroused." Rogers feared that they were "in for considerable trouble." The duke, in a cypher telegram, commented on his ambivalent feelings about Etienne Dupuch: "Am afraid that Etienne Dupuch's aggressiveness in the *Daily Tribune* is more inspired by personal vanity than by true aspirations of the mass of the Negro population. He is dangerous and unpredictable, but must be reckoned with."[100]

Finally, after some pressure from the Colonial Office, the Bahamian legislature gave in and passed the act in 1946 (no. 19 of 1946). However, agitator for nonwhites Robert M. Bailey noted in a letter to the *Tribune* on 3 August 1946 that the passage of the bill was a step in the right direction but left much to be accomplished. The whole process of preparing the Register of Voters and other details were sorely needed. He also mentioned the tactics that white candidates used to intimidate voters. In one case Bert Cambridge, while accompanying another black candidate (Willie Weeks) on an election tour of Bimini and West End, Grand Bahama, was "reliably informed that an ex-member of the House, a white man as a candidate for re-election, had told the voters, that should they elect a colored man, they would not get any more jobs."[101] Bert Cambridge also cited instances in Watlings Island and Exuma, where voters were discouraged from voting for blacks as they were incapable of properly representing them and, further, could do little to help them. Bailey and Cambridge had courage to speak their "mind on the question of race."[102]

Besides its recommendations regarding labor and the secret ballot, the Russell Commission also called for an adjustment of import duties, the consideration of income tax and death duties, a land tax, and the control of land, especially cultivatable acreage on the Out Islands. It urged that the population be educated in agriculture and fishing and that the Out Island conditions be improved in order to stop the drift to Nassau. The commission favored the introduction of birth control in view of the high birth rate of 34.7 per thousand in 1943 and suggested some reform in the outdated constitution.[103] As far as a more equitable form of taxation and birth control were concerned, the recommendations did not get further than the Executive Council. The duke was personally in favor of birth control "from a humane point of view" but was warned by the Executive Council that it would be unwise to broach the subject since blacks viewed "this beneficial measure as a subtle way of gradually exterminating their race," so he dropped the idea. Introduction of income tax was vehemently opposed by two unofficial members of the council, Ralph Collins and Harold G. Christie. Their view apparently was shared by most of the other politicians, black and white, who feared that if introduced, income tax would discourage wealthy people from settling in the Bahamas.[104]

The Contract

Despite the calm that had rapidly returned to the city after the riot, Nassau and colonial whites and middle-class nonwhites had been frightened by the black uprising. Never before in the history of the colony had there been such collective violence. The duke, fearful of further trouble, was also cognizant of the fact that jobs were becoming scarcer as the construction of the bases neared completion. There were layoffs as early as September 1942. As the duchess wrote confidently to her Aunt Bessie: "The negroes are busy complaining now that the base is nearing completion and some of them are being laid off. I should not be surprised to see more trouble—but this time one is somewhat prepared and there is enough fire-power on the island to deal with the situation."[105]

The duke, learning from his American contacts of the dire agricultural labor shortages in the United States created by World War II, moved quickly on his own initiative to negotiate an agreement in March 1943 with the American government for recruitment of Bahamian laborers in the British West Indies Labor Programme.[106]

Negotiations resulted in a series of agreements whereby the Bahamian government would supply temporary agricultural laborers to the United States. Popularly called either "the Project" as an extension of the work on the bases, or "the Contract," the scheme lasted for twenty-two years and had significant social effects. As Tracey Thompson stated, "the United States government managed the American side of the programme until 1947," after which it was taken over by the Bahamas Employer Committee until the scheme ended in 1965. Recruitment for the Contract began in April 1943 at the Labor Bureau in Nassau, which later sent out recruiters to the Out Islands. In order to qualify, one had to be eighteen or older and physically fit enough to pass a medical examination supervised by the American authorities. Transportation costs within the Bahamas and to the entry point in the United States were borne for laborers by the home government. While in America, however, travel expenses including the cost of returning the worker to the place of entry into the country were taken care of by the United States government. Ensuring that wages would be no less than 30 cents an hour, the agreement also vainly promised that the Bahamians would not be discriminated against because of their race, creed, color, or natural origin.[107] By May 1943 more than 2,500 Bahamian workers had left for the Contract, joining Mexicans, Jamaicans, and Barbadians in the United States. In August the full quota of 5,000 had been reached. Numbers peaked in July 1944, when 5,762 Bahamians were employed on the Contract, roughly a tenth of the Bahamian population.[108] Between 1943 and 1947 a total of 15,241 workers were recruited.[109]

Initially Bahamian laborers were employed on farms and plantations in Florida, but within a short time some were transferred north in groups of between 300 and 400 persons. Bahamians were soon widely scattered throughout the eastern United States, as far north as New York and as far west as Indiana. In the early years of the Contract women were mostly excluded, but they gradually became accepted. Volunteers were predominantly black unskilled laborers, but approximately ninety white Bahamians, mostly from the Out Islands, were recruited for dairy work. Finding the working and climatic conditions too severe, the majority of them returned to the Bahamas by 1946.[110] According to George Roberts, a black man of New Providence interviewed by Olga Culmer Jenkins in the late 1990s, whites were discouraged from applying. Roberts opined that "they didn't want no white people doing it. You had to be a certain complexion (laughter). White people who applied were turned down. . . . But the lower-class people, this Contract was made specifically for them."[111]

Bahamians working on the Contract were to be employed in agriculture. None were to be considered for military service. At the age of twenty-one, Sir Clifford Darling—who would in due course go on to serve as speaker of the House, minister, and governor general—decided to go on the Contract. He admitted that he had never farmed but said "he saw 'The Contract' as a way to get away from Nassau . . . and wanted to explore."[112] Finding the food and living conditions "deplorable," he and others staged two demonstrations, and he commented that after their demonstrations, living conditions improved. Nevertheless, the workers with whom he lived decided to elect three persons to represent their interests. Clifford Darling was the youngest to be elected. As a representative he was not required to do any farm work and had the privilege of using an army jeep. Working along with a mechanic, he was part of the team that cleaned canals, and he also learned how to drive a tractor. Sir Clifford's experiences would stand him in good stead when he returned to the Bahamas and became secretary and later president of the Taxi Cab Union.[113]

Long Islander John Newman stated his reason for going on the Project: "There was nothing going on in Long Island. Because all we had to do here was to farm for corn, peas, bean, and take care of our sheep and goat. There was not much money in it. Therefore, we see that we have a chance of going to the States and helping ourselves more." On the Contract he "picked apples in Virginia, peaches in Georgia, cotton in Arkansas, beans in Tennessee, and tomatoes in Ohio."[114]

A Cat Islander who was a plumber, and who claimed to have been employed for about $3 an hour by the Pleasantville Company, was nonetheless jealous of his friends going to the United States: "All my friends them was ready going. I hear the boys say 'man we going!' In spite of they want me to stay and be a maintenance plumber. I say 'no man. I ain't being no maintenance plumber. I gotta to go over there and see Uncle Sam's place.'"[115]

Individual contracts with similar stipulations were taken out with each worker. More detail was given to the question of wages and to the system of deductions in the personal agreement. It was understood that 75 cents would be withheld daily from the worker's wages, which varied between $3 and $5 a day—much more than they could earn in the Bahamas. The money so deducted would be paid as a family allowance to the worker's family in the Bahamas or deposited on behalf of the worker in the Post Office Savings Bank of the colony. Additionally, many workers made voluntary additional payments that were deducted from the wages. Such remittances were given to the laborer's wife each month if he were married. If he were single the money accumulated in a Post Office Savings account until he returned. Between April 1943 and the beginning of 1944, Bahamian employees working in the United States earned more than £300,000. Of this amount, more than £60,000 were transferred to the Bahamas as family allowances or savings. The numbers of workers engaged in the Contract at one time fluctuated between 4,500 and 5,000 workers. In 1953 Bahamians earned just over £481,609.[116]

The Contract, while increasing the earning power of thousands of black laboring Bahamians and the ability to save, also took its toll on the Out Islands. Many laborers spent six- to nine-month periods on the Contract in the United States and then returned home. Others, however, deserted their communities, settling permanently in Nassau or in the United States. Some Out Islands settlements were left with a scarcity of men, usually in their most productive years. Women and children were left in charge of the farms, and some learned to cope with the heavy work of cutting the fields. Because of the scarcity of manpower, farming, except for subsistence, was often neglected. In the absence of their spouses, women gained more independence. These women, at least temporarily, became head of their household and were solely responsible for its smooth running and the rearing of the family. Some wives, appreciative of how the earnings eased hardships on the islands, carefully kept records of the money sent home by their husbands. Others, because of the lengthy absences of their husbands, became involved with other men, sometimes carrying their children, and in many cases the traditional family broke down altogether.[117]

Many men (and a few women) on the Contract lived frugally, saving and supplying their families with funds and other necessities. Some were able to save enough money from their earnings to "lay the foundations of financially more secure lives." As Tracey Thompson states: "Remelda Bodie was able to buy a house," and "Calvin Bethel was able eventually to purchase fifty acres of land and build a citrus grove in Vero Beach, Florida."[118]

Others, however, were wasteful. As the thrifty Samuel Whateley of Bramley, Cat Island, remembered: "Some fellows they just go over there and squander away with the money and have a big time, you know, (spend) as they make it. They figure they got allowance coming home to the family and they ain't worrying with the money that they make. What they make they just blow it out."[119]

Experience gained through the Contract was significant in shaping the Bahamian view of America and life in general. Out Island laborers on the Contract, some of whom had never even visited Nassau, much less the United States, found the journey from their isolated communities to their various destinations an event in itself. While many had traveled by boat, some had not seen or heard of an airplane before. Receiving a smallpox vaccination warranted comment by some laborers. Cat Islander Edward Dempster, for example, said the injection had to do with the "climate of the cities."[120]

Once in the United States, most laborers lived in army-style labor camps, the majority of which were equipped with showers, laundries, and sanitary facilities. Spartan by American standards, they were considered "plush" by laborers unaccustomed to running water, showers, or inside toilets. There were also serviceable tables, chairs, beds, and radios and efficient stoves. As noted, however, some found the living conditions deplorable, including Clifford Darling, who had left a comfortable home.[121]

Though Bahamians were conscientious, their new regimen was very different from what they knew, especially where a piecework system applied. On Bahamian Out Islands, farming was usually completed in the morning, with the rest of the day set aside for other household chores. In the United States, laborers were obliged to work on farms from 7:00 a.m. until 8:00 p.m. Instead of being responsible for all phases of farming, they were now employed for the most part simply for the harvesting. Though not often given the responsibility of operating machinery, the migrant workers frequently worked in conjunction with harvesting equipment and were in effect animate parts of a larger machine.[122]

As John Newman explained: "Well, how we worked. I'll say six days. But most of the work was piecework. And you worked to your leisure, but you have to put in those days. The faster you worked, the more money you got. When you weren't working, the foreman, he always look out for a job for you from another farmer. So you never be out of work, still occupied with work."[123]

In addition to the new environment, Bahamian laborers were introduced to new and unaccustomed living arrangements and social relationships with strangers, from other islands, colonies, and many parts of the United States. On the Contract, Bahamian workers interacted socially with strangers "in their own living areas."[124]

Some on the Contract had very positive relationships with their American employers, even in the Deep South. Remelda Bodie said of her white Virginian employer, "He was very nice to us. We used to take our food on the farm and cook and then he used to say, come in the house and look around. He was the best white man I ever see to be that nice."[125] H. R. Bethel worked in Vero Beach, Florida, and "became the protégé of an employer who entrusted him the management of his several hundred employees, the power to sign checks on his behalf, and the trading of his securities on the New York Stock Exchange."[126]

Although the agreement between the United States and the Bahamas stipulated that Bahamian laborers were not to be discriminated against in any way while in America, thus extending the "protection of President Franklin D. Roosevelt's Executive Order No. 8802, also known as the Fair Employment Act (1941)," which "prohibited discrimination in employment because of race, color or national origin in an effort to support the war effort."[127] This was either ignored or purposely not enforced.

Most Bahamian laborers, especially Out Islanders from the all-black settlements, were shocked at the legally enforced Jim Crow segregation then common throughout the South. Many Bahamians were called "nigger" for the first time by whites. Some were afraid to venture from the labor camps for fear of arrest "just for being black." Ordinary white citizens taunted them in their efforts to "have fun" at the local bars, and they were sent to the back of liquor or grocery stores and always served last. Black Bahamian women also complained of the refusal of store clerks to let them try on shoes without wearing stockings or hats without a head covering. While traveling, black Bahamians were sometimes denied a place to eat or sleep, and if offered facilities, these were usually below acceptable standards. Some confrontations between blacks and whites resulted in the blacks being incarcerated, along with the loss of their privilege to work in the United States. The harsh discriminatory practices deeply affected Bahamian labourers.[128] As Samuel Whateley stated,

> [The people were] kind of mean on colored people. Oh, in Florida, they used to lynch colored people. Colored people had no right in Florida ... in fact you couldn't go to no fun, to no dances around. In Florida the law would be there to get you. Take you to jail and make you pay some money ... after I see that, I stay in my camp.[129]

As Donald Rolle recalled, the town sheriff did not allow blacks to be in town after 6:00 p.m.[130]

Gratuitous harassment by white overseers was intolerable to proud Bahamians. "We had this fella," recalled Samuel Miller forty years later, "he would come and go and he would check each (piece of) fruit. [He] had to see if you had the right size. . . . So what he would do, he would kick the box—you done pick a whole box of fruit—kick it over, check 'em, an' he leave 'em on the ground till you pick 'em up. He wouldn't put his hand [in the box], he'd kick it over, check every one o' 'em, then he would [say]: 'Pick that up, boy.'"[131]

Another Cat Islander, while noticing the American whites' brutally prejudiced treatment of all blacks, also observed the difference between Bahamian black workers and their American counterparts. On the whole it seems that

Bahamians were more conscientious. Some Bahamian laborers considered American blacks both lazy and craven, and this attitude produced tension between them, resulting in fights that sometimes ended fatally. The American blacks worked "just to get a few dollars and go to the beer joint," claimed a Cat Island veteran of the Contract. Bahamians, on the other hand, "don't leave til sundown. They's work (because they are) away from home. They come to make money."[132]

Working on the Contract significantly affected a sizable proportion of the black Bahamian population and helped eventually to change the structure of the society. Besides enabling a larger percentage of the population to accumulate cash, bringing more money into circulation, the Contract exposed thousands of Bahamians to cultural differences, exposing them to new types of food, modes of dress, customs, and modern facilities. Along with the deep impression that southern racial policies made on Bahamian laborers came the pleasurable and occasionally dangerous experiences in the large cities. Some workers enjoyed listening to radios and saw movies for the first time, while others were initiated into the game of pool. More adventurous types encountered risks when frequenting brothels, quickly learning how to protect themselves against pickpockets and other dishonest types.

Bahamian laborers experienced new farming methods and were exposed to mechanization. Those returning to the Out Islands, however, found it difficult to apply the newly acquired techniques, due to the rocky soil and lack of machinery. Some, after the taste of city life, were unable to resettle in their quiet and isolated villages. A great number remained in the United States, some sending for their families, while many more moved to Nassau.[133]

Wartime Nassau

The Bahamian capital, temporarily rid of the potentially explosive element of unemployed labor, became a prosperous wartime Royal Air Force base. A large number of airmen began arriving in late 1942 to take up station at the Operational Training Unit (OTU) at Oakes Field, even before the base had been completed. Thousands of trainees familiar with single-engine aircraft passed through the Bahamas as they learned to master the more advanced twin-engine Mitchells and the four-engine Liberators. More than 3,000 men were on the permanent staff of OTU No. 111, turning out more than 5,000 trained airmen and over 600 crews. The No. 113 Wing Transport Command was stationed at Satellite or Windsor Field.[134]

As already described, Nassau's white elite took pride and pleasure in catering to and entertaining the troops at the IODE and duchess's canteens. Besides the regular informal gatherings when spontaneous sing-songs often took place, members of the IODE usually held monthly dances for the airmen. The troops also enjoyed special social evenings at the Royal Victoria, Yacht Club, and Jungle Club, entertained by the RAF Dance Band, which played regularly at the United Nations Officers' Club, located at what had been the exclusive Emerald Beach Club. The RAF station at Oakes Field also sponsored its own parties, which were held in the large gymnasium. Occasionally outside entertainers appeared. At such events only whites could be invited from outside the base. A strict policy of segregation precluded inviting nonwhite women, or at least those with "pronounced negro features." The troops, who were allowed out of the base every two weeks, were forbidden to "consort with colored women." The white troops could not walk in the company of a nonwhite woman; neither could they stand about talking with a nonwhite woman or visit her at her house. Troops were allowed to be served by a nonwhite woman employed at a reputable café or shop and were not decreed culpable of "consorting" if sitting next to a nonwhite woman by chance in a bus or church.[135]

The rule often went unobserved. Many servicemen broke rank, visiting infamous clubs and bars. Radio operator Roy Smith, who was posted to Nassau in 1942, recalls that the "trips to town were not used to the best advantage . . . invariably most of our pittance of service pay was dispensed to various bartenders in such genteel places as the Quarterdeck."[136] Others went further, visiting brothels or clubs known for their disreputable clientele. In October 1943 the Executive Council noted that prostitution was becoming a menace, and policemen were ordered to clear women of ill repute off Bay Street. At the same time it was discovered that there was a high percentage of venereal disease among RAF personnel in Nassau. The Venereal Diseases Act, passed less than two years later in 1945, was indicative of the high local rate. It also signaled the treatment of the disease by penicillin, which came into widespread clinical use following World War II.[137]

Before the end of the hostilities, however, many lasting relationships were made between the troops and Bahamians, mainly white. Certain nonwhite Bahamians, mostly light skinned, were also occasionally invited to the base at Oakes Field, predominantly to play table tennis and watch boxing matches. The Bahamians, in turn, despite the color restrictions, reciprocated the hospitality and entertained their friends from the forces in their homes. After the war ended, many friendships endured, mainly by means of correspondence and the occasional visit.[138]

More than a dozen servicemen, especially soldiers of the Scottish High-landers, made Nassau their permanent home by marrying white or near-white Bahamian women. Wartime weddings included those of George Evans to Agnes French, James Millar to Peggy Moseley, and Cyril Loughran to Margaret Brownrigg. RAF servicemen, including Dutch Holland and Henry Scates, also found lasting romance. The latter married Helen Lloyd, the very fair-skinned niece of Rowena Hill Eldon.[139]

Wartime life in Nassau offered relative gaiety and a peaceful and fairly prosperous atmosphere, though interrupted by a downtown fire, the Oakes murder, and occasional trouble caused by rowdy servicemen, who were quickly disciplined by the military police. The location of the bases in Nas-sau ensured that adequate supplies of food were maintained throughout the war. Shortages, including of canned meats, fish, and grits, occurred later in the war and did not significantly affect the population. Dwindling supplies of kerosene resulted in long queues in Nassau and brought total darkness at night to some houses in the Over-the-Hill district and on the Out Islands. Gasoline shortages did not affect the majority of people, as cars were still luxuries.[140]

Two notable distractions were a major fire in downtown Nassau less than four weeks after the riot and the mysterious murder of the wealthy developer and philanthropist Sir Harry Oakes on the stormy night of 7–8 July 1943. The fire, started by a struggling shopkeeper who resorted to arson, spread over more than two blocks. Fortunately extra fire engines at the base and a num-ber of enthusiastic but frantic volunteers, including the Duke of Windsor, saved the city from complete destruction. Sir Clifford Darling described the scene in his memoirs:

> The Duke worked alongside the men, hosing down the fires and at-tempting to save what could be saved from the shops and houses in the blaze. There he was, the former King of England, dressed in a pair of khaki shorts, his face and fair hair smeared with soot, pulling the fire hose. Near him was a black man, also pulling the hose, who was not at all pleased with the effort the Duke was putting forth. Not recognizing the Duke, the fellow shouted at the Governor. "You little Conchy Joe S.O.B., why don't you pull the hose properly?" Another black fellow near-by said to him, "Boy don't you know who that is? That's the Duke of Windsor!" The first man immediately dropped the hose and took off. The Duke remained at his post and was very helpful in putting out the fire.[141]

The white incendiary was convicted and sent to jail for seven years, a similar sentence being handed down to most of the sixty-seven persons convicted for participation in the riot.[142]

Perhaps the most disturbing wartime event in the Bahamas was the brutal and still unsolved murder of Sir Harry Oakes. The duke and duchess were in the United States when it took place and were shocked, as were most Bahamians. Windsor tried to impose an embargo on news leaving the colony, but the proprietor of the *Tribune*, Etienne Dupuch, who had arranged to visit Oakes's home "Westbourne" that morning to inspect Sir Harry's sheep, got hold of the news and flashed it around the world. Not confident of the local police, Windsor, with undue haste, acquired the services of two Miami police officers, Melchen and Barker, who had been assigned to him on one of his trips to the United States. Windsor wrote in August 1943, "The older and more conservative elements and the whole negro population suspect [Count] de Marigny's guilt but above all wish the murderer, whoever he is, pay the supreme penalty for so dastardly a crime, which caused the death of a fine old man and great benefactor—the best friend the Bahamas ever had."[143] The Duke of Windsor disliked de Marigny and his circle, which led him to call de Marigny the leader of "a quite influential, fast and depraved set of the younger generation, born of bootlegging days, and for him they have an admiration bordering on hero worship. This unsavory group of people would therefore like to see de Marigny escape the rope at all costs, whether guilty or innocent—but if the colored people are ever given the slightest reason to suspect the jury, then the consequences may be grave."[144] Melchen and Barker's case against the accused, the Mauritian Alfred, Count de Marigny, husband of Oakes's daughter Nancy, hinged on what were believed to be incriminating finger prints. Bahamian lawyers Godfrey Higgs and W.E.A. Callender, in defending the accused, were able to discredit the finger-print evidence on which the Crown's case depended. Count de Marigny was acquitted following a sensational trial. Despite the "not guilty" verdict, de Marigny was deported. The debates, hypotheses, and speculation about the murder continue still.[145]

Dame Doris Johnson in her book *The Quiet Revolution* commented:

> It didn't seem to have any bearing on the case that the watchman for the Oakes Estate was found dead shortly after. As Over-the-Hill gossip went, however, he knew too much to be allowed to live. . . . Many Bahamians today still say they believe that Sir Harry was killed because he was so generous and fair to Bahamian laborers and had vowed to bring about the downfall of one of the "Bay Street Boys."[146]

Eva McPherson Williams, in an interview with Olga Culmer Jenkins, stated: "The Duke made a really big mistake when Sir Harry was murdered. He didn't think much of our police force. They were always recruited from Barbados and other West Indian islands, so they were all coloured."[147] Another person interviewed, who withheld his name, said he knew who had had Oakes killed and that the actual killer was shipped out. Leading black lawyer A. F. Adderley, who de Marigny wanted to defend him, was appointed as prosecutor for the Crown. The unnamed interviewee believed that if A. F. Adderley had taken the case, Marigny would not have been acquitted. The person who hired the killer "didn't want Adderley on that case. 'Cause all of them woulda went to jail, too."[148]

Postwar Years

Celebrations were held to mark the end of the war in Europe. When Churchill on 7 May 1945 announced the unconditional surrender of the German forces, twelve rounds were fired from Government House. Church bells rang out all over New Providence and a festive air prevailed. Public offices and businesses closed for two days and a large crowd, headed by Anglican bishop Spence Burton, gathered in Christ Church Cathedral to give thanks. On Sunday, 13 May, a victory parade along Bay Street attracted hundreds of onlookers.[149]

When the RAF withdrew its last airmen in September 1946, it left an important legacy to the Bahamian people. The two well-constructed airfields were to prove of great significance in the years that followed. Unofficially led by Stafford Sands, a member of the House of Assembly and the Executive Council and described by Governor Murphy as "probably the ablest Bahamian of his generation," the government turned its energies to developing tourism.[150] Britain's economic woes made the Bahamas a popular haven for a new generation of financial émigrés. The Duke of Windsor, in summing up his governorship shortly before his departure, wrote euphorically and with some exaggeration that since the United States had entered World War II, "there had developed a state of prosperity as has never been experienced, and the remarkable feature of this prosperity is that it has come mainly through the labor of the working classes who never before in the whole history of the Colony have earned as much money as in the last two years."[151] Fears that the Bahamas would return to its prewar depressed state proved groundless, as the Contract was renegotiated with more generous terms, and both tourism and foreign investment were revived and would reach undreamed of dimensions.[152]

Investments were made in many properties, tremendously boosting real estate prices. Bay Street property trebled in value in less than a decade. Properties on the Out Islands and on Cable Beach in New Providence also rose dramatically, spurring a rise in the cost-of-living index. British capital, some of it supplied through Barclays Bank, established in Nassau in 1947, enabled the elite and a number of the nonwhite middle class to finance family homes, mainly in the eastern suburbs. The Bahamas also prospered from the setting up, by sophisticated, mainly white accountants and lawyers, of "suitcase" companies and tax-sheltering trusts for Americans wishing to avoid an increasingly systematic Internal Revenue Service. This trend would continue, making the Bahamas a prosperous tax haven even after the sterling bloc was dismantled.

The chief beneficiaries were white lawyers and realtors, epitomized by the brilliant and ubiquitous Stafford Sands and the less flamboyant Harold Christie, who in the late '20s and '30s had encouraged investments from such developers as Guy Baxter, Sir Oliver Simmonds, Sir Herbert Holt, and Sir Harry Oakes. Guy Baxter developed Orange Hill and the Grove in western New Providence. Sir Oliver constructed the Balmoral Beach Hotel and engaged in other businesses. Sir Herbert developed properties along the eastern coast.[153]

By the late 1940s Bay Street lawyers' office fronts featured checkerboards of locally registered companies in the thousands, just as the number of banks and trust companies rose from one of each in 1939 to dozens in the 1950s and more than seventy in the mid-1960s. The setting up and maintenance fees were substantial, and lawyers also benefited from the rule that required local representation on the board of any locally registered company.

Bay Street was able to sustain its hegemony by its control of patronage, the trickle-down effect of economic prosperity, and "the promulgation of the myth that it alone could sustain the flow of wealth."[154] Reactionary Bay Street politicians were led by Stafford Sands, whom Seel, assistant under-secretary of state with special responsibility for the West Indies, described as "able, physically and oratorically commanding, ruthless and inflexibly opposed to reform except to entrench his class."[155]

Bay Street was determined to return the colony to peacetime prosperity but was not interested in radical change. It allowed the underdevelopment of education, which made for a lack of political sophistication and a shortage of nonwhite professionals and perpetuated the age-old habits of dependency and lack of self-confidence on the part of the black majority. The nonwhite middle class realized the injustices in the society but lacked the political will or the machinery to effect change.

Most important to the growth in tourism was the Development Board, established in 1914 and energized by chairman Stafford Sands. By the late 1950s the board received a larger share of the budget than the entire education system. Its chief concern was the development and encouragement of foreign investment. Sands also changed Nassau's tourism from a quality venture to a mass tourism resort by extending the season into the summer months. Between 1949 and 1953 there was a spectacular increase in air arrivals. The total arrivals in the latter year, numbering 90,485, mainly Americans, more than trebled the figure for 1949.[156]

Oakes Field served as the first commercial airport in the Bahamas. Its transfer by the Royal Air Force to the Bahamas government in 1946 prompted appointment of the director of civil aviation early the next year. At first Pan American Airways provided only a daily flight to and from Miami in the winter season. But flights increased eightfold by 1950, with three daily flights during the summer months. Longer-haul Nassau-Bermuda-London flights, introduced by British South American Airways in 1947, were taken over three years later by the restructured British Overseas Airways Corporation, which introduced its Stratocruiser and Constellation aircraft services between Nassau and London. That November BOAC inaugurated a direct weekly New York-Nassau-Bermuda flight. Such vital air connections were to stimulate unprecedented growth in the tourist industry, with the tourist season extending into the summer months after 1950.[157]

As tourism surged, it increasingly attracted Americans. Mass tourism on the Out Islands was pioneered by British entrepreneur Billy Butlin, who attempted to operate a superior version of his popular British holiday camp at West End, Grand Bahama, where he had purchased a large tract of land in 1948. Supported by several large British companies, he began construction in 1949, but delays caused by a dock strike in Britain hampered the development, and it was far from complete when it opened in February 1950. Nevertheless more than 18,000 tourists visited the Butlin village in early 1950. The camp closed that autumn after only one season, putting many Bahamians out of work. Historian Peter Barratt commented that "it was essentially the right development in the right place—but it was about ten years too soon."[158]

Other more modest developments on the Out Islands included Roland Symonette's "French Leave," a cluster of holiday cottages accommodating about thirty people, located between Governor's Harbour and Palmetto Point, Eleuthera, and E. C. Davis's Lighthouse Club at Fresh Creek, Andros, which became famous for its yachting and deep-sea fishing.[159] Two major farming operations financed by American entrepreneurs existed in Eleuthera in the forties and early fifties. The Hatchet Bay Company was developed by Austin Levy, a wealthy American textile manufacturer, who purchased two thousand acres at Alice Town in 1936 and created a model dairy and chicken farm. Two years after Levy's death in November 1951, Hatchet Bay was considered "the most important undertaking in the colony." Hatchet Bay employed two hundred local people and supplied water and charged reasonable prices in the company-owned store. The company did practice segregation. White staff and managers lived in "special houses" paid for by the company in an area known as "downtown" or "white town," and white children attended their own school there. Black Bahamians lived in the settlement and were discouraged from frequenting the "white town" areas.[160]

At Rock Sound, South Eleuthera, American Arthur Vining Davis, chairman of the Bahamas Trust Corporation, also invested heavily. Acquiring 5,000 acres of land just north of Rock Sound in 1939 through realtor Harold G. Christie, he developed the Three Bays Farm, similar to the Levy operation. Concentrating on tomato production, he gave steady labor to many Eleutherians, not only in farming but also in the canning factory he built there.

Following the war, Davis, who had acquired 30,000 acres (most of the land in the southern third of Eleuthera) began further development of South Eleuthera Properties, as the venture became known.[161] Developing a fashionable resort in cooperation with the Bahamas government, he also extended roads, electricity, running water, and a telephone system in Rock Sound. In May 1950 Davis sold most of his Eleutheran holdings to the Colonial Development Corporation. The corporation, hoping to assist the country as it was ineligible for assistance under the Colonial Development Welfare Act of 1940, planned to develop a full-blown holiday resort. When the venture failed in 1954, Davis bought back most of his holdings at a profit.[162]

In Inagua the Ericksons were successful in expanding their salt operation with a substantial loan from Barclays Bank, to improve plant machinery and also establish reliable markets in Canada and the United States, where industrial plants such as the Dupont Company helped to absorb its output. Inaguans and a small number of Turks Islanders earned a minimum of nine shillings and six pence a day and were described in 1951 as "well off."[163]

So too were the majority of laborers who worked in the lumber industry. The Abaco Lumber Company, which had operated at Wilson City and Norman's Castle, moved to Pine Ridge, Grand Bahama, in the autumn of 1944.[164] A branch of the company also operated out of Stafford Creek, Andros, rivaling the Bahamian-owned lumber camp at Mastic Point. The latter, operated by Karl Claridge, produced lumber for export as well as charcoal for domestic purposes. The majority of Bahamians cooked over wood fires and depended on hot charcoal to heat the "flat" or "goose" irons to iron clothes. Coal was also used as a substitute for kerosene during the war.[165]

The Abaco Lumber Company relocated about five miles east of Hawksbill Creek at Pine Ridge and was the most elaborate in the Bahamas, soon boasting one and a half miles of railway linking the dock on the north coast to the settlement. The machinery of the lumber camp was powered by steam, including the locomotive, which eventually had about fifteen miles of railway track. The methods employed in the two sawmills to convert pine trees into weather-boarding planks and rectangular section beams were highly organized. Most wood was exported, but some was used locally.[166]

During the mid-forties the operation received a boost in the person of Wallace Groves, a Virginian financier who had served a prison sentence in the United States for mail fraud; he purchased it in 1946 and replaced all steam equipment (except locomotives) with diesel-driven machinery. By 1950 the Pine Ridge operation employed nearly 1,800 people and had exported more than 10 ten million board feet of lumber. A year later the Groves company was awarded a contract from the National Coal Board in Britain to provide it with pit props. By this time Groves was already planning to construct a deep-water harbor at Hawksbill Creek, a move that foreshadowed the phenomenal development of Freeport in the late 1950s.[167]

Crawfishing was also an important industry in Grand Bahama. In the early 1940s, Wenner-Gren established General Seafood (Bahamas) Ltd. at West End, putting the industry on a sound commercial footing.[168]

The Bahamas government in 1946 also farmed out more than 48,000 square miles of land and underwater concessions to various oil companies, including the Standard Oil Company and Shell Overseas Company. Drilling and prospecting for oil, however, were not pursued.

Health and Education

In line with the British Labour government's efforts to bolster services in its colonial territories, and following some of the recommendations of Professor Henry Richardson's government-sponsored *Review of Bahamian Economic Conditions and Postwar Problems* (1944), the Bahamas experienced some improvements in the health and educational fields. The work of infant welfare clinics continued, catering mainly to the nonwhite population. The duchess had made improvements during the war, setting up three weekly clinics for children. Through private funding two clinics had been built, one on Balliou Hill Road and the other in Bilney Lane in the eastern district. This was a boon to dedicated nonwhite nurses such as Alice Hill Jones, who profited from better-equipped facilities in which to reduce infant mortality and to teach mothers pre- and post-natal care.[169]

Stimulated by wartime developments in medicine, some improvements took place in the treatment of the two most serious health hazards in the Bahamas: venereal disease and especially tuberculosis, the incidence of which was considered the highest in the West Indies. By 1953 a 33-bed isolation ward for tuberculosis patients was established in the former RAF hospital built during the war at Prospect Ridge and a new 200-bed Bahamas General Hospital was opened in May. The treatment of venereal disease was improved by the use of penicillin.

Planning for the construction of a new mental hospital began in 1947. The old structure was dilapidated, and the methods used were primitive. One report stated: "The mental hospital in Nassau dates from the days when lunatics were treated like criminals, and they still occupy small cells with heavy iron bars across windows. The violent cases having heavily weighted iron chains tied to their legs."[170] When Polish psychiatrist Dr. Henryk Podlewski arrived to head the mental institution in the early 1950s, he admitted that during a rainstorm he was forced to take cover under an umbrella in order to protect himself and the papers on his office desk.[171]

The improvements made in Nassau were not evident in the majority of the Out Islands, which continued to suffer from a dearth of qualified medical staff. In 1953 there were only four government doctors outside New Providence, located mainly at settlements where foreign investment development was taking place. Similarly, there were only twenty qualified nurses and twelve registered midwives serving the entire Out Island chain.[172]

Many problems also beset the educational system, although significant steps were taken in postwar years to improve it. Provision was made for two scholarships of £44 per annum for three years to enable students to enter universities of their choice within the British Empire. Over the next five years the Board of Education was active in arranging for in-service training for its personnel at institutions in the United Kingdom. After much debate the House of Assembly finally agreed that provision be made for a director of education. Subsequently, T. E. Hutchinson was appointed.[173] Evening classes were begun on a regular basis, and in 1949 a small Technical School was opened at Oakes Field. In order to improve standards in public schools, a small training College established at Oakes Field in 1950, with an initial intake of thirty trainees, mainly teachers. Attached to the institution was a training school with accommodation for 260 children.[174]

While the Education Amendment Act of 1951 increased the board's powers by authorizing it to conduct vocational, technical, continuing education, and adult classes and to conduct teacher training, among other ancillary services, it failed to give the board control over secondary education.[175] The Government High School in 1953 was the only wholly government-financed secondary school. Increasing demands, especially for the growing nonwhite middle class, led to the establishment of two church-sponsored schools. St. John's College on Market Street, opened in January 1947 by the Anglican Diocese, was attended predominantly by mixed-race and black children. St. Augustine's College, situated in Fox Hill and founded in 1945 by the Roman Catholic priests of the Order of St. Benedict, was a racially mixed school for boys. For the first time the Roman Catholic authorities, who generally adopted American methods of education in their schools, were preparing students, most of whom came from Catholic homes, for the British GCE O-level examinations.[176] Roman Catholic priest Father Marcian Peters admitted that there was "quite a bit of anti-Catholicism exhibited in so many ways. We were just not accepted for the best, and our schools were looked down upon as being second class or third class."[177]

Also established in the 1940s was the racially segregated St. Andrew's School, formed in 1948 by a "group of parents who wished to provide . . . an education comparable to that supplied by private schools in England."[178] St. Andrews School was a limited company that numbered among its shareholders the parents of every child enrolled. Original shareholders included lawyer Godfrey Higgs, merchants W.H.H. Maura, Basil and John Burnside, and Girl Guide leaders Eulalie M. Higgs and Veronica M. Higgs.[179] By establishing the school in this way the shareholders controlled the intake of students. It was run exclusively for white children and was not integrated until the 1970s. Among the first nonwhite children accepted were the grandchildren of Sir Milo Butler.

Conclusion

The small improvements made by the government did not alleviate the growing sociopolitical dissatisfaction within nonwhite Bahamian society. Though there was not as yet a united opposing force to challenge the Bay Street regime, deprivations and discrimination were resented and a cause for concern. Reverend H. H. Brown, a black Methodist minister, in a remarkable sermon delivered at Governor's Harbour, Eleuthera, on 14 January 1946, attacked the entrenched position of the wealthy merchants in the legislature. He asserted:

> I doubt there is anywhere else on earth masquerading as "democracy" a less representative government. . . . Instead of "government of the people, for the people" we have "exploitation of the many, for the privileged, by the few." That a people have the kind of government that it deserves is almost axiomatic. A criticism of the local government is therefore a criticism of the entire local population. Until people awaken to their own responsibilities, they will not have a responsible government. But nothing can possibly justify the attempt of any government to keep the people asleep. Who has learned the lesson of the [1942] riot? Not the Governor with his recent appalling appointment [Stafford Sands] to the Executive Council. Not those members who repeatedly block the simpler efforts for economic improvement, political development, or educational expansion. Not an administration which sends thousands of men overseas on "projects" and does nothing to prepare for their return home. I venture one sure word of prophecy: Unless the powers that be consider a little less of the world of self, and unless the ordinary citizen awakens to the responsibilities of democracy, the riot of 1942 will seem pale and insignificant in comparison with its successor.[180]

When challenged, Reverend Brown claimed that "the colored population, the entire Out Island population and even (though very few) White Nassauvians, are 100 per cent behind the utterance." Surprisingly, Alvin R. Braynen, "a very active member of the House of Assembly and of Trinity Church" said that in his opinion it was "the finest stand taken by a minister in my time." He challenged the members of the government to refute it but opined that "of course, they can't because every word is true."[181]

7

The Formative Years, 1950–1958

Political Organization, Race, and Protest

People had marched on Emancipation Day in 1938 to press for labor reforms and for the secret ballot, and as we have seen, the secret ballot had been implemented provisionally in 1939 in New Providence (chapter 5) and was declared permanent in New Providence in 1944. The Russell Commission had recommended extending the secret ballot to the Out Islands. However, its general extension to the Out Islands did not come into effect until the general election of 1949 (chapter 6). While the pact among the various nonwhite groups dissolved, what remained were the bitter feelings between whites and nonwhites. The white population had been solidly against extending the secret ballot to the Out Islands because they felt the people were too illiterate to use it. Blacks and browns had united, inspired by a cause that was becoming increasingly racial.

The Citizens' Committee

Most concerned with the extreme discrimination upheld by the Nassau white elite was the Citizens' Committee. Established in December 1950, it was a mixed-race and black middle-class organization headed by Maxwell J. Thompson. Dentist Cleveland W. Eneas, Baptist minister A. E. Hutcheson, businessman Leon McKinney, and Federation of Labour head Charles Rodriguez also served on its executive board. Other professionals who joined the organization included dentist Jackson Burnside, locally trained lawyers Gerald Cash and Randol Fawkes, and the recently returned Cambridge-educated Kendal Isaacs, youngest son of the late restaurateur Edward A. Isaacs. (Other founding members included Percy Pinder, Edgar Bain, Charles Dorset, Samuel White, Samuel O. Johnson, William A. Swain, W. M. Albury,

Harcourt W. Brown, Samuel McPherson, Cyril Tynes, Marcus Bethel, and Bertram Cambridge.)

The formation of the organization was triggered by the government's refusal to let Bahamians see three films: *No Way Out, Lost Boundaries,* and *Pinky,* all of which explored the "Negro problem." The group also aimed to address injustices in society more generally. Its constitution, moderate and vague in tone, vowed that it would "generally protect, improve, preserve and defend the economic, educational and political rights and liberties of all Bahamians."[1]

When the showing of *No Way Out* at the Capitol Theatre in Grant's Town was advertised in Nassau, the Censorship Board banned it and the other two movies they found to be racially sensitive. A. F. Adderley, the only non-white member of the board, resigned; the other members were Gurth Duncombe, Oswald Moseley, and the commissioner of police. According to dentist Cleveland W. Eneas, the black population had looked forward to seeing Sidney Poitier, a son of the Bahamas, in one of his first starring roles. Poitier played the part of a physician, "trained and educated as well as any doctor of the day . . . not a servile Negro."[2] Eneas, writing in 1976, stated: "The Bay Street Boys and leaders of the white supremacy movement in the Bahamas were not ready to allow the Negroes of the Bahamas to see that this was possible for them. This stood to ruin all their 'careful planning.' This was not a part of their strategy, and the Negroes who were under their servitude were not to be enlightened to the fact that such a thought existed in the world. They, through their power stopped it." Dr. Eneas saw that this "awakened the most militant" and energized them in their determination to wrest power from Bay Street. This would take some time, and they realized that they needed "economic, political and intellectual" power to succeed.[3]

Not able to get a satisfactory answer from the Censorship Board, the Citizens' Committee met with the acting governor, F. A. Evans, who referred the matter back to the Censorship Board, who refused to reverse their decision. Subsequently, on 9 November 1950, the Citizens' Committee convened a meeting that was well attended. Several members spoke, including Chairman Maxwell Thompson, Bertram Cambridge, A. Leon McKinney, Marcus Bethel, Cleveland Eneas, and William Swain, outlining the aims, objectives, and policy of the committee. Maxwell Thompson stressed the need for racial equality, for extending educational opportunity to all young Bahamians, raising the standard of living for the masses, lending assistance to the Out Islands, encouraging a free press, and defending economic, educational, and political rights and liberties for all Bahamians.[4]

Following the speeches Kendal Isaacs, chairman for the evening, solicited signatures for a petition requesting a court of appeal and the appointment of more nonwhites on public boards and committees. Some Out Islanders also sent in petitions on these issues. A number of the Citizens' Committee members were also signers of the unsuccessful petition sponsored in April 1950 by the Old Scholars Association of the Government High School, requesting the House of Assembly to reconsider affiliation with the University College of the West Indies. When invited to do this in 1946, the white-dominated government had refused. Gerald Cash, then representing the western district of New Providence, made the motion for a Select Committee. Among those supporting it were William Cartwright, a light-skinned mixed-race Long Islander, Dr. C. R. Walker, and Bertram Cambridge. Among reasons given by the white oligarchy for the rejection of the affiliation with the University College of the West Indies were that the Bahamas was not part of the West Indies geographically and that such venture was premature; that the Bahamas should concentrate on elementary education; and that the university would become a breeding ground for young communists.[5]

In the late 1940s Dr. Walker had founded an anti-establishment newspaper, the *Voice*, which lasted until the late 1950s, but a file was not systematically kept and few copies exist. In order to alert Bahamians of the work of the Citizens' Committee, the *Citizens' Torch*, a small newspaper edited by Dr. Cleveland Eneas, was established in 1951. Eneas believed that through its publication the Citizens' Committee "carried a burning torch for many a year in these islands, lighting the way for Black people to follow in their march towards first class citizenship." It was able to sensitize Bahamians to the pernicious system of racial segregation then present in the Bahamas. In the second issue of the *Torch* Cleveland Eneas wrote in an editorial entitled "Race Segregation Must Go":

> Our efforts will not be for the few, but for the benefit of all citizens of this community. . . . It will not only make life better for us Negroes, but for every citizen of the country. . . . It should be insulting to each and every one of us to be obviously barred from any place because we're black. . . . It is a difference altogether when people are discriminated against because of behavior, but in our town, the insults leveled against us brand all of us as being ill-bred, ill-mannered, and lacking good behavior.[6]

In another editorial entitled "Pride and Dignity," Eneas scolded nonwhites for tolerating the treatment handed out by whites:

In many ways, we Negroes in The Bahamas are particularly devoid of pride and dignity and consequently we are blatantly disrespected by the white people of the community. . . . Why do I say that we have no pride and dignity? In spite of the degrading treatment that we received, the Jim Crow counters of J. P. Sands are still crowded with us. Nine out of every ten customers of the Stop-N-Shop are still Negroes.[7]

A subcommittee of the Citizens' Committee reinforced Eneas's editorials, concluding that segregation and discrimination were "practiced openly and flagrantly in Nassau, for example, in hotels, Amusement centers such as the Jungle Club, The Spider, Paradise Beach, Black's Candy Kitchen and the Grand Central Restaurant." Additionally, discrimination was practiced in some businesses, such as that of J. P. Sands; in schools, particularly St. Andrew's; in sports at Garfunkel field; and in banks, some mail boats, and the Savoy Theatre on Bay Street.[8]

The celebrated American mixed-race writer Langston Hughes, while on a visit to Nassau in the summer of June 1954, described his impressions:

There is a colour line—very much, so I hear, like that of Bermuda—since it is so near our American South. The deluxe hotels, restaurants, and beaches are not open to Negro patronage. . . . But there are no WHITE or COLOURED signs such as Florida has, only an hour away, and no Jim Crow buses or taxis, and none of the red-necked rudeness in public services common to our mainland. . . . And the people—I mean the colored people (I did not meet a single white soul)—are very nice people. I want to go back to Nassau.[9]

In another article Hughes wrote that unlike posh hotel facilities in Kingston, Jamaica, and Port-au-Prince, Haiti, which accommodated nonwhites, "The big hotels in Nassau do not welcome Negroes. For colored people there are some pleasantly comfortable guest houses, and a number of clean but otherwise colored hotels."[10]

The Citizens' Committee brought the pernicious system of segregation into the open, challenging whites, and tried to educate nonwhites to its evils. It recommended competing with whites as a form of boycotting white-owned stores on Bay Street, but there were too few brown and black people who could afford to compete with the Bay Street merchants. Hartley Saunders contends that the ideas "expounded" by the Citizens' Committee were not "well received by the masses." He also argued that some members of the organization were not fully committed to its cause, and it soon died.

Many of those involved struggled economically, and young mixed-race and black middle-class professionals found it difficult to make a decent living in Nassau. Lawyers, for example, stood little chance of attracting wealthy clients and the lucrative corporate business dominated by Stafford Sands. Less well-paid criminal matters usually went to older, more experienced nonwhite lawyers, such as Adderley, Toote, and until 1949 to W.E.S. Callender. Moreover, young nonwhite professionals competed with their white counterparts, such as Geoffrey Johnstone, Peter Christie, and Peter Graham, who were well connected. They were all called to the Bahamian Bar in 1950.[11] On his return home from the University of Cambridge in England in 1950, Kendal Isaacs set up modest chambers in the Kelly Building on Bay Street. Business was so bad that he could not afford to pay a secretary, and his sister, Sybil Thompson, obligingly helped him with his clerical work. When by 1952 conditions had not improved, he joined the civil service as a stipendiary and circuit magistrate—the first nonwhite to be appointed in that position.[12] Isaacs later served as solicitor general and attorney general before entering private practice.

A substantial number of members of the Citizens' Committee and the *Voice* were also involved in the establishment on 5 April 1952 of the Penny Savings Bank, an all-black institution. Prominent among its promoters was A. Leon McKinney, originally from Long Cay in the southern Bahamas. Educated in Miami, McKinney worked as an insurance agent and at various other jobs there before returning to the Bahamas in 1937, after working as a stock manager at the Erickson-owned West Indian Chemical Company in Inagua. He moved to Nassau for some years and was accepted in the position of assistant manager of the Community Industrial Life Insurance Company.[13]

McKinney's dream, born out of his American experience, was to establish a bank that would cater to low- and middle-income Bahamians. The bank began with capital of six thousand pounds "divided into six thousand shares at one pound each." Its holdings were at the beginning "a lot of land and a dilapidated house on the corners of Market and McPherson Streets in the Southern District of New Providence."[14] It was strategically located in the south but not too far south. Symbolically it stood opposite the Southern Recreation Ground, where all mass meetings took place.

Enlisting the aid and support of Cleveland Eneas as vice-president, Randol Fawkes as secretary and legal advisor, Edgar Bain as treasurer, and Percival Hanna as assistant secretary—all dark-skinned nonwhites—McKinney presided over the official opening of the Penny Savings Bank on 21

November 1952. Attending the ceremonies were representatives of the Royal Bank of Canada and Barclays Bank and also respected nonwhite leaders A. F. Adderley and Eugene Dupuch, the member of the House of Assembly for Crooked Island, and men, women, and children from the various black "villages." McKinney stated at the opening: "We are not seeking what is profitable for the few. . . . We are thinking in terms of the many . . . this institution, at present, does not boast of being a bank but rather a school of 'thrift' where any man, woman or child may take the first step towards self-sufficiency by opening an account with an amount as small as a penny."[15]

Despite many difficulties, especially in its early years, the Penny Savings Bank was still a viable operation into the 1970s, when it still stood "as a fortress of financial strength and a landmark in the struggle of the black man for greater dignity and self-respect through good business practices." Indeed the bank gave confidence to mixed-race and black people who were too awed to enter the two white-staffed, foreign-controlled banks on Bay Street. Many Bahamian youngsters opened their first accounts at the newly formed Penny Savings Bank, and the bank also assisted many nonwhite Bahamians to start businesses and build homes; in fact, to "get their start on the road to independence." According to Randol Fawkes, "the Penny Savings Bank Limited lasted for forty years, until in 1992 it became a part of the Government's national savings institutions."[16]

Socioeconomic Conditions in 1953

The Bahamas in 1953 was very different from that of the 1880s. The impact of worldwide technological improvements, especially in transportation and communications and accelerated by two world wars, had brought global events closer to the Bahamas, and to a certain extent the Bahamas had entered the mainstream of the world.

Yet the change was only relative, partial, and far from beneficial to most Bahamians. What changes had occurred were extremely uneven in their application, exacerbating and pointing up the deep divisions in the society. Within Nassau itself this was especially clear. Due in part to an increasing birth rate, but mainly to accelerated migration from the Out Islands and other parts of the region, numbers were pressing on limited resources. Many new buildings were going up in the most desirable locations, but the town spilled out into ill-managed Over-the-Hill suburbs that were underprivileged slums compared with the "quaint and bustling" hub of downtown Bay Street or the seaside villa strips to the east and west. Similarly, there was an increasing division between the colony's capital and the neglected Out Islands.

Moreover, this double dichotomy, between downtown Nassau and its teeming suburbs and between the developing metropolis of New Providence and the underdeveloped outer islands, was evidence of an intensifying split between the white plutocracy—the Bay Street Boys and their poor white "Conchy Joe" clients—and the disadvantaged black majority. White paternalism and the intermediate and intermediary roles of the mixed-race and black middle class meant that changes had been delayed. Yet the greediness of the leaders of the white elite, the self-centered naiveté and impotence of most of the intermediate class, and continuing poverty of the black majority in the face of rising expectations meant that the Bahamas in 1953 stood on the brink of fundamental socioeconomic and political changes.

Attainment of a higher education was becoming increasingly important in determining status. A significant number of mixed-race and black people, benefiting from the facilities for public secondary education established in 1926, now sought professional careers, especially in the legal and medical fields. Included among these were lawyers Gerald Cash, Kendal Isaacs, Randol Fawkes, and Lynden Pindling and dentist Cleveland Eneas. In 1953 nearly a third of those in the legal profession were nonwhite. Two of the five dentists were black, while five out of the seventeen private doctors were nonwhite. Additionally, another mixed-race doctor, Dr. Ricardo DeGregory, held the post of anesthetist at the Bahamas General Hospital. Exposure to education and travel was also a means of upward mobility for some blacks. In addition, church leadership, particularly in the disunited but locally controlled Baptist church, gave status and respectability to nonwhites, especially Out Islanders. The latter, in fact, by 1953 were the dynamic force within the leadership of the Baptist faith in Nassau. Mixed-race migrants similarly provided the impetus for accelerated political developments.[17]

Middle-class mixed-race and black women were employed in the traditionally nonwhite-dominated professions and within clerical ranks of the civil service. By 1953 girls were being encouraged to pursue higher education, especially in medical-related fields. Returning home to a nursing sister's post at the Bahamas General Hospital in 1953 was highly qualified Hilda Bowen, daughter of stone mason Irvin Bowen; she was the first Bahamian black woman to hold such a high post.[18] Still studying nursing in Great Britain were Patricia Fountain, Dorothy Davis, and Olivia Jarvis, members of the mixed-race and black middle class. At the same time Clarice Sands, daughter of Baptist minister Talmadge Sands and his wife Dora, was studying radiography at the Sheffield Royal Infirmary, while Keva Eldon, daughter of Rowena and Sidney Eldon, was preparing to enter Girton College, Cambridge.[19]

While the infrastructure including the road system was improved, especially in downtown Nassau, black areas were largely disregarded. The modernization of the city, aimed at pleasing an increasing tourist clientele, also benefited the white elite who controlled the political and economic machinery. Although other people might have been marginally better off, the value of land had appreciated so greatly it was farther out of reach for ordinary people than ever before. In Nassau, foreign and local whites who could afford the most attractive properties largely bought up hillside and seaside acreages, some for speculative purposes. Prohibitive costs and subtle segregation practices by realtors excluded mixed-race and black people, forcing them inland. Similarly, on the Out Islands large areas of land were bought by local and foreign investors alike, while land tenure practices for the brown and black majority remained uncertain and confused. Traditional methods of farming persisted, and agriculture, in many cases for subsistence, remained an important part of Out Island life.

In economic terms the wealth of the white elite, gained mainly through modern developments in tourism and finance, created a wider than ever cleavage between the races. While the white elite effectively limited the power and size of the British official class by keeping the salaries of higher posts within the civil service low, they also welcomed wealthy whites and sometimes members of the reactionary North American "international set." Imitating their habits, the white elite developed elaborate and expensive lifestyles. They upheld racial integrity, refusing to have social relations with the mixed-race and black middle class, which itself was stratified by shade differences.

The definition of a nonwhite person in the Bahamas was still ambiguous in 1953, varying greatly according to a person's family or attitude. Subtle distinctions relating to color increased class and racial divisions. Some whites called anyone with a drop of African blood "a colored person," while some nonwhites called anyone with an appreciable amount of European blood "white." Terms such as mulatto, "a yellow person," and "bright-skinned" were still commonly used to classify the various gradations of color. Methodist missionaries were often startled at having to reclassify those whom they considered "predominantly black" (but obviously with white ancestry) as those "who consider themselves white."[20] In many cases the explanation of a dark skin was an Indian ancestor, much more acceptable than an African.

Proximity to the southern United States and the development of tourism did not help racial attitudes. Exposure to so many whites tended to emphasize the already innate feelings of inferiority among nonwhites. Many of the mixed-race and black middle class absorbed white values and tried to overcome their racial identity by straightening their hair, while some light-skinned persons "passed." A hierarchy was thus created within the nonwhite community, where not only color but hair quality and facial structure mattered. While "a light skin, straight hair, thin lips and a narrow nose" were considered "good," "a dark skin, kinky hair, thick lips and a flat nose" were "bad." "Good" hair might compensate for a dark skin, but physical features mattered most.[21] With poor images of themselves, mothers often pulled their children's noses to make them more pointed.[22]

The expansion of tourism as the major industry after the Prohibition years increased the value of land, attracting both developers and speculators. While a number of developments beneficial to the black laboring population had materialized, especially at Eleuthera, Andros, Grand Bahama, and Inagua, large areas of land were often bought for speculative purposes, remaining undeveloped for years. Influential realtors such as Harold Christie, attracted by the promise of handsome profits, continued buying up huge parcels of land, both on New Providence and on the Out Islands. Wielding economic and political clout, Christie justified speculation by the developments that materialized. He was able to obtain privately owned land because so many of the owners were poverty-stricken, but it seemed that he was also able to get any Crown lands he wished because of a complacent regime at the Crown Lands Office, which then, perhaps by no accident, was dominated by non-Bahamians.[23]

Land purchased at nominal prices sold for huge profits. Some purchasers of beachfront land declared many of the best beaches private. Entire cays, especially in the Exumas, were sold to foreigners and the wealthy white elite. The posting of "No Tresspassing" signs on the cays was indicative of trends of the time. Beach and seaside property was becoming the reserve of wealthy whites. The birthright of Bahamians was steadily being eroded.[24]

The drift of population away from the Out Islands exacerbated this situation and the already complicated land tenure system. Squatters, commoners, and owners of generation property often left the land vacant or uncultivated in order to seek their fortunes in Nassau. Even those who farmed the land discovered that when they tried to establish title, it was by no means as certain as they thought. Demonstrating two different concepts in regard to land ownership would be the celebrated Bowe case, heard in the Nassau Supreme Court in 1961. James Maxwell Bowe, a well-off mixed-race stock farmer who had inherited the Forest Estate from his father and had owned it in fee simple since 1920, was challenged in 1961 by twenty-eight residents who claimed that they were entitled to the entire Forest Estate through squatters' rights. The resident sharecroppers, who traced their occupation of the Forest settlement back to slavery, worked the land and were supposed to have paid annual rent of a third of the crops produced. They claimed that for thirty years they had had access to the whole of the Forest Estate in Exuma "at will," farming and herding their "creatures" without supervision from Maxwell Bowe or his father. Their claim, however, was broken in the courts because Bowe was able to prove that all the claimants were sharecroppers or had not farmed any single piece of the land for twenty years.[25]

The sharecropping system and the uncertain land tenure practices helped to keep the majority of Out Islanders poor and economically dependent. No systematic plan was made at this time to solve the complicated land situation or to improve traditional methods of farming. Many peasants left the land, seeking better opportunities in Nassau and the United States. Whereas in the late 1880s and early 1890s, nearly 20 percent of the population had been directly employed in agriculture and fisheries, by 1953 only 10.6 percent were so employed.[26] Many who remained on the Out Islands were involved in wage labor rather than being self-employed.

Those who migrated to Nassau were mostly unskilled and were initially employed in menial jobs, primarily as laborers and domestics at low wages. Meager earnings did not keep abreast with the spiraling cost of living in Nassau—the highest in the Caribbean.[27] The expanding tourism industry, while generating jobs and keeping unemployment to a minimum, also necessitated increasing importation of food and luxury items, not only for tourists but also for the local population, who preferred imported goods. Indirect taxation through customs duties—the main source of revenue—and the refusal of the House of Assembly to introduce income tax maintained the inequitable tax system, which put the burden on the poor and low-income earners.

While the majority of the white mercantile class were faring increasingly well, and profiting from the tax structure and the commercially oriented economy, the black laboring population, poor and middle-class whites, and a large proportion of the mixed-race class suffered most, although over time, some members of the middle strata managed to purchase their own homes with inherited money or by securing mortgages.[28] Poor whites, especially those from Harbour Island and Abaco, stood better chances than the black laboring class. Often related or known to white businessmen, Out Island and Nassau whites were more easily trusted. Moreover, because of their color, they secured jobs in Bay Street businesses, and their reliability and connections assisted them in obtaining bank loans and various other credit facilities.

On the other hand, blacks, especially immigrants from the Out Islands, were not considered a good risk. Credit facilities and bank loans were hard to obtain. Blacks' mobility to and from the United States perhaps discouraged whites from transacting business with them. More often than not, hard-pressed blacks, including West Indian policemen, resorted to black and mixed-race money lenders. Often fronting for better-off and more respectable mixed-race men, some money lenders charged exorbitant interest and refused to give receipts for interest payments.[29] Other blacks, as well as some mixed-race people, joined the traditional *asue* savings clubs in order to accumulate small amounts of capital. Some also opened small accounts at the Penny Savings Bank. Because of their reputations and "respectability," middle-class mixed-race and black people, often on meager government salaries, were able to secure small loans and credit facilities from the more sympathetic but astute white merchants. A few were even given references to foreign-owned banks.[30]

Although changes were beginning to take place, the economy was increasingly controlled by the white elite. As members of the House of Assembly, the white politicians devoted much time and energy to public affairs, especially to promoting tourism, but the benefits largely accrued to themselves and their relatives and friends.[31] Tourism, which yielded very high revenues to the rich and powerful, succeeded in creating "private wealthy empires" while widening the gap between the rich and poor. As Gordon Lewis succinctly stated: "In effect, the Bahamas government was deliberately kept a poor government in a rich economy," with "the resultant contrast between private affluence and public squalor, between elegant hotels and gift shops on Bay Street and the shacks of the Negro proletariat that works in them 'over the Hill.'"[32]

By the 1950s the white population in the Bahamas had shrunk in proportion to the mixed-race middle class and the black laboring class, although still large in comparison to other British West Indian colonies except Bermuda. Whereas in 1888 it was estimated that a quarter of the population was white, by 1953 and only 12.6 percent was classified as being of European origin. At the same time, 14.1 percent was described as being mixed and 72.6 percent as African (i.e., black).[33] By upholding an archaic constitutional framework and perpetuating corrupt election practices, the white elite had acquired increased powers within the elected House of Assembly and the legislature generally. Still elected as independents, white members, although at times highly individualistic, generally united on major policy issues. By the early 1950s and even before that, many white members were influenced by the able, powerful, and reactionary Stafford Sands, the unofficial leader of Bay Street.[34]

Political representation in the Lower House had not dramatically changed in ethnic terms since the turn of the century. Whereas in 1889 six nonwhites sat in the House of Assembly, by 1953, in spite of the introduction of the secret ballot, there were still only seven, including the mixed-race journalists William Cartwright and Etienne Dupuch, lawyers Eugene Dupuch and Gerald Cash, musician Bertram Cambridge, physician Dr. Claudius Walker, and undertaker Marcus Bethel. For voting purposes the group included Long Islander Henry M. Taylor, whom some, including himself, considered white.[35]

The Progressive Liberal Party

By the early 1950s the nonwhite (including mixed-race and black people) population was ready for change. The formation of the Citizens' Union in the 1920s and 1930s, a prelude to the explosive 1942 riot and followed by a series of strikes later in that decade, the Women's Suffrage Movement in the late 1940s and early 1950s, and the ballot box activism and Citizens' Committee in the 1950s were evidence of the growing dissatisfaction among nonwhites. Although mixed-race persons did not seemingly take part in the Nassau riot, they too suffered from racial discrimination, humiliation, and the inequities in the strictly stratified society. Moreover, they and dark-skinned nonwhites realized that Bay Street could be challenged and was not "invincible."[36]

It is not certain who initiated the idea of forming the Progressive Liberal Party (PLP), the first successful political party in the Bahamas. A group of anti-establishment and idealistic light-skinned (near-white) Bahamians, many of whom were Roman Catholic with roots in the Out Islands, met in early October 1953. Most prominent among them were Henry M. Taylor, junior member of the House of Assembly for Long Island; William Cartwright, junior member of the House for Cat Island; and Cyril St. John Stevenson; the latter two became owner and editor respectively of the *Herald* after the death of Stanley Lowe in January 1953. Taylor was from a poor background in Clarence Town, Long Island, where he lived with his great aunts. As a youngster, deprived of a good secondary education, he read avidly, especially political histories. He also taught at Out Island schools for several years before drifting into Nassau, where he took a course in accounting and worked at various jobs in the private and public sectors. Randol Fawkes described Taylor as a poorly dressed "ne'er-do-well accountant." As a boy Taylor had become aware of corrupt election practices and was determined to change the status quo. According to Fawkes, during the 1949 elections, while the "Bay Street Boys" used "fleets of ships, planes and helicopters, H. M. successfully walked, cycled and 'donkeyed' his way to a seat in the House of Assembly for the Long Island constituency."[37]

Cartwright, also a Long Islander, migrated to Nassau, where he struggled to teach himself journalism. In 1947, following a brief but fairly successful career in real estate, he established a publishing business, the *Bahamian Review*, the Bahamas' first monthly news magazine, which flourished "despite the efforts of Bay Street to withhold advertising."[38] Critical of the House of Assembly's policies, he successfully contested the all-black constituency of Cat Island in 1949. He described his experience during his campaign in the "totally Negroid constituency" that for many years had returned white realtor Harold C. Christie. Cartwright was assisted by black physician Dr. Claudius Walker. Together they visited the "patriarch" of the island, Sammie Swain, soliciting his vote. After an eloquent statement from Dr. Walker, Cartwright asked whether Swain would vote for him in the morning. "Brother Swain" replied: "Well Mr. Cartwright . . . I like all two-a-yinna, so dis what I decide to do. . . . I ga vote for Mr. Christie (the white man) and pray for you Mr. Cartwright."[39]

Stevenson, a Nassauvian whose mother was from Long Cay, worked as a reporter with the *Nassau Guardian*. He became affiliated with Cartwright's *Bahamian Review* magazine. More important to the PLP was Cartwright's purchase of the biweekly *Herald,* formerly edited by Jack Stanley Lowe and, after Lowe's death in January 1953, by Holly Brown. Stevenson later purchased the paper and took over its editorship. The *Herald* became the official propaganda organ of the PLP. In addition to his duties as secretary-general of the PLP operating on "a shoestring," Stevenson published the *Nassau Herald*, delivering seething criticisms of the white oligarchy and accusing its members of "corruption and mal administration." Fawkes opined that the *Herald*, a weekly publication, "became a flaming sword and a shield fighting for the people's rights and protecting them against human rights abuses of a colonialist regime . . . until Bay Street shuddered at the mere mention of its name."[40]

The three founders of the PLP, a group of "outsiders," were courageous in challenging the powerful white mercantile elite, opening themselves to victimization. Journalist P. Anthony White stated in an article after the death of the last surviving member of the group, William Cartwright, in June 2012: "Cartwright, Taylor and Stevenson, all mulattos (sic), suffered greatly at the hands of Bay Street for having dared to spearhead an organization of largely black Bahamians whose common and greatest enemy was Bay Street."[41] According to William Cartwright, he used his own money to visit England and Jamaica in order to gather information about party organization in order "to fight the Bay Street Boys."[42] On his and Cyril Stevenson's return from Jamaica, according to H. M. Taylor, they called Taylor requesting that they meet to form a political party. He agreed and became the chairman of the new organization. Cartwright was elected to the position of treasurer and Stevenson as secretary-general. Among the other charter members of the party were John S. Carey, an Eleutherian bookkeeper who became vice chairman; Urban Knowles, a Nassau printer, as chaplain; and Clement Pinder, a clerk, also from Nassau, who was appointed assistant secretary-general. In addition, appointed as executive members were Felix N. Russell, a black-skinned Cat Islander and small businessman; Holly H. Brown, a near-white Nassauvian, World War I and II veteran, and founder of the *Herald*; and Paul Farrington, a Nassau printer (who soon bowed to pressure from Bay Street). Charles Rodriguez, who had served as the president of the Federation of Labour in 1942, was associated with the party as well.[43]

A Women's Branch was also established in about 1953. The branch met regularly at the Silver Slipper and was headed by some of the suffragettes: Georgina Symonette, Eugenia Lockhart, Madge Brown, and the Heastie sisters, with roots in Acklins. One of the chief aims of the Women's Branch was to raise funds for the fledgling party.[44]

Shortly after the formation of the PLP, Lynden Pindling, who had recently returned from London, visited Cyril Stevenson at the *Herald's* office in mid-November and joined the PLP as its legal adviser. He and F. N. Russell were the only black-skinned men in the early PLP's executive. Pindling was born in Nassau in 1930, the only son of Viola (Bain) Pindling, who hailed from Acklins, and Arnold Pindling, a Jamaican who served on the police force before building a house and starting a grocery business on East Street. Lynden Pindling attended the Government High School, the only government secondary school, between 1943 and 1946. He worked for two years at the Post Office Savings Bank before going to London to read law at the University of London at Middle Temple.

There Pindling met and hobnobbed with many who later became political leaders of Caribbean and other Commonwealth countries. Many of them were anti-establishment and socialist. He was exposed to the new nationalistic ideas associated with the decolonization process. His interest in politics was aroused, and he realized that his service to the Bahamas was not only as a lawyer but as someone who must "delve into the life of this (Bahamian) community . . . and unravel the mysteries of unrest and dissension and assist in the promotion of a good life for his fellows citizens."[45] Politics gave him an appreciation of how "white minorities used their political and economic power to perpetuate minority rule . . . and entrench their wealth . . . at the expense of the black majority." He realized that the PLP had the potential to "break that cycle in the Bahamas and allow democracy to bloom and flourish."[46]

During its early years the PLP grew slowly and steadily under Taylor's leadership. It drew up and published a constitution and platform that enunciated its aims and policies. Demanding political and social change, it pledged itself as a party for all men, whether rich or poor, black, brown or white, and of whatever religious creed. It called for wider representation in the House of Assembly, the enfranchisement of women, the reduction of House terms from seven to five years, and the introduction of municipal government for Nassau. Among the party's aims were control of immigration and improvements in higher education, teacher training, school facilities, and health services. It promised a New Deal for the neglected agricultural Out Islands and more enlightened labor legislation. Labeled a leftist party, it vowed its opposition to Communism, of which it was to be accused by its detractors.[47]

Both daily newspapers, the *Nassau Guardian* and the *Nassau Tribune*, were critical of the party and its officers, as were many of the nonwhite middle class. The editor of the Bay Street–owned and controlled *Guardian* was skeptical of its membership, and the *Tribune*'s mixed-race editor and proprietor, Etienne Dupuch, although traditionally a critic of Bay Street, questioned the timing of the party system, arguing that political parties were too sophisticated for the Bahamas of the day.[48]

Dr. Cleveland Eneas was convinced that the "mulattoes" or near whites who established the PLP never intended to be dominated by blacks. They refused to invite the "racially radical" members of the Citizens' Committee, which, as noted, had been formed in reaction to the Nassau elite's refusal to see three films exploring black-white relations. Eneas believed that the "mulattoes" despised the black-skinned majority and wished "to wrest the power" from Bay Street to the exclusion of the black majority.[49] Perhaps Eneas exaggerated, but the founders of the PLP seemed to desire compromise. As Hartley Saunders explained, William Cartwright, in an article describing the formation of the party, stated that "it was not his intention to destroy white people, take their property or force them out of the country, nor was it his intention to replace incompetents or under-qualified people simply because of colour." H. M. Taylor had similar views, wishing to "broaden the scope of the membership to include a large divergence of political opinion, whose voices could be expressed on their governing body."[50] In fact, the PLP failed to attract a broad cross section of the community. Very few whites joined; John Purkiss, a Welshman married to a Bahamian, and Clive Cavill, an Australian engineer, were two of the few exceptions. The mixed-race and black middle class generally did not take the PLP seriously in its early years; many had little respect for the leadership. Upwardly mobile and working-class blacks, who had little to lose, were attracted to the PLP, seeing it as a means of liberation from discrimination and the iniquitous social structure.

Early in December 1953 a series of meetings was held to establish PLP branches. The first rally took place in Kemp Road at the St. James Masonic Lodge in the eastern district of New Providence. It was attended by about two hundred persons, who were addressed by Taylor, Pindling, Cartwright, and Urban Knowles, an early supporter. Taylor spoke on the evolution of the party system, explaining it as an "acceptable democratic" form of government. Pindling was critical of certain laws that retarded progress and had "roots deep in class discrimination." Cartwright bemoaned the high cost of living and how it affected the average family, and Urban Knowles referred to discriminatory practices. Two days later a meeting was held at the private residence of Richard E. Farquharson in Coconut Grove in the southern district, where twenty-one persons registered. The following evening more than a hundred gathered at the Girls Lydia Club on East Street; thirty persons became members of the party.[51] During the early days the four branches in New Providence—East Street, Balliou Hill Road, Kemp Road, and the Grove—all predominantly black, were active and were helped financially by William Cartwright.

Taylor, Stevenson, and Pindling traveled together in the mid-1950s to form additional branches in New Providence and the Out Islands. By 1956 they had attracted several black members with potential for leadership. These included Clarence Bain, an Androsian and strong supporter of Pindling, and Milo Butler, a successful politician and Nassau businessman and fiery orator, who brought creditability to the party. Others included Samuel White, a restaurateur in the Over-the-Hill area; Randol Fawkes, maverick trade union leader; Samuel Isaacs, a Nassau plumber and civil servant; Grant's Town merchants Charles A. Dorset and Charles Rodriguez; and Arthur Hanna, recently qualified in Britain as a lawyer and a friend of Lynden Pindling.

Most supporters were black and enthusiastically embraced the fledgling party. Bay Street politicians and their supporters took note, determined to destroy the movement. They began by pressuring the executives of the British South American Airways in London to act against PLP leader Taylor, an assistant accountant with the company in Nassau, who had been accused of dishonesty while in the public service and also of slander against P. E. Christie, a former member of the House of Assembly.[52] The Nassau manager of the airline, against his wishes, had no choice but to terminate Taylor in 1954. Taylor remained unemployed for some time but stayed with the party.[53] William Cartwright, one of the financial backers of the PLP, was also victimized by Bay Street and his creditors, who pressured him, forcing his resignation from the party. According to Hartley Saunders, who interviewed him, he was put in prison for fraud and was further intimidated by several Bay Street representatives, who tried to get him to label Stevenson and Pindling as communists.[54]

During 1954 the PLP met with members of the Bahamas Taxi Cab Union in order to persuade union members to join the party. After some deliberations, all the members who were financially able to do so joined the PLP. As Hartley Saunders opined, this union was advantageous as "it gave the PLP a very stable base because most of the taxi cab drivers were independent of the Bay Street Boys . . . not subject to direct intimidation."[55] The PLP also established a number of branches in the Out Islands. The first one opened on 28 March 1954 in Fresh Creek, Andros, led by Clarence Bain as chairman.[56] By the beginning of June that year Taylor announced that several other branches had been established in the Out Islands, including in Bimini; settlements in Stanyard Creek, Andros; the Bight, Cat Island; and Deadman's Cay, Long Island. Representatives from each branch, including Clarence Bain, were elected to attend the party's first political convention, which was held on 11 June 1954 in the Aurora Lodge Hall at the top of Charlotte Street in Nassau. The PLP platform had been published in both daily newspapers.[57]

The steadily increasing strength of the PLP continued to alarm the Bay Street establishment. In September 1954 an official at the Colonial Office in London informed Colonial Secretary A. G. Gardner-Brown in Nassau that the *New Commonwealth* of 19 August 1954 warned of "the possibility of colour trouble owing to the failure of the 'Bay Street Merchants,' either to explain their point of view or share undoubted prosperity with the coloured people. The point of view referred to here is that as Bay Street men have provided skill and money to develop the tourist industry, they are entitled to the lion's share of the proceeds." N. L. Mayle, the writer, was apprehensive that as the PLP developed, color troubles might arise. Gardiner-Brown was then asked to give an "assessment of the risk of colour trouble in The Bahamas within the next three or four years." He replied: "If my guess is better than yours, I would say that racial bitterness will increase and will, through the PLP, enter more and more into politics . . . if white Bahamians continue to believe that every coloured man has his price and that, with the payment of that price, life will go on as happily as before."[58]

Despite such activity, the PLP continued to grow. Colin Hughes opined that the PLP actually benefited from "the attacks of its enemies." The culmination of the printed attacks appeared in the *Nassau Guardian* under the pseudonym "C. Frank Candour." It questioned the party's claim to 450 members, scoffed at its lack of finance, and bitterly attacked leading PLP members including Stevenson and Taylor.[59] An angry PLP supporter, Henry Bowen, defended the leadership and retorted: "Nassau is stink with discrimination. I might go so far as to say that we have more racial discrimination here than anywhere else in the Caribbean or even some of the southern United States." He claimed that "C. Frank Candour" was in fact a Bay Street member of the House of Assembly and even named him. Hughes asserts that this "allegation" was never denied. Bowen, whose letter was published on the front page, added: "The Progressive Liberal Party is the black man's party, the same as the Chamber of Commerce is the white man's party. If the PLP fails in 1956, God help the Bahamian people."[60] In the *Herald* Cyril Stevenson also attacked Robert Symonette, president of the *Guardian,* who he claimed had written under the pseudonym, and alluded to his questionable racial antecedents.[61] Colonial officials whose assessment was that the PLP was "dying quietly" opined that it had received a "a revivifying transfusion from a most unexpected source." Additionally, they believed the "racial character of its propaganda" had hardened, and its "ultimate appeal to the electors and to the masses" was founded on racial discrimination.[62]

Etienne Dupuch, concerned about the PLP's "hate propaganda" and still very critical of the Bay Street politicians, was determined to oppose them. He spearheaded a new party, the Bahamas Democratic League (BDL), of which he became chairman. The BDL consisted of a number of moderate Bahamian nonwhites and whites, mainly young Englishmen. Three members of the House of Assembly joined the BDL, including Dupuch. The white lawyer and historian Colin Hughes, who was born in the Bahamas, was secretary while Dupuch was chairman. They both believed that Bahamians "need not be divided by racial differences." Hughes admitted that "at the time the overwhelming dominance of Bay Street seemed a much greater danger to

Bahamian racial harmony than did the handful of PLP members."[63] The first meeting of the BDL was held early in 1955 at the offices of the *Tribune*. Many persons from differing backgrounds turned up and seemed enthusiastic. Besides Dupuch and Hughes, these included blacks—Cleveland Eneas, A. Leon McKinney, Robert M. Bailey, M. Willie Rahming, and Samuel E. McPherson—the mixed-race Nigel Jones, and whites Hon. Reginald Farrington, Leslie Higgs, J. S. Johnson, Captain Leonard Thompson, and Englishman Trevor Marshall.[64] Dupuch was disappointed, however, that most of the nonwhites who had encouraged him to start the movement, and whom he nominated for various committees, did not attend, failing even to become members. He wrote later of his disappointment, concluding: "Had these men supported the Bahamas Democratic League, we might have had a respected and responsible racially integrated Opposition in the country today."[65]

Hughes reports that "a Memorandum of principles was prepared," and in February the BDL was officially established. Committees were appointed and contributed to the party's platform, which was completed in March 1956.[66] Dupuch presented several petitions to the House of Assembly on behalf of the party. One of the first to be laid on the table in the House of Assembly concerned the Collins Wall. As noted in chapter 5, bootlegging millionaire Ralph Collins, using nonwhite Bahamian laborers, had built a high wall topped with broken glass, nails, and rough-edged shells around his large estate just east of the city of Nassau. By the 1940s developers had purchased much of the area and proceeded to build several "suburban residential estates."[67] A wide road known as Collins Avenue was constructed from north to south of the development. Lots were sold to whites, mixed-race buyers, and upwardly mobile blacks. The area held the "germ of a new middle class," comprising migrants from the Out Islands and mixed-race and black people who were considered "respectable."[68] Collins's mansion was turned into a private racially segregated school, St. Andrews, after the Methodist school committee began to integrate Queen's College. The area became known as Centreville, and the residential suburban shopping center, constructed in part of the eastern section of the Collins estate, was called Palmdale. Just west and south of the wall were densely settled black areas, including part of the Over-the-Hill district. Lots were sold and purchased with the assumption that the wall, which was unbroken on the western side and partially intact to the south, would remain. As Nicolette Bethel demonstrated: "Almost immediately, therefore, the wall came to symbolize the segregation of Nassau, providing a physical barrier between the people considered 'respectable' by the society at large (many of them white and coloured) and others of 'suspicious' pedigree (the majority of them black)."[69]

Many of those who lived south and west of the wall worked as domestics and in other capacities. Rather than take the longer route to Palmdale and other eastern areas, they installed ladders at strategic points along the wall that were used by men, women, and children. It was not long before accidents occurred. A pregnant woman suffered a miscarriage after a fall and a boy broke a leg. Both were black and lived Over-the-Hill west of the wall. In 1955 the Bahamas Democratic League petitioned the House of Assembly on behalf of that neighborhood requesting that the wall be opened to allow pedestrian traffic. Dupuch, who had presented the petition, was appointed chairman of the committee but received no support from the other members, including Roland T. Symonette, who was one of the representatives for the eastern district. They argued that the landowners were opposed to the idea and had purchased the property with the certainty that the wall would not be torn down. Symonette presented a counter-petition from one hundred Centerville residents "asking that the wall be retained unbroken," arguing that "there was no occasion for access to the thickly populated areas west of the wall."[70] Dupuch was replaced as chairman, losing the initiative, and when a new select committee was appointed three subsequent petitions failed, all asking for the wall to be opened. The wall was not fully breached until 1959.[71]

The pro-establishment *Nassau Guardian* was critical of Dupuch and the *Tribune*. The *Guardian* defended the status quo:

> Any action by the House which does not support the position of these landowners will create a most dangerous precedent; it will render future real estate planning and development impossibly insecure; it will cause grave doubts in the minds of all present and future property owners of the inviolability of guarantees of privacy upon which their purchases were contingent in large measure. If there is an expectant mother, in this day and age, who displays such total disregard for her own health and that of the child she carries that she "jumps over" a wall—well a gate isn't going to solve her problems.[72]

The 1956 Resolution on Racial Discrimination

Five years before the 1956 resolution, musician and politician Bert Cambridge, representing the southern district, presented in the House of Assembly a petition "from certain citizens of New Providence re: discrimination against coloured Bahamians." The petition noted that in Canada, in Jamaica and other West Indian colonies, in many cities in the United States, principally the State of New York, and in the "Mother Country," laws had been passed to outlaw discrimination. Moreover, nonwhite Bahamians had fought in both World Wars and some continued to fight in Korea. Reviewing the discrimination that still existed in the colony against people of color—refusal of accommodation in hotels, failure in public business places to serve "decent and respectable citizens . . . because of the texture of their skin"—the petition requested that members of the House of Assembly enact laws to prohibit "discrimination on grounds of colour." The petition was signed by all white House members, priest Milton E. Cooper, lawyers K.G.L. Isaacs and Orville A. Turnquest, businessmen H. C. Carter, Edgar E. Bain, and U. J. Mortimer, J. P., and 802 others. Cambridge's request for the appointment of a select committee to consider the matter was defeated thirteen to seven by the Bay Street representatives, including Stafford Sands and R. T. Symonette. Interestingly, George W. K. Roberts, a Bay Street merchant, voted in favor of the petition.[73]

Complaints about racial discrimination continued. Both the PLP and the BDL abhorred the humiliating treatment of nonwhites. The PLP had included the elimination of racial segregation in its platform and was convinced that Bay Street politicians were unlikely to reverse their policies in this regard. The BDL was more moderate and perhaps did not "realize how deep racial prejudice had penetrated the core of Bahamian society."[74] Hartley Saunders believed the society was so divided that "there was no room for a moderate Party. It had to be one or the other and not an in-between."[75] Many members of the Citizens' Committee and other nonwhites felt uncomfortable with the militancy of the black adherents of the PLP. Their philosophy was to overthrow the Bay Street regime completely. Some thought the mixed-race members who dominated the leadership of the PLP were too moderate. Black leaders such as Milo Butler and Lynden Pindling, influenced by the civil rights movement in the United States and the nationalist movements in the West Indies, used racial issues in appealing to the black majority. Politics in the Bahamas was becoming polarized on color rather than purely class lines.[76]

Black labor leader and lawyer Randol Fawkes, who was later suspended from practicing law for two years, announced in February 1954 that he was petitioning the queen regarding a client, a "black man" who he thought had been sentenced unfairly, by an "all white" jury, to ten years for fraud in the post office. Fawkes, indignant and calling for a royal commission, saw this as "only one incident in a pattern of mal-administration experienced by black people in the Bahamas."[77] In May that year H. M. Taylor voted against increasing a grant to the Imperial Order of Daughters of the Empire's hospitality committee because it practiced racial discrimination. Taylor's request for a select committee was refused.[78]

The issue of racial discrimination not only affected nonwhite Bahamians; it caused embarrassment to Dupuch and others when foreign blacks, especially West Indians, suffered the indignity of the Bahamian discriminatory policy. Dupuch became personally involved in an incident in 1953 when Hugh Springer, eminent Barbadian barrister and registrar of the University College of the West Indies, was a victim of the Bahamas color bar. On an unscheduled stop at Nassau on a British Overseas Airways Corporation flight, Springer was unable to dine at the Prince George Hotel on Bay Street. While other passengers were taken to the hotel, Springer was invited to have dinner at the airport cafeteria. To avoid further humiliation, Springer contacted Etienne Dupuch, whom he had met in London. Dupuch hosted him to dinner and put him up for the night.[79]

The incident, widely publicized in the British press, brought protest from the West Indies, including a sharp letter to the Colonial Office from Sir Hugh Foot, governor of Jamaica.[80] The principal of University College of the West Indies, W. W. Grave, wrote to Sir Robert Neville, governor of the Bahamas, informing him of the incident, and launched a formal protest against "the treatment accorded to Mr. Springer."[81] Nearly two years later a similar incident occurred involving two well-known Jamaicans, physician Lenworth Jacobs and his wife. Traveling on BOAC, Dr. Jacobs and his wife had to spend a night in Nassau because of mechanical difficulties with an airplane. Local BOAC manager B.G.W. Wiggett was aware of other embarrassing incidents and discrimination suffered by nonwhites in Nassau, especially Jamaicans. The incidents had drawn criticism from the press in the United Kingdom and the Commonwealth and from Jamaica's governor, Sir Hugh Foot, and its Executive Council, which considered BOAC responsible for making arrangements to prevent such incidents taking place.[82] B.G.W. Wiggett, in a letter to the Bahamas governor, the earl of Ranfurly, advised that the airline was "firmly opposed to racial segregation and, as International carriers of high reputation, have responsibility to its passengers to provide first class hotel accommodation when required without regard to race, colour or creed." He further explained that BOAC had been able to protect "non-European passengers from discrimination and discourtesies, but only as a result of the individual goodwill and cooperation of certain hoteliers; but the absence of any firm policy to cover such eventualities makes each occasion one of anxiety and hazard." He pleaded with Ranfurly to take appropriate measures to prevent the continuation of further discriminatory incidents.[83]

Governor Ranfurly, clearly embarrassed, corresponded with H.R.H. Princess Alice, countess of Athlone and chancellor of the University College of the West Indies. He explained that he thought adequate arrangements had been made with the hotels "to cater for coloured travelers." Explaining that while he would "never have considered the arrangements perfect, they went as far as my Executive Council were prepared to go at this time, and the fact is that for two years now, with the cooperation of certain hotels, we have managed to avoid these disgraceful incidents." Ranfurly outlined what had happened. One hotel was closed for repairs; two others "were genuinely full." Dr. and Mrs. Jacobs, who were separated from the rest of the passengers, were taken by the commissioner of police to the Fort Montagu Hotel, where the manager, who had agreed to accept them, "knowing that they were coloured and who welcomed them at the door of the hotel, denied them accommodation as soon as the Commissioner of Police had left." The governor also stated that BOAC would not normally have used this hotel because its management "is notoriously bad . . . and because it has always adopted an anti-coloured attitude."[84]

The government of Jamaica also demonstrated its displeasure regarding discrimination in Nassau and Bermuda, where similar incidents had occurred affecting Jamaicans traveling on official business, including the Jacobses. Chief Minister Norman Manley, in early December 1955, issued a statement inviting BOAC to give "a positive assurance" that passengers traveling on routes that included Nassau and Bermuda "would never be exposed to insults of that kind." An official report from the Bahamas was sent to the Jamaican government, the result of action by the governor, BOAC, and a subcommittee appointed by the Executive Council, stating that all leading hotels in Nassau had issued statements to the press "saying that no discrimination will be permitted in these hotels in future." Additionally, the president of the Bahamas Hotels Association issued a public statement deeply regretting the Jacobs incident and giving assurance that members of the hotel association "agreed to accommodate all airline passengers without discrimination in future."[85]

Etienne Dupuch, had commented cautiously on the 1953 Springer episode that it was "just another one of those unpleasant incidents that should give thoughtful people in this community cause for serious pause." He warned in early January 1956: "The time has come when discrimination in all licensed public places in this British Colony will no longer be tolerated by the people at whom this indignity is leveled. Our people have been tolerant, patient under years of crushing insult. Their patience is now at a breaking point."[86] This was true of Dr. Cleveland Eneas, who forcefully expressed his opinion in reply to an uncomplimentary remark in the *Nassau Guardian* by columnist "Dinghy Joe," who implied that the tourist industry was of utmost importance and might suffer if public places were integrated. Eneas replied that he deplored the idea that Bahamians should "sacrifice everything that is principled on the altar of the tourist business. That I must creep and crawl and teach my children to creep and crawl in their own land so that we may attract tourists."[87]

Dupuch in 1956, more widely traveled and aware of the civil rights movement in the United States, was more outspoken. Having attended meetings of the Commonwealth Press Union in New Zealand, he met "Jerry" Fletcher, a Jamaican of English parentage and managing editor of the Jamaica *Gleaner*. Fletcher taunted him, showing him a clipping of the front page of the *Gleaner*'s account of the Jacobs incident in Nassau: "What kind of country do you live in, Etienne?" Dupuch, embarrassed, realizing that discrimination in public places had to be stopped, promised Fletcher that when he returned to Nassau he would "bust this business wide open or die in the attempt."[88]

Upon his return to Nassau, Dupuch began writing articles about discrimination in Nassau hotels and alluded to the Springer and Jacobs incidents. Criticizing the government for merely exploring the problem as it related to travelers passing through Nassau, he reiterated the urgency of the issue. During the first two weeks in January 1956, numerous letters on racial discrimination appeared in the *Tribune*. A. Leon McKinney, black businessman and founder of the Penny Savings Bank, questioned whether it was right for the Bahamas Hotel Association to offer accommodation to colored travelers and not Bahamians. He suggested that the government appoint a commission to study and report on the whole problem of segregation and discrimination and make recommendations to the legislature.[89] This letter probably inspired Dupuch.

Henry Taylor, chairman of the PLP, was also moved by the Springer and Jacobs incidents. The PLP in its platform vowed to eliminate racial discrimination in the colony. Taylor took immediate action, tabling a number of questions on the subject to the leader of government.[90] Speaker of the House of Assembly Asa Pritchard delayed putting the questions on the agenda for several meetings, and when he did they were not answered immediately.[91]

In the interim, Taylor states that he discussed his plan of action with several of his friends, including McKinney, who was also a friend of Dupuch. According to Taylor, Dupuch, who faced stiff competition from the PLP, was worried about his chances of being reelected in the eastern district, which he had represented since 1949. Dupuch felt he needed to impress voters in his nine-month-old party, the BDL, which had made little progress. His opponent in the eastern district was the handsome and popular Sammie Isaacs, a newcomer to politics but already a member of the National General Council of the PLP.[92]

Dupuch also discussed his chances with friends, including A. Leon McKinney, who Taylor states advised him to do something "spectacular," like bringing the question of discrimination to the floor of the House to gain support. McKinney warned Dupuch of Taylor's intention to do likewise and advised him to move swiftly. Dupuch gave notice on 17 January 1956 that he would move an anti-discrimination resolution in the House at its next meeting.

The resolution asked for a commission of inquiry to investigate all matters relating to discrimination in the colony: "Resolved that this House is of the opinion that discrimination in hotels, Theatres and other places in the Colony against persons on account of their race or colour is not in the public interest. Resolved further that this House is of the opinion that a commission Of Enquiry should be appointed under the Commissions of Enquiry Act to investigate all matters relating to such discrimination in the Colony with power to make recommendations for eliminating this evil by Legislation or otherwise."[93]

Taylor recalls that it was "an opportune move on the part of Mr. Dupuch and a well timed one. . . . Although Mr. Dupuch had 'beaten me to the deal' I was prepared to support his resolution." Indeed, the PLP made it known at public meetings that the resolution would be moved and debated on the floor of the House on 23 January. Hundreds of people, many of them supporters of the PLP, descended on the House "en masse," filling the galleries, the stairs, the lobby downstairs, and also the sidewalks and streets outside.[94] As Dupuch related: "Every seat in the gallery was occupied by coloured men and women. Halls and passage ways were crowded, and hundreds of coloured people milled around in the public square and streets outside the House of Assembly building the night I moved my resolution."[95]

Dupuch made an impassioned and lengthy speech. Requesting a public declaration whether Bahamians were one or two groups of people, he recalled meeting a young Bahamian in London recently who was ashamed to admit he was from the Bahamas because of its blatant color bar discrimination. Comparing the Bahamas with other West Indian tourist resorts and the United States, he deplored the Bahamas' notorious reputation for its callous treatment of nonwhite visitors and the humiliation suffered by Bahamians, and he dared the House to discuss a subject it had always avoided.[96] Bertram Cambridge, who himself had presented a similar petition, acknowledged that he was himself a victim of discrimination: "I have worked in hotels in this island and I know that common prostitutes are admitted to places on Bay Street because they are white and decent coloured people are refused admission."[97]

Other nonwhite members who endorsed the motion included Gerald Cash, Henry M. Taylor, Marcus Bethel, Eugene Dupuch, and C. R. Walker. Cash and Taylor recounted embarrassing incidents of discrimination that had recently occurred in Nassau. Cash, noting that people were reluctant to talk about racial issues, called for an open discussion.

The majority of whites maintained an "eloquent silence" but surprisingly, two supported Dupuch. Donald McKinney admitted that the racial problem was the biggest question facing the colony and queried whether the effect of discrimination on tourism might not be exaggerated. Dr. Raymond Sawyer saw no harm in appointing a commission to consider the matter. Frank Christie moved and it was carried by 11–9 that the resolution be referred to a select committee. This was the usual way of killing a motion.

When the speaker appointed Frank Christie as chairman of the committee, Dupuch sprang to his feet and protested. He recalled that "something in me cracked. I had promised Jerry Fletcher in New Zealand that, if necessary, I would die in the attempt. I knew the time had now come to throw discretion to the winds. I stood up, stepped back from my seat, and made the bitterest speech of my whole life."[98] The speaker ordered Dupuch to sit down. He refused, and the speaker threatened to have a police sergeant remove him. Dupuch continued his protest, but the speaker repeated his threat. Dupuch, who was pounding on the table, replied defiantly: "You may call the whole Police Force, you may call the whole British Army. . . . I will go to jail tonight, but I refuse to sit down, and I am ready to resign and go back to the people."[99]

The crowd, including many PLPs, suddenly rose in loud protest, declaring that Mr. Dupuch "would not be touched by anyone." A roar went up from those gathered in the square, and the House of Assembly was in turmoil. Donald McKinney, anxious that there be no violence, moved quickly for an adjournment. The speaker's procession from the chair was interrupted by the crowd, who surged protectively around Dupuch, their hero. In fact, although he denied it, according to eyewitnesses the crowd lifted Dupuch on their shoulders and carried him around the square. PLP leaders took advantage of the moment and addressed the people rallying in the square.[100]

It was ironic, as H. M. Taylor and other leaders of the PLP recognized, that Dupuch, a strong critic of the party, had gained mileage by supporting a plank in the PLP's platform. The PLP had made progress in enhancing public awareness among the masses through its meetings and the columns of the *Nassau Herald* edited by Cyril Stevenson. Public opinion had changed and had become more racially charged. While Dupuch was being lauded, members of the Bay Street clique were booed and heckled by a large crowd as they emerged from the House. Leading white lawyer and parliamentarian Stafford Sands and his wife were followed down Bay Street by a crowd of some sixty or seventy people "booing and jeering in choruses."

Stafford Sands, incensed, along with other members of the House including Speaker Asa Pritchard and Frank Christie, met with the governor the next morning to lodge a protest and followed it up with a four-page letter in which he reiterated his views and a request that "similar disturbances will not occur in the future." He threatened that "if there is any repetition in this matter," he would have no choice but to visit London to seek support from British parliamentarians. Sands also stated that he could not help feeling that "the lack of firmness on the part of the Police encouraged the crowd to further vociferation." He and the other members of the group felt that "at the present moment there is a very serious situation developing, and that any lack of firmness on the part of the Police or any impression in the minds of the general public of weakness on the part of the Police may well permit more serious conditions to develop." Sands and his colleagues, however, did not see the incident as "a widespread demonstration" but rather as one "stemming entirely from a small group," perhaps no more than two hundred, but opined that if left unchecked, "many will develop into the leaders of mob-disturbance."[101]

There was almost immediate reaction from the majority of the Nassau hotels and restaurants. They issued statements in the newspapers informing the public that their doors were open to all, regardless of race. Most denied that there had ever been discrimination and said, as did Charles Wong, proprietor of the Golden Dragon, that regardless of color, anyone who was well behaved, properly dressed, and able to pay would be welcome.[102]

The Bahamas Hotel Association, in early February after discussion with a subcommittee of the Executive Council, had acknowledged that the Jacobs incident was "regrettable" and was due to a misunderstanding over the reservations made by BOAC for its passengers. At that time all members of the association had agreed to accommodate in-transit airline passengers.[103]

When the House met the following evening, Dupuch observed that there were "larger crowds in the Square" than the night before. "The atmosphere was tense," and the speaker was furious. He quickly called the newly arrived commissioner of police, Englishman Colchester-Wemyss, and ordered him to "clear the corridors of the House." Fearful that the commissioner might overreact, precipitating violence, Dupuch "kept quiet." The House recessed for a week.

Frank Christie called several meetings of the anti-discrimination committee. In the *Tribune* Dupuch assured the public that considerable progress was being made, exhorted people to "be patient . . . but vigilant," and advised that legislation from other countries and colonies was being obtained by the committee, which gave an interim report to the House of Assembly on 20 February 1956.[104] The resolution returned by the committee on 29 February was practically the same as the first part of Dupuch's, which condemned discrimination in "public" places on grounds of race and color. This part of the resolution was unanimously passed by the House.

The committee's resolution, however, had rejected Dupuch's original request for a commission of inquiry and Gerald Cash's argument that legislation was necessary. Cash brought a minority report and stated that

> while I cannot disagree with the resolution as a first interim report, I am certain that the resolution in itself is not the solution to the problem of discrimination in public places. I am convinced that legislation should be enacted to assure the public their rights. To protect those rights and to provide remedies in the event of a breach of any of those rights of not being discriminated against in hotels, theatres and other public places in the Colony because of race or colour, I do advocate and will support such legislation. The resolution does not do that and is merely a record of the opinion of the House which is not in any way binding on hotels, theatres, and public places.

Etienne Dupuch disagreed with Cash, abandoning the second part of his resolution. At the time he admitted that legislation might be needed later. In retrospect, Dupuch declared that the resolution almost overnight changed the whole social structure of the colony without a single disturbance or drop of blood.[105]

Dupuch's moderation and compromise were severely criticized by the

PLP. Taylor, its chairman, like Cash, said that the resolution was a step forward but no solution; it did not go far enough.[106] A commission of inquiry would have exposed the severe racism that existed and those who perpetuated it, namely the majority of House members. Bay Street politicians obviously feared the repercussions of opening up the racial issue, and Etienne Dupuch, who could have gained political mileage among blacks, also faced economic and political realities. He needed to make a decent living and support his large family and did not wish to upset his few white liberal benefactors, who kept him afloat financially in 1956 when he suffered a serious loss of business. He admitted in his autobiography, *Tribune Story*: "At the political level were Sir George Roberts and the Hon. Godfrey Higgs. These men fought my battles in and out of season . . . at the business level, Mr. John Burnside of the General Hardware, Mr. Bert Kelly of Kelly Motor Co., Mr. Neville Sands of The Tiny Shop, and Mr. Joseph Garfunkel of the Home Furniture Co. didn't say a word to me. All they did was quietly increase their business with *The Tribune*."[107]

Taylor, writing later, admitted that "many responsible people" wished for gradual and more moderate change as far as racial issues were concerned. But he conceded that "this was not to be," as "the racial propaganda put out by the party, not only did not subside but eventually there was an abortive attempt to put the discrimination process in reverse."[108]

The 1956 resolution, as Hughes and Doris Johnson argued, demonstrated a new determination by blacks. They had made their presence felt around the House of Assembly and could force Bay Street to back down: "The barriers had begun to fall." Doris Johnson attributed this new confidence felt by black Bahamians to the PLP.[109] The successful passage of half of the resolution also exploded the myth that desegregation would turn tourists away and destroy the economy. Tourism in fact increased dramatically after 1956.

The incident also demonstrated the intransigent attitude of the mercantile elite—their unwillingness to yield unless pushed and their determination to do all in their power to secure their own ends. The select committee refused to consider the second half of the resolution, which would have allowed for a commission of inquiry to air the whole issue and possibly recommend the passage of legislation. Dupuch did not insist on an anti-discrimination bill, as he believed that "the change could be brought about by custom and there was an old saying 'custom is stronger than law.'"[110]

According to Dupuch and Doris Johnson, immediately after the passage of the resolution, mixed-race and black people flocked to the hotels, restaurants, and the Savoy Theatre. Johnson commented: "The resolution was enough to kindle the courage of thousands of black Bahamians. Jubilantly, they converged on Bay Street almost at once and began testing the anti-discrimination proposal by entering places forbidden to them until now. Many registered at hotels and enjoyed one night of comparative luxury before returning to their small wooden houses 'over the hill.' ... The PLP had created a climate in which almost miraculous things could happen. Sweetly encouraged, the black Bahamian was walking tall in his homeland at last." However, this trend did not continue, because as Dupuch observed, most blacks could not afford to frequent such places and were not comfortable in all-white establishments.[111]

Despite Dupuch's claim that there was revolutionary change in the social structure after the passing of the resolution, discrimination in public places took some time to be completely broken down. The hotels claimed that they did not discriminate because of color, but certain establishments did not welcome blacks. They subtly practiced segregation by making excuses; for example, scantily clad white tourists would be served in some establishments, but blacks would be turned away because "they were improperly dressed" or "it was a membership club." Sir Clifford Darling, a PLP senator at the time, said that as late as 1964 he was refused service in a downtown restaurant.[112]

Real estate was governed by restrictive covenants in certain areas, such as Westward Villas and the Grove off West Bay. Realtors, who were predominantly white, did not even show certain properties to nonwhites. As late as the early 1970s a black couple answering an advertisement for the sale of apartments in the exclusive Cable Beach area visited the complex and were told that none were available. The next day a young English lawyer who was a friend of theirs inquired and was given red carpet treatment. Not only were several apartments available, but so was financing.[113]

With few exceptions, among them the Penny Savings Bank, banks and other financial institutions did not employ nonwhites as tellers or executives. In 1958 the only blacks hired were cleaners and messengers. The St. Andrew's School color bar was not broken until 1967, when Milo Butler's grandchildren were admitted with urging from the Progressive Liberal Party.[114]

The Colonial Office, while noting that discrimination in hotels and public places had ceased, acknowledged that private clubs were another matter. It seemed satisfied with this position, admitting that "it was up to the membership." Membership clubs such as the Nassau Yacht Club did not admit blacks or mixed-race persons until the late 1960s, while the Royal Nassau Sailing Club maintained white membership until very recent years. In the Out Islands the Peace and Plenty Hotel discriminated on the basis of color and had to be advised by Governor Arthur in 1959 of the passage of the 1956 resolution.[115] Racial discrimination persisted in the Bahamas well into the 1970s, and some would argue it still exists.

The 1956 General Election and Its Aftermath

Having made its presence felt around the House of Assembly, the PLP exuded new confidence in its 1956 election campaign. The membership was said to have grown to about five thousand, with nine branches in New Providence and thirty in the Out Islands.[116] At its second convention in 1955, it had amended its platform to include a plan of attack against racial discrimination. PLP leaders continued their criticism of racial discrimination, which still existed despite Dupuch's resolution. They encouraged crowds to congregate and demonstrate in a racially charged atmosphere, thus creating near hysteria on the part of the white population, a section of whom demanded that a warship be present in the port of Nassau on polling day.[117] Governor Ranfurly stated "the racial issue predominates. . . . Tension in some quarters is undoubtedly high." He expressed concern about "the government's ability to maintain order should riots occur." He inquired what assistance would be available if reinforcements were needed from the outside, and he concluded that "the state of alarm which exists amongst a large portion of the white community cannot be entirely ignored."[118]

Secretary of State Alan Lennox-Boyd felt obliged to acquaint Prime Minister Anthony Eden with Ranfurly's concerns and the threat of possible violence leading up to the elections scheduled for between 8 and 20 June. Describing the archaic constitution, he stated that reforms in social, administrative, and labor legislation were difficult due to the disinterest of the ruling class of mostly white businessmen "who have been notably selfish and narrow minded in their attitude." Should riots occur, he thought the local police force might "prove inadequate" but informed Prime Minister Eden that two companies of British infantry battalions could be flown in from Jamaica in case of emergency.[119]

Henry Taylor, chairman of the PLP, also expressed concern about the racial propaganda being promulgated by some factions in the party and "finding fertile soil." Personally, he was opposed to it altogether and worried that "a hate campaign" would damage his popularity: "It was a fire that was lying dormant and had been present in the hearts and minds of the Bahamian coloured people for years and generations. They consciously did not know it was there and smouldering within them." Other members of the party and other Bahamians, including Etienne Dupuch, had similar feelings. Taylor was caught in a difficult position, as the PLP was drawing thousands of black Bahamians who were attracted by the racial rhetoric. He felt that any protest to this "approach" toward the masses would be committing political suicide. As he admitted, "The PLP's racial propaganda increased and got stronger in the ranks of the organization. The stronger it got, the more it was being accepted by the masses."[120]

The PLP fought its first election as a party in 1956, nominating fourteen candidates, three of whom failed to nominate as candidates, while the pro–Bay Street group fielded twenty-six candidates. The latter's campaign, while capitalizing on their achievements in bringing prosperity to the Bahamas, warned against PLP's "mess of promises" and also the PLP's alleged plan to introduce income tax, always anathema to Bahamians. A letter writer signing himself "Truth" stated: "The Bay Street group, which has the majority of members in the old House, is the backbone of the Colony."[121] Bay Street politicians also issued a personal attack against the *Herald's* editor Cyril Stevenson in the *Nassau Guardian*, copies of which were distributed in the Andros constituency.[122]

According to Ranfurly, the campaign "was fought, to all intents and purposes, on a racial basis and much bitter feeling was aroused which is likely to display itself for some time to come."[123] His observation was accurate. The *Nassau Guardian's* editor, Benson McDermott, following the results of the election, and critical of the lack of experience among the leadership of the PLP, demonstrated his strong support for the Bay Street candidates, stating that since the Bahamas economy was based principally on the tourist industry, "the Assembly should have among its members a strong contingent of men with wide business experiences."[124]

Six days before the elections in New Providence, Lynden Pindling, contesting a seat for the first time, wrote an article in the *Nassau Herald* that revealed the plight of the masses. He emphasized the economic and social problems facing the black majority, deploring the conditions under which they lived: "We see that our people should not be allowed to live in the squalor of two-room shacks, some of which are less strong and less healthy than some chicken coops we know." Pindling was convinced that health and education were among the "greatest problems" facing Bahamians. He believed it was government's duty to develop its people but explained: "our Government has been somewhat unique in that it has thought more of the developments of sun, sand and sea than the development of the lives of human beings. . . . We must have more schools and teachers . . . to fit our children for tomorrow." Pindling stressed that the public school system should include "Secondary School subjects." Addressing health he stated: "Hand in Hand with the education of its people goes the health of its people. To develop them to the fullest, care must be taken that they have good food and medical attention." There were oblique references to race: "Now more than any time in our history . . . a great awakening is sweeping across our people. . . . Once a blind people, we are now washing the scales from our eyes. . . . Once a tortured and crippled people, we are now loosening the shackles that bound us and stepping forth into the world as honourable and free and equal men. We have nothing to lose but our chains of second-class citizenship and lack of opportunity."[125] The PLP gave no apologies for playing the race card.

The PLP won six of the twenty-nine seats in the House of Assembly in the 1956 elections, four being in New Providence and two in Andros. Despite its failure to change the House of Assembly's racial composition, the election was important, the PLP winning one-third of the votes cast. Randol Fawkes and Lynden Pindling won the two seats in the southern district of New Providence; Samuel (Sammie) Isaacs and Milo Butler were successful in the eastern district and western district respectively. In the Out Islands Cyril Stevenson and Clarence Bain defeated two "right wing" candidates and were elected for Andros. In Long Island just the opposite occurred. Taylor, the leader and chairman of the PLP, and Ragged Islander Lochinvar Lockhart lost to Bay Street candidates D. E. D'Albenas and Peter D. Graham. Dupuch's moderate middle-class party, the Bahamas Democratic League, was soundly rejected. Dupuch's defeat brought comment from Ranfurly: "The Right Wing accomplished its objective of getting him out of the House, but wisdom in their tactics is open to question. Dupuch was a moderate and as things have turned out he could have wielded considerable influence on the new Left Wing opposition."[126] However, it is doubtful that Dupuch could have had any influence on the new leadership of the PLP. While in New Providence elections were held for the first time on the same day, those on the Out Islands were spread over more than a two-week period, giving the advantage to the powerful Bay Street oligarchy by using an outdated plural electoral system.

More significantly, Taylor's defeat heralded the rise of Pindling, who was chosen over Fawkes as parliamentary leader of the PLP. Randol Fawkes was the obvious choice for leader. Highly respected, he was popular and had worked tirelessly to change the antiquated labor laws. Taylor thought him the "most popular" and "respected member" of the six elected, although he was considered to be a loner and sometimes erratic. Taylor and Stevenson met to discuss the matter. Taylor advised that Stevenson deserved to be considered for the leadership, being a founding member of the PLP, and said he would have suggested Stevenson for the post but for his fair complexion: he thought Stevenson "would not have a chance to win an election in the Council." Taylor and Stevenson, despite their respect for Fawkes, were more impressed with Pindling and engineered his election as parliamentary leader of the party. Fawkes was disappointed, was often at odds with the PLP, and was in and out of the party.[127]

Pindling, more of a "man of the people, darker in complexion than Taylor, less Anglicized than other university graduates like [Paul] Adderley and [Orville] Turnquest, and still a successful professional man with whom the rising Negro middle class could identify," was a natural leader with outstanding ability. Having met many of the leaders of the emerging nations, he was aware of the struggles of colonial subjects and was determined to change the status quo. In a speech made at his call to the Bahamian Bar, he stated that the traditional view of a lawyer's task as "a defender of criminals or a draughtsman of wills . . . today . . . is far greater. He must reach forward out of the realm of pure law and delve into the life of this community; he must unravel the mysteries of unrest and dissension and assist in the promotion of a good life for his fellow citizens."[128] Politically astute and charismatic, Pindling also showed personal moderation and pragmatism, which combined with his knowledge of constitutional matters to make him a successful leader. He realized that the racial factor was an important tool in achieving power. At the PLP's victory parade in 1956 he declared that "a new Negro was born on June 8th; a Negro who has been knocking on the door asking for representation . . . a Negro who said 'If others will not represent us, we will represent ourselves.'"[129]

As Clifford Darling stated, the 1956 election, however, "was not without its problems"—the usual bribery and corruption. After the 1956 election women on at least one Out Island could be seen wearing £5 notes on their dresses. In the Abaco district a charge of bribery was made by "a disgruntled candidate" against former deputy speaker Frank H. Christie, who was charged in the Magistrate's Court. The case was adjourned and eventually dropped.[130] But Jonathan Rolle of Cedar Harbour, a resident of Cooper's Town, gave a vivid account of the corruption that was endemic in the Bahamas for generations. The usual procedure began with the candidate acquainting the organizer that he and his colleagues were contesting the election and that "he must do his best to get the boys [seemingly all black] to support himself and Mr. Johnson." No suggestion was made that any money was involved. Shortly before the election a further meeting took place between Christie and the organizer, on a boat. Questions were asked if everything was alright and if he "had the boys together." He was told he had to pay "the boys for their day." Later the organizer returned to the boat and collected the money, "which was to be distributed to the boys after they had voted." The payments were not distributed on Election Day but the following day. The "boys" were paid £10 each and also received rum, beers, and sodas. Those receiving money were named by Jonathan Rolle, who gave a sworn statement to police officers in Cooper's Town on 20 June 1956.[131] Clifford Darling commented: "At last, the fresh, new political climate in The Bahamas made it possible for someone to stand up and bear witness to the election bribery that the Bay Street Boys had used for years amongst the black Bahamians to assure them of their continued, iron-fisted control of the Colony."[132]

Corruption, it seemed, was also perpetuated by some ministers of religion (presumably Protestant and black), who at election time would accept large sums of money from politicians depending on them to influence the votes of their congregations. According to Doris Johnson, "Pop" Symonette, as he was affectionately called, leader of the Bay Street Boys, openly declared it was the "Black Baptists, who kept them in power."[133] Bribery was common in New Providence and the Out Islands. Etienne Dupuch in the *Tribune's* editorial of 12 May 1956, shortly before the election, called for "honest and decent leadership from their ministers." He "deplored ministers 'who accepted dispersed bribery'" as "a great betrayal and degradation of the people when it is their duty to uplift."[134] The editor of the pro-establishment *Nassau Guardian* defended the ministers, stating: "It would seem unthinkable for anyone who cares for the good of the community to try to drag religious prejudices into a political campaign, but it has happened right here in Nassau."[135] Accusing Dupuch, a Roman Catholic and a candidate, of "religious prejudice," and of making "a desperate effort to stave off defeat," the *Guardian's* editor continued the attack: "In what appears to be a pretty clear effort to pit church against church, it has in fact pitted race against race."[136]

The House of Assembly met on 9 July 1956, when for the first time, newly elected members of a political party attended and were sworn in. After the PLP members had taken the oath of allegiance, Pindling rose and informed members that for the first time in Bahamian history persons belonging to a political party had been elected, and its members represented more than half the population of the Bahamas. His request for full recognition of the Progressive Liberal Party, its platform, and himself as parliamentary leader was refused by Speaker Asa Pritchard. The party in return began its opposition by voting against the election of the speaker and deputy speaker.

The following day the international press described the opening of the House, including a Reuters dispatch datelined Nassau, 10 July 1956 and headed with one word: "Deterioration." In a speech opening the House of Assembly, Ranfurly "deplored what he described as the noticeable deterioration in human relations between whites and coloured people in the colony. Outside the House, hundreds of coloured men and women gathered in Parliament Square to shout 'PLP all the way' slogan of the Progressive Liberal Party, which secured six seats in the 29-member House in last month's election." The governor was distressed by the deterioration as he had "a profound belief in the natural friendliness and kindness of the Bahamian people." He, like Pindling, informed members that the six seats won by "the leftwing P.L.P., whose candidates were running for the first time, embrace more than half of the Colony's population."[137]

Similarly, the *Daily Mail* of 11 July 1956 published an article with the headline "Trouble Brews in Our Paradise Isles." Reporter Christopher Lucas wrote of Ranfurly's call for sweeping reforms following the demonstration of about 3,000 "coloured" people outside the Parliament building demanding "equal rights." He appealed to all Bahamians to lay aside any bitterness recent elections might have engendered. Then, to the amazement of white members, he called for direct taxation for the Bahamas and urged local businessmen to contribute a larger share to the "island's revenue instead of placing the major burden on poorer people crippled by heavy taxes on food, clothing and daily necessities." Lucas concluded that he had spoken to "an influential resident" who told him on the telephone: "There is no evidence of rioting or strikes so far. But the present unrest could develop into trouble." Erroneously, he stated, "It is the first time the coloured people ever started putting up a fight for their rights."[138]

At the second meeting of the House, PLP supporters were again out in full force. Ranfurly, fearing the outbreak of lawlessness, described the scene: "PLP supporters thronged the precincts of the House and cheered whenever they could catch a glimpse of one of their Members in action. Unpopular Right Wingers were booed on coming out of the House and had to push their way through a hostile crowd. Fortunately, no incident occurred, but the Speaker found the occasion sufficiently menacing to ring me up at 1 a.m. and ask me to listen to the roar of the crowd."[139] The Bay Street politicians were worried about such behavior and the openness with which black people were expressing themselves. Their uneasiness about possible violence led them to send a delegation to Government House to complain and to inform Ranfurly that "protective measures proposed were completely inadequate."[140]

Ranfurly did not appear to be worried but nevertheless took action to pacify the Bay Street contingent and to protect them from the jeers and ridicule of the demonstrators. He stated at the time: "In view of the emotional state of both races and of the fact the P.L.P. were undoubtedly encouraging crowds not only to congregate but also to demonstrate, it became necessary to restrict certain areas in the vicinity of the House during the hours that members were arriving, sitting and leaving."[141] The PLP reacted immediately by sending a telegram to the Colonial Office protesting the governor's action as "undemocratic in the current stage of political development and also highly provocative." Taylor, Stevenson, and Pindling demanded immediate action by the Colonial Office.[142]

After meeting with the PLP leaders, Ranfurly advised them that "interruptions of the business of the House and molestation of the members could not be tolerated, and that it was therefore necessary to close to the public the area in the immediate vicinity of the House." However, the governor indicated that "orderly gatherings" were permissible, and in the case of a very large crowd (300 to 400 people), supervision of "a strong body of Police" would be necessary. He also informed the Colonial Office that the Bay Street men admitted they had overreacted, adding that their "predictions were without foundation."[143] Nevertheless, the "Right Wing" adjourned the House of Assembly until January 1957.

Asked by the Colonial Office to give his views on the colony's situation "in the days to come," Ranfurly initially refused but then commented truthfully on its position during the summer of 1956. He stated that there was a need for the "majority" to compromise and for the "'minority' whose sole approach at present is the racial angle" to cooperate.

Appeals to mob hysteria will, I anticipate, continue until such a time as things have had a chance of settling down, but for the present have no reason whatever to believe that the PLP itself is interested in disorder or violence in achieving its ends. The leaders have themselves stated to me that although fully conscious of their weak position as a minority party in the House, they are interested only in constitutional methods of achieving their "platform." They also say, as no doubt they would, that they expect the next Election to return them as the majority party.[144]

Encouraged by the growing support, mainly among blacks, but annoyed by the long adjournment of the House, PLP leaders prepared to visit London on the "Crusade for Freedom." In early October 1956 a delegation made up of Pindling, Taylor, and Butler met with officials, including the head of the West Indies section of the Colonial Office and the parliamentary undersecretary, Lord Lloyd, in London to complain about the "widespread bribery and corruption which has long been associated with elections in the Colony" and to press for constitutional and electoral reforms. Colonial officials were diplomatic but noncommittal. Taylor highlighted the major difficulties of the electoral system, namely, the restricted franchise—limited to males, the plural vote, the company vote, and the existence of bribery and corruption. Milo Butler, emphasizing the racial inequalities, stated: "If the PLP did not get what it wanted they would have to seek it for themselves which would not be a pleasant process." He added that "The PLP was the tool to end them."[145] Pindling stressed the party's intention to do everything possible by constitutional means "but as the representative of a very turbulent constituency himself, he could not hide the truth of what Mr. Butler had said."[146] Acting Governor of the Bahamas K. M. Walmsley opined that the "Crusade," although used basically to bring constitutional issues to the attention of the British government, also served to keep the leaders "in the public eye during so long an adjournment."[147]

Following the meetings in London Philip Rogers, an officer in the Colonial Office, in a secret and personal letter to Governor Ranfurly written on the instructions of ministers and dated 17 October 1956, expressed concern about possible future developments in the colony. The consensus was: "The Bahamas is heading for racial and political trouble through the present 'policy' being pursued by the Bay Street gang." There was fear that "unless the moderate elements of the P.L.P. receive some encouragement and have some success all experience suggests that they will be outbidden and driven out by extremists."[148]

Rogers proposed in the letter that it might be a good idea to meet with the Bay Street group to determine their plans and whether they would be willing to make some concessions. The manner in which he ended the letter was not very optimistic. "While we are under no illusion about the possibility of achieving miracles by changing the whole attitude of Bay Street, such a visit would, we think, afford an opportunity for some straight talking which might make a little dent in the 'old guard's' armour."[149] Ranfurly replied, confessing that he could make no "predictions." Admitting that there were troublesome elements in the colony, he categorized them as electoral inequities, constitutional ambitions, a few unprincipled "rabble-rousers," an "extremely ignorant and easily led electorate, which is predominantly coloured," and perhaps most difficult of all, "a recalcitrant, stubborn and politically obtuse right wing—not very numerous but extremely powerful in the material sense and pretty unscrupulous."[150] Ranfurly was alarmed to learn that some of the "right wingers" commented that "the Colony has got on very well during the last six months with the House adjourned, and they can see no reason for the House to meet for any length of time in January, as the essential matters can be disposed of quickly and the remainder can be assigned to Committees. Anything more likely to offend the P.L.P, I cannot imagine."[151]

However, Ranfurly characterized the "right wingers" as "awful cowards" who were frightened during and after the general elections in 1956 but had "regained their confidence." He believed that certain factors could decrease political tensions, including the prevailing prosperity and, in his opinion, the "virtual" nonexistence of racial discrimination. The governor acknowledged that while it was "easy to say that every white appointment to office is discrimination against colour, and it is true that the majority of whites will always continue to oppose the encroachment of coloured people into public office . . . that is about all it amounts to, and whoever is administering the Government should be able to maintain a reasonable balance between the two races, at least to the extent that racial discrimination should never be a very genuine issue."[152] In Ranfurly's opinion, Bay Street politicians would "do just enough in the next few years to keep the pot from boiling over . . . they will try to move towards a more responsible form of Government, but with the main object of getting more power and control into their own hands and no-one else's. The pot will therefore continue to simmer until the next General Election is on the horizon, and then I have little doubt there will be trouble."

He had a low opinion of Bahamians generally, at least the Bay Street group, describing them as "venal people; commerce and piracy are in their blood; politics are a profitable business; and I don't see how one could give too much responsibility until men of integrity and morality begin to show themselves far more than they do at the present time."[153]

In February 1957 what seemed a trivial incident was blown out of proportion, demonstrating the prejudice and attitude of the white elite. Assistant Secretary of State for the Colonies F. Kennedy visited Nassau and, along with Colonial Secretary F. A. Noad, was hosted by the PLP leaders at a private dinner. It had been agreed that politics would not be discussed. After a series of toasts, including one to "Our guests" from Cyril Stevenson, Kennedy replied with the toast to "the PLP." He was rudely criticized by the *Nassau Guardian*, and the majority of Bay Street politicians took exception to his "interference" in Bahamian affairs and his "sociability" with and "legitimation" of the

PLP. Blaming Noad for this so-called indiscretion, they withheld half of his gratuity when his contract ended. Not only did this annoy the PLP followers—it received a strong reaction from Dupuch, who challenged "this brand of boorish intolerance [of] which the *Guardian* is so often guilty."[154]

Later in 1957 Taylor and Pindling wrote to the new governor, Sir Raynor Arthur, and again met with Colonial Office officials, submitting their views on constitutional reform, which included universal adult suffrage, abolition of the plural and company vote, reduction of House of Assembly terms from seven to five years, and establishment of one-member constituencies. They also requested reforming the Legislative and Executive Councils and asked for the introduction of a ministerial system of government and semi-responsible government.[155] These requests were mainly opposed by the Bay Street politicians, but under pressure from the governor and the Colonial Office, they appointed a Select Committee on Constitutional Reform. However, Arthur, writing confidentially to Secretary of State Lennox-Boyd, described their report as "an attempt to ensure the effective political power should be exercised forever by the group of rabid white reactionaries which at present has a majority in the House of Assembly, which is locally called the Bay Street Group."[156]

Taylor, leader of the PLP, wrote to both Lennox-Boyd and Lord Lloyd at the Colonial Office expressing the PLP's desire for constitutional change but stressing the party's disagreement with the report. In his letter to Lloyd he explained that the PLP had ousted a member (Fawkes) for "for non-co-operation," and for signing the report, thus embarrassing the party.[157] It is interesting to note that realtor Harold Christie, on a visit to Philip Rogers at the Colonial Office, informed him that the Bay Street men "think that they only have a 5 to 7 year period (until the next election) before their predominance is very seriously threatened by, and perhaps lost to the coloured members. They have put forward their plan for constitutional change in order to enable them in that time to entrench their position in certain respects." Christie, though, was in favor of modifying the proposals and making some concessions to "the coloured Left Wing group."[158] Colonial Office officials looked forward to meeting with a Bay Street delegation. An unforeseen and dramatic event would "serve as a catalyst" to introduce reforms urged by the PLP and the Colonial Office.

8

※

THE 1958 GENERAL STRIKE
AND ITS AFTERMATH

The 1942 riot had demonstrated the deep dissatisfaction of the masses with the status quo. Small improvements were passed, including trade union legislation, but it was defective and severely restricted membership in a union. Politically though, the PLP, the first successful party to be established in the Bahamas, was making progress. Buoyed by winning six seats in 1956, the party made demands for electoral reform and constitutional advances. Also using the *Herald* to spread their agenda, they lashed out against injustices in the society. Additionally, the PLP held rallies at which fiery speeches were delivered, sponsored public demonstrations in downtown Nassau while the House was in session, and debated furiously in that chamber. Frequent cables and a delegation of protest were also sent to the Colonial Office in London. Labor union matters resulting in confrontation and the general strike would give the PLP, to which many union members belonged, the opportunity to assist in forcing change.

Significant and guarded progress had been made on the race issue following the 1956 resolution. While "overt acts of social discrimination (in the late '50s) had become rare," subtle discriminatory practices persisted.[1] Both in Nassau and the Out Islands, white communities sought to preserve their racial integrity by isolating themselves from brown and black people as much as possible. Private clubs, elite societies, and charitable organizations still practiced segregation, as did some business houses (including banks) and certain schools, especially the racially exclusive St. Andrews and to a lesser extent Queen's College. Nonwhites were never promoted to certain top posts in the civil service. Mixed-race and black leaders felt indignant about the lingering discriminatory practices in Nassau, while the Colonial Office recognized that color and class were closely linked to economics: "As it happens there are very few, if any coloured Bahamians who have the financial means to keep up with those who constitute the Colony's 'Upper set,' and they are not likely to achieve the necessary riches if the ruling class has anything to do with it."[2]

Racial tension was real during and following the 1958 general strike. Politics and labor unions converged. The PLP and the Taxi Cab Union, supported by many other unions, became the catalysts for the strike. H. M. Taylor was still leader of the party, but according to Arthur Hanna, a close friend and colleague, from 1956 Pindling saw himself as leader of the PLP.[3]

Randol Fawkes, also from Over-the-Hill, was a graduate of the Government High School. He trained locally as a lawyer under Thaddeus A. Toote, one of the early Bahamian black lawyers, and joined the PLP as well but was more aligned to the labour movement. Fawkes, like Tubal Uriah Butler in Trinidad, was obsessed with a sense of mission in seeking to bring more dignity to the black masses. Fawkes defended a mixed-race post office clerk who had been charged (he thought unfairly) with misappropriating money from the treasury. When an all-white jury brought in a guilty verdict, the clerk was sentenced to prison for thirteen years. Fawkes criticized the judge and appealed the verdict. This angered the legal establishment, and Fawkes's enemies were pleased when Fawkes was found guilty of misconduct regarding a will, before Chief Justice Sir Oswald Bancroft, and was suspended from practicing at the Bahamian Bar for two years. Fawkes spent a self-imposed exile in New York. There he experienced the beginning of the civil rights movement and was inspired by a speech Emperor Haile Selassie delivered while visiting Harlem in July 1954 and by the singing of powerful black entertainer Paul Robeson. Fawkes returned home to Nassau determined "to overthrow the white oligarchy" and, like Moses, deliver his people.[4] Both Pindling and Fawkes, members of the House of Assembly since 1956 for the south, were deeply influenced by the civil rights movement in the United States. They followed Martin Luther King Jr.'s philosophy of nonviolence and met with him. Fawkes invited King, while on a private visit to the Bahamas, to speak to a capacity audience of members of the Bahamas Federation of Labour (BFL).

Fawkes sought to bring about change through the mobilization of the trade union movement. Establishing an employment agency, the first of its kind, he attracted workers from all fields; he organized them "into craft unions and successfully negotiated on their behalf for better working conditions." Finally, under pressure from the Bay Street merchants and the government, who tried to "suppress the movement," in 1942 Fawkes had established the BFL, which was an affiliation of unions and members of individual trade unions divided into branches according to their trades. The Taxi Cab Union, although self-governing, was affiliated with and paid dues to the BFL.[5] The membership of the Taxi Cab Union and the BFL was predominantly black and generally supported the PLP.

Clifford Darling, born in Acklins in the southern Bahamas, migrated to Nassau, where he would later become the president of the Taxi Cab Union. Earlier he had learned the electrical trade from his brother and trained as a barber. The 1942 riots left an indelible impression on Darling. Attracted by the opportunity to "get away from Nassau," he volunteered for the Contract in the United States, beginning his sojourn in Florida. Legalized discrimination during work and free time was almost "intolerable." Darling had grown up in Crooked Island, near his birthplace in Acklins, where there was no discrimination: "Racial prejudice was something I never encountered until the thirties when I came to Nassau to live. . . . At that time there was grave discrimination in Nassau."[6] On Darling's return to Nassau in 1946, he was "committed to bringing about changes in the pattern of discrimination" in his homeland. Seeking financial independence, he decided to become a taxi driver and immediately joined the Bahamas Taxi Cab Union, then consisting of about forty-five members. The union was made up of drivers who owned their vehicles and technically worked for themselves. Colonial Office officials did not consider the Taxi Cab Union a trade union in the strict sense.[7]

In his memoirs Darling admitted that when he first began driving a taxi, he "did very little taxi work." Most of his time was spent on his three-year crusade to "convince the taxi men that we had to break down racial discrimination in The Bahamas . . . so that we could become first class citizens in our own country." He met some opposition, discovering that "some black people in The Bahamas were content to live with discrimination here. A lot of them did not want to rock the boat. They would say that the Lord would take care of it." Gradually, however, Darling convinced them, and they in turn converted others to the idea. Gaining respect for Darling, the Taxi Cab Union members elected him as secretary of the union in 1949.[8]

Soon after his election, campaigning began for the general election of 1949. Darling described an incident that occurred during the campaign. Joseph Baker, a white lawyer and Bay Street merchant, was running for the southern district against two black candidates, Dr. C. R. Walker and Bert

Cambridge. Baker hired eight taxi drivers and offered to pay them eight pounds for transporting voters to the polls on election day. On hearing of this, Darling reminded them that Baker "did not respect black people" and that as black people they should not support him. Walker and Cambridge won by a landslide, while Baker lost his deposit. Apparently the taxi drivers also assisted the victorious candidates, angering Baker, who refused at first to pay them. Darling, after some harsh words had passed between them, persuaded Baker to reimburse the drivers.[9]

The Colonial Office was kept abreast of political and union developments. Traditionally it had been reluctant to interfere in local affairs in the colony. It avoided upsetting the Bay Street clique, which had brought sustained prosperity to the Bahamas through development of tourism. However, the fear of black anger and the growing militancy of the unions and the PLP, whose leaders were then considered left-wing extremists, would force Britain to reexamine its position on political developments in the Bahamas. A secret Bahamas Political Report of September 1954 sent to London contained unflattering information about individual members of the PLP and revealed the increasing attachment between the Taxi Cab Union and the new party.[10]

The original dispute that led to the general strike in January 1958 occurred on 2 November 1957. For some years there had been tension between the Taxi Cab Union and the operators of hotel and tour bus companies. Several hotels had been operating their own transportation to and from the airport, and tour companies began to follow the same pattern. The Taxi Cab Union complained that there was little business left for taxis, "be they Union or non-Union vehicles."[11] The official opening of the new airport at Windsor Field, more than eleven miles west of Nassau, was scheduled for 16 November 1957. The problem might perhaps have been resolved but for the discovery by the union of negotiations that begun between the Hotel Association and Meter Taxi Cab firm, owned by Edward Legatt, a British resident whose board included Bay Street representatives, and a local company operated by black Long Islander Dan Knowles. He had migrated to Nassau many years earlier and established the Dan Knowles Taxi, Livery and Bus Service. The intention was that the local bus company and taxi firm would be given "franchises" to convey passengers between the airport and the hotels. Such a scheme would have led to a "considerable increase of the seating capacity of hotel vehicles" and would probably have ended in a monopoly that excluded the Taxi Cab Union entirely.[12]

Government became involved in the dispute because the Airports Board controlled parking regulations at the airport. For the hotels to succeed in this "franchise" project, the Airports Board had to allocate large areas of parking space for the franchise operators. The government realized that such a move would be unpopular with the Taxi Cab Union and that "a large body of opinion in Nassau resented what was alleged to be another move by wealthy Bay Street merchants to squeeze out the small operator."[13] On the other hand, the Airport Board could not agree that the Taxi Cab Union should have a monopoly on collecting passengers from the airport. The board decided that the system whereby the hotel buses and tour company cars were allowed to transport passengers from the Oakes Field airport (the original airport), should continue.

By 26 October 1957, the government learned that the Taxi Cab Union intended to make trouble on the day of the unofficial opening of Windsor Field on 2 November. According to Acting Governor K. M. Walmsley's correspondence to the Colonial Office in London, a transport subcommittee of the Executive Council was convened, under the chairmanship of Attorney General L.A.W. Orr, to try to settle the dispute. The Taxi Cab Union was said to have been represented by Pindling and Darling, president of the union. The tour operators were represented by Knowles and Legatt, president of the Meter Taxi Cab firm. The attorney general persuaded the Hotel Association to agree that the hotels and their drivers would not increase total seating capacity of their vehicles beyond the level that had been established at Oakes Field. According to Walmsley's account, Darling agreed with the compromise. Darling vehemently denied this and stated that not only did he not attend the meeting, which he dubbed fictitious; he said he had no knowledge of it.[14] The government is supposed to have told Darling that a tally of the numbers of passengers traveling in hotel buses and taxis would be supplied to the union. However, the union was not satisfied. The lack of accurate statistics "as to the established share of traffic in the past" had caused the breakdown of previous negotiations.[15]

On the morning of 2 November when the new airport opened to traffic, the Taxi Cab Union decided to show their dissatisfaction, led by Darling, Nick Musgrove, Lochinvar Lockhart, Jimmy Shepherd, and Wilbert Moss. Nearly all the 193 union drivers arrived at the airport determined to force the withdrawal of hotel transportation. When the first batch of visitors arrived and tried to enter hotel transportation, the Taxi Cab Union drivers approached the vehicles and persuaded the passengers to travel by taxi. Darling stated, "We are here . . . to protect our interest—the small man's interest against big monopolies and a few individuals who wish to destroy us."[16]

According to the official account, with which Darling disagreed, the "attitude of the drivers was surly and uncompromising," and the chairman of the Airports Board temporarily refused to allow hotel transportation to operate. After checking with government officials, however, hotel vehicles were allowed, resulting in a blockade of all roads to and from the airport by the Taxi Cab Union drivers. Union drivers not only parked their cars "across the roads in groups of twenty"; they also locked the vehicles, effectively closing the roads. Encouraged by government workers, including those from customs, immigration and civil aviation, they defied police orders to move their vehicles. Junior police officers obviously sympathized with the demonstrators, who were also encouraged by PLP supporters.[17]

Frank Christie, chairman of the Airports Board, gave assurance that he and his members would "enter into discussions" with the union and that the hotels "would comply" with union demands. There would be an eight-week "cooling off period" when hotels would not send transport to the airport. Meanwhile, the transport subcommittee, under the attorney general, would attempt to obtain a permanent settlement.[18] Only then would Darling agree to end the blockade by ordering "the taxi drivers to move their cars," nearly thirty hours after the action began.[19]

Approximately thirty Taxi Cab Union drivers were charged in the Magistrate's Court with obstruction and three with assault. Charges against Darling and Wilbert Moss, a senior member of the union, were dismissed. However, several of their colleagues, including Oswald Barnard, James Glinton, and Leon Bowe, were found guilty of obstruction and assault and were fined. In addition James Shepherd was found guilty of refusing to move his vehicle; Jerome Hutcheson was found guilty of obstruction and refusing to move; and James Pratt, a seventy-four-year-old driver, was found guilty of assault. However, none of those convicted were imprisoned. Darling opined: "Given the mood in the country at that time and the fact that such an overwhelming [black] majority of the public stood behind us, not to mention the sympathy we engendered from the other Unions, . . . I believe if Magistrate E. P. St. George had sentenced any of us to jail, there would have been a big uprising."[20] Race relations were worsening. Union members defended their actions when questioned by Solicitor General K.G.L. Isaacs. "The attitude of the men . . . was that they were protecting their livelihood in the best way they knew"—their "bread was at stake," and they represented "people fighting for equal rights."[21]

Many people, however, especially wealthy whites, "took a serious view of the incident at the airport," and were fearful that it would negatively affect the tourist industry on which the "colony's prosperity depends." There had been a "good deal of uncertainty and considerable tension before the cases came to trial." Dupuch wrote: "The time has gone when any section of the community will be satisfied to accept the crumbs thrown from the master's table."[22]

Meetings were held between the government representatives, the Taxi Cab Union, the Hotel Association, and the tour companies during the same week as the incident. Pindling was legal advisor for the union. It seemed that an agreement had been reached in December. Nineteen of the twenty points put forward had been agreed upon. Tour companies were allowed to supply three vehicles each in transporting passengers from the airport and hotels. However, point twenty, the original bone of contention, still gave tour companies exclusive rights in transporting passengers from Nassau to the airport in cars of their own choice. Refusing to accept this, the union demanded a "first come, first served" system whereby the first drivers on the line would be assured of a fare. The tour operators and the Hotel Association refused to "budge from their position," thus causing a breakdown of the negotiations.

The demonstration of the Taxi Cab Union won the support of the PLP and the Bahamas Federation of Labour. Assistance also came from a highly respected labor leader for Britain, Sir Vincent Tewson, and Martin Pounder, Caribbean representative for the Trade Union Congress, who both visited the Bahamas in early December 1957, giving advice to the Taxi Cab Union, the BFL, and PLP party leaders.[23] Tewson held a press conference at the Royal Victoria, met with Governor Arthur, and spoke at a very well-attended meeting sponsored by the BFL at the Roman Catholic Benedict's Hall. Darling observed that the hundreds of people who had come to hear Tewson spilled onto the priory grounds. Emphasis was placed on "the principles" of trade unionism and the avoidance of "irresponsible action at all costs." Negotiation was key, and a strike should be a last resort.[24]

On 8 January Darling demanded and got the appointment of a three-man tribunal to attempt to break the deadlock. However, the Taxi Cab Union objected to all three proposed members: Leonard Knowles, who was retained by Dan Knowles Taxi and Bus Service in an action "pending in the Supreme Court against the Taxi Cab Union"; C. C. Richardson, who had acted as a mediator in a dispute between the union, the tour operators, and the Knowles company on previous occasions; and Brigadier Torrance, who was considered unfamiliar with local conditions.[25] Their decisions, the union thought, would be biased in favor of the tour companies. The union's request to have Fawkes as arbitrator failed as the tour companies objected, thus bringing negotiations to a standstill. Fawkes and Pindling subsequently met with the governor, unsuccessfully attempting to persuade him to appoint an impartial commission to investigate the causes of the dispute.[26] Darling then appealed to the BFL for "active assistance," stating that "the situation is very grave indeed, as negotiations have completely broken down."[27]

Fawkes called a meeting of the BFL and affiliate unions at their new headquarters located in the Bodie Building on Wulff Road on 11 January 1958. Also present were Pindling, Bain, Butler, and Rhodriquez. Darling records that at first, Fawkes "was adamantly opposed to taking strike action, preferring to continue to negotiate." According to James Shepherd, secretary of the Taxi Cab Union, Fawkes thought the strike would be illegal because all the drivers were businessmen in their own right. Pindling informed the meeting that it was legal to strike. After being threatened by the Longshoremen's Union, a powerful affiliate of the BFL, and his own officers that they were prepared to strike without him, Fawkes "reluctantly agreed" to take the strike vote, and the membership "overwhelmingly voted in favour of calling a General Strike to support the Bahamas Taxi Cab Union and to protest long-standing ingrained injustices to all workers of The Bahamas." The PLP was at first ambivalent to the idea of the strike. Shepherd stated that Pindling backed it because he was the union's legal adviser. He conferred with the PLP leader, Taylor, and Shepherd thought the "PLP took advantage of the strike for political purposes."[28]

Darling stated that the Bahamas Federation of Labour "took it from there," emphasizing, though, that "it was not Randol Fawkes who instigated the Strike. . . . It was without doubt, the Bahamas Taxi Cab Union that orchestrated and administered the General Strike."[29] A password was agreed. At 8:30 a.m. on Sunday 12 January, Pindling and Fawkes entered the Emerald Beach Hotel. Resting their right hands on the right shoulder of Saul Campbell, president of the Hotel Workers' Branch Union, they whispered "Now!" This was repeated at other hotels throughout New Providence. By that evening all the major hotels were virtually closed, and the Taxi Cab Union had withdrawn all its taxis. The hotels tried to carry on with white staff and loyal black helpers, but tourists soon left the colony. By Wednesday 15 January, workers had not returned, and all hotels were closed. Additionally, many construction workers, bakers, garbage collectors, airport porters, employees of the Electricity Corporation, a number of employees at the Public Works Department, and some private employees had already stopped work. The general strike had begun.[30] When Governor Arthur opened the legislature on Tuesday 14 January, there was a "demonstration" by a crowd of about 800 to 1,000. Arthur and the Bay Street politicians were booed (the first time a governor of the Bahamas had been booed in public), while Fawkes, Pindling, and other members of the PLP were cheered on their arrival at the House. The governor described them as "extremist left wing political leaders." Butler daringly walked through the public square and shouted to the crowd around the PLP members: "These are your representatives . . . get rid of white man rule in this country."[31] Arthur stated that "there was no violence." However, after he left the legislature "the police had considerable difficulty in controlling the crowd and the Riot Squad Reserve was summoned, but did not have to be used."[32] The next morning McDermott, editor of the *Nassau Guardian*, commented indignantly in an editorial: "This is no labour dispute—and it never was; it is the carefully engineered outcome of all the race and class hatred that has been preached for years in this community. If the Government ever doubted that, the insult on Tuesday morning to the Queen's representative should clear the thinking of all who still, officially, control the future of this Colony."[33]

Following the opening of parliament, a mass prayer meeting was held at the Southern Recreation Grounds at 3:00 p.m. A handbill distributed to supporters explained the purpose of the meeting "for bread, for peace, for freedom." Officials from the Taxi Cab Union, the BFL, and the PLP "addressed the crowd," urging nonviolence. The details of the disagreement were explained to the crowd, as was the planned boycott of certain white-owned institutions—for example, the Capital, Nassau, and Meeres theaters, the entrances of which were being picketed to prevent patrons from entering and to ensure that no films could be shown. Most Bay Street businesses, fearing violence, had battened down their windows and doors. After the prayer meeting people wandered about in the southern district "almost aimlessly" but excitedly. Magistrate St. George ordered all bars closed "for an indefinite period." Bay Street, however, was empty. Journalist Majorie Noble described the effect: "Over Bay Street today hung a death-like pall. The pall of vanished prosperity. The workers know it too."[34] In the *Tribune* on Tuesday 14 January, a "lover of Nassau" similarly expressed his apprehension regarding the strike. Acknowledging that strikes had occurred in England, he reminded Bahamians that their livelihood depended on the tourist trade: "No visitors, no money coming into the economy. It has taken many years to build up Nassau's reputation as a place where people are kind, polite and contented. . . . Once that reputation has gone, who knows where they will prefer to go?"[35]

In the early hours of Wednesday 15 January 1958, when most residents were asleep, a company of the Royal Worcestershire Regiment previously stationed in Jamaica arrived in Nassau, wearing battle dress and helmets.

They were heavily armed, some with 30 mm rifles with fixed bayonets, while others had automatic weapons. Arthur, fearing that the tense racial situation might descend into in violence, which Darling later admitted was a possibility, had alerted the commander of the Caribbean area and asked for a company of troops to be sent.[36] The governor had also given instructions that the press was not to be given any information. Many press representatives were held hostage at the airport for over an hour.[37]

There was some interruption in the electrical supply at Prospect Ridge, tampering with high tension wires in Oakes Field, and unauthorized entry and tampering with circuit breakers at the Bernard Road switching station. Additionally, "a stick of dynamite" was found attached to an isolated switch on the golf course.[38] Soldiers were stationed at strategic locations including the electrical department and the telecommunications offices. A government announcement was made the next morning explaining the rationale for the presence of the troops. Their purpose was for the protection of "life and property" and from "intimidation."[39] The visible presence of the troops, who patrolled downtown Nassau, its suburbs, and the entire island, gave the white Bay Street merchants confidence enough to reopen their shops and had a sobering effect on the populace generally. The *Tribune* reported that there was optimism that the Taxi Cab Union and the tour operators would "break the deadlock."[40]

There were also outrageous rumors, including one printed in the *Guardian* stating that the "troops are here to *slay* the people."[41] A 2,200-ton antisubmarine frigate, H.M.S. *Ulster,* arrived a few days later with technicians to maintain essential services and public utilities and presumably to supply reinforcement if necessary.[42] While most people felt more secure, as the strike wore on for a second week Darling stated that "feelings of hostility" began to "run very high." Occasional dynamite incidents and attempts at sabotage of the electrical power continued. Hotel workers, collectors of garbage, and street sweepers, among others, were still on strike. Several small guesthouses were open for tourists who chose to stay.[43] By 21 January, however, the tourist trade had ceased. At least 17,000 persons were without jobs because of the strike.

Some visitors and Bahamians expressed their feelings. Majorie Noble was critical of the strike leaders, accusing the taxi drivers of being selfish and pointing out that even if the strike ended soon, a great part of the Bahamas' livelihood had disappeared. She also, much to Darling's chagrin, characterized "the Bahamas Taxi-Union and its leaders as ignorant and naïve people who were manipulated by evil outside forces."[44] A letter writer with the pen name "A sorry citizen" stated: "God made all, coloured and white, and put us in these ever beautiful islands. Why don't we live as one, share with one another, and love one another. . . . He made us all, we are his children—brothers and sisters—but do we act that way? No. So don't go around here with a stuck up nose—keeping on one side of the line. Remember THERE IS NO COLOUR LINE IN HEAVEN."[45]

Comments, some critical, also came from nonwhite Bahamians. Audley Humes, for example, observed that when the Taxi Cab Union went on strike, "I thought they were fighting for point 20, but now I'm not quite sure." Additionally, he strongly criticized Fawkes, accusing him of distracting the public "from the true root cause of the strike" in his "attempts to seize the opportunity to try to unionize the hotels and other businesses." Humes continued: "In the first place, he [Fawkes] should never have ordered a general strike. If the hotel struck in sympathy with the Taxi Union, there goes our whole economic structure. What else is there to wreck? There are no guests in the hotels, no building going on. . . . The B.F.L. had no differences with government or the other enterprises on the island, yet their President called a general strike against them"[46]

Dupuch commented in the *Tribune*'s editorial of 16 January 1958 under the headline "Tension Slacks Off." Describing Nassau as a "Ghost Town," he anticipated that there should be a settlement soon. The strike had fanned racial animosities, which reached "fever" proportions. To Dupuch this was a pity as "coloured" Bahamians, usually "so gentle and kind," were in an "ugly mood." Indeed, as editor and proprietor of the *Tribune* he had warned the public following the 1942 riot but now bemoaned inaction: "Because the white people of this community have been so absorbed in making money that they have failed to realize that there are things in life—and especially in the field of human relations—that are more important than weighting their souls down with gold that can only drag us all down to hottest hell."[47] Castigating the wealthy whites for not addressing the known "injustices," "unfairness," and "deep spiritual wounds" suffered by the majority in the community, he opined that they had failed. Dupuch continued: "The tragedy of it all is that all this unnatural hatred has been produced by the greed and avarice of a few men in the community." While this crisis would "pass," he expected that "then you'll forget again—and just go merrily on chasing 'the pot of gold at the rainbow's end' until one day it will destroy you . . . and me too . . . and all of us."[48]

Negotiations between the unions, tour companies, and government continued, as did the rallies at the Southern Recreation Ground and Windsor

Park on East Street and Wulff Road. Pickets that had been located in isolated areas, including George Street in the west, Mackey Street in the east, and five movie theatres, spread by 20 January to Bay Street. Some picketers were injured, being "knocked down" by cars. A white Bahamian, Emmett Pritchard—son of Asa Pritchard, the House speaker and proprietor of the John Bull store on Bay Street—was charged in the Magistrate's Court "with causing harm, assault and negligent driving." The case was adjourned to 31 January by Magistrate Maxwell Thompson. A number of picketers were charged with intimidation, but their cases were also adjourned.[49] Racial tension was real, and Darling opined that Asa and Emmett Pritchard's "feelings for the strikers were obvious." Leaders of the strike became concerned for the safety of the picketers. Governor Arthur also took note, confidentially informing the secretary of state in London of the situation: "Picketing has been orderly but tension rose yesterday in consequence of violent demeanour of the Speaker of the House of Assembly, Pritchard and family, whose shop was picketed."[50] Racial hostilities and "deeply felt emotions" ran high as the strike continued into its second week.[51]

News of the strike was reported in the British, Canadian, and American press. The latter suggested that political issues were the real cause of the strike. The *New York Times* reported that "negroes have been demanding welfare legislation and modern laws. Efforts of the Governor and the British Colonial Office to obtain reforms have been blocked by a Legislature dominated by a small group of wealthy whites."[52] Press reaction embarrassed the British Embassy in Washington, where officials feared that supporting the Bahamas' legislature would bring international ridicule. Colonial Attaché Douglas Williams, in a confidential letter to the Colonial Office, asked for advice on the official policy on the Bahamian situation. Williams stated that there was "interest in the events in Nassau throughout the Carolinas, Georgia and Florida," where the merchants of Bay Street were "regarded as the biggest gang of pirates yet unhung." The embassy's official line was that while it had little sympathy with Bay Street group, it was difficult to intervene in their affairs. From the media's point of view "this issue seems to be the hottest thing since Mau Mau."[53]

Pressure on the Bahamian government and support for the unions came from American and international labor leaders, including those in other West Indian colonies, even though the Bahamas was not part of the West Indies Federation. Fawkes spoke to labor organizations in New York, whose leaders telegraphed the secretary of state, pledging support both moral and financial and urging the British government to establish democracy in the

Bahamas.[54] Several foreign labor officials visited to offer advice and assistance, among them Ken Sterling, a black Jamaican, representing the International Confederation of Free Trade Unions; Wesley Wainwright of the National Worker's Union in Jamaica; Thossy Kelly, president of the Jamaica National Workers Union; and Martin Pounder, Trade Union Congress representative for the Caribbean. Sterling also addressed the crowd at a rally, stating: "The Bahamas is too small for two worlds to exist. They have to realize that the Bahamas would have to belong to Bahamians, or perhaps, to nobody at all." Pounder and Sterling were shocked to discover that the dispute that had given rise to the strike was not a trade dispute but a disagreement between two conflicting commercial interests. Despite this, however, they assisted in settling the strike, particularly Pounder.[55]

Support for the unions and PLP also came from other British Caribbean colonies. The Jamaican House of Representatives unanimously passed a resolution condemning the "disgraceful and outmoded system and attitude" in the Bahamas and calling for the establishment of a royal commission of inquiry. Chief Minister of Jamaica Norman Manley cabled this information to the Colonial Office in London.[56] As Hughes stated, the general strike cemented "relations between the PLP leaders and their West Indian counterparts."[57]

After tough negotiations between the governor, the Taxi Cab Union, and the tour car operators, assisted by Pounder, Thossy Kelly, Pindling, Shepherd, Fawkes, and Darling, the general strike was called off on 29 January 1958. An agreement favorable to the Taxi Cab Union was reached. Several days before, employees of the electrical corporation resumed work and by Tuesday 28 January, all public health workers and two-thirds of the striking Public Works Department employees had returned to work. By 30 January there was a general resumption of work and a return to normal, although major hotels remained closed for a few days until tourist traffic resumed.[58] The strike caused a severe setback in the tourist industry. At first recovery was slow, but it accelerated by the end of 1959. While all government employees were accepted back, not all hotel workers were reemployed.

Due to internal events, strong local public opinion, and sustained international criticism, Arthur pressed the Colonial Office to take urgent action in insisting on instituting reforms in the Bahamas.[59] The governor personally deplored the colony's constitution, seeing it as "morally indefensible" and a "hopeless anachronism." In an earlier communication, while disagreeing with Bay Street's request to keep the troops in the Bahamas indefinitely, Arthur was reluctant to see them go immediately, noting "the nervousness of the white population and the slackness of the Police," rather than the potential for a renewal of violence. However, he was afraid that if the Colonial Office pressed for constitutional change before any labor and political reforms were made, it might turn the Bahamas into "a little South Africa."[60] Arthur was convinced that the Bay Street politicians "should start getting their house in order in the eyes of the world," and he wondered "how long should we back up Bay Street with British bayonets."[61] Rogers added that American opinion was also "critical" of the Bay Street group, "so there is nothing to be gained by Bay Street trying to play off the USA against the United Kingdom on this."[62] The troops remained in Nassau for two years.[63]

Arthur's appeal to the Colonial Office, which probably embarrassed but deeply concerned the British government, finally brought results. In March 1958 it was announced that Alan Lennox-Boyd, secretary of state for the colonies, would visit the Bahamas in early April for a week to investigate the underlying causes of the strike and to make recommendations for the solution to the problem.[64] Labour members of the British Parliament pressed for answers to problems in the Bahamas and in its outdated constitution.[65] The British government could not reform the Bahamas' antiquated constitution except by passing an act of Parliament, which it felt was extreme.[66] However, it had to be seen to promote democracy, and Arthur persuaded his colleagues in London that something must be done to liberalize the Bahamas' constitution. The governor recognized the reactionary mold of the Bay Street politicians who had by this time (March) formed themselves into the United Bahamian Party (UBP) led by Roland Symonette, whom he thought he might successfully sway. Stafford Sands, whom he recognized as the "dominant" and, in his opinion, "obdurate" leader, would be more difficult. In fact younger members of the UBP, according to Symonette's son Robert, then deputy speaker of the Assembly, felt that change was needed.[67] In the meantime, PLP leaders Taylor and Pindling had met with officials at the Colonial Office and offered sound suggestions for constitutional advance. A viable opposition to Bay Street was emerging. Recognizing the existing antagonism and acknowledging the successful tourist industry, the Colonial Office wished Bay Street to make the necessary reforms to avoid trouble and possible bloodshed in the future.

By the time of Lennox-Boyd's visit, Arthur had brought together the Taxi Cab Union and tour companies to sign an agreement providing more equitable transportation to and from Nassau's International Airport. This was significant as in the "public mind taxi drivers signified the 'coloured under privileged' majority and the Tour car operation, the white, politically over-privileged, minority."[68] Arthur also promised that legislation would be passed allowing hotel and agricultural workers to unionize and that a labor department and a Bahamas transport authority would be established, which resulted in the passage of the Road Traffic Act 1958 relating to motor vehicles and public transportation and provided for the establishment of a Road Traffic Authority.[69] The governor's well-received speech over the local radio station, ZNS, on the night following his announcements, urged all parties to work together, forget the past, and look to the future. His attempt to introduce an Emergency Power Act during the following week, giving him overriding powers, was opposed by Bay Street politicians, who cherished their power and independence. Following the debate in the House of Assembly it was referred to a select committee, where it died.[70]

As Hughes has opined, the strike "brought Bahamian problems to the front pages of the world's press for a day or two, and shook the Colonial Office off the fence it had straddled so long." It also strengthened relations "between the PLP leaders and their West Indian counterparts," as already noted. Pindling and Fawkes were able to garner some support for "their demand for a royal commission" from the chief minister of Jamaica and Jamaica's House of Representatives, which adopted a resolution in support of an investigation into the strike.[71] Eric Williams, chief minister of Trinidad and Tobago, sent a personal message of support.[72] It was Lennox-Boyd's visit to the Bahamas that accelerated change and had a significant impact on Bahamian constitutional and political development. The recommended reforms eased much of the tension that might have led to violence and ultimately resulted in the "Quiet Revolution"—the peaceful transition to majority rule. His presence was also significant in that no British representative of his stature had ever visited the Bahamas in a working capacity. During a week's stay Lennox-Boyd met with leaders of the UBP and PLP and representatives from the BFL. He also visited several Out Islands, including Eleuthera, Crooked Island, Acklins, and Exuma.

After consulting with all the groups he informed the UBP that the British government was serious about reform and issued a warning that it was determined to support a majority opinion regardless of the House of Assembly's makeup. If the Bahamian government failed to implement the proposed reforms, "no one is in doubt to the ultimate authority of the Imperial Parliament."[73] Lennox-Boyd reiterated the Colonial Office's view that if the Bay Street men did not reform their constitution, they might end up with one they did not like. A year earlier in London, Arthur had discussed the matter of constitutional change with Roland Symonette and Stafford

Sands. The subject of British honors arose and might have served as an incentive for the two most powerful men in the House of Assembly, who were later knighted. They were able to coerce the House into supporting the suggested electoral changes.[74]

Lennox-Boyd's intervention was an important milestone. The Colonial Office, besides demanding electoral changes, examined labor matters and also investigated educational, medical, and housing conditions and the cost of living. Two important Colonial Office–sponsored reports were produced, the Houghton Report on Education and the Hughes Report on Medical Services. The Houghton Report, critical of the inefficiency of the board system and political influence wielded on it, recommended that new comprehensive education legislation be enacted, an advisory council on education be appointed, and a sixth form be established at Government High School and perhaps at Queen's College. The government-appointed Board of Education did not exercise any supervision over secondary schools. Government High was controlled by a Board of Governors, Queen's College by the Methodist Synod, Xavier's College and St. Augustine's College by the Roman Catholic Church, St. John's College by the Anglican Diocese, and the Bahamas Junior Academy by the Seventh-day Adventists. St. Andrew's School, a limited company, was still racially segregated. A Teacher's Training College established in 1950 was functioning in 1955. Because of a dearth of trained and efficient teachers, the college was temporarily closed in 1957.[75]

The Government High School, however, made considerable contributions to public service, especially the teaching profession and private enterprise. Six members of the 1957 House of Assembly were former pupils of the Government High School.[76] According to a 1958 report, in terms of real facilities the Bahamas ranked third, well behind Barbados and Trinidad and Tobago, but considerably ahead of Jamaica and Antigua. But the quality of teaching in Jamaica, Trinidad, and Barbados was much higher than in the Bahamas.[77] Hughes's report on medical services decried, among other problems, the lack of qualified doctors on most Out Islands. Healthwise though, the Bahamas compared favorably with the other larger Caribbean islands. In fact, in terms of the availability of medical resources, the Bahamas ranked among the best. Both reports, however, recommended sweeping reforms.[78]

Shocked by the first setback to tourism since the war, Bay Street, now formally constituted as the UBP, was jolted into accepting some long overdue changes, while at the same time redoubling its efforts to divide and discredit the opposition made up of the Taxi Cab Union, the PLP, and the Bahamas Federation of Labour. After some pressure and assistance from the British and West Indian trade unionists and labor experts at the Colonial Office, the Bahamas' House of Assembly passed the Trade Union and Industrial Conciliation Act in July 1958, which brought the Bahamas in line with Jamaica, Trinidad and Tobago, and Barbados. Besides laying down rules for union organization and industrial action, the act set up a Labour Department headed by a chief industrial officer and a Labour Office responsible for all matters connected with workers' wages, insurance, and welfare and family allotments as well as continuing to recruit and organize workers on the Contract—all under the authority of a Labour Board appointed by the governor.[79]

Significant electoral reforms were incorporated in the General Assembly Election Act of 1959. Limited adult suffrage was introduced, giving all males over twenty-one years of age the right to vote; the company vote was abolished, and the plural vote, which allowed one person to vote in every constituency, was limited to two. In order to bring the constituencies into line with the movement of population, four additional seats in New Providence were created (two in the south and two in the east), with provision to be made for by-elections as soon as possible. Lennox-Boyd, strongly influenced by his discussion with the PLP, made these latter recommendations in an attempt to redress the imbalance of representation between Nassau and the Out Islands. Lennox-Boyd and the governor may have been influenced by F. M. Collett's observation a couple of years earlier: "A Bahamian Out-Island is very much a man's world. The local men were definitely opposed to votes for women. They told me they did not think women were educated enough to vote. Secretly, I think, they feared that votes for women would mean less rum and cash handed out at election time. The white politicians were, I consider, opposed to votes for women as it would double their election expenses."[80] Neither saw the need or evidence of widespread demand for granting women the vote. Lennox-Boyd's visit, however, highlighted the women's suffrage movement that had existed since the early 1950s.

Women's Suffrage Movement

As Marion Bethel argued, the suffrage movement in the Bahamas "had its origins in the emerging black middle-class of the Over-the Hill area of Nassau."[81] Bethel also noted that some Bahamian women, especially members of lodges, were aware of the enfranchisement of women in the English-speaking Caribbean, namely Jamaica (1944), Trinidad and Tobago (1946), and Barbados (1950).[82] White, brown, and black middle-class women seemed to have little interest in getting the vote. They focused on promoting charitable organizations and social work, which gave them the opportunity for public service and satisfied their sense of noblesse oblige. Two of the pioneers of the suffrage movement, Mary Ingraham and Mabel Walker, were exceptions. They were probably more informed about West Indian developments since their husbands, Rufus Ingraham and Dr. C. R. Walker, were members of the House of Assembly. As early as 1948 Bahamian women began calling for the right to vote. Three years later Mrs. Ingraham sponsored a petition imploring her representative in the House, Stafford Sands, who presented it although admitting he could not give it his support. The petition was referred to the Constitution Committee chaired by Sands, and there it died.[83]

In 1952 another petition drafted by the Daughters of the Improved Benevolent and Protective Order of Elks of the World and other residents of New Providence was presented to the speaker of the House. Signatories of the petition included Mary N. Ingraham, Lillian Isaacs, Mabel Isaacs, Myrtle E. Wray, Effie Archer, Mamie Astwood, Jennie Smith, and 438 others. Later in the year the United Nations General Assembly adopted a Convention on the Political Rights of Women, which entitled women "to vote in all elections on equal terms with men without discrimination."[84] Obviously Bahamian women were aware of these developments. Sylvia Laramore, a Cat Islander, who had assisted in preparing the original petition, published letters in the *Tribune* during October 1954 demanding the passage of legislation on the enfranchisement of women.[85]

The Progressive Liberal Party's establishment in 1953, and the election of six of its members in 1956, impacted the women's movement. Two of its leading members, Eugenia Lockhart and Georgiana Symonette, were also members of the Women's Branch of the PLP. They campaigned for the party in the 1956 election and were determined to gain the vote for women. It appears that the women's suffrage movement was officially established in 1957. Mary Ingraham—whose husband was a candidate in the 1949 election and would align himself with the United Bahamian Party in 1958—was elected president in that year.[86] Other officers included Georgiana Symonette as vice-president and Eugenia Lockhart as secretary. All three officers were mixed-race women identifying closely with the black community. The suffrage movement participants met in Dr. Walker's Rhinehart Hotel on Baillou Hill Road in Grant's Town. Other leading members were Mabel Walker and Althea Mortimer. Few white women supported the movement. Those who did included Veronica Higgs (wife of George V. E. Higgs), June Stevenson (wife of Cyril Stevenson), and Beryl Hanna (wife of Arthur D. Hanna); all were of English origin, married to Bahamian men, and two of the men, Stevenson and Hanna, were nonwhites and PLP members.

In their struggle to obtain the vote for women, these women bombarded the House of Assembly with petitions demanding the franchise for women. Following the 1958 strike, Lennox-Boyd's visit to the Bahamas resulted in the granting of full male adult suffrage. During his visit the suffragettes demonstrated on Bay Street with placards demanding the vote for women and were given an audience with Lennox-Boyd, only to be disappointed with his negative attitude regarding their request for the right to vote.

Doris Johnson, who returned to Nassau in 1958 after receiving bachelor's and master's degrees (she would later obtain a doctorate from Columbia University), energized the suffrage movement, giving it the militancy that it needed. She mobilized the movement into a fighting force and was one of the founders of the National Council of Women, formed in September 1958 and "born out of a lecture given by Mary McLeod Bethune," founder of Bethune-Cookman College in Florida. Dr. Johnson was not among the founders of the suffrage movement and some, including Eileen Dupuch, editor and publisher of the *Tribune*, think she "saw a political opportunity and grabbed it."[87] Leading suffragettes, including the founder and president Mary Ingraham, Georgina Symonette, Mabel Walker, and Eugenia Lockhart, also joined the council, which was an affiliate of the International Council of Women. Johnson, a former teacher in government schools, was a recipient of a Bahamas government scholarship that she lost as a result of her active participation in the suffrage movement. Johnson states that Stafford Sands, whom she dubbed the "boss of the UBP," declared that "women would get the vote over his dead body."[88] She recognized two major problems: the difficulty of getting women to support the movement, especially those in the Out Islands, and the victimization of members of the movement by the UBP.[89] Nonetheless, in 1958 the women's suffrage movement, pressing for the enfranchisement of women, produced a new petition signed by more than 2,500 persons. Gerald Cash, member of the House, with the support of Milo Butler, presented the petition to the speaker and members of the House of Assembly on 1 December 1958.[90]

Early in 1959 Doris Johnson demanded an opportunity to address members of the House of Assembly in their chamber. Her request, which was debated by the House, was refused by the speaker, Robert Symonette, as she was in parliamentary language "a stranger." To grant her permission to speak in the House would have established a precedent. Lynden Pindling presented a petition on Doris Johnson's behalf. Randol Fawkes gave an eyewitness account of what followed. According to his account, immediately following Symonette's decision, six members of the UBP "bolted from their chairs and headed for the stairway where they were confronted by a group of angry straw vendors" and other militant supporters. In face of this demonstration, the members hurried back to their seats, and the speaker consented to allow Johnson to speak in mixed-race magistrate Maxwell Thompson's court.[91] Suffragettes demonstrated, carrying placards with the words: "No Nation Can Risk Higher Than the Status of Its Womanhood." On 19 January 1959 Doris Johnson, dressed in black, delivered a forty-minute "impassioned plea" on behalf of 54,000 women, then more than half of the adult population of the Bahamas. Assuring members of the House that women had achieved leadership roles in many areas of society and had learned democratic techniques in various organizations, she expressed concern over the lack of representation of women on juries and boards, the incarceration of very young delinquent girls, and the failure to appoint females as commissioners and justices of the peace. Johnson stressed that in spite of their wide experience, women still suffered gross inequalities, and she demanded that women be given the vote. She likened the situation for women in the Bahamas to the American colonists before the War of Independence, who suffered taxation without representation. However "putting aside our grievances, we women raise our hearts and heads to loftier things: our willingness and readiness to participate as full citizens in the affairs of our country. We women are ready, willing and able. *You must no longer deny us our rights.*"[92] Despite this moving and eloquent speech, nothing was done.

The very next day Mary Ingraham led a group of suffragettes and their supporters, including Symonette, Lockhart, Doris Johnson, Mildred Donaldson, Shirley Sands, Willamae Saunders, and Mary Stuart, to Government House to present a petition requesting the governor to insist that the law be changed, allowing women to vote.[93] They received international support from British Labour Member of Parliament Eirene White, Conservative MP Joan Vickers, and Helen Tucker, president of the National Council of Women of Canada, all of whom visited Nassau.[94]

Kim Outten-Stubbs states that 1960 "proved to be a turning point for the Movement." The six PLP members of the House "rallied" behind the movement, taking the women's cause to Windsor Park, the Southern Recreation Grounds, and the Out Islands.[95] Lynden Pindling, parliamentary leader of the party, presented a petition for the immediate franchise of women. Support also came from the lodges, especially the Elks organization, which had primarily black membership. The coming to power of the British Labour

Party, which promised its support, also was of significance. Encouraged by the growing local and international support, but disappointed with the lack of local governmental action, the women's suffrage movement dispatched a delegation consisting of Doris Johnson, Eugenia Lockhart, and Henry Taylor, then chairman of the PLP, to London to seek help. There they met with Ian McLeod, secretary of state for the colonies, at a conference attended by female parliamentarians and supporters Eirene White and Joan Vickers. McLeod was optimistic that attitudes were changing and that new legislation would soon be passed.[96]

The suffragettes nevertheless continued to demonstrate. When the legislature opened in January 1961, representatives of the movement picketed on Bay Street. With pressure from all sides except the majority of white women, who did not publicly express their opinion, UBP members capitulated despite their fear that enfranchised women would increase the number of black and PLP voters. Almost immediately, a select committee was appointed and reported in favor of the vote for women, with effect from January 1963. Seven UBP members signed, but the PLP and independent members objected to the delay and refused to do so. Lynden Pindling then presented a petition demanding the immediate enfranchisement of women.[97] Arthur Hanna also submitted a petition, requesting the amendment of the Election Act that would enable universal adult suffrage. The bill allowing women to vote was passed on 23 February 1961 and came into effect on 30 June 1962, and women voted for the first time in the 1962 election.[98]

The struggle for the vote for women was racially charged. Although according to Eileen Dupuch, UBP leader Sir Roland Symonette "was determined" to let Doris Johnson be heard, the majority of UBP members, representing the white community, had opposed the black and mixed-race membership of the suffragette movement and their sponsors, particularly the predominantly black Progressive Liberal Party.[99] Aware that most women were black, they feared losing support. The *Herald* newspaper hammered away at white Bay Street. In October 1960 it made the PLP's policies clear, declaring,

Make no mistake about it Bahamians. Our struggle was never more deeply defined. Regardless of what anyone may say, this struggle is white against black, and we did not produce the rules—they did. . . . The Negro majority is now engaged in a death battle with the white minority. Before any efforts can be made towards racial harmony in this country, we are going to have to destroy their vicious and twisted concept of racial superiority; bring them crumbling to the ashes of defeat, smash their little harbours of arrogance and complacency. . . . Only then will we be able to start all over again—on terms that are truly equal—to build a decent society where racial divisions are of no consequence and where the colour of a man's skin bears no relevance to his position in any segment of that society. . . . But the task cannot even begin until everything represented by the United Bahamian Party has been obliterated.[100]

Developments between 1960 and 1962

The 1960 by-election was fought in a racially charged atmosphere with resounding success for the PLP, which won all four seats. The *Tribune* and *Guardian* saw it as a "crushing vote of 'no confidence' in the ruling UBP." The *Guardian* lamented that the prosperity brought by the UBP meant nothing to the majority of the population in New Providence, who "wish to be governed by their own kind . . . purely on the basis of racial affiliation."[101] An "unexpected windfall" contributed to PLP success. Cyril Stevenson printed a document in the *Herald* in October 1959, supposedly written by Peter Knaur, an American journalist working for the *Guardian*. Known as a propaganda advisor to the UBP, Knaur insulted the black population in an article that reflected the "idea of racial superiority." It also stated "this is the white man's society, and the Negro does not have the self-confidence to destroy it." Knaur's "Master Plan" revealed how the UBP could ingratiate itself among black people and win their support.[102] The *Tribune* countered: "It reflected an attitude of mind that dies hard among a very small group of people in this community . . . an idea of racial superiority that has defeated every effort to weld our people into a solid unit of Bahamians."[103] But the *Guardian* in a front page editorial brazenly questioned: "Race hatred? You can search Peter Knaur's writing—including his report—from end to end and you will find none. . . . 'This is a white man's society.' Think carefully. Does anyone seriously think that it is not? Is it an African society? Anyone who says so is insulting the people of the Bahamas who for centuries have been British—in name, in language, in custom, education and culture. In everything, in fact, except origin." The *Guardian* then sarcastically asked the *Herald* if it would advocate "that the streets of Nassau should echo to the beat of the tom-tom, or witness the primitive rites of voodoo and black magic?" It was sure that the *Herald* would not agree because the people of the Bahamas "have had centuries of civilization" and cannot be compared to "their brothers across the ocean who are for the most part only one generation removed from savagery. . . . This is why Peter Knaur said 'This is a white man's society.' But he meant it in a sociological, not racial, sense."[104] Dupuch, although he held no brief for the PLP, was critical of the *Guardian*'s disparaging remarks about Africa. The *Guardian* "retorted that the PLP was using African developments to catch votes while Ghana rushed towards dictatorship."[105]

After the 1960 by-election Taylor, who won a seat, claimed that relations between Pindling and himself became strained, and Pindling's attitude "changed completely." In fact Pindling was taking control. Still chairman, Henry Taylor had been out of the House of Assembly for a term, while Pindling as parliamentary leader and Fawkes as union boss had gained mileage during the strike. Pindling actively assisted Fawkes in mobilizing the striking hotel workers and took an active part as legal advisor in the unions' negotiations. Although Fawkes was still tremendously popular and was still the crowd's hero, Pindling was increasingly wooing the same crowd. For a variety of reasons Fawkes's political career waned after the strike. This was important for Pindling because the masses had considered him their Moses. Pindling and the PLP eventually eclipsed the Bahamas Federation of Labour, and he replaced Fawkes as the crowd's hero.[106]

Part of the problem was race. While the *Herald* tried to continue its appeal to all Bahamians "regardless of race," Taylor in an article asked the question: "Is the PLP a Negro Party?" He "concluded that it had to be because no whites had the courage to support it." He admitted that racial exclusiveness had not been the intention of the PLP founders and that the plank "attacking Jim Crowism" had not been a part of the original and was inserted later. The plank condemned Jim Crow policies and pledged to eradicate such policies, promising anti-discrimination and anti-segregation legislation and that the party would strive to end discrimination in the Bahamas.[107]

PLP members of the House of Assembly and the *Herald* were very critical of any actions that discriminated against nonwhites. As Hughes demonstrated, since the 1956 resolution against racial discrimination, "overt acts of social discrimination had been rare." But the PLP pounced on any hint of racism. When the majority in the House voted only £5,000 for drought relief at Andros but twice as much to assist wealthy white racehorse owners, and £120,000 to provide accommodation for British troops still stationed in Nassau, the *Herald* headlined the article: "'Conchy Joe' Representatives Vote to Feed Horses—Vote to Starve Negroes." It reminded readers of Bay Street's "inhumanity to man, of their hatred for Negroes and their treachery to their country."[108]

Clarence Bain reminded Bay Street politicians or Conchy Joes that although they did not "own slaves in the direct sense," indirectly "they have had the way of life of these islands so manipulated that the Negroes worked and developed the wealth of the country while the Conchy Joes reaped the reward." Hughes interpreted Bain's remarks as an attack on the present leaders, hinting that they were "former white trash" or perhaps were of mixed parentage and had made their money recently, for example from bootlegging, and were not descendants of the "old slave owners."[109] At the same time, PLP leaders denied they were preaching "race hatred or were anti-white," contending that "it is not our desire to bring the white race down; it is our desire to raise our people up." They used race so that they could educate their "people" to respect their heritage and learn to support their own politically, as whites were "taught to support their own people."[110] Race relations, however, worsened. In January 1960 the English matron of the public hospital was assaulted in her "quarters." The *Tribune* started a reward fund attempting to apprehend the culprit. Critical of the outcry the incident caused, the *Herald* wrote that if the victim had been a "coloured" woman, no such action would have taken place, concluding with: "When a coloured Bahamian is involved they couldn't care less and they discuss it with a shrug by saying that it was probably her own fault."[111] *The Guardian*, however, touted the growing prosperity and the fact that the Bahamas was better off materially than the rest of the greater Caribbean and warned that the PLP's campaign of race hatred would be to the disadvantage of the colored people they pretended "to champion."[112]

Following the by-election held in May 1960 giving the PLP ten House members, the National General Council (NGC) of the PLP was enlarged, and according to Taylor, Pindling sponsored many of the aggressive newcomers, including London-trained lawyer Paul Adderley, chief laboratory technician Clement Maynard, locally trained lawyer Orville Turnquest, realtor Jeffrey Thompson, and bookkeeper Warren Levarity. Most of these men were dark-skinned and identified more readily with Pindling than with Taylor. Pindling's influence with the new group was "exceptionally high." Taylor accused him of "consciously or unconsciously building up a following to himself." This eventually divided the council into "two camps."[113]

The expanded NGC was changing. Among the new group were several militants, including Thompson, Levarity, journalist Arthur Foulkes, retired policeman Spurgeon Bethel, science graduate Sinclair Outten at the Telephone Company, and medical student Eugene Newry. In late 1958 or early 1959 they formed a pressure group, the National Committee for Positive Action (NCPA). According to Thompson, their purpose was to get rid of a white minority government and to open up opportunities for all Bahamians. "We decided we would do whatever we considered necessary to accomplish that purpose."[114] The NCPA was determined to rid the PLP of the "old conservative guard." Thompson and Turnquest confirmed that Taylor, Stevenson, and the original founders "would have been satisfied with a better deal for the majority black population, but perhaps were not [as] convinced as they were that blacks could run the affairs of the country."[115]

It was surprising and perhaps naive, therefore, that Sir Raynor Arthur, in a speech to the Chamber of Commerce at the end of his three-year term as governor, denied that "there was any cause for racial feeling in the Bahamas, and warned against the emergent party system being allowed to divide on racial grounds." He compared the PLP with the British Labour Party, "which based its appeal to the electorate on class hatred" and "has suddenly found itself out on a limb because class distinctions have disappeared and this appeal evokes no response from the public."[116]

The racially charged political atmosphere that spilled over into social life intensified between the May 1960 by-elections and the general elections in November 1962. The new "intellectual" forces within the PLP, particularly the NCPA members, caused dissension within the party hierarchy as they worked to oust Chairman Taylor, who claimed he was verbally attacked and that racial slurs were cast against him. Gradually the NCPA members gained almost complete control of the council and introduced more aggressive campaign tactics. According to Taylor, "goon squads," agitators, and loudmouth proponents of the PLP broke up UBP meetings. The *Herald* continued its racially focused propaganda, harking back to the insulting Knaur report—as earlier noted, in October 1960 it had stated that the "struggle is white against black. . . . The Negro majority is now engaged in a death battle with the white minority."[117]

The UBP, on the other hand, appeared to have a change of heart. In 1961 members voted to open the Collins Wall, a symbol of racial separation, and supported the vote for women, for which pressure had been initiated by the PLP. A House Committee recommended that no public beaches be sold in the future, and in April 1962 the House of Assembly agreed to reduce its term from seven years to five. The PLP, skeptical of this about-face, pressed on with its propaganda, promising to "promote racial harmony by outlawing discrimination."[118] Like the UBP, it also promised an early constitutional conference and other positive changes in the fields of education, health, and social welfare.

From the beginning, however, the PLP had reservations about the Hawkesbill Creek Agreement (1955) and the later supplementary agreement signed in 1960 between the Grand Bahama Port Authority, headed by Wallace Groves, and the Bahamas government, which gave the Port Authority much power and control over the governance of Freeport, including immigration, social services, and education.

The majority of workers lived outside the boundaries of Freeport proper. There developed a class and color divide, as nearly all those living in Freeport-Lucaya were wealthy or well-paid whites, many of them foreign, whereas workers living outside the boundaries were almost exclusively blacks. Some of the more skilled laborers and white collar workers employed by the Port Authority and living in the concession area, however, were American southerners and white Bahamians. They needed no encouragement to use their color to their advantage and to discriminate against nonwhites. American "rednecks" demonstrated their prejudice, calling all nonwhite manual workers "Haitians." During the 1960s there developed a form of class and racial separation and a general tone reminiscent of South African apartheid. While Freeport grew into the "second city," also dubbed the "Magic City"—with the growth of industrial plants like the BORCO oil refinery, the cement works established by U.S. Steel, and residential and tourist developments in the 1960s—slums developed behind the oil refinery and the chain of settlements farther west, including Eight Mile Rock.[119]

Despite the UBP's actions, its racial propaganda machine was well oiled during the election campaign. It attacked PLP candidates as inexperienced and irresponsible and bragged of its success in tourism and the prosperity it brought to all Bahamians. It used the *Guardian's* columns to counteract the PLP's mention of being in slavery: "Take a drive through the most populous sections of New Providence, through areas where the PLP would have you believe that the Negro is kept in 'slavery' by white 'masters.' Did you ever see so many 'slaves' driving around in automobiles? . . . [Or] accomplish the construction of so many large modern buildings . . . [or] own businesses, from banks to garages to grocery stores."[120]

A correspondent signing himself as "A coloured Carpenter" warned blacks and especially women that "we are all poor" and depend on the "white man for jobs . . . so if the PLP gets the majority of seats in the House of Assembly, you know that only they and their families will be taken care of."[121] The writer was obviously aware of the growing prosperity brought by tourism, banking, and the emergence of the Bahamas as a tax haven. However, the PLP was concerned about the increasing number of non-Bahamians hired to meet the demand for jobs created by these developments. The National

Committee for Positive Action established a new newspaper in August 1961, the *Bahamian Times*, edited by Arthur Foulkes, a journalist formerly with the *Tribune*. Foulkes and other NCPA members, wishing to take a different approach to that of the *Herald*, read voraciously, books about politics, economics, and African history. They used such knowledge to educate the masses about politics, economics, and African history, their loss of self-confidence, and their need to regain self-respect and to restore black dignity.[122] They nevertheless continued the assault on racial discrimination, citing the example of qualified "Negroes . . . being passed over for the light skinned foreigner."[123] With the election imminent, both parties were on the attack. The PLP's suggestion in the House of Assembly to abolish or reform the Legislative Council and "secure an Executive Council elected by the House" met with the negative comment from Deputy Speaker R. H. Symonette that the "PLP wanted the UBP to do the work now so that they could take over as dictators later." He also accused the PLP of showing signs of Communism and "undermining authority and overthrowing the Constitution."[124] The PLP continued its attack when Stafford Sands stated that the government would seek "permanent residents" from Europe. The PLP warned that such a policy would "convert Nassau into a new Johannesburg and the colony into a new Kenya," resulting in "Negro Bahamians," if they were fortunate, getting "jobs as servants in homes of their white European masters."[125]

That racial tension was intensifying in Nassau was illustrated by an incident when a nine-year-old black newspaper vendor was blocked by the twelve-year-old son of a white employee from reentering the air-conditioned shop where he had been selling papers. The paper vendor fell and injured his head, was treated at the hospital, and discharged. However, a rumor quickly spread that the younger boy had been killed, causing a crowd to gather outside the shop and the calling out of the riot squad. Milo Butler addressed those gathered. A letter writer later wrote that someone declared, "We need to get about a dozen white people and string them up." Early that afternoon a letter was sent to the *Tribune* recommending that all British persons connected with the incident be deported.[126]

Both parties supported internal self-government. While the UBP pledged to promote good will between classes and races and equal opportunities for all, the PLP promised to encourage harmonious race relations and forbid discrimination. The PLP declared that it represented the majority of the Bahamian population. Milo Butler claimed: "We have been run by the UBP and their forefathers for 300 years and it is time we ran ourselves. . . . There are 88 per cent of the population who look like you and me and only 12 per cent who look like the UBP people. . . . No rhyme or reason why people who look like that should go on ruling us."[127] Some violence occurred during the racially heated campaign. Both the *Tribune* and *Guardian* supported the UBP and blamed the violence on the "PLP goon squads." The *Herald* used the "race card" again, once more evoking the Knaur report. The UBP and its supporters warned the public that the PLP were inexperienced and would destroy the Bahamas' economy. Etienne Dupuch's *Tribune* cautioned: "These people don't want to come in to learn government—which is the biggest business in the world . . . they want to take over a happy and prosperous country with perhaps the most delicate economy in the world. In short—they want to experiment with your bread and butter."[128] When Eugene Dupuch commented that "the PLP had created a monster—that is, racism"—a PLP supporter designed a poster declaring: "Let the Monster Live, Good Lord." Almost immediately his landlord of twenty years cancelled his tenancy.[129]

Such victimization was common as campaign rhetoric grew more vitriolic. Milo Butler was quoted as saying: "All these years these people have had their feet on our necks—now you have a chance to throw them off. 300 years ago our pride was ripped out of us slaves in a nasty manner. They beat us until we lost our pride and our language. Now if a man of the other race should kick you, you should kick back, and then you will know you have your pride back."[130]

The 1962 general election held on 27 November was a devastating defeat for the PLP, dashing the hopes of optimistic members of the party. However, the party claimed that it had polled more total votes than the UBP and had lost because of the UBP's stranglehold on the Out Islands, which had twenty-one seats to New Providence's twelve. While the UBP won nineteen seats, the PLP secured eight, a loss of two seats. There were four pro-UBP independents, and two "idiosyncratic independents," Alvin Braynen and Randol Fawkes.[131] Of significance for the PLP was Pindling's retention of his seat and Taylor's defeat. This was the beginning of the end for Taylor. Relations between himself, Pindling, and the National General Council deteriorated. After a series of altercations with the NGC and in order to avoid further humiliation, at the party's eighth convention in 1963 Taylor and Stevenson stood down from the chairmanship and secretaryship, respectively. Pindling was elected chairman as well as parliamentary leader, consolidating his position as the undisputed leader of the PLP with the blessing of the NGC and the NCPA, most of whom were his close friends and allies. Craton argues that the "response of the PLP was to turn itself unequivocally into the party of the black majority, adopting the extreme rhetoric and tactics of the Black Power movement in the United States."[132]

Expressing disappointment and "shock and surprise" at the PLP's defeat, the pro-PLP *Herald* stated that it seemed much more work was needed to open "the eyes of a people kept so long in darkness that they are unwilling to emerge."[133] The main reason for the PLP's setback was almost certainly fear of the consequences of black majority rule, shared not only by the white minority and nonwhite middle classes but by many blacks themselves, including the recently enfranchised women. This was the first election held under universal adult suffrage, a disappointment to the PLP, which had supported the women's suffrage movement, but a relief to the members of the UBP. The latter had feared that the newly enfranchised women would stand by their opponents, who they believed benefited by the abolition in 1958 of the property, plural, and company vote. Obviously, lack of confidence in their fellow blacks (or as PLP pundits preferred to define it, lack of self-confidence or false consciousness and self-hatred) contributed to the defeat. Moreover, many Bahamians feared that the PLP was incapable of maintaining the stability and prosperity they were experiencing under the UBP.[134]

CONFRONTING A DIVIDED SOCIETY

It was not until the establishment of the Progressive Liberal Party in 1953 that organized opposition was felt in the Bahamas, and it would take another fourteen years for the black majority to win political power. Beginning with improved secondary and tertiary education and escalating with the protests of the 1942 riot, the 1956 resolution, and the general strike in 1958, changes underscored racial issues and raised expectations among the black laboring population. Politically, the Bahamas was on the brink of change in 1962. Although that year's election was an overwhelming victory for the United Bahamian Party because of the unbalanced distribution of constituencies, the predominantly black Progressive Liberal Party had won more votes than the white-dominated UBP. Five years later, elections would end in a tie.

By the early 1960s modernity had come to New Providence, if not to the Out Islands. The economy based mainly on tourism and financial services continued to expand. The dominant North American culture brought in by visitors, investors, and Bahamian Project or Contract workers greatly affected the Bahamas. Many who had lived and worked in the United States, having adjusted to higher wages and modern facilities, found it difficult to readjust to traditional Out Island life. With more capital and heightened expectations, many Out Islanders left their settlements to seek employment in Nassau, at Pine Ridge, and later at Freeport in Grand Bahama. Community patterns were changing.

Demographic Forces at Work

Between the 1880s and early 1960s the population of the Bahamas had almost tripled, rising from 43,500 in 1881 to more than 130,000 in 1963.[1] A high birth rate and in-migration from the Out Islands and the West Indies resulted in a tremendous increase in New Providence particularly. Nassau accommodated the greatest number of whites and most of the migrant and non-Bahamian population. The concentration of the population was influenced by the neglect of agriculture and the establishment of tourism as the major industry. After 1953 more than half the Bahamian population lived in New Providence.

Also significant was that people indigenous to New Providence formed only 45.5 percent of its population by 1953; nearly 42 percent were Out Island born.[2] By 1963 foreign-born residents constituted 12 percent of the burgeoning population of New Providence, including West Indians (3 percent), chiefly policemen, and especially Barbadians, who had joined the Bahamas Police Force in large numbers between 1946 and 1952.[3]

Out Islands with declining populations included Abaco, Harbour Island, and Eleuthera in the north, and Cat Island, Rum Cay, Long Cay, and San Salvador in the southern Bahamas. Decline in the Andros population brought on by the demise of sponging was offset by the development of the lumber industry and tourism. Similarly, outside investments stimulated growth in Grand Bahama's population. Having declined before World War I, it showed positive growth due to West End's importance as a base in the clandestine bootlegging trade during Prohibition. After 1944 the development of the lumber industry at Pine Ridge and the subsequent phenomenal growth of Freeport had a decided impact on the expansion of Grand Bahama's population.[4]

Statistics on racial categories provided in the 1943 and 1953 censuses did not appear in the 1963 census. Racial assignments in the censuses of 1943 and 1953 were self-identified as opposed to those given by enumerators. The 1943 census recorded 11.5 percent as Europeans (whites), 83.3 percent as "African (black)," and 4.7 percent as "mixed." "Mongolians" made up 0.3 percent, "others" 0.2 percent, and 67 persons did not state their race. Ten years later in 1953, 12.6 percent classified themselves as whites, an increase probably due to the recent immigration of Americans, Canadians, Britons, and Europeans. Significantly, only 72.6 percent now called themselves black, while 14.2 percent said they were mixed.[5] A decrease of more than 10 percent in the proportion of self-defined blacks and the quadrupling of the actual number calling themselves mixed is surprising. We can perhaps speculate that with the white oligarchy determined to sustain its hegemony in an expanding economy, racial categories would tend to become polarized on the American model to ensure that all who could possibly pass as white would do so.

Paradoxically, though, favorable economic opportunities provided incentives for the mixed-race middle class to distance itself from the black majority, especially the new immigrants from the West Indies, and in particular the Barbadians and Haitians.

Cultivating Solidarity

Black solidarity was also advancing, however. Two institutions that strengthened the nonwhite community were the Baptist Church and the various lodge organizations. Since the late nineteenth century the Baptist faith in the Bahamas had gained in membership and developed a more educated and respected leadership. Reverend Talmadge Sands's appointment as head of Zion Baptist Church in 1931 was of great significance: a Bahamian, a nonwhite, and an Out Islander at that.

Despite the differences between native Baptist churches and Zion, which was linked to the Baptist Missionary Society in London, his appointment served as an example for others.[6] Several early Baptist ministers in New Providence were Out Islanders. Harcourt W. Brown from Eleuthera served at Bethel Baptist Church from 1939 and later at St. John's Native Baptist Church.[7] His successor, Reverend Timothy E. W. Donaldson, was born in Cat Island and began his career as a teacher before migrating to the United States, where he became a citizen. Upon his return in the early 1920s, Donaldson was ordained and given superintendence of various churches on the Out Islands affiliated with St. John's. In the early 1950s he was back in the United States and was awarded a doctor of divinity degree from Bishop McGuire Theological Seminary of New York. His leadership at St. John's saw the promotion of local music and drama. Mixed-race and black youths with natural talent, including Winston V. Saunders, were allowed expression that had hitherto been difficult in the race- and class-conscious Bahamas.[8]

Eleuthera-born Jerome E. Hutcheson headed the Metropolitan Baptist Church, a splinter church of St. John's located in Hay Street, Grant's Town. Another splinter church of St. John's, the Mission Baptist Church on East Street, was headed by Exumian Reuben E. Cooper. In 1933 Enoch Backford, a Long Islander who immigrated to Nassau in the 1920s, was appointed head of Salem Baptist Church, a splinter church of Zion. Backford had received his training at Morehouse College in Atlanta, Georgia, and at the Florida Memorial College in St. Augustine.[9]

The dynamic black leadership within the Baptist Church in the Bahamas attracted respect, and links to southern U.S. Baptist congregations were growing. The bonds were cemented after 1942, when the main Baptist groups combined for a time under the title Bahamas Baptist Mission and Educational Convention, to plan an educational system. In 1944, already in contact with the National Baptist Convention of Chicago and the Southern Baptist Convention of Nashville, Tennessee, the Bahamian Educational Convention received financial assistance from its American affiliates to establish three schools catering to nursery, preparatory, and elementary school children. A Baptist High School was not established until 1961.[10]

Similar in doctrine and American in origin was the Church of God, which also attracted blacks. Akin to the African Methodist Episcopal Church or Shouter Chapel established in Nassau in the mid-nineteenth century and which still existed in some form in the 1950s, the Church of God was a branch of the American institution of the same name. It was originally led in the Bahamas by Bishop W. V. Eneas. Its first church was built Over-the-Hill in the early 1920s, on a street later to become known as Eneas Jumper Corner.[11] As with the Baptists, leadership and congregational autonomy were paramount. This led to divisions, and the Church of God splintered into many groups, including the Church of God of Prophecy, known familiarly as the "Jumper Church." Even in the 1950s it attracted tour operators so that visitors could witness how members in sustained periods of "exaltations" could "ketch the Sperret."[12]

The traditional secular friendly societies formed by liberated Africans, freed slaves, and their descendants grew more sophisticated and were associated with black Freemasonry lodges and such fraternal organizations as the black versions of the Elks, Buffaloes, and Odd Fellows. Many blacks belonged to several organizations, each with its particular character, rituals, and regalia. Elite white men sometimes ridiculed the imitative pretensions of the black societies, failing to recognize the significance of these organizations: "With their arcane mysteries and mimic hierarchies, the blacks were psychologically displacing the alienation and deprivation imposed by the dominant social order. Few whites, moreover, acknowledged the degree to which membership in the societies and the performance of ritualized mysteries provided an institutional link to the kinship and community rituals and ceremonies of aboriginal Africa." Like church participation, membership in the secular black organizations offered leadership roles that "helped to facilitate and shape black political activity in the twentieth century."[13]

Ongoing Disparities in Housing and Land

As in most biracial communities in the Bahamas, residential segregation prevailed in New Providence. During the 1950s while the white population was still largely confined to Nassau and the northern shores, there were also several pockets of whites in Centreville and Sears Addition on the eastern edge of Nassau. As more mobile middle-class mixed-race and black people moved out of their traditional areas, some acquired land to the south of the recently settled white areas. The majority of whites involved, often from Abaco and Harbour Island, were located on the northern side of the suburban developments, generally on hill top and main street lots. Mixed-race persons aspired to such choice properties but either could not afford them or were never offered them by realtors.

To avoid subtle discriminatory practices, some mixed-race couples approached the property owners directly. Some were willing to sell to certain nonwhites if they obtained the necessary financial backing. In most cases this was difficult, so the majority of mixed-race families had to settle for the property in the valley or "middle section." Blacks, because of economic constraints and discrimination by white real estate agents, were relegated to the "back" or southern areas.[14] Sir Orville Turnquest, born and raised in Grant's Town, observed: "The mass of the black population also expanded, as their numbers increased, into areas outside the original Over-The-Hill neighbourhoods into . . . Coconut Grove, Shirley Heights, Culmersville, Sears Addition, Greater Chippingham, Pinewood Gardens and others."[15] Beginning about 1956, Turnquest stated, "many second generation family members would have been getting a better education, jobs, and leaving their parents in Grants Town and Bain Town."[16]

Blacks also settled in the wholly black area of Engleston and on Wulff Road, which in the early 1950s was little more than a cart track. When relocating, more mobile blacks put their Over-the-Hill houses up for rent, often to immigrants. By 1953, 36 percent of the houses in New Providence were tenant occupied.[17] As Doran and Landis have demonstrated, most leased properties fell into disrepair.[18] S.E.V. Luke, one of the assistant secretaries at the Colonial Office, wrote in 1951: "Behind Nassau's picturesque old-world streets and princely mansions along the East and West shores are slums as bad as any in any West Indian Colony, and far worse than anything Bermuda can show." He added that he was "shocked by a personal tour of Nassau's slums with the Governor"—not because they were worse than slums "existing on a larger scale in every West Indian Colony but because it is disgraceful that [such] conditions should exist in so rich an island."[19]

Not all residents would have agreed with this negative report. Turnquest saw the area in 1962 as "the most developed community of the black Bahamian population," though conceding that some zones could perhaps be characterized as slums.[20] Arlene Nash Ferguson noted that deterioration was more pronounced later.[21] Rosemary Hanna's *Pictorial History and Memories of Nassau's Over-the-Hill* (2013) highlights the "tremendous contributions" of Over-the-Hill toward development of the Bahamas.[22]

But infrastructure had not kept pace with the population. Most blacks in New Providence lived in three-roomed wooden houses without running water or sewage disposal. In 1963, 56 percent of all Bahamian houses were of wood construction, some 14 percent of stucco or loose freestone, and 26 percent of concrete block. In New Providence 37 percent of houses had piped public water in 1963, but 12 percent depended on private wells or tanks, and 50 percent had only public standpipes.[23] The majority of Bahamians still depended on water tanks, wells, and public standpipes.

In contrast, substantial improvements in housing had been made among the white elite, better-off whites, and the mixed-race and black middle class. Two- and three-bedroom concrete houses with running water and inside plumbing were becoming common, especially in the predominantly white areas of Centreville and Sears Addition. By 1963, 30 percent (up from 22.3 percent in 1953) of all houses in New Providence were built of concrete.[24] As the population moved from the city into the suburbs, older areas were left more crowded and dilapidated than before.

Residential segregation likewise still prevailed among Out Islanders, the majority living in unpainted wooden houses without running water or inside sanitary facilities.[25] Some communities where substantial foreign or tourist investment had occurred had benefited from installation of public water systems.[26]

Communications and transportation had seen some improvements. Nassau had fairly efficient international telegraph service with cable connections with Bermuda and Fort Lauderdale, Florida; it also operated six radio telephone circuits with the American Telegraph and Telephone Company in Miami, linking it with London. Internally, Nassau was connected to thirty-four Out Island settlements by radio telegraph and had telephone links with twenty-seven of them. It also had ship-to-shore radio circuits in operation at Nassau, Inagua, Cat Cay, and Pine Ridge, Grand Bahama.[27]

As described in chapter 6, Oakes Airfield—where angry laborers had gathered on the morning of 1 June 1942 before rioting in downtown Nassau—became the first commercial airport in the Bahamas.[28] Pan American Airways had Miami-Nassau flights, and British South American Airways launched Nassau-Bermuda-London service that evolved into BOAC's weekly New York-Nassau-Bermuda flights.[29] The road system was improved in the center of Nassau but lagged elsewhere.[30] In the early 1950s most Out Islands still had only rudimentary road systems, although Eleuthera had a seventy-mile asphalted road, and a few other islands had concrete roads within settlements.[31] By 1953 most islands were serviced by motorized mail boats that called weekly.

As improved mail boat service provided more reliable supplies of food, land ownership became less necessary for survival. In monetary terms land had appreciated greatly in value, but its acquisition eluded the majority. Crown lands still amounted to considerable acreages, and land policy had not changed appreciably since the 1890s.[32] Most people were unable to meet the long-standing stipulations reinforced in 1948 that required certain minimal improvements to be made before freehold title was given.[33]

The imperial government's primary land policy objective was to ensure that land leased or sold by the Crown was used for development and not merely held for speculative purposes—a vain hope. Prohibition and tourism drove up land values, which resulted in land being bought for speculative purposes and remaining undeveloped. Influential realtor Harold Christie bought large parcels at nominal prices and sold some for huge profits; the Crown Lands Office was dominated by non-Bahamians.[34] Large holdings prevented expansion by local inhabitants, and fine beaches became private.[35] Some foreigners and local white elites bought their own cays: William Cay in the Exumas, for example, was purchased in 1953 by Hume Cronyn and Jessica Tandy of theatrical fame. During the same year local white businessman Herbert A. McKinney bought Crab Cay, the largest cay in Great Exuma's harbor.[36]

The majority was excluded from the boom. Intricacies in the land tenure system (chapter 1), combined with migration from the Out Islands, meant that owners of generation property left land vacant, and even those farming the land found it difficult to establish title, as in the case of J. Maxwell Bowe's resident sharecroppers (chapter 7).[37] No systematic plan was made before 1962 to resolve the land tenure situation or support traditional farming, and the percentage of people working in agriculture steadily declined.[38] At the same time, wage labor failed to keep pace with the spiraling cost of living.[39]

Enforcing and Eroding Segregation

Prohibition not only enriched certain families, mainly white, but also established a pattern determining the basis of the Bahamas' economy: a strong commercial rather than agricultural bias. The pattern widened the gap between classes and races. Wealthy white Bay Street merchants continued to dominate Bahamian life in every sphere until 1967. American influence exacerbated the situation as Bahamians were further exposed to segregation practices by migrating to Florida and by the presence of thousands of American tourists in Nassau and some Out Islands. As Colin Hughes has argued, race relations in the Bahamas resembled those in the southern United States more than those in the West Indian colonies.[40]

Indeed, the color line hardened. The society was deeply divided by race. Color more than class separated the different sectors. Some upward mobility among poor whites and the black laboring population had occurred, and a small white middle class had emerged, comprising some Nassau whites but mainly Out Island immigrants from Abaco and Harbor Island. But there remained a cleavage between rich and poor even within the white society, although because of their color, poor whites had better chances of obtaining jobs from the white elite.

The economy continued to be tightly controlled by the white elite. As members of the House of Assembly, the white politicians devoted much time and energy to promoting tourism and the financial sector, with the benefits largely accruing to themselves and their relatives and friends. Tourism and financial services yielded high revenues to the rich and powerful, creating "private wealthy empires" and widening the gap between the rich and poor.

Some of the wealthy elite, such as Sir Stafford Sands and Sir Harold Christie, emulated the lavish lifestyles of the winter residents, occupying "palatial homes" and entertaining their friends at "gargantuan dinners and cocktail parties."[41] They employed a host of domestic personnel, which included household servants, cooks, butlers, and chauffeurs.[42]

The traditional elite such as the Duncombes, Adderleys, and Moseleys still held respected positions in the society, but they entertained on a more modest scale and lived more simply, as did the new white middle class made up of professionals, small businessmen, and civil servants. For traditional elite men, the regular Saturday night supper at the Club had ceased when that venerable institution closed in 1946.[43] The segregated St. Andrew's Society and the Royal Victoria Masonic Lodge remained bastions of Nassau's white elite men. The Boy Scout movement under the presidency of Godfrey Higgs was also dominated by the elite.

Elite women were staunch members of the Bahamas Red Cross, the Imperial Order of Daughters of the Empire, and the recently reorganized Girl Guide Association. In the early 1960s the Red Cross Society was headed by wives of the white elite but included several token mixed-race spouses of politicians or successful nonwhite professional men. Charitable work formed part of the ethos of the ruling class and spread gradually to the middle class in the form of noblesse oblige, the notion that it is the duty of the upper class to do good works for the unfortunate of the lower classes. This notion, of course, reinforced social distinction.

Members of the conservative and exclusively white IODE built their own headquarters in 1952 and continued to cater to the armed forces by entertaining officers from the Royal Navy ships that frequently visited Nassau. In addition to the upkeep of the Royal Air Force Cemetery, a relic of World War II, they also performed various charitable works.[44] Many IODE members were associated with the Girl Guide movement, which had been revived by the governor's wife, Lady Murphy, in 1945. Leadership was predominantly white, although the organization encompassed members of both races. Nonwhites included as treasurer Rita Toote, wife of T. A. Toote. Until the mid-1950s Girl Guide companies were strictly segregated by race. The Second Nassau Girl Guide Company in the early '50s was white. Several light-skinned middle-class girls were allowed to join about 1955. However, when the company leader invited darker middle-class girls to join in 1961, most white parents withdrew their daughters. When Arlene Nash (Ferguson) joined in 1961, there was one white guide, Teresa Rae, daughter of liberally minded British civil servant Richard Rae.[45]

Racial segregation also existed in sports. In the 1950s and early 1960s softball and basketball were played at Garfunkel Field in the recently developed suburb of Palmdale. Players were mostly white, although some light-skinned mixed-race men were members of teams. Spectator areas, however, were strictly segregated. Whites sat in an enclosed wired-off section with bleachers on the basketball court, while nonwhites sat in their cars or on a low stone wall outside the compound.[46]

Whites played tennis at the Nassau Lawn Tennis Club, while mixed-race persons and blacks could join the Gym Tennis Club, established in the 1920s. By the early 1950s it had built its own clubhouse on the corner of Wulff Road and Mackey Street. Cricket was attractive to mixed-race people, the black middle class, and a growing number of upwardly mobile West Indians. Sporting clubs including St. George's, St. Albans, St. Bernards, the Westerners, the Vikings, and St. Agnes belonged to the Bahamas Cricket Association, headed in the 1940s by A. F. Adderley and after his death in 1953 by Kendal Isaacs.[47]

Similarly, whites segregated themselves in their church attendance. Most traditionally belonged to the congregations of the Anglican Christ Church

Cathedral, the Methodist Trinity Church and Ebenezer, and the Presbyterian St. Andrew's Kirk. At the Kirk, at least in the 1940s, separate Sunday schools were held for whites and nonwhites.[48] This practice was slightly relaxed by 1962. Similarly, up until the late 1950s and early 1960s, Christ Church, which had a large middle-class mixed-race following, held separate Sunday schools. White children attended on Saturdays, while mixed-race and black children received religious instruction on the Sabbath. At Ebenezer, whites and nonwhites entered through separate doors and sat on different sides of the church.[49]

For the majority of Bahamians, the Board of Education's public educational facilities left much to be desired, with inadequate buildings, short supplies, and few trained teachers. Despite the existence of evening continuation classes and the training college established in 1950, the majority of teachers in that year had no formal training.[50] As late as 1956 half of all Bahamian teachers had received no professional training and lacked even the minimum of academic qualifications.[51] Unsatisfactory primary education resulted in poor performance in secondary schools, with concomitant school certificate results. Very few candidates attempted the Higher School Certificate, and those who did, with few exceptions, were unsuccessful.

However, a number of mixed-race and black persons benefited greatly from the improved standards of the Government High School, which moved out of its cramped quarters in 1960 into a modern purpose-built building at Oakes Field, becoming a crucial factor in the growth of the professional nonwhite middle class. Additionally, the Anglican and Roman Catholic churches had opened high schools including St. John's College Anglican School (1945), which catered to the upwardly mobile nonwhite middle and lower classes. St. Augustine College Catholic School for boys was opened in 1945, and St. Francis Xavier, a high school for girls, had been established in 1890. Both catered to whites and also the upwardly mobile nonwhite middle class. Secondary education, although limited to those who could afford it, was the salvation of nonwhite Bahamians. By 1953 a third of Nassau's legal profession was nonwhite, including A. F. Adderley, Gerald Cash, Eugene Dupuch, Randol Fawkes, Kendal Isaacs, William Swain, Maxwell Thompson, Paul Adderley, Orville Turnquest, and Lynden Pindling.[52]

During the early 1950s a substantial number of mixed-race and black persons were studying in professional fields, including medicine, dentistry, law, and engineering. Those already qualified included five dentists, of whom two were black: Jackson Burnside and Cleveland Eneas. Five out of seventeen doctors were nonwhite, and another nonwhite, Dr. Ricardo DeGregory, held the post of anesthetist at the Bahamas General Hospital.[53] Several Out Islanders and some of West Indian descent also held important positions in the public service. West Indians were usually better educated and more aggressive and upwardly mobile than Bahamians. For example, Clement T. Maynard, the son of a Barbadian artisan, was appointed chief laboratory assistant in the Bahamas General Hospital in 1952.[54] On the other hand, Out Islanders with poorer educational backgrounds were also energetic and upwardly mobile. Inagua-born mixed-race World War II veteran Wenzel Granger, by 1951, occupied the rank of assistant superintendent of the Bahamas Police Force.[55]

A growing number of Out Islanders also succeeded in private enterprise. Long Islander William Cartwright owned a publishing company, while black Exumian E. J. Rolle in 1953 established the Exotic Gardens, a floral and landscaping firm on Marlborough Street in Nassau. Rolle, from Forest in Exuma, had emigrated to Nassau in 1936. After working in Nassau for several years, he attended the Tuskegee Institute in Alabama between 1944 and 1946, training as a horticulturist. On his return to Nassau, he became known for his landscaping abilities.[56]

Women likewise made notable advances through pursuing higher education: Hilda Bowen trained in Britain and became a nursing sister at the Bahamas General Hospital in 1953 and matron in 1962.[57] Other members of the nonwhite middle class who trained professionally overseas were Patricia Fountain, Dorothy Davis, Olivia Jarvis, Clarice Sands, and Keva Bethel (see chapter 7).[58] In the late 1950s and early 1960s Dawn Thompson read geography at the University of Durham, and her sister Jeanne studied law at the University of London. Both sisters were graduates of Wolmer's Girls School in Jamaica, where they completed their Higher School Certificate. Jeanne was the third Bahamian woman to be called to the Bahamas Bar.[59]

Many of the older generation of the mixed-race and black middle class, bound by economic and family responsibilities, continued to work in the civil service, which particularly attracted women, to the dismay of many governmental heads.[60] Nonwhites, now dominating Out Island commissioners' posts, were also beginning to occupy senior posts within the civil service departments. Better educational opportunities and the shortage of suitable whites led to the appointment of mixed-race and black staff. Not many nonwhites held the top posts, however. An exception was the fair-skinned Sidney Eldon, a career civil servant, who held the post of comptroller of customs in 1953, having been appointed seven years before.[61] Many nonwhites felt that discriminatory policies rather than capability excluded such men from holding even more responsible posts. Eldon's long experience in the Treasury Department and as assistant treasurer made him the obvious candidate (before his transfer to customs) for promotion to the receiver generalship and a position in the Executive Council. But even he could advance only so far before meeting the inevitable obstacle of the color barrier. If promoted to the post of receiver general, he would have needed to be invited to Government House and rub shoulders with the wives of the white elite. Eldon was, however, appointed to the Legislative Council in 1951.[62]

For the mixed-race and black middle class, social life had broadened. The white elite benefited most from the developments in tourism, banking, and land investment, but some money filtered down to the middle class. With extra money, rising expectations, and more leisure time, there was an increase in travel and participation in social and sporting clubs. Mixed-race and black middle-class persons were conscious of the poorer nonwhites and had their own idea of noblesse oblige. "Mother Butler," parent of Milo Butler, held in Malcolm's Park an annual treat for the poor, which by the early 1950s had almost become an institution. Following her example were members of the mixed-race elite, including Rita Toote and Ethel Adderley, who spearheaded the Christmas Cheer Fund, a similar but more elaborate charity. Similarly, Lillian Archer's Girl's Lydia Club assisted mixed-race girls who came from humble backgrounds.[63]

Although most whites chose careers in business, an increasing number were entering professional fields. Law traditionally was attractive to a minority of the Nassau elite, but other less prestigious fields such as agriculture and teaching began to attract some. Oris Russell, for instance, studied agriculture at the University of Florida and returned to take up a post in the Department of Agriculture.[64] Similarly, Colin Kelly read French at the Sorbonne and came home to a teaching career.[65] In addition a new consciousness was growing among middle-class whites, some of whom descended from Out Islanders and sought training in less appealing areas. Philip Kemp, for example, received instruction in Kentucky in funeral direction and embalming and returned to Nassau to establish his own business in 1951.[66] Similarly, Albert Russell from Cherokee Sound, Abaco, attended the Florida School of Barbering in the late 1940s and on his return to Nassau in 1949 was employed in the Prince George Hotel's barber shop.[67] Many middle-class whites earned the respect of mixed-race and black persons.

Fundamentally, though, local white views about color had not changed. The Queen's College School Committee, although pressured by the London Methodist Society to integrate Queen's College, admitted the bare minimum of nonwhite children by the late 1950s and early 1960s, fearing that massive numbers would lead to intermarriage, which was to be avoided at all costs.[68] White thinking, subtly upheld by Mary Moseley in the *Nassau Guardian*, was unlikely to be shaken by the paper's new owners, headed by Robert "Bobby" Symonette, a member of the House of Assembly and the son of Sir Roland T. Symonette.[69]

Bobby Symonette had a "tincture" of African "blood" but considered himself white and did not sympathize or mix freely with nonwhites. As described in chapter 7, the definition of a mixed-race person remained an ambiguous matter of subtle distinctions and identifying terms.[70] An Indian ancestor, for example, was more acceptable than an African one.[71] Tourism, exposure to American whites, Garveyism, and postwar egalitarian trends all fed into the mix, and a hierarchy pertained within the black community.[72] Details of physical appearance could count for a lot.[73]

The Politics of Identity

Peter Graham, a white UBP member of the House of Assembly elected in 1956 and 1962, stated that in the latter year, "the Bahamas was racially divided."[74] Sir Arthur Foulkes, who at that time was an active member of the PLP, opined that since the riot of 1942, attitudes of the white ruling class in Nassau had stiffened. He described Stafford Sands in particular as being "uncompromising and more aggressive" than the "old ruling class."[75] Similarly, in the late '50s and early '60s, social stratification in biracial Out Island Bahamian communities hinged on color, with whites occupying dominant positions in the society.

While skin color was important among mixed societies such as those in Tarpum Bay and many communities in Long Island, so too were social attitudes and positions in society. Even if quite dark, "a person is white when he thinks more of white people than of black people. We say his heart is white or her heart is white."[76] A Long Islander might be married to someone black, but if he was a doctor or had "good hair," he was acceptable. In the racially mixed society of Mathew Town, Inagua, there was no segregation as such. The Ericksons, however, had a separate compound where white foreign workers lived.[77] Within all-white and all-black communities, divisions were more dependent on wealth and status. With the adoption of wage labor, class distinctions began to be made according to economic positions dependent on jobs, possessions, power, and social status. Admiration for American imported goods stimulated development of the money economy.

Wage labor was rapidly replacing the old subsistence economy in many Out Island communities, and the massive migration of Out Islanders into the capital caused fundamental changes in Bahamian society, which assisted in eventually breaking down rigid color lines.

While the chief beneficiaries of Nassau's prosperity were the white elite, the expanded mixed-race and black middle class, mainly through a heightened consciousness and increased educational opportunities, made limited material gains. Some middle-class nonwhites were also doing quite well professionally or in business.[78] Worst off were members of the black laboring class, most of whom struggled to sustain their existence, living primarily in poor conditions in Over-the-Hill Nassau.

Improved wage rates in Nassau were neutralized by the increasingly high cost of living caused by the "price-cost structure generated by the tourist economy" and the economic dependence on customs revenues.[79] Catering to tourists, mainly from the caste-conscious United States, bolstered white attitudes in Nassau. Moreover, poor but conservative Out Island whites, who because of their color were at an advantage in the city, looked down on nonwhites. Traditionally fearing intermarriage, whites displayed hostility to any member of their race who dared openly fraternize with a mixed-race or black person. This attitude, almost equivalent to apartheid, was clearly demonstrated in the admissions policy of the local Methodist Church, the Queen's College School Committee, and St. Andrew's School.

Nassau whites disliked the British expatriate officials and took subtle measures to control their numbers. The House of Assembly also legislated to control immigration generally. As Howard Johnson demonstrated, most Bahamians were particularly hostile to West Indians, whom they regarded as "both arrogant and opportunistic."[80] Bahamians generally refused to recognize themselves as West Indian, which to them stood for something "subversive and dangerous."[81] Howard Johnson states: "Ironically in a society long divided along racial lines, class and colour lines, resentment of the outsider provided an element of cohesion which transcended those divisions."[82] The development of tourism and the financial sector had lessened the insularity of the colony and strengthened ties with the United States, with which the Bahamas increasingly identified.

During the 1960s and 1970s, the search for a Bahamian identity began in earnest, with emphasis on an exploration of the African experiences. It can be argued that in the Bahamas the most important element in the search for "self-definition" was racial identity. This emphasis, as Howard Johnson demonstrated, was particularly poignant in view of the marginalization of nonwhites and the severe discrimination suffered until at least the 1960s.[83] Wealth and power continued to be equated with race, which affected every aspect of Bahamian life.

The Election of 1967

In August 1961 the National Committee for Positive Action launched its monthly newspaper the *Bahamian Times*, determined to remove the PLP's conservative old guard, suspecting that this group doubted the ability of blacks to govern. Racial propaganda grew more intense, and public speeches, along with articles in the *Herald* and *Bahamian Times* on the topic of race, were used to stir the emotions of the masses.[84] Sir Arthur Foulkes stated that race was not used by the PLP as "a tactic"—race was "the issue."[85]

Nonwhite Bahamians were "a proud and aspiring people" with a strong, sophisticated black society and a thriving social and cultural life.[86] Yet they had quietly endured discrimination for many years, accepting a sense of inferiority passed on to them by their parents.[87] The mixed-race middle class, acutely aware of the racial divide, began to resent the degrading, unjust treatment and indignities meted out by whites and, in some cases, near whites. The nonwhite population's tolerance for inequality based on racial grounds was steadily eroding. By the 1960s all these forces combined to make race relations a serious issue that the PLP used in their campaign.

After the 1962 election changes began in earnest, in spite of the fact that the Bay Street oligarchy was still in control. A new constitution framed in London in 1963 introduced ministerial government, which came into effect on 1 January 1964, giving nominal protection against discrimination on the grounds of race, place of origin, religion, and political opinion. The PLP, pushing against the discriminatory policies of the governing United Bahamian Party, led a demonstration on 27 April 1965 criticizing unfair constituency boundaries that favored the white minority. Spearheading the demonstration, which came to be known as "Black Tuesday," was opposition leader Lynden Pindling, who in protest hurled the mace from the House of Assembly through an open window. This action was continued by a protest march at the time, and again on 24 May 1965, followed by a visit to New York during August that year for a session of the United Nations Committee on Colonialism. After the demonstration in 1965, the Progressive Liberal Party was "unequivocally . . . the party of the black majority."[88]

Further, PLP supporters were addressed by black American politician Adam Clayton Powell, who warned that they would remain "second class citizens" if they did not unite. The PLP continued its assault on conflict of interest matters, such as those regarding Freeport, Grand Bahama, whereas Development Board chairman, and later as minister of finance, Stafford Sands was privately profiting from consultancy fees from the Port Authority. The PLP held public meetings and demonstrations, with speakers severely criticizing the UBP. Preceding the 1967 elections the PLP petitioned the queen complaining about the "undemocratic allocation of seats in the House of Assembly and the unfair delimitation of electoral boundaries, conflict of interest involving Ministers," and even accusations of "criminal elements of this hemisphere thus endangering our ancient heritage as a God fearing Christian community."[89]

An external factor that assisted the opposition in awakening political consciousness was the civil rights movement in the United States under the dynamic leadership of Martin Luther King Jr. and his close associate Dr. Ralph Abernathy. King visited the Bahamas in 1958, 1960, and 1964, when he met with the PLP leadership. By the mid-1960s Stokely Carmichael's Black Power philosophy also was affecting Bahamians and the PLP leadership.

The 1967 election was fiercely fought. The PLP used the theme from the movie *Exodus,* and the American civil rights anthem "We Shall Overcome" became very popular. According to Dame Doris Johnson, Martin Luther King's famous "I Have a Dream" speech also echoed from juke boxes across New Providence. Black celebrities such as Sidney Poitier and Harry Belafonte lent their support. The emphasis on race had intensified under Pindling's leadership from 1963 with the support of the NCPA within the PLP, led by Arthur Foulkes, Warren Levarity, and Jeffrey Thompson, whose aim was to get rid of the white minority government and open up opportunities for all Bahamians.[90]

Enough nonwhites had the courage to vote for the predominantly black opposition PLP in January 1967 for the election to end in a tie, and Lynden Pindling was able to form the first PLP government with the support of the sole labor candidate Randol Fawkes, who took over the Ministry of Labour, and former UBP member Alvin Braynen, who ran as an independent and agreed to become speaker.[91]

In April 1967 at a Teachers Union banquet, Father Bonaventure Dean, a radical black Roman Catholic priest and headmaster of St. Augustine's High School, made a profound statement.[92] Cognizant of the Detroit race riots in the United States, he declared: "In the Bahamas we do not have Black Power because this implies a 'power' within a country which lacks the legitimate power to achieve its goals. In the Bahamas we have black men in power.

Whether or not their exercise of power will develop in this country a black nation as opposed to a Bahamian nation depends on how well we teach a lesson in the correct meaning of *justice* and equality *for all.*" He continued: "That black men have been treated unjustly by white men is *an uncontestable fact.* It would be wise for white men to admit this. They may have done so in ignorance but they have done so none the less. I believe that an admission that they have acted wrongly will help to blunt the edge that could too easily become a sharp instrument of revenge in the black man." Bonaventure then exhorted black men to be just, to avoid the "evil of the past," and to choose the "correct system of education" that could "pave the way to this because it will be based on the *individual personal worth of each human being* regardless of colour, race or creed."[93] To a large extent successive Bahamian governments have followed his advice.

⁘

As the new premier, Lynden Pindling hardly put a foot wrong during his first year in office. His moderation and shrewdness, and the same qualities in his government, ensured the maintenance of free enterprise, the continued expansion of the tourist industry, and the training of Bahamians to fill as many posts as possible, while recognizing the need for qualified expatriates. The PLP government also made it clear that health services would be improved. Fearful of reprisals and reverse discrimination, a small number of Bahamians left the Bahamas, most notably Stafford Sands and Donald D'Albenas, members of the opposition UBP.[94]

Pindling and the PLP government now generally tried to avoid the encouragement of racial rhetoric. Members of the party were embarrassed when popular black singer Nina Simone urged Bahamians to be more militant "and to take back the land the English had taken from them and stop being frightened of expressing themselves."[95] Dr. Trevor Munroe, a lecturer at the University of the West Indies, visited Nassau in 1970. During his address to the left-leaning Unicomm organization in Nassau, he encouraged its members to follow "a revolutionary rather than reformist ideology," observing that a "black premier did not ensure black government." Pindling, "a reformist" like most new Caribbean leaders in the period surrounding Independence, disagreed with Munroe, remaining convinced that the Bahamas' problems could be solved "within the existing democratic system and under the rule of law."[96] He favored a gradual and peaceful transition from white leadership and discouraged discrimination against citizens of

European descent. His moderation and astuteness ensured that the majority of Bahamians were not alienated or victimized.

On behalf of the PLP, Pindling gave assurances that they would continue to expand tourism and maintain stability. This bolstered confidence and led to a substantial PLP victory and devastating defeat for the UBP in the 1968 general election, called due to the death of PLP member Uriah McPhee. The election results clearly demonstrated the polarization of the Bahamian electorate by racial origins.

Following the election and building on the constitution of 1963, which introduced ministerial government, further constitutional advance was obtained in 1969. This strengthened the colony's independent authority and also augmented the power of the ruling party. The Senate was enlarged, and for the first time the Bahamas government was given the right to negotiate trade and migration agreements with other governments, while the police and internal security were placed under control of a cabinet minister.

The Bahamas government provided new opportunities for Bahamians while actively promoting tourism. It tightened up on the operations in Freeport, which was described as "a foreign outpost," and began the Bahamianization of that city, taking control of immigration to make certain that Freeport became an integral part of the Bahamian community. Emphasis would also be directed at expansion and improvement in the educational system, including the establishment of the College of the Bahamas in 1974.

In 1968 the annual flow of tourists to the Bahamas surpassed the million mark for the first time. Despite the depression in early 1969 and during the 1970s, the general election on 19 September 1972, fought on the issue of Bahamian independence, brought a landslide victory for the PLP, which would remain in power until 1992. As Craton and Saunders explained: "For the first time, the opposition openly acknowledged that the Bahamas belonged to the black majority and attempted to fight the election on issues other than race."[97]

Notes

Abbreviations

ANG	Archives printed by the *Nassau Guardian*
Bahamas Acts	Laws of the Bahamas, Bahamas Archives, Nassau
CO	Colonial Office Records, National Archives, U.K., Kew
conf.	confidential
MMS	Methodist Missionary Society
NC	Neville Chamberlain Papers
NQMP	*Nassau Quarterly Mission Papers*
PRO/EDU	Ministry of Education Records, Bahamas Archives, Nassau
Russell Commission	*Report of the [Russell] Commission . . . 1942*, ANG
WMMS	Wesleyan Methodist Missionary Society

Foreword

1. Craton and Saunders, *Islanders in the Stream*. The second volume won the prestigious Elsa Goveia Prize of the Association of Caribbean Historians in 1999. See also G. Saunders, *Bahamian Society after Emancipation* (2003). This is a revised and expanded edition of the book originally published in 1990 and republished in 1994.

2. C. Hughes, *Race and Politics*.

3. For a fairly recent survey, see G. Saunders, "Recent Developments in the Historiography of the Post-Emancipation Anglophone Caribbean," and Bolland, "Historiography of Decolonization in the Anglophone Caribbean."

4. H. Johnson, *The Bahamas from Slavery to Servitude*.

5. W. Johnson, *Post-Emancipation Race Relations*.

Introduction

1. Lewis, *The Growth of the Modern West Indies*, 62.

2. Craton and Saunders, *Islanders*, 2:56.

3. Ibid., 2:55–73.

4. Ibid., 2:55.

5. Ambrose Shea to Lord Knutsford, 6 April 1889, CO23/231/219–19a, Original Correspondence, Bahamas Governor's Dispatches, 1881–1962, Colonial Office Records, National Archives, United Kingdom, Kew (all Colonial Office records are hereafter cited as CO, with accession numbers); microfilm copies are in the Bahamas Archives, Nassau.

6. Johnston, *Bahamian Jottings*, 11.

7. Bahamas Archives, *Settlements in New Providence*, 18.

8. James A. Archer to MacDonald, Nassau, 11 December 1899, Wesleyan Methodist Missionary Society (hereafter WMMS) Papers, 1883–1946, Bahamas box 22, School of African and Oriental Studies, University of London.

9. Report of Dr. A.H.B. Pearce, Chief Medical Officer, 2 July 1923, encl. Cordeaux to Amery, 20 February 1925, CO23/296.

10. Rawson, *Report on the Bahamas Hurricane of October 1866*, 2, archives printed by the *Nassau Guardian* (hereafter ANG). Many official documents, including votes of the Legislative Council and House of Assembly, were published by the *Nassau Guardian* but are not necessarily stored there; most are housed in the Bahamas Archives, Nassau.

11. Stark, *Stark's History and Guide to the Bahama Islands*, 107.

12. Report on the Census of the Bahama Islands, taken in April 1881, ANG (all 1881–1963 census reports cited in these notes are in this collection); *Colonial Annual Reports, Bahamas, 1881–1907*, 76; *Report on Blue Book for 1887*, 5.

13. Peters, "The American Loyalists," 62-63.

14. Sharer, "The Population Growth of the Bahama Islands," 40–43.

15. Report on the Census of the Bahama Islands, taken on 27 June 1891, ANG.

16. Appendix to the Votes of the House of Assembly, 1890, 33, Archives printed by the *Nassau Guardian* (ANG), held at the Bahamas Archives and the House of Assembly, Nassau.

17. Report on the Census of the Bahama Islands, taken in April 1881, ANG.

18. Stark, *Stark's History and Guide to the Bahama Islands*, 14.

19. Brodber, *A Study of Yards in the City of Kingston*.

20. Savishinsky, *Strangers No More*, 71.

21. Eneas, *Bain Town*, 2–7.

22. *Nassau Quarterly Mission Papers* (hereafter *NQMP*) 6, no. 23 (December 1891): 73.

23. Brathwaite, *The Development of Creole Society in Jamaica*, 306–11.

24. Brereton, *Race Relations*, 3.

25. Ibid., 3–4.

26. H. Johnson, *The Bahamas from Slavery to Servitude*, 99.

27. Themistocleous, "'Merchant Princes of Nassau,'" 144.

28. Ibid., 143.

29. Kiernan, *Lords of Human Kind*, 201.

30. Brereton, *Race Relations*, 5.

31. Craton and Saunders, *Islanders*, 2:52–54.

32. H. Johnson, *The Bahamas from Slavery to Servitude*, 83.

33. Ibid., 60.

34. Craton and Saunders, *Islanders*, 2:11.

Chapter 1. The Bahamas in the Post-Emancipation Period

1. G. Saunders, *Slavery in the Bahamas*, 206.
2. Burn, *Emancipation and Apprenticeship in the British West Indies*, 366.
3. Ibid., 368.
4. Themistocleous, "'The Merchant Princes of Nassau,'" 48–49.
5. Craton and Saunders, *Islanders*, 2:3.
6. Ibid., 2:4.
7. Craton, *History of the Bahamas*, 197.
8. H. Johnson, *The Bahamas from Slavery to Servitude*, 89.
9. Laws of the Bahamas (hereafter Bahamas Acts), 2 Vic. 1, c. 2 (1839), held at the Bahamas Archives and the House of Assembly, Nassau.
10. Bahamas Acts, 3 Vic., c. 3 (1840).
11. Wakefield, *A View of the Art of Colonization*, 328–29; Craton and Saunders, *Islanders*, 2:48.
12. Rogers, "The Wages of Change," 97.
13. Besson, "A Paradox in Caribbean Attitudes to Land."
14. N. Bethel, "Generation Property"; Craton, "White Law and Black Custom."
15. Besson, "Family Land as a Model for Martha Brae's New History." See also Besson, "A Paradox in Caribbean Attitudes to Land."
16. N. Bethel, "Generation Property," 16.
17. Craton and Saunders, *Islanders*, 2:50.
18. Ibid., 2:51.
19. Ibid.
20. Ibid., 2:51–52.
21. Bahamas Acts, 59 Vic., c. 14 (1896); *Statute Law of the Bahamas, 1799–1965* (ed. Hone), 123.
22. Craton and Saunders, *Islanders*, 2:52.
23. Blayney Balfour to Lord Stanley, 19 February 1834, CO23/91/111.
24. H. Johnson, *The Bahamas from Slavery to Servitude*, 84.
25. Ibid., 93. See also W. Haynes-Smith to Joseph Chamberlain, 7 July 1896, no. 76, CO23/244.
26. H. Johnson, *The Bahamas from Slavery to Servitude*, 93.
27. Memorandum of Agreement, 14 August 1865, between Alexander Forsyth, Agent for William Marshall Esq., Attorney of the heirs and Owner of the landed Estate of Charles Farquharson, late of Watlings Island deceased, of the first part, and Jacob Deveaux Senior, Farmer of Watlings Island, O'Brien Collection, Bahamas Archives, Nassau.
28. H. Johnson, *The Bahamas from Slavery to Servitude*, 95–97.
29. G. Saunders, "Social History of the Bahamas," 25.
30. H. Johnson, *The Bahamas from Slavery to Servitude*, 98–99.
31. Ibid., 99.
32. William Colebrook to Baron Glenelg, 3 February 1836, no. 10, CO23/96.

33. H. Johnson, *The Bahamas from Slavery to Servitude*, 100.

34. Ibid.

35. Craton and Saunders, *Islanders,* 2:39.

36. Ibid.

37. Craton and Saunders, *Islanders,* 2:45; see also H. Johnson, *The Bahamas from Slavery to Servitude,* 105–6.

38. Powles, *Land of the Pink Pearl,* 88; Saunders, "Social History of the Bahamas," 27.

39. H. Johnson, *The Bahamas from Slavery to Servitude,* 111.

40. Shedden, *Ups and Downs in a West Indian Diocese,* 111.

41. H. Johnson, *The Bahamas from Slavery to Servitude,* 111.

42. W. Haynes-Smith to Joseph Chamberlain, 7 July 1896, no. 76, CO23/244.

43. H. Johnson, *The Bahamas from Slavery to Servitude,* 113, 115–16.

44. Lewis, *The Growth of the Modern West Indies,* 311.

45. G. Saunders, *Bahamian Society after Emancipation,* 98–100.

46. See Brereton, *Race Relations,* 24.

47. *Colonial Annual Report, Bahamas,* 1890, 3.

48. W. Haynes-Smith to Chamberlain, 4 July 1896, Duplicate Governor's Dispatches, 1893–97, folios 431–39, Bahamas Archives, Nassau.

49. Bahamas Acts, 22 Vic., c. 9, An Act securing the erection of an Hotel in the Island of New Providence, 30 April 1859; Bahamas Acts, 20 Vic., c. 15, An Act to promote and encourage steam Navigation between the Port of Nassau . . . and the Port of New York and to provide in part for the expense of conveying the Mails between those ports, 3 April 1857; Craton, *History of the Bahamas,* 212.

50. Craton and Saunders, *Islanders,* 2:80; Powles, *Land of the Pink Pearl,* 182.

51. *Statute Law of the Bahamas,* 1929 (ed. Harcourt G. Malcolm, printed by Waterlow and Sons, London), xliv–xlv.

52. T. Thompson, "Constitutional Authority in the Bahama Islands, 1946–1947," 20.

53. Malcolm, *Manual of Procedure in the Business of the General Assembly,* 113–24; *Bahamas Blue Books,* 1844, 64, 66, Bahamas Archives, Nassau; T. Thompson, "Constitutional Authority in the Bahama Islands, 1946–1947," 21; Dupuch, "Government in the Bahamas," 125. The *Blue Books* are a compilation of colonial government statistical records. The Bahamas Archives had the *Blues Books* transferred from the Colonial Secretary's Office, Nassau, to the Bahamas Archives.

54. Themistocleous, "'Merchant Princes of Nassau,'" 172; Duke of Buckingham and Chandos to Rawson, no. 4053, 6 May 1868, CO23/192/158–61.

55. Bahamas Acts, 10 Geo. IV, c. 10, An Act to amend an Act, entitled An Act for consolidating the several acts for regulating elections and qualifications of members of the General Assembly of these islands and of electors, and for ascertaining and describing the limits and bounds of several islands and districts within the government, which send representatives to the General Assembly, and for other purposes therein mentioned, 11 January 1830.

56. Craton, *History of the Bahamas,* 120.

57. Sands, *The Anglican Church and Education in the Bahamas*, 80.

58. Police Act, 31 December, Laws, Duplicate Manuscript, 1814–22, Bahamas Archives, Nassau; Craton and Saunders, *Islanders*, 2:322.

59. District Chairman to MMS (Methodist Missionary Society), 4 August 1838, quoted in Cash, Gordon, and Saunders, *Sources of Bahamian History*, 144. See also W. Johnson, *Post-Emancipation Race Relations*, 80.

60. Craton and Saunders, *Islanders*, 1:334.

61. Symonette and Canzoneri, *Baptists in the Bahamas*, 13–14.

62. Kirkley Sands, "Religion in the Bahamas," notes for lectures used at the College of the Bahamas, 2004.

63. Lowenthal, *West Indian Societies*, 115.

64. Powles, *Land of the Pink Pearl*, 159; Stark, *Stark's History and Guide to the Bahama Islands*, 239; Craton and Saunders, *Islanders*, 2:102.

65. Williams, *Methodist Contribution*, 107.

66. Sir Rawson W. Rawson to the Duke of Buckingham and Chandos, 4 May 1868, CO23/191/434–39.

67. Bahamas Acts, 32 Vic., c. 27 (1869); King, *Addington Venables*, 28–29.

68. Gordon, *A Century of West Indian Education*, 1, 10.

69. Williams, *Methodist Contribution*, 52.

70. Ibid., 52-53.

71. Gordon, *A Century of West Indian Education*, 10.

72. Bahamas Acts, 6 Wm. IV, c. 17 (1836). See also William Colebrooke to Lord Glenelg, 14 May 1836, CO23/96/481–82.

73. Williams, *Methodist Contribution*, 54–55.

74. Bahamas Board of Education Annual Report, 1838, PRO/EDU/5/28, 2, Ministry of Education Records, Bahamas Archives, Nassau (hereafter cited as PRO/EDU with relevant accession numbers).

75. Bahamas Acts, 2 Vic., c. 1.15 (1839); Williams, *Methodist Contribution*, 54.

76. Williams, *Methodist Contribution*, 152.

77. Craton and Saunders, *Islanders*, 2:27.

78. Craton and Saunders, *Islanders*, 2:28; W. J. Woodcock, Popular Education in the Bahamas, Nassau, 1851, CO23/140, 71–80.

79. Craton and Saunders, *Islanders*, 2:27.

80. John Gregory to Earl Grey, 1 January 1852, CO23/140, 5–9; February 1852, 52–54.

81. Bahamas Acts, 10 Vic., c. 1 (1864).

82. Craton, *History of the Bahamas*, 200–1.

83. Williams, *Methodist Contribution*, 61.

84. *Bahamas Almanac*, 1894, 113; Williams, *Methodist Contribution*, 61.

85. Craton and Saunders, *Islanders*, 2:30, 95.

86. Report of the Board of Education and Inspector of Schools, 1870–71, p. 7, PRO/EDU/5, 3, 2–6.

87. Report of the Inspector of Schools 1875–1876, p. 1, PRO/EDU/5/4/6.

Chapter 2. Bahamian Society in the Late Nineteenth and Early Twentieth Centuries

1. C. Hughes, *Race and Politics*, 24–37; L. Braithwaite, "Stratification in Trinidad"; Smith, *The Plural Society in the British West Indies*, 162–75; Furnivall, *Netherlands India*; Furnivall, *Colonial Policy and Practice*; Lowenthal, *West Indian Societies*, 91.

2. C. Hughes, *Race and Politics*, 24–25.

3. Smith, *The Plural Society in the British West Indies*, 162–75; Smith, *A Framework for Caribbean Studies*,60.

4. C. Hughes, *Race and Politics*, 26.

5. Ibid.

6. Powles, *Land of the Pink Pearl*, 120. See also Dupuch, *Tribune Story*, 20–21.

7. Ambrose Shea to Knutsford, 21 May 1888, CO23/230/206–207a.

8. Haynes-Smith to Chamberlain, 7 July 1896, CO23/244/104–20.

9. Powles, *Land of the Pink Pearl*, 316–17, 318.

10. *Bahamas Blue Book*, 1894 and 1897, Bahamas Archives, Nassau; also in Colonial Office Records, National Archives, United Kingdom, Kew.

11. *Nassau Guardian*, 4 and 9 May 1892.

12. *Nassau Guardian*, 14 May 1892.

13. Shea to Knutsford, 21 May 1892, CO23/234/282.

14. *Nassau Guardian*, 21 May 1892.

15. Northcroft, *Sketches of Summerland*, 56.

16. Austen Chamberlain to Joseph Chamberlain, 23 November 1890, Neville Chamberlain Papers, NC/1/6/102, University of Birmingham, United Kingdom (hereafter cited as NC with accession numbers).

17. *NQMP* 33, no. 129 (June 1918): 12.

18. *Nassau Guardian*, 19 April 1905 (R. H. Sawyer's obituary); the post-nominals CMG signify appointment to the rank of Companion in the chivalric Order of St. Michael and St. George.

19. Dupuch, *Bahamas Handbook and Businessman's Annual*, 1975–76, 16–25.

20. Encl. Allardyce to Bonar Law, 16 December 1916, CO23/278/264.

21. See Armbrister, Recollections (1947–57), P.W.D. Armbrister Papers, Bahamas Archives, Nassau; see also Ruth Bowe, "Honourable Percy William Armbrister, 1862–1957," *Journal of the Bahamas Historical Society* 3, no. 1 (October 1981): 20–22.

22. Craton and Saunders, *Islanders*, 2:209.

23. Rev. T. Raspass, Nassau, to Rev. C. Osborn, Methodist Missionary Society (hereafter MMS), 15 September 1890, West Indies Correspondence, Bahamas, School of African and Oriental Studies, University of London.

24. Powles, *Land of the Pink Pearl*, 41.

25. Ives, *The Isles of Summer*, 291.

26. Powles, *Land of the Pink Pearl*, 126.

27. Northcroft, *Sketches of Summerland*, 55.

28. Powles, *Land of the Pink Pearl*, 129.

29. Neville Chamberlain Papers, 1890–98, Sunday, 18 January 1891, NC 3/2/1.

30. Bruce, *Memoirs of Peter Henry Bruce*, 400.

31. *Bahamas Almanac*, 1894, 26.

32. *Bahamas Almanac*, 1892, 25.

33. Dupuch, *A Salute to Friend and Foe*, 28, 30.

34. *Bahamas Almanac*, 1892, 18–19.

35. Churton, *Island Missionary of the Bahamas*, 96–97.

36. Gostwick to McDonald, Nassau, 10 February 1898, MMS, West Indies Correspondence.

37. Dupuch, *Tribune Story*, 64.

38. Brereton, *Race Relations*, 193.

39. Banton, *Race Relations*, 38–54

40. Bolt, *Victorian Attitudes to Race*, 134–37, 143.

41. Northcroft, *Sketches of Summerland*, 64.

42. Dupuch, *Tribune Story*, 20.

43. Ives, *Isles of Summer,* 292.

44. Powles, *Land of the Pink Pearl*, 120–21.

45. Ibid., 123.

46. Ibid., 121, 123.

47. G. Saunders, *Bahamian Loyalists and Their Slaves*, 7.

48. Northcroft, *Sketches of Summerland*, 61.

49. Powles, *Land of the Pink Pearl*, 105, 108–9, 309: Powles to Holland, 29 July 1887, CO23/229/621–32; Blake to Holland, 12 September 1887, CO23/229/448–49; Powles to Holland, 29 July 1887, CO23/229/625–30.

50. Encl. in Taylor (Administrator) to Holland, 19 August 1887, CO23/229/427.

51. Powles, *Land of the Pink Pearl*, 112. See also Votes of the House of Assembly, 1887, 12–13, ANG; Bahamas Acts, 50 Vic., c. 3, 1887, Act to Indemnify all persons who have acted contrary to Acts of Assembly relating to erection of wooden buildings to provide against further violations of the said Acts.

52. *Nassau Times*, 9 and 23 April and 15 June 1887.

53. Henry Blake to Holland, 12 July 1887, CO23/229/361–62.

54. Powles, *Land of the Pink Pearl,* 309; *Nassau Guardian*, 5 September 1887; Wilmot, "Race and Justice in the Bahamas: The Case of Lewis Powles."

55. Henry Blake to Holland, 25 June 1887, CO23/229/236–37.

56. Northcroft, *Sketches of Summerland,* 62.

57. Dupuch, *Tribune Story*, 37.

58. Interview with Rowena Eldon, 3 May 1983, Nassau.

59. Lowenthal, *West Indian Societies*, 90.

60. Cox, *Caste, Class, and Race*, 361–62.

61. Themistocleous, "'Merchant Princes of Nassau,'" 138.

62. Ibid., 167.

63. Henry Blake to Earl of Derby, 10 May 1884, CO23/224/208–12.

64. Extract from a private letter to L. D. Powles, unsigned and undated, CO23/235/279–85, and enclosed in Powles (London) to Marquis Rippon, 29 October 1892, CO23/235/277–78.

65. Craton and Saunders, *Islanders*, 2:95–96.

66. G. Saunders, *Social Life in the Bahamas, 1880s–1920s*, 18–19.

67. *Bahamas Almanac*, 1901, pages with list of names unnumbered.

68. Interview with Cecil V. Bethel, 1 May 1984, Nassau.

69. Dupuch, *Tribune Story*, 20–23.

70. Neville Chamberlain's Diary, 1890–98, NC2/2/1.

71. Powles, *Land of the Pink Pearl*, 101.

72. Cited in Themistocleous, "'Merchant Princes of Nassau,'" 221. See *Nassau Guardian*, 25 September–10 November 1886.

73. Themistocleous, "'Merchant Princes of Nassau,'" 220. See also James Carmichael Smith Papers, Royal Commonwealth Society Library, Cambridge University.

74. E. B. Taylor to Lord Knutsford, 14 August 1889, CO23/231/502–8, and Ambrose Shea to Lord Knutsford, 5 November 1889, CO23/231/630–32; Votes of the House of Assembly, 1883, 50, ANG.

75. Votes of the House of Assembly, 1885, 103, ANG.

76. Votes of the House of Assembly, 1889, 193–95, ANG.

77. Ambrose Shea to Lord Knutsford, 23 November 1889, CO23/231/356–57.

78. Lowenthal, *West Indian Societies*, 105, 110.

79. Interview with Cecil V. Bethel, 1 May 1984, Nassau.

80. Ambrose Shea to Rippon, 29 April 1893, CO23/236/256–63; see also *Nassau Tribune*, 24 November 1924 (hereafter cited simply as *Tribune*).

81. Shea to Rippon, 29 April 1893, Co23/236/263.

82. *Tribune*, 24 February 1951; letter, Ian Duffield, Dept. of History, University of Edinburgh to Mr. Simpson, Royal Commonwealth Society, n.d., RCMS 113/27/28, Manuscript Section, Royal Commonwealth Society Library, Cambridge University.

83. Lowenthal, *West Indian Societies*, 113.

84. Ibid., 111.

85. Craton and Saunders, *Islanders*, 2:98.

86. McDermott, "L. W. Young: Formidable Force from Fox Hill," 15.

87. Interviews with Rowena Eldon, 3 May and 8 December 1983.

88. Craton and Saunders, *Islanders*, 2:98.

89. H. Johnson, "Friendly Societies in the Bahamas, 1834–1910," 184–86.

90. Craton and Saunders, *Islanders*, 2:116.

91. Lowenthal, *West Indian Societies*, 115.

92. E. C. Bethel, "Music in the Bahamas," 55.

93. Ibid., 55–56.

94. McCartney, *Ten, Ten, the Bible Ten*, 56.

95. *NQMP* 11, no. 43 (December 1896): 79.

96. Craton and Saunders, *Islanders*, 2:118.

97. Henry Blake to Granville, 20 March 1886, no. 32, Duplicate Governor's Dispatches, 8 December 1881, 25 July 1887, 419, Bahamas Archives, Nassau.

98. Eneas, *Bain Town*, 46.

99. Edwards, *Bahamas Songs and Stories* (1895), 17–19.

100. Northcroft, *Sketches of Summerland*, 71.

101. E. C. Bethel, "Music in the Bahamas," 124.

102. *NQMP* 10, no. 39 (December 1895): 84.

103. E. C. Bethel, "Music in the Bahamas," 125–26. See also *NQMP* 10, no. 39 (December 1895): 84; Powles, *Land of the Pink Pearl*, 148.

104. Powles, *Land of the Pink Pearl*, 147

105. Northcroft, *Sketches of Summerland*, 66.

106. *Nassau Times*, 31 July 1880 and 3 August 1881.

107. Eneas, *Bain Town*, 32.

108. Interview with Dr. C. R. Walker, 31 July 1970, Grant's Town.

109. *Nassau Guardian*, 10 August 1886.

110. E. C. Bethel, "Music in the Bahamas," 217.

111. Powles, *Land of the Pink Pearl*, 147–48.

112. Farquharson, *A Relic of Slavery*, Wed., 26 December 1832, 36.

113. *Nassau Guardian*, 29 December 1886.

114. *NQMP* 4, no. 16 (March 1890): 245.

115. E. C. Bethel, "Music in the Bahamas," 219.

116. *Nassau Guardian*, 24 December 1890.

117. Bahamas Acts, 62 Vic., c. 31, 1899; E. C. Bethel, "Music in the Bahamas," 220.

118. *Nassau Guardian*, 27 December 1899.

119. McDermott, "L. W. Young: Formidable Force from Fox Hill," 34–35.

120. Detailed Sanitary Report on the area between Victoria and Church Street, 21 June 1923, encl. in Cordeaux to Amery, 20 February 1924, CO23/296.

121. Interview with Jennie Cancino, 12 January 1984, Nassau.

122. Rawson, *Report on the Bahamas Hurricane of October 1866*, 2, archives of the *Nassau Guardian*.

123. Interview with Sybil Thompson, 25 April 1984, Nassau. See also Powles, *Land of the Pink Pearl*, 212.

124. *NQMP* 28, no. 109 (June 1913): 26; Lester to Hartley, 27 June 1893, MMS, West Indies Correspondence; see also *NQMP* 4, no. 16 (March 1890): 250.

125. Craton and Saunders, *Islanders*, 2:156. See also Bahamas Archives, *The Salt Industry of the Bahamas*.

126. H. Johnson, *The Bahamas from Slavery to Servitude*, 113.

127. Bahamas Archives, *The Bahamas in the Nineteenth Century, 1870–1899*, 15.

128. Eric, "'Buckra Land' Land: Two Weeks in Jamaica," 5. The name Allan Eric is a pseudonym for C. W. Willis; cited in H. Johnson, *The Bahamas from Slavery to Servitude*, 113–14.

129. H. Johnson, *The Bahamas from Slavery to Servitude*, 115.

130. Powles, *Land of the Pink Pearl*, 59.

131. Report on the Census of the Bahama Islands, taken on 27 June 1891; Report on the Census of the Bahama Islands, taken on 14 April 1901, ANG.

132. *NQMP* 12, no. 47 (December 1897): 76.

133. Craton and Saunders, *Islanders*, 2:147.

134. Powles, *Land of the Pink Pearl*, 204.

135. Ibid., 111–12. See also Craton and Saunders, *Islanders*, 2:149.

136. Powles, *Land of the Pink Pearl*, 219.

137. Dodge, *Abaco*, 72.

138. Craton and Saunders, *Islanders*, 2:150.

139. *NQMP* 4, no. 13 (June 1889): 154.

140. Mills, "The Study of a Small and Isolated Community in the Bahamas," 877.

141. *Nassau Times*, 28 July 1880.

142. Tull, "Colour Pride in Tarpum Bay," 71.

143. Stark, *History of and Guide to the Bahama* 39.(139)

144. Haynes-Smith to Chamberlain, 7 July 1896, CO23/244/117.

145. Powles, *Land of the Pink Pearl*, 70.

146. Stark, *History of and Guide to the Bahama* , 138.

147. Interview with Dame Ivy Dumont, former governor general, 22 October 2009, Nassau.

148. *NQMP* 9, no. 34 (September 1894): 56; Holm, "African Features in White Bahamian English," 53; Craton and Saunders, *Islanders*, 2:158–60.

149. *NQMP* 27, no. 112 (March 1914): 128; *NQMP* 11, no. 42 (September 1896): 40; Neville Chamberlain to Joseph Chamberlain, 25 December 1890, NC1/6/10/10.

150. *NQMP* 11, no. 44 (March 1897): 112. See also Otterbein, *The Andros Islanders*, 136; La Flamme, "Green Turtle Cay"; Gelda and Griffin, "Dyadic Relationships within the Bahamian Family."

151. Penrose, "Sanitary Conditions in the Bahamas," 410–11.

152. Ibid., 409.

153. Interview with Drs. John and Sonia Lunn, 10 September 1984, Nassau. See also Dorland and Arey, *Dorland's Illustrated Medical Dictionary*.

154. Interview with His Excellency, the Honourable Arthur D. Hanna, 16 March 2010, Nassau; see also interview with Percival Hanna, 22 February 1984, Nassau.

155. William Aranha to Acting Colonial Secretary, 17 August 1932; Aranha to Acting Colonial Secretary, 25 March 1933, Colonial Secretary Papers, Bahamas Archives, Nassau; Orry Sands, pers. comm., Nassau, 12 June 2012.

156. Otterbein, *The Andros Islanders*, 71, 74.

157. Ibid., 77.

158. Smith, *West Indian Family Structure*, 247.

159. Otterbein, *The Andros Islanders*, 84.

160. *NQMP* 9, no. 34 (September 1894): 55.

161. *NQMP* 8, no. 30 (September 1893): 34.

162. Shedden, *Ups and Downs in a West Indian Diocese*, 144–45

163. Defries, *In a Forgotten Colony*, 81–83.

164. Powles, *Land of the Pink Pearl*, 72

165. Craton and Saunders, *Islanders*, 2:160.

166. *NQMP* 4, no. 15 (December 1889): 218.

167. *NQMP* 11, no. 44 (March 1897): 122.

168. Neville Chamberlain to Ida Chamberlain, Andros, 25 December 1893, NC1/16/2/24.

169. *Nassau Guardian*, 1 January 1897.

170. Bahamas Archives, *Junkanoo*, 15.

171. *NQMP* 3, no. 10 (September 1888): 54. See also Craton and Saunders, *Islanders*, 2:167.

172. Edwards, *Bahama Songs and Stories* (1942), opposite 18 and 90.

Chapter 3. Gradual Changes in the Bahamas, 1880–1914

1. Thomson, *England in the Twentieth Century*, 24.

2. Ibid., 22–23.

3. Williamson, *A Notebook of Commonwealth History*, 225.

4. Ibid., 240; Thomson, *England in the Twentieth Century*, 31.

5. Lewis, *The Growth of the Modern West Indies*, 64.

6. Ibid., 63.

7. Blake to Derby, 12 August 1884, CO23/224.

8. Craton and Saunders, *Islanders*, 2:145.

9. Powles, *Land of the Pink Pearl*, 92; Craton and Saunders, *Islanders*, 2:145.

10. Bahamas Archives, *The Pineapple Industry of the Bahamas*, 18–20.

11. Bahamas Acts, 52 Vic., c. 22 and c. 25 (1889).

12. Shea to Knutsford, 6 April 1889, CO23/231/217–18.

13. Shea to Knutsford, 21 April 1891, Duplicate Governor's Dispatches, 1887–93, 366, Bahamas Archives, Nassau.

14. Shea to Ripon, 24 April 1894, CO23/239/218a; Shea to Ripon, 23 April 1894, Duplicate Governor's Dispatches, 1893–97, 129, Bahamas Archives, Nassau.

15. Rev. F. B. Mathews to Archdeacon Wakefield, 28 February 1894, NC3/7/24.

16. Feiling, *The Life of Neville Chamberlain*; Neville Chamberlain's Diaries, 25 November 1890, 2 June 1891, NC2 2/1.

17. Austen Chamberlain to Joseph Chamberlain, 3 January 1891, NC1/6/10/11.

18. Neville Chamberlain to Joseph Chamberlain, 2 July 1891, NC1/6/10/19.

19. Neville Chamberlain to Joseph Chamberlain, 15 July 1891, NC1/6/10/20.

20. Ambrose Shea to Ripon, 24 April 1894, CO23/239/218–19.

21. Neville Chamberlain to Joseph Chamberlain, 8 November 1895, NC1/6/10/102, 110, 114.

22. Out Island Commissioner's Report, Nicoll's Town, Andros, 1915, Bahamas Archives, Nassau; Craton, *History of the Bahamas*, 238.

23. H. Johnson, *The Bahamas from Slavery to Servitude*, 114.

24. Dupuch, *Tribune Story*, 21; *Watchman*, 5 November 1901 and 5 December 1903.

25. See 4 of 1907, *Bahamas Statute Law*, c. 242, in *Statute Law of the Bahamas*, 1929 (ed. Harcourt G. Malcolm); Grey-Wilson to Elgin, Duplicate Governor's Dispatches, 17 July 1907, 206–8, Bahamas Archives, Nassau.

26. Out Island Commissioner's Report, Fresh Creek, Andros, 1919, Bahamas Archives, Nassau.

27. *Freeman*, 5 April 1887.

28. Brereton, "'The Development of an Identity,'" 280.

29. Paul Adderley, *From Pompey to Pindling*, Inaugural Sir Lynden O. Pindling Memorial Lecture, Nassau, 22 March 2001, DVD, Bahamas Archives, Nassau.

30. R. Adderley, *"New Negroes from Africa,"* 227.

31. H. Johnson, "Friendly Societies in the Bahamas," 184–86.

32. Quoted in ibid., 194. See also *Nassau Guardian*, 3 August 1887.

33. R. Adderley, *New Negroes from Africa*, 227.

34. Ibid.

35. *Freeman*, 21 February 1888.

36. Ibid.

37. *Freeman,* 21 February 1888, meeting of the Anglo-African League; *Freeman*, 20 March 1888, meeting of the Anglo-African League.

38. *Freeman*, 20 March 1888.

39. *Nassau Guardian*, 14 April 1888.

40. Votes of the House of Assembly, Nassau, 20 March 1888, ANG.

41. R. Adderley, *New Negroes from Africa*, 234; Cash, Gordon, and Saunders, *Sources of Bahamian History*, 228–30.

42. R. Adderley, *New Negroes from Africa*, 235.

43. Eneas, *Bain Town* (1988), 36.

44. H. Johnson, *The Bahamas from Slavery to Servitude*, 119.

45. *Bahama Herald*, 24 December 1858; published 1849–77.

46. Bayley to Newcastle, 11 February 1861, CO23/165/19.

47. C. L. Johnson, "The Strategic Importance of the British West Indies, 1882–1932," 25–26; see also H. Johnson, *The Bahamas from Slavery to Servitude*, 119–30.

48. Lees to Kimberley, 29 July 1882, CO23/222.

49. H. Johnson, *The Bahamas from Slavery to Servitude*, 121.

50. Encl., undated, in Henry Blake to Frederick Stanley, 19 September 1885, confidential (hereafter conf.), CO23/226.

51. H. Blake to F. Stanley, 8 August 1888, conf., CO23/226.

52. Powles, *Land of the Pink Pearl*, 113, 114–15.

53. Shea to Knutsford, 22 November 1888; Winfield to Kimberley, 19 December 1888, CO23/230; H. Johnson, *The Bahamas from Slavery to Servitude*, 122.

54. Knutsford to Ambrose Shea, 19 January 1888, conf. (draft), CO23/230, cited in H. Johnson, *The Bahamas from Slavery to Servitude*, 124.

55.Bahamas Acts, 54 Vic. c. 14 (1891); H. Johnson, *The Bahamas from Slavery to Servitude*, 125.

56. Brereton, *Race Relations*, 127–28.

57. Shea to Rippon, 1 May 1893, CO23/236/408, 409–10; 8 July 1893, CO23/237/135.

58. Encl. in Shea to Rippon, 8 July 1893, CO23/237/107–38.

59. Jackson to Rippon, 17 July 1893, no. 101, Duplicate Governor's Dispatches, 4 May 1893–3 August 1897, folio 44, Bahamas Archives, Nassau; Jackson to Ripon, 20 July 1893, CO23/237/176–79.

60. Evidence of Reverend Willerup, encl. in Administrator H. Jackson to Ripon, 20 July 1893, CO23/237/187; see also enclosed Notes of Evidence taken by the Committee of Enquiry into recent disturbances on 15 April 1893, CO23/237/175–89.

61. H. Johnson, *The Bahamas from Slavery to Servitude*, 128; Shea to Ripon, 8 July 1893, CO23/237/98–106.

62. H. Johnson, *The Bahamas from Slavery to Servitude,* 129–30.

63. *Tribune*, 3, 4, 18 February, 10, 20 August, 2, 20 September, 21 October 1911, 18, 19, 21 June 1913.

64. *Nassau Guardian,* 5 August 1914*; Tribune,* 5 August 1914.

65. *Colonial Annual Reports, Bahamas,* 1918–19, encl. Allardyce to Milner, 16 January 1920, conf., CO23/286/84.

66. Bahamas Acts, Edward VII, c. 8, (1907); *Colonial Annual Reports, Bahamas,* 1946, 30–31.

67. An Act to Provide for the Control of the Ice House and to regulate the supply and the sale of ice, 1923, *Statute Law of the Bahamas,* 1799–1929, vol. 2, c. 240.

68. *Tribune,* 3, 5 January 1911; Bahamas Acts, 2 and 3 Geo. V, c. 8 (1912); *Strombus Magazine* 1, no. 2 (February 1913): 1.

69. Glinton-Meicholas, *From the Void to the Wonderful,* 27.

70. Interview with Herbert McKinney, 8 November 1975; Malone and Roberts, *Nostalgic Nassau,* 59.

71. Bahamas Acts, 7 and 8 Edward VII, c. 31, An Act Regulating the Law as to Motor Cars in the Island of New Providence, 8 June 1908; *Tribune,* 4 June 1911.

72. Bahamas Acts, Medical Act; For the Registration of Medical Practitioners, 5 and 6 Edward VII, 1906, c. 7.

73. Ibid.

74. Medical Report 1912, encl. Haddon-Smith to Harcourt, 17 June 1913, CO23/271/271.

75. Medical Report 1914, encl. Hart-Bennett to Harcourt, 7 April 1915, CO23/275/211–12, 218–22; Bahamas Acts, Pharmacy Act, 3 and 4 Geo. V (1913).

76. Cottman and Blassingame*, Out Island Doctor.*

77. William Allardyce to G.E.A. Grindle, 30 March 1916, private, CO23/279/101.

78. Dupuch, *Tribune Story,* 24–25.

79. Grey-Wilson to Harcourt, 2 January 1912, CO23/269/9.

80. Bahamas Acts, 1 and 2 Geo. V, c. 7, An Act to consolidate and amend the Law

relating to Public Medical Officers, 13 July 1911; 17 of 1914, An Act to Make provision for securing the Public Health, 22 June 1914.

81. Haddon-Smith to Harcourt, 17 June 1913, CO23/271/279.

82. Bahamas Acts, 17 of 1914, An Act to Make provision for securing Public Health, 22 June 1914.

83. Medical Report 1914, encl. Hart-Bennet to Harcourt, 7 April 1915, CO23/275/209–10; Medical Report 1912, encl. Haddon-Smith to Harcourt, 17 June 1913, CO23/271–72.

84. Medical Report 1919–20, encl. Grant to Milner, 6 October 1920, CO23/287/16–18.

85. *Report of the Commission on Venereal Diseases* (Nassau: Nassau Guardian, 1918), 4, Bahamas Archives, Nassau; Bahamas Acts, 3 and 4 Geo. V (1913), Pharmacy Act; 4 Geo. V, c. 13 (1914), Immoral Traffic Act.

86. *Nassau Guardian*, 10 May 1916.

87. Haddon-Smith to Harcourt, 1 January 1914, conf., CO23/269/304–6.

88. Dodge, *Abaco*, 83–86; *Colonial Annual Reports, Bahamas*, 1916–17.

89. Tinker, *Migration of Peoples*, 137.

90. Out Island Commissioner's Reports, Cherokee Sound, Abaco, 1912, Bahamas Archives, Nassau; Wesleyan Methodist Missionary Society (WMMS) Papers, Foreign Field VII, 1910–11, 167, School of Oriental and African Studies, University of London; Williams, *Methodist Contribution*, 179; Dodge, *Abaco*, 84; Nancy Albury, "A Preliminary Review of the Abandoned Settlements and Logging Operations at Wilson City and Whitesville, Great Abaco, the Bahamas, 2010," Bahamas Archives, Nassau.

91. Haddon-Smith to Harcourt, 1 January 1914, CO23/273, 4–7; *Tribune*, 17 December 1913; *Colonial Annual Reports, Bahamas*, 1913–14; Asa Paine, General Manager, Bahamas Timber Co., to Haddon-Smith, and Bernard L. Wyatt to Commandant R. H. Crawford, 21 December 1913, CO23/273/8, 9.

92. *Colonial Annual Reports, Bahamas*, 1916–18; Dodge, *Abaco*, 85–87, 98–103.

93. Report on the Census of the Bahama Islands, Taken 2 April 1911, ANG.

94. Quote from Bayley to Newcastle, 25 April 1860, no. 38, CO23/163; see also H. Johnson, *The Bahamas from Slavery to Servitude*, 154; and Cash, Gordon, and Saunders, *Sources of Bahamian History*, 245.

95. Blake to Stanley, 8 August 1885, CO23/226.

96. Cash, Gordon, and Saunders, *Sources of Bahamian History*, 96.

97. Ibid., 96–97.

98. Parks, *Miami: The Magic City*, 87–88; speech of Governor Grey-Wilson, 5 February 1907, Votes of the Legislative Council, 5 February–8 July 1907, 8, ANG; letter from "Twist Back," *Tribune*, 19 January 1911; H. Johnson, *The Bahamas from Slavery to Servitude*, 155.

99. H. Johnson, *The Bahamas from Slavery to Servitude*, 154–55.

100. British Ambassador, Washington, to Colonial Office, 13 April 1911, Colonial Office Records, U.K., and copy in Bahamas Archives, Nassau; Out Island Commissioner's Report on the Bight, San Salvador (Cat Island), 1912, Bahamas Archives, Nassau (Cat Island was once called San Salvador); Cash, Gordon, and Saunders, *Sources of Bahamian History*, 161.

101. Commissioner's Report on the Bight, Cat Island, 1912, Bahamas Archives, Nassau; appendix to the Votes of the Legislative Council of the Bahama Islands, 15 February 1921–16 January 1922, 206, ANG.

102. H. Johnson, *The Bahamas from Slavery to Servitude*, 163; letter by R. J. Bowe, *Tribune*, 12 January 1922; Myers, "'I love my country bad, but . . .'"

103. H. Johnson, *The Bahamas from Slavery to Servitude*, 158; petitions from Bahamians in Florida, 27 October 1911, no. 188, CO23/268 (cited by H. Johnson).

104. Parks, "The History of Coconut Grove, Florida, 1821–1925"; Mohl, "Settlements of Blacks in South Florida," 121–24. See also Larry Smith, "Coconut Grove: Bahamian Roots in Florida," *Tribune*, 12 October 1977.

105. Methodist District Chairman to WMMS, 25 July 1921, and Methodist Minister for Florida to WMMS, 26 May 1921, in Cash, Gordon, and Saunders, *Sources of Bahamian History*, 99.

106. Cash, Gordon, and Saunders, *Sources of Bahamian History*, 99.

107. *Tribune*, 14 August 1911; Hurston, *The Florida Negro*, 12, 22; Hurston, *Dust Tracks on a Road*; Mohl, "Settlements of Blacks in South Florida," 121–22.

108. H. Johnson, *The Bahamas in Slavery and Freedom*, 158–59.

109. Appendix to the Votes of the Legislative Council, 11 January–6 June 1910, 86, ANG.

110. Craton and Saunders, *Islanders*, 2:100, 235.

111. Ibid., 2:221–22.

112. *Nassau Guardian*, 3 and 15 December 1879; H. Johnson, *The Bahamas from Slavery to Servitude*, 140.

113. *Nassau Guardian*, 28 December 1887; H. Johnson, *The Bahamas from Slavery to Servitude*, 134; Bahamas Archives, *The Sponging Industry*, 16.

114. H. Johnson, *The Bahamas from Slavery to Servitude*, 139–40.

115. Ibid.

116. Glinton-Meicholas, *From the Void to the Wonderful*, 15.

117. Kirkley Sands, assistant professor, notes for lectures used at the College of the Bahamas, 2012.

118. Glinton-Meicholas, *From the Void to the Wonderful*, 18.

119. Ibid., 31; Barry, *Upon These Rocks*, 11.

120. Bahamas Acts, 1 and 2 Geo. V, Roman Catholic Vicar Forane Incorporation Act, 13 July 1911.

Chapter 4. World War I and Prohibition

1. Proclamation Act and Emergency Relief Act, Bahamas Acts 5 Geo. V, c. 1 and c. 2 (1915).

2. Haddon-Smith to Harcourt, 13 August 1914, CO23/274/4–6; *Nassau Guardian*, 8 August 1914.

3. The Bahamas chapter of the IODE was founded in 1901 and flourished long after World War II. Eventually it disbanded and gave its headquarters to the Bahamas Historical Society. G. Saunders, "Social History of the Bahamas," 198–99; P. Albury, *Story of the Bahamas*, 172.

4. *Nassau Guardian*, 11 September 1915.

5. *Tribune*, 22 September 1914, 24 November 1915.

6. Haddon-Smith to Harcourt, 16 December 1914, CO23/274/394–95.

7. *Tribune*, 17 October 1914, 7 November 1914.

8. Dupuch, *A Salute to Friend and Foe*, 31–32.

9. Ibid., 64.

10. Allardyce to Bonar Law, 9 August 1915, CO23/276/52; Asquith to Bonar Law, 16 June 1915, CO23/276, 49–53, 408.

11. Dupuch, *A Salute to Friend and Foe*, 33.

12. *Nassau Guardian,* 11 September 1915.

13. Holmes, *The Bahamas during the Great War*, 42, 175–80. See also encl. in H. W. Grant to Viscount Milner, 3 November 1920, CO23/287/93–199.

14. *Nassau Guardian*, 24 November 1915, 10 May 1915, 5 August 1916; Holmes, *The Bahamas during the Great War*, 122. See also Craton, *History of the Bahamas*, 248. He states that fifty died in active service.

15. The Development Board, created in 1914, was held in abeyance until after the war, as were other planned public works such as the deepening of the harbour. Hart-Bennett to Harcourt, 23 February 1915, CO23/275/117.

16. Allardyce to Bonar Law, 19 April 1916, CO23/277/176; Allardyce to Long, 5 February 1918, 79–81, 83–92, CO 23 series, Bahamas.

17. Allardyce to Long, 26 January 1918, 5 February 1918, CO23/282/46, 236. See also Votes of the House of Assembly, 24 January 1918: War Contingent Act, no. 15 of 1916, ANG.

18. *Nassau Guardian*, 21, 24 August 1918; Allardyce to Long, 31 July, 24 August 1918, CO23/282/124–26, 163.

19. Allardyce to Long, July 1917, conf., CO23/280.

20. Dupuch, *A Salute to Friend and Foe*, 31–106.

21. Ibid., 33.

22. Dupuch, *Tribune Story*, 27.

23. Dupuch, *A Salute to Friend and Foe*, 54–55.

24. Ibid., 100.

25. Ibid., 55.

26. Ibid., 99–106; Dupuch, *Tribune Story*, 189–92.

27. Allardyce to Long, , 28 July 1917, conf., Co23/280/326–27; Allardyce to Long, 4 March 1918, conf., CO23/282/348–50; Allardyce to Long, 13 November 1918, CO23/283/331–33.

28. Allardyce to Long, 25 November 1918, conf., CO23/283/254; *Tribune*, 24 November 1918; McDermott, "L. W. Young: Formidable Force from Fox Hill," 24–25.

29. *Tribune*, 24 February 1911.

30. *Tribune*, 24 February 1911, 25 October 1917; Allardyce to Long, 29 October 1917, conf., CO23/281/53; *Nassau Guardian*, 3, 7 November 1917.

31. *Nassau Guardian*, 24 August 1918; Allardyce to Long, 24 August 1918, CO23/283/163, CO23/283/163.

32. Interview with Audrey V. Isaacs North, 20 June 1984.

33. C. Hughes, *Race and Politics*, 14.

34. G. Saunders, "Social History of the Bahamas," 215–16, 282; Craton and Saunders, *Islanders*, 2:220.

35. *Tribune*, 5 May 1920.

36. Hill, *The Marcus Garvey and Universal Improvement Association Papers*, 3:513.

37. Police Commandant Whebell to Colonial Secretary, 13 July 1921, Colonial Secretary Papers, Bahamas Archives, Nassau.

38. Philip Bailey to Burnet, Key West, 26 May 1921, WMMS Papers. See also Cash, Gordon, and Saunders, *Sources of Bahamian History*, 99.

39. Cash, Gordon, and Saunders, *Sources of Bahamian History*, 99.

40. T. Martin, *Race First*, 16, 371.

41. The Seditious Publications Prohibition Act 1919 banned the *Negro World* absolutely. See Colonial Secretary's minutes, 20 May 1920, Colonial Secretary Papers, Bahamas Archives, Nassau.

42. E. E. Turner, Commandant of Police to Acting Colonial Secretary, 13 May 1920, Colonial Secretary Papers, Bahamas Archives.

43. Richard S. Barrett to Major E. E. Turner, Commandant of Police, 4 August 1920, Minute Paper, Colonial Secretary Papers, Bahamas Archives.

44. Prospectus of the Union Mercantile Association, encl. Minute Paper, Colonial Secretary File May–July 1920, Colonial Secretary Papers, Bahamas Archives. See also *Nassau Guardian*, 24 July 1920.

45. They included David A. McKennon, a carpenter, as president; Samuel H. Tinker, carpenter, vice president; Caleb J. Gibson, tailor, treasurer; and Eustace E. Duvalier, merchant, secretary. Among its supporters were Reuben Bethel, tailor, nicknamed "the Honourable Marcus Garvey"; Dr. C. H. Knight; Christopher C. Smith, merchant; A. F. Adderley; and Oscar E. Johnson, nicknamed "Marcus Garvey II."

46. Major E. E. Turner, Commandant of Police, to Acting Colonial Secretary, Nassau, 29 May 1920, conf., Minute Paper, Colonial Secretary Papers, Bahamas Archives.

47. Richard Barrett to Major Turner, Commandment of Police, 4 August 1920. Minute Paper, Colonial Secretary Papers, Bahamas Archives.

48. Minute Paper, 21 January 1921, Colonial Secretary Papers, Bahamas Archives. See also *Nassau Guardian*, 19 June 1921.

49. *Nassau Guardian*, 3, 19, 26 May 1921.

50. *Tribune,* 21 July 1921.

51. *Tribune,* 21 January and 10 September 1928; Paul Adderley, *From Pompey to Pindling*, Inaugural Sir Lynden O. Pindling Memorial Lecture, Nassau, 22 March 2001, DVD, Bahamas Archives, Nassau.

52. *Tribune,* 27 October 1928; H. Saunders, *The Other Bahamas*, 144–45.

53. *Tribune*, 21 November 1928.

54. *Negro World,* 2 April 1927.

55. *Tribune,* 21 November 1928.

56. Ibid.

57. Report on the Census of the Bahama Islands, Taken on 2 April 1911; Report on the Census of the Bahama Islands, Taken on 24 April 1921, ANG; *Strombus Magazine* 2, no. 2 (1914): 55–58.

58. Interview with Rowena Eldon, 3 May 1983.

59. Allardyce to Grindle, private, 5 October 1918, CO23/283/205.

60. *Bahamas Blue Book,* 1914–15, Bahamas Archives, Nassau.

61. McDermott, "Opinionated, Warm-Hearted, Autocratic," opposite page 22.

62. *Tribune,* 19 January, 23 February, and 23 April 1921; *Tribune,* 9 August 1919.

63. Shedden, *Ups and Downs in a West Indian Diocese,* 181; Richards to Burnet, 2 March 1926, Nassau, MMS, West Indies Correspondence; *Tribune,* 15 and 19 February 1930; interview with Rowena Eldon, 3 May 1983.

64. Votes of the House of Assembly, 21 January–6 May 1926, introductory page, ANG.

65. *Tribune,* 27 September 1924.

66. *Tribune,* 28 July 1928.

67. *Tribune,* 7 and 11 July 1928.

68. *Nassau Guardian,* 7 July 1928.

69. Burns to Amery, 12 July 1928, CO23/390/5.

70. Freeston to Grindle, Office Note, 27 July 1928, CO23/390/3.

71. H. Saunders, *The Other Bahamas,* 149–50.

72. H. Johnson, "National Identity and Bahamian Culture," 16–17 .

73. Ibid., 17.

74. H. Johnson, "Labour on the Move." See also H. Johnson, *The Bahamas in Slavery and Freedom,* 149; *Tribune,* 18 October 1924, 4 April 1925.

75. Cordeaux to Thomas, 28 April 1924, conf., CO23/295; Cordeaux to Amery, 11 June 1925, conf., CO23/296.

76. Cordeaux to Churchill, 15 March 1922, conf., CO23/290/98–99; Cordeaux to Churchill, 12 May 1922, CO23/309–19, 353.

77. Cordeaux to Churchill, 15 March 1922, CO23/290/347.

78. Dupuch, *Tribune Story,* 32–33.

79. Ibid., 33.

80. *Nassau Guardian,* 5 and 7 December 1922.

81. H. Johnson, *The Bahamas from Slavery to Servitude,* 131–33.

82. Ibid., 131–32; Votes of the House of Assembly, 11 May 1925, 413; see also Votes of the House of Assembly, 30 April 1925, 361, ANG.

83. Executive Council minutes, 18 January 1927–19 December 1928, Governor's Office 1/39, stored at Bahamas Archives, Nassau.

84. Johnson, *The Bahamas from Slavery to Servitude,* 148.

85. Holmes, *The Bahamas during the Great* War, 153. See also encl. in Grant to Milner, 3 November 1920, CO23/287/93–199.

86. Holmes, *The Bahamas during the Great War,* 123, 134–35, 156–59.

87. Dupuch, *A Salute to Friend and Foe,* 31.

88. Craton, *History of the Bahamas,* 250; P. Albury, *Story of the Bahamas,* 176.

89. *Colonial Annual Reports, Bahamas,* 1919–20, 40.

90. Cash, "Colonial Policies and Outside Influences," 58.

91. Craton, *History of the Bahamas*, 251.

92. *London Times,* 3 March 1920.

93. Cash, "Colonial Policies and Outside Influences," 59, 140; *Bahamas Blue Books,* 1919–20, 1918–46, Bahamas Archives, Nassau.

94. Cash, "Colonial Policies and Outside Influences," 140; *Bahamas Blue Books,* 1918–46, Bahamas Archives.

95. *Nassau Guardian,* 1 September 1921, 14 and 19 September 1922; 13 and 23 January 1923; Cash, "Colonial Policies and Outside Influences," 67; telegram, Geddes to Curzon, 4 August 1921, A5728/3560/45; Cordeaux to Churchill, 3 October 1921, A297/170/45, Colonial Office Records, National Archives, United Kingdom, Kew, microfilm in Bahamas Archives, Nassau.

96. Hughes to Geddes, 26 June 1922, CO23/292 Misc.

97. Cordeaux to Churchill, 18 October 1921, CO23/289/212; Cordeaux to Churchill, 18 October 1921, secret, CO23/289/215–16.

98. Encl. Cordeaux to Amery, 31 December 1925, conf., CO23/297.

99. Bell, *Bahamas: Isles of June,* 190, 192–93.

100. Cash, "Colonial Policies and Outside Influences," 61–62; Chilton to Foreign Office, 11 May 1921, A3560/3568/45, Foreign Office 371 5699 (cited by Cash, 62).

101. Encl. Chamberlain to Amery, 24 March 1927, private, CO23/344.

102. Ibid.

103. Interview with E. Basil North and Audrey North, 31 July 1984. See also Hughes to Geddes, 26 June 1922, CO23/292.

104. Hughes to Geddes, 26 June 1922, CO23/292, Misc.; Grant to Churchill, 31 August 1922, conf., CO23/291/215; Nellie Symonette to Devonshire, 29 December 1923, CO23/294, Misc.

105. Cordeaux to Geddes, 2 April 1923, CO23/294; *Tribune,* 16 December 1983.

106. *Tribune,* 16 December 1983. See also Votes of the House of Assembly, 1935, ANG.

107. Van de Water, *The Real McCoy,* 93–94.

108. *Tribune,* 11 September 1926.

109. Bell, *Bahamas: Isles of June,* 184.

110. *Nassau Guardian,* 30 September 1922.

111. *Year Book of the West Indies and Countries of the Caribbean,* 1929, 134.

112. *Tribune,* 15 April, 23 September 1925, 17 July 1926, 11 January 1927; *Nassau Guardian,* 3 February 1923, 29 December 1926.

113. Cordeaux to Churchill, 10 April 1922, CO23/290/216–17; *Colonial Annual Reports, Bahamas,* 1928, encl. in CO23/405; *Colonial Annual Reports, Bahamas,* 1931, encl. in CO23/454.

114. *Colonial Annual Reports, Bahamas,* 1928, 1931, encl. CO23/405 and CO23/454.

115. *Tribune,* 17 June 1925.

116. H. Albury, *Man-O-War,* 89, 92.

117. Aspinall, *Pocket Guide to the West Indies,* 64.

118. Craton and Saunders, *Islanders,* 2:245.

119. *Colonial Annual Reports, Bahamas,* 1931, CO 23/297.

120. *Nassau Guardian,* 3 and 21 February 1925; *Tribune,* 13 February 1924, 6 February 1926, and 16 December 1983.

121. *Colonial Annual Reports, Bahamas,* 1933, 14; 1938, 18–19, 22–23.

122. Encl. Allardyce to Milner, 11 February 1919, CO23/284/47.

123. *Colonial Annual Reports, Bahamas,* 1925, encl. CO23/297.

124. Cordeaux to Darnley, 8 August 1925, private, CO23/296.

125. Craton and Saunders, *Islanders,* 2:246.

126. Barratt, *Grand Bahama* (1972), 75–140.

127. *Colonial Annual Reports, Bahamas,* 1925, CO23/297.

128. Cordeaux to Darnley, 8 August 1925, private, CO23/296.

129. Burns to Amery, 20 November 1926, conf., CO23/297.

130. Conveyance, 5 June, 1937, between Guy Robert Brooke Baxter the Vendor and the Baxter Estate, Bahamas Archives, Nassau.

131. Burns to Amery, 20 November 1926, conf., CO23/297; Moseley, *Bahamas Handbook,* 35.

132. Burns to Amery, 20 November 1926, conf., CO23/297.

133. *Nassau Guardian,* 6 March 1923.

134. *Tribune,* 20 January 1923, 24 November 1924.

135. Peggs, "A History of Bahamian Education," 267.

136. Williams, *Methodist Contribution,* 67. See also Board of Education Annual Reports, PRO/EDU/5–23, 26, Ministry of Education Records, Bahamas Archives, Nassau.

137. Williams, *Methodist Contribution,* 67; Orr to Amery, 2 September 1927, CO23/342.

138. Richard P. Dyer, note on "The Problem of Queen's College," Archives of Queen's College High School, Nassau.

139. Clifford to Beckett, 12 April 1934, CO23/508.

140. Barry, *Upon These Rocks,* 382.

141. G. Saunders, "The Ambiguous Admission Policy of Queen's College High School," 19; Northcroft to MacDonald, Hope Town, Abaco, 11 July 1890, MMS, West Indies Correspondence.

142. Richard P. Dyer, "The Problem of Queen's College," 1 November 1926, encl. in Richards to Burnet, 20 January 1927, MMS, West Indies Correspondence; Minutes of the Adjoined Meeting of Queen's College, 15 May 1961.

143. Richard P. Dyer to Dr. Gascoyne S. Worrell, 17 October 1928 (courtesy of Hon. Paul L. Adderley); G. Saunders, "The Ambiguous Admission Policy at Queen's College High School," 13.

144. Richards to Burnet, 20 January 1926, MMS, West Indies Correspondence; see also Dyer, "The Problem of Queen's College."

145. *Nassau Guardian,* 16, 19 April 1919 and 15 July 1922.

146. Williams, *Methodist Contribution,* 181; minutes of the Education and (Queen's College) School Committee, 15 January 1924, MMS, West Indies Correspondence.

147. Searle to Andrews, 11 April 1925, Nassau, MMS, West Indies Correspondence.

148. Beveridge, *Report on the Public Health*, 48, encl. in CO23/359.

149. Ibid., 41.

150. Ibid, 45.

151. Ibid, 26.

152. Encl. Cordeaux to Thomas, 21 March 1924, CO23/295; Cordeaux to Amery, 31 March 1926, CO23/297; Medical Report, 1924, encl. Cordeaux to Amery, 20 February 1925, CO23/296.

153. Beveridge, *Report on the Public Health*, 37; Smith to Harcourt, 17 June 1913, CO23/271/289.

154. *Tribune,* 15 March and 24 November 1924; *Nassau Guardian*, 28 February 1925.

155. Report on the Census of the Bahama Islands, Taken on 26 April 1931, ANG.

156. Cordeaux to Amery, 11 June 1925, conf., CO23/296; Richards to Burnet, 2 March 1926, Nassau, MMS, West Indies Correspondence.

157. Cordeaux to Amery, 9 April 1926, CO23/297 and CO23/383; *Tribune,* 17 March 1926, 14 May 1927; Bell, *Bahamas: Isles of June,* 188–89.

158. Burns to Amery, 28 July 1928, CO23/391; *Nassau Guardian*, 28 July 1928.

159. *Report of the Commission on the Prison Department,* Nassau: Nassau Guardian, 1928, 36–48, ANG.

160. *Nassau Guardian*, 5 September 1922; *Report to Enquire into the Establishment of an Industrial School, January 1923*, Nassau: Nassau Guardian, 1923; encl. Cordeaux to Thomas, 12 March 1924, CO23/295.

161. *Report to Enquire into the Establishment of an Industrial School, January 1923,* 19, 28.

162. *Nassau Guardian*, 29 October 1921.

163. Ibid.; *Report to Enquire into the Establishment of an Industrial School,* 35–36.

164. Williams, *Methodist Contribution*, 68; see also Board of Education Annual Reports, PRO/EDU/5–24,3, Ministry of Education Records, Bahamas Archives, Nassau.

165. Lewis, *The Growth of the Modern West Indies,* 311.

166. G. Saunders, *Bahamian Society after Emancipation,* 10–11; *Year Book of the West Indies and Countries of the Caribbean,* 1926–27, 91.

167. *Year Book of the West Indies and Countries of the Caribbean,* 1926–27, 91.

168. Bahamas Archives, *A Selection of Historic Buildings of the Bahamas,* 42.

169. *Tribune,* 24 November 1924; *Bahamas Blue Books,* 1901–2, 1908–9, 1920–21, 1931, Bahamas Archives, Nassau.

170. Richard P. Dyer, "Note on the Problem of Queen's College," 1 November 1926, MMS, West Indies Correspondence.

171. *Nassau Guardian*, 22 January 1921, 10 December 1921; *Tribune,* 27 January 1926.

172. *Nassau Guardian*, 13, 15 December 1921.

173. A. Thompson, *Economic History of the Bahamas,* 28.

174. Interview with Percival Hanna, 22 February 1984, Nassau.

175. Interview with E. Basil North, 31 July 1984, Nassau.

176. *Nassau Guardian*, 23 September 1922. See also *Tribune,* 9 April 1921; A. Thompson, *Economic History of the Bahamas,* 22.

177. Advertisement in Moseley, *Bahamas Handbook*; A. Thompson, *Economic History of the Bahamas*, 22; Interview with Maxwell Thompson, 17 January 1984.

178. *Tribune*, 26 December 1923; Interview with Maxwell Thompson, 17 January 1984, Nassau.

179. Interview with Dr. Terry North, London, 5 August 1983.

180. Interview with Cecil V. Bethel, 1 May 1984, Nassau.

181. Interview with E. Basil North, 31 July 1984, Nassau.

182. Bell, *Bahamas: Isles of June,* 193.

Chapter 5. The 1930s and the Depression

1. Noble, Horowitz, and Carroll, *Twentieth Century Limited*, 224; A. Thompson, *Economic History of the Bahamas*, 41, 44.

2. Pelling, *Modern Britain, 1885–1955*, 111–13; D. Thomson, *England in the Twentieth Century*, 145.

3. Pelling, *Modern Britain, 1885–1955*, 114; D. Thomson, *England in the Twentieth Century*, 145.

4. Ayearst, *The British West Indies*, 39, 199.

5. West Indian Royal Commission Report 1938–1939, June 1945 (Cmd. 6607), British Sessional Papers, House of Commons, 1944–1945, 6:279.

6. P. Albury, *Story of the Bahamas*, 183–84.

7. Dundas to Passfield, 21 October 1929, CO23/416, 16 July 1929, CO23/412; Cash, "Colonial Policies and Outside Influences," 201.

8. *Colonial Annual Reports, Bahamas*, 1930–31 and 1934–35.

9. Bahamas Archives, *The Sponging Industry,* 23.

10. G. Saunders, *Bahamian Society after Emancipation*, 26–27.

11. Peter Deveaux, "The Story of Centreville and Collins Wall," *Nassau Guardian*, 17 October 1983.

12. Craton and Saunders, *Islanders*, 2:268.

13. "Sir Harry Oakes: The Man behind the Myth," *Bahamas Handbook,* 1976–77, 21, 23–24, 25–27, 28, 29.

14. Bahamas Acts, 1 Edward V111 and 1 Geo. V1, c. 32 (1936).

15. "Sir Harry Oakes," 27.

16. *Tribune*, 16 May 1933, 21 October 1933.

17. Clifford to Thomas, 13 January 1936, CO23/555, and 24 August 1937, CO23/555; *Tribune*, 13 April 1935.

18. *Tribune*, 19 November 1930; see also *Tribune*, 2 September 1931.

19. Clifford to Thomas, 13 January 1936, CO23/555.

20. Ibid.; *Tribune*, 13, 17, 24 April 1935.

21. Report on the Census of the Bahama Islands, Taken on 26 April 1931; encl. in Clifford to Thomas, 13 January 1936, conf., CO23/555.

22. Report on the Census of the Bahama Islands, Taken on 26 April 1931, ANG; Clifford to Cunliffe-Lister, 14 April 1932, CO23/369.

23. Telegram, Clifford to Cunliffe-Lister, 24 June 1932, CO23/469.

24. Telegram, Clifford to Cunliffe-Lister, 14 November 1932, CO23/474. It was also reported in the *Daily Telegraph* in England on 11 November 1932. See also Clifford to Cunliffe-Lister, 1 December 1932, CO23/474.

25. Clifford to Thomas, 15 February 1936, CO23/540.

26. C. Hughes, *Race and Politics*, 15.

27. Clifford, *Proconsul*, 194.

28. Clifford to Cunliffe-Lister, 16 October 1934, CO23/516.

29. Dupuch, *Tribune Story*, 76–77.

30. *Colonial Annual Reports, Bahamas*, 1934–35; Cash, "Colonial Policies and Outside Influences," 202.

31. Clifford to Cunliffe-Lister, 23 July 1935, CO23/462; Clifford to Cunliffe-Lister, 30 December 1932, CO23/463.

32. *Tribune*, 22 May 1933 and 24 January 1934.

33. *Nassau Magazine* 1, no. 4 (1934): 10.

34. Craton and Saunders, *Islanders*, 2:264; *Nassau Magazine* 2, no. 4 (April 1935): 4.

35. Forbes, *A Unicorn in the Bahamas*, 138; *Who's Who* 2, no. 40 (1935): 22; *Bahamas Handbook*, 1971–72, 42; *Tribune*, 26 and 30 July 1935.

36. Interview with Rowena Eldon, 3 May 1983.

37. Craton and Saunders, *Islanders*, 2:265.

38. Interview with Maxwell Thompson, 17 January 1984.

39. Ibid.; interview with Alphonso Blake Higgs, 30 June 1982.

40. *Tribune*, 12 May and 9 August 1932, 30 December 1933, and 12 February 1934.

41. Interview with Alphonso Blake Higgs, 30 June 1982.

42. K. Thompson, *An Eye for the Tropics*, 155; see also 132–53.

43. *Tribune*, 11 January 1935, 3 December 1935, 26 December 1935.

44. E. C. Bethel, "Music in the Bahamas," 230.

45. Burns, *Colonial Civil Servant*, 84.

46. H. Johnson, *The Bahamas from Slavery to Servitude*, 147–48.

47. A. Thompson, *Economic History of the Bahamas*, 49–50.

48. Cash, Gordon, and Saunders, *Sources of Bahamian History*, 285.

49. Ibid., 51, 144, 278–79.

50. F. Taylor, "The Tourist Industry in Jamaica, 1919–1939," *Social and Economic Studies*, 22 (1973): 205–28.

51. Ibid., 216.

52. Cited in Lowenthal, *West Indian Societies*, 72.

53. Brereton, "Social Organization and Class," 43.

54. Curry, *Bahamian Lore*, 76; Votes of the House of Assembly, 21 November 1935–1 June 1936, 226, ANG.

55. Burns, *Colonial Civil Servant*, 84.

56. Malone and Roberts, *Nostalgic Nassau*, 42.

57. Dahl, *Literature of the Bahamas*, 64–65.

58. Rex Nettleford, "Cultural Impact of Tourism," in *Report of a Regional Confer-*

ence on Tourism and Its Effects, Nassau, 24–28 November 1975. See also Lewis, *Main Currents in Caribbean Thought*, 7. Quashie can be described as an unsophisticated or gullible black male peasant.

59. Burns, *Colonial Civil Servant*, 84.

60. *Tribune*, 12 March 1930.

61. *Tribune*, 4 October 1933.

62. Dundas to McDonald, 11 July 1938, conf., CO23/653.

63. *Tribune*, 8 June 1935.

64. Ibid.; Votes of the House of Assembly, 21 November 1935–1 June 1936, ANG.

65. A. Thompson, *Economic History of the Bahamas*, 49, 50, 69.

66. Interview with Basil and Audrey North, 10 August 1984, Nassau.

67. A. Thompson, *Economic History of the Bahamas*, 49; G. Saunders, "Social History of the Bahamas," 359.

68. Clifford to Cunliffe-Lister, 29 January 1934, CO23/504.

69. Clifford to Shuckburg, 25 February 1933, CO23/477; *Tribune*, 12 April, 15 November 1930; 4 April 1934.

70. W. Paget to E. W. Thompson, 11 June 1934, Queen's College, conf., MMS, West Indies Correspondence, 1932–37; E. W. Thompson to E. V. Paget, 25 May 1934, MMS West Indies Correspondence, 1932–37.

71. Clifford to Shuckburg, 25 February 1933, CO23/477.

72. Williams, *Methodist Contribution*, 69; Fawkes, *Faith That Moved the Mountain* (1979), 10.

73. *Bahamas Handbook*, 1980, 31.

74. G. Saunders, *Bahamian Society after Emancipation*, 35–36.

75. *Tribune*, 30 September 1935, 1, 2, and 4 October 1935.

76. Jenkins, *Bahamian Memories*, 77.

77. Interview with E. Basil North, 8 January 2004.

78. G. Saunders, "Profiles of Several Outstanding Bahamian Women."

79. *Tribune*, 2, 3, and 13 July 1935, 2 August 1935, 14 and 18 September 1935.

80. Interview with Holly Brown, 10 September 1984.

81. *Report of the [Russell] Commission Appointed to Enquire into Disturbances in the Bahamas which took place in June 1942*, Nassau: Nassau Guardian, 1942 (hereafter Russell Commission), ANG.

82. Bahamas Acts, 1 Edward VIII, c. 7 (20 Jan. 1936–11 Dec. 1936), 1 Geo. VI, c. 32 (1936–1952).

83. Interview with Holly Brown, 10 September 1984, Nassau.

84. Ibid.; C. Hughes, *Race and Politics*, 41.

85. Extract from Report, 11 October 1938, received from Langston Jones, Inspector of Imperial Lighthouse Service, CO23/653. It is not clear from the records how a Defence Corps could have been secretly formed.

86. Dundas to Parkinson, 11 July 1938, conf., CO23/653.

87. Russell Commission, 1, 10.

88. Craton and Saunders, *Islanders*, 2:269–70.

89. Encl., Dundas to Ormsby-Gore, 21 February 1938, conf., CO23/638.

90. G. Saunders, *Bahamian Society after Emancipation*, 144; Bolland, *Politics of Labour*, 295.

91. H. Johnson, *The Bahamas from Slavery to Servitude*, 115.

92. Report on the Census of the Bahama Islands, Taken on 26 April 1931, ANG.

93. G. Saunders, *Bahamian Society after Emancipation*, 141.

94. Bolland, *Politics of Labour*, 297.

95. Encl., Dundas to Ormsby-Gore, 18 March 1938, CO23/638.

96. Appendix to the Votes of the House of Assembly, 18 October 1937–21 February 1938, 215–16, ANG.

97. Ibid., 217–18; see also telegram, Jarret to Ormsby-Gore, 18 March 1938, CO23/638.

98. *Tribune,* 13 October and 5 and 22 November 1937; see also G. Saunders, *Bahamian Society after Emancipation*, 143.

99. *Daily Express*, 26–27 August 1937; *Evening Standard,* 27 August 1937, and *Manchester Guardian*, 27 and 30 August 1937.

100. *Tribune*, 13 October 1937.

101. Bolland, *Politics of Labour*, 298

102. Police Charge Book, 1938–39, Bahamas Archives, Nassau; G. Saunders, *Bahamian Society after Emancipation,* 144–45.

103. Votes of the Legislative Council, 1937–38, 42–43, ANG.

104. Bolland, *Politics of Labour*, 298.

105. Report by Commissioner J. A. Hughes, "Inagua Disturbance and Present Conditions," 23 February 1938, encl. in Dundas to Ormsby-Gore, 19 March 1938, CO23/638.

106. E. Robinson, Colonial Office, note of conversation with Mary Moseley, 25 July 1938, CO23/653.

107. Dundas to McDonald, 11 July 1938, conf., CO23/653.

108. Dundas to McDonald, 9 August 1938, CO23/653.

109. *Tribune,* 2 June 1939.

110. H. Saunders, *The Other Bahamas*, 169; see also *Tribune*, 8 May 1939.

111. Dundas to Parkinson, 6 June 1939, CO23/659; see also Votes of the House of Assembly, 12 July 1939, ANG.

112. *Tribune,* 7 June 1939.

113. H. Saunders, *The Other Bahamas*, 170, 172.

114. Dundas to Lloyd, 8 August 1940, CO23/678, cited in Cash, "Colonial Policies and Outside Influences."

Chapter 6. World War II and the 1942 Nassau Riot

1. P. Albury, *Story of the Bahamas*, 212–13; *Nassau Magazine* 12, no. 1 (December 1945): 9.

2. Richardson, *Review of Bahamian Economic Conditions*, 94.

3. Fishing for fish with horny overlapping plates or scales that protect the skin.

4. Craton and Saunders, *Islanders*, 2:276.

5. Ibid.; Cash, "Colonial Policies and Outside Influences," 267.

6. Bloch, *Duke of Windsor's War*, 154–57

7. Pye, *The King over the Water*, 15–131.

8. Craton and Saunders, *Islanders*, 2:280.

9. Forbes, *A Unicorn in the Bahamas.*

10. Forbes, *Appointment with Destiny*, 108.

11. Cited in Craton and Saunders, *Islanders*, 2:285; Poitier, *This Life*, 15–36.

12. Poitier, *This Life*, 15–36.

13. "H.R.H. the Duke and Duchess of Windsor in North America," *Nassau Magazine* 9, no. 1 (December 1941):8–9, 25, 28, 36–37.

14. See Lee, *Colonial Development and Good Government*, 47–48; Bahamas Acts, 3 and 4 Geo. VI, 9 May 1940, 12 August 1940; Dundas to Lloyd, 18 June 1940, conf., CO23/692; *Colonial Annual Reports, Bahamas*, 1946, 5.

15. P. Albury, *Story of the Bahamas*, 207.

16. *Nassau Magazine* 11, no. 1 (December 1943): 26, 34; Dupuch, *Tribune Story*, 50.

17. Windsor to Stanley, 24 January 1944, CO23/734.

18. *Nassau Magazine* 11, no. 1 (December 1943): 33.

19. Dupuch, *Tribune Story*, 52.

20. Bloch, *Duke of Windsor's War*, 118. See also "His Royal Highness the Duke of Windsor," *Nassau Magazine* 10, no. 1 (1941):11; "H.R.H. the Duke and Duchess of Windsor in North America," *Nassau Magazine* 9, no. 1 (December 1941):8–9, 25–29; Pamela Murry "Government House Redecorated: The Duke and Duchess of Windsor's Official Residence," *Nassau Magazine* 8, no. 4 (March 1941):8–10, 30–31.

21. Ibid., 147.

22. Ibid., 138.

23. *Tribune*, 20 July 1951; interview with Alphonso Blake Higgs, 30 June 1982.

24. Bloch, *Duke of Windsor's War*, 138.

25. Ibid.

26. Craton and Saunders, *Islanders*, 2:279.

27. Bloch, *Duke of Windsor's War*, 138.

28. Dupuch, *Tribune Story*, 83–85.

29. Ibid., 35; Bloch, *Duke of Windsor's War*, 139–40.

30. Bloch, *Duke of Windsor's War*, 128.

31. Ibid., 126; Craton, *History of the Bahamas*, 259–60.

32. *Nassau Magazine* 9, no. 2 (January 1942): 8–9; interview with Rowena Eldon, 3 May 1983.

33. Interview with Rowena Eldon, 3 May 1983; "Years in Nassau," *Bahamas Handbook*, 1978–79, 76–77.

34. "War Years in Nassau," *Bahamas Handbook*, 1978–79, 77.

35. Ibid.

36. Bloch, *Duke of Windsor's War*, 283.

37. Interview with Rowena Eldon, 3 May 1983.

38. A. Taylor, *English History, 1914–1945*, 459–63; Pelling, *Modern Britain, 1885–1955*, 156.

39. It was later headed by Londoner Major D'Arcy Rutherford. See *Colonial Annual Reports, Bahamas*, 1956, 5.

40. *Nassau Guardian*, 4 March 1944.

41. *Colonial Annual Reports, Bahamas*, 1946, 5; P. Albury, *Story of the Bahamas*, 210–11.

42. Jenkins, *Bahamian Memories*, 206.

43. *Nassau Guardian*, 9 September 1943; Dyer to Friends, circular letter, 1 November 194, 1, and Dyer to Johnson, 25 February 1942, WMMS Papers; *Nassau Magazine* 9, no. 3 (February–March 1942): 16; vol. 10, no. 1 (December 1942): 22; vol. 11, no. 1 (December 1943): 12.

44. *Colonial Annual Reports, Bahamas*, 1946, 5; *Nassau Magazine*, Anniversary Number, 1942, 22; "War Years in Nassau," *Bahamas Handbook*, 1978–79, 69.

45. *Nassau Magazine* 8, no. 2 (January 1941): 18.

46. Evidence of Richard J. A. Farrington to Russell Commission, 271–76, ANG. See also Executive Council minutes, 17 September 1941, Bahamas Archives, Nassau.

47. G. Saunders, *Bahamian Society after Emancipation*, 151–52.

48. Dupuch, *Tribune Story*, 86.

49. Evidence of Karl Claridge to Russell Commission. See Executive Council minutes, Bahamas, Meeting no. 23, 4 January 1940–31 December 1941.

50. Executive Council minutes, 17 September 1941.

51. Russell Commission, 9.

52. Ibid., 1–3.

53. Select Committee, Votes of the House of Assembly, 1942–43, 316, ANG.

54. Evidence of Bertram Cambridge to Russell Commission, 92.

55. Evidence of Karl Claridge to Russell Commission, 229.

56. Evidence of Karl Claridge and Leonard Storr to Russell Commission, 230, 182–83.

57. Evidence of Charles Rhodriquez and A. F. Adderley to Russell Commission, 145 and 93.

58. Report of the Select Committee, Votes of the House of Assembly, 1942–43, 313, ANG.

59. Evidence of A. F. Adderley and Bertram Cambridge to Russell Commission, 145, 93.

60. Interview with Sir Randol Fawkes, 22 November 1982, Nassau.

61. Russell Commission, 31.

62. Evidence of Leonard Storr Green to Russell Commission, 182–86.

63. Fawkes, *The Faith That Moved the Mountain* (2003), 25.

64. Russell Commission, 39–40.

65. Report of the Select Committee, Votes of the House of Assembly, 1942–43, 311–15, ANG

66. Evidence of Percy Christie to Russell Commission, 25; Evidence of A. F. Adderley to Russell Commission, 149; Evidence of Richard Holbert to Russell Commission, 31–32; Evidence of Bernard J. Nottage to Russell Commission, 333–34.

67. Evidence of Nottage to Russell Commission, 333–34.

68. *Tribune*, 4 June 1942; telegram, Windsor to Stanley, 4 June 1942, CO23/731/3, 12, 24.

69. Telegram, Windsor to Stanley, 4 June 1942, CO23/731/25.

70. Fawkes, *The Faith That Moved the Mountain* (2003), 34–35.

71. Telegram, Windsor to Stanley, 4 June 1942, CO23/731/25.

72. Executive Council minutes, 14 January 1942, Bahamas Archives; see also Foreign Office telegram, passed onto Colonial Office, CO23/73/44; telegram, Heape to Stanley, 20 June 1942, CO23/731/43; Russell Commission, 39–40.

73. Dr. Claudius Walker to Russell Commission, 475.

74. G. Saunders, *Bahamian Society after Emancipation*, 159.

75. Evidence of Frank Field, Mary Moseley, Dr. Roland Cumberbatch, and John Damianos to Russell Commission, 137–38, 249–58, 476, 296.

76. Craton and Saunders, *Islanders*, 2:288.

77. Evidence of Eric Hallinan to Russell Commission, 515.

78. Windsor to Cranborne, 9 December 1942, CO23/731.

79. Select Committee, Votes of the House of Assembly, 1942–43, 330, ANG.

80. C. Hughes, *Race and Politics*, 251.

81. D. Johnson, *Quiet Revolution*, 15.

82. Roker, *Vision of Sir Lynden Pindling*, 162; Martin and Storr, "'I'se a Man,'" 73.

83. G. Saunders, *Bahamian Society after Emancipation*, 165; C. Hughes, *Race and Politics*, 251–52; Martin and Storr, "'I'se a Man.'"

84. See Bolland, *Politics of Labour*, 382–88.

85. *Tribune*, 6 March 1943.

86. *Tribune*, 11 March 1943.

87. *Tribune*, 13 March 1943.

88. *Tribune*, 19 April 1943.

89. H. Saunders, *The Other Bahamas*, 215.

90. *Tribune*, 29 April 1943.

91. H. Saunders, *The Other Bahamas*, 216.

92. *Tribune,* 18 May 1946.

93. H. Saunders, *The Other Bahamas*, 216; *Colonial Annual Reports, Bahamas*, 1949, 8, 10.

94. Closing Speech to the Legislature, 14 September 1943, Votes of the House of Assembly, 1942–43, 195, ANG; Bahamas Acts, An Act Relating to Trade Unions, 31 March 1943, no. 9 of 1943; Act to Provide for payment of compensation for injuries suffered in the course of their employment, no. 25 of 1943.

95. *Tribune,* 3 July 1944.

96. *Nassau Guardian*, 4 July 1944.

97. *Nassau Guardian*, 5 July 1944.

98. Ibid.

99. Windsor to Stanley, 12 July 1944, CO23/798.

100. Cypher telegram, Windsor to Stanley, 17 September 1944, CO23/798/15. Cypher meant it was written in a secret code.

101. H. Saunders, *The Other Bahamas*, 221.

102. Ibid., 222.

103. Vital Statistics, 1942–43, CO23/131.

104. Windsor to Stanley, 10 August 1943, CO23/734; Executive Council minutes 8 and 9 January 1943; see also Windsor to Stanley, 30 January 1943, CO23/733/20.

105. Duchess of Windsor to Aunt Bessie, 26 September 1942, cited in Bloch, *Duke of Windsor's War*, 281.

106. Executive Council minutes, 17 March 1943; T. Thompson, "Remembering 'the Contract,'" 7.

107. Appendix to the Votes of the House of Assembly, 1943, 302–5, ANG; Darling, *Sir Clifford Darling,* 1:57.

108. Craton and Saunders, *Islanders*, 2:292; T. Thompson, "Remembering 'the Contract,'" 9.

109. T. Thompson, "Remembering 'the Contract,'" 9.

110. Murphy to Hall, 23 January 1946, CO23/814; Murphy to Hall, 19 June 1946, CO23/814; Windsor to Stanley, 10 August 1943, secret, CO23/760/51; see also Greenberg, "The Contract," 30–32, 205.

111. Jenkins, *Bahamian Memories*, 210.

112. Darling, *Sir Clifford Darling*, 58.

113. Jenkins, *Bahamian Memories*, 208.

114. Ibid.

115. Greenberg, "The Contract," 176.

116. Richardson, *Review of Bahamian Economic Conditions*, 28–29; *Colonial Annual Reports, Bahamas,* 1950–51, 7, Bahamas Archives, Nassau; Bahamas Administrative Reports, 1953, CO23/156.

117. Greenberg, "The Contract," 172, 193, 204.

118. T. Thompson, "Remembering 'the Contract'"; C. Bethel, pers. comm., 1 January 1992, 11.

119. Greenberg, "The Contract," 193.

120. Ibid., 175.

121. Darling, *Sir Clifford Darling*, 58.

122. Craton and Saunders, *Islanders*, 2:294–95.

123. Jenkins, *Bahamian Memories*, 208.

124. Greenberg, "The Contract," 201.

125. R. Bodie, pers. comm., 15 January 1993, in T. Thompson, "Remembering 'the Contract,'" 5.

126. H. R. Bethel, pers. comm., December 1991–January 1992, in T. Thompson, "Remembering 'the Contract,'" 10.

127. Ibid.

128. Greenberg, "The Contract," 191, 201.

129. Ibid., 201.

130. Ibid.; Donald Rolle, pers. comm., 19 December 1991, in T. Thompson, "Remembering 'the Contract,'" 10–11.

131. Samuel Miller, pers. comm., 18 December 1991, in T. Thompson, "Remembering 'the Contract,'" 10.

132. Ibid. For fights between Contract workers and black Americans, see Murphy to Hall, 23 January 1946, CO23/814.

133. Greenberg, "The Contract," 204.

134. P. Albury, *Story of the Bahamas*, 212; *Nassau Magazine* 12, no. 1 (December 1945): 9.

135. R. N. Waite, Group Captain, R.A.F. Station, Nassau, telegram to the Duke of Windsor, 31 December 1943, and telegram, Windsor to Stanley, 4 January 1944, both in Governor's Office, Secret no. 120: "Colour Bar" unofficial file, 24 September 1943–4 July 1959, Bahamas Archives, Nassau.

136. "War Years in Nassau," *Bahamas Handbook*, 1978–79, 78.

137. Bahamas Acts, The Venereal Diseases Act 1945 (21 of 1945); telegram, Windsor to Stanley, 4 January 1944; Executive Council minutes, 28 October 1943.

138. Interview with E. Basil North and Audrey V. North, 10 August 1984.

139. "War Years in Nassau," *Bahamas Handbook*, 1978–79, 73; interview with Rowena Eldon, 3 May 1983.

140. "War Years in Nassau," *Bahamas Handbook*, 1978–79, 78; *Nassau Guardian*, 10, 13 January, 3 May 1943, 29, 31 July 1943, and 1 April 1944.

141. Roker, *Sir Clifford Darling*, 54.

142. Supreme Court Criminal minutes, 7 April–30 July 1942 and 29 April–1 August 1942, S.C. 20/90; Magistrate's Court Criminal minutes, 15 April–30 July 1942, MAG 7/104, Bahamas Archives, Nassau.

143. Windsor to Oliver Stanley, 10 August 1943, quoted in Bloch, *Duke of Windsor's War*, 312.

144. Ibid.

145. Craton, *History of the Bahamas*, 262.

146. D. Johnson, *Quiet Revolution*, 26.

147. Jenkins, *Bahamian Memories,* 170.

148. Ibid.

149. *Colonial Annual Reports, Bahamas*, 1946, 7–8.

150. Cash, "Colonial Policies and Outside Influences," 336–37.

151. Windsor to Stanley, 28 November 1944, CO23/770.

152. Craton and Saunders, *Islanders*, 2:300.

153. A. Thompson, *Economic History of the Bahamas*, 46.

154. Craton and Saunders, *Islanders*, 2:301.

155. G. F. Seel, "Note on Visit to the West Indies," 7 November 1949, CO23/858.

156. Bahamas Administrative Reports, 1951, CO23/154.

157. *Colonial Annual Reports, Bahamas,* 1946, 219; Bahamas Administrative Reports 1951, CO26/154; Cash, "Colonial Policies and Outside Influences," 343.

158. Barratt, *Grand Bahama* (1982), 71–72.

159. Neville to Lyttelton, 14 November 1952, CO1031/138; *Nassau Magazine* 6, no. 1 (Fall 1953): 13.

160. Interview with Edith Stirrup, 3 July 2012.

161. Bregenzer, *Trying to Make It*, 33–34.

162. Ibid., 34.

163. Encl. Neville to Luke, 1 October 1951, CO23/889.

164. Dodge, *Abaco*, 86; see also 83–87.

165. Evidence of Karl Claridge to Russell Commission, 228–32; Richardson, *Review of Bahamian Economic Conditions*, 86.

166. Barratt, *Grand Bahama* (1983), 65–66.

167. Ibid., 66–67, 69–70, 75–160; encl. Neville to Luke, 1 October 1951, CO23/889.

168. Richardson, *Review of Bahamian Economic Conditions*, 88–90.

169. Medical and Sanitary Report, 1940, CO23/727; Bahamas Administrative Reports, 1953, CO26/156; Bloch, *Duke of Windsor's War,* 183.

170. Extract from Lord Listowel's Report on the West Indies, 1949, CO23/888.

171. Interview with Henryk Podlewski, 9 September 1984, Nassau; Report on the Bahamas in 1949 by Governor Murphy, September 1949, encl. Murphy to Creech Jones, 30 September 1949, CO23/868; Annual Medical and Sanitary Reports, 1953; Bahamas Administrative Reports, 1953, CO26/156.

172. Report on the Bahamas in 1949 by Governor Murphy, September 1949, encl. Murphy to Creech Jones, 30 September 1949, CO23/868; Votes of the House of Assembly, 22 July 1946, 438, ANG; *Colonial Annual Reports, Bahamas*, 1950–51, 21.

173. Williams, *Methodist Contribution*, 69.

174. Bahamas Acts, Education Amendment Act, 1951 (26 of 1951); Williams, *Methodist Contribution,* 70.

175. *Colonial Annual Reports, Bahamas,* 1950–51, 207; Williams, *Methodist Contribution,* 71.

176. Barry, *Upon These Rocks*, 346.

177. Ibid.

178. Williams, *Methodist Contribution*, 108

179. Memorandum of Association of St. Andrews School, 11 November 1948, Registrar General's Department, Nassau.

180. H. H. Brown, Sermon at Governor's Harbour, 14 January 1946, quoted in Cash, Gordon, and Saunders, *Sources of Bahamian History*, 291.

181. H. H. Brown to Wesleyan Methodist Missionary Society, 29 January 1946, quoted in Cash, Gordon, and Saunders, *Sources of Bahamian History*, 291.

Chapter 7. The Formative Years, 1950–1958

1. Constitution of the Citizens' Committee, Eneas Collection, Bahamas Archives, Nassau.

2. Eneas, *Let the Church Roll On*, 47–48.

3. Ibid.

4. H. Saunders, *The Other Bahamas* 231–33.

5. Votes of the House of Assembly, 3 April 1950, 354, ANG; Fawkes, *The Faith That Moved the Mountain* (2003), 48–49.

6. H. Saunders, *The Other Bahamas*, 235.

7. Ibid., 235–36.

8. Ibid., 236.

9. Langston Hughes, "Nassau a Flower Garden Island Just for Tourists," *Chicago Defender*, 19 June 1954.

10. Langston Hughes, "Nassau Rum, Conch Salad Calypsos, and Night Clubs," *Chicago Defender*, 26 June 1954.

11. *Tribune*, 31 March and 9 June 1950.

12. Interview with E. Basil North and Audrey V. North, 10 August 1984.

13. *Bahamian Review Magazine* 13, nos. 5–10 (1971): 25; Fawkes, *Faith That Moved the Mountain* (1997), 57, 60–61.

14. Fawkes, *Faith That Moved the Mountain* (2003), 62.

15. Ibid., 64.

16. Ibid., 65–66.

17. Craton and Saunders, *Islanders*, 2:304–8.

18. "Hilda Bowen, M.B.E. Portrait of the Week," *Tribune*, 1 November 1983.

19. *Tribune*, 3 October 1951 and 21 October 1953.

20. Denyer to Noble, 10 April 1947, Governor's Harbour, Eleuthera, WMMS Papers; Dyer to Noble, 7 November 1953, Nassau, WMMS Papers.

21. Lowenthal, *West Indian Societies*, 97.

22. Interview with Winston V. Saunders, 10 November 1984.

23. McDermott, "Harold Christie," 22–23.

24. *Tribune*, 11 November 1953.

25. Judgement in the Case of the Petition of James Maxwell Mitchell Bowe under the Quieting of Titles Act, 1959, concerning the Forest Estate, Bahama Islands Supreme Court, Equity Division, no. 137 of 1961, Bahamas Archives, Nassau.

26. Report on the Census of the Bahama Islands, taken on 27 June 1891; Report on the Census of the Bahama Islands, Taken on 6 December 1953, ANG.

27. *Colonial Annual Reports, Bahamas*, 1952–53, 6–7.

28. Interview with Sybil Thompson, 25 April 1984, Nassau.

29. Interview with Sir Henry M. Taylor, 18 September 1984; interview with Percival Hanna, 22 February 1984, Bahamas Archives, Nassau.

30. Interview with E. Basil North and Audrey V. North, 10 August 1984.

31. Pridie to Luke, 12 November 1950, CO23/888.

32. Lewis, *The Growth of the Modern West Indies*, 320.

33. Shea to Knutsford, 6 April 1889, CO23/231/219–19a; Report on the Census of the Bahama Islands, taken on 6 December 1953. ANG.

34. Pridie to Luke, 12 November 1950, CO23/888; Murphy to Creech Jones, 20 July 1949, CO23/861.

35. *Year Book of the West Indies and Countries of the Caribbean*, 1953–54, 69–70.

36. H. Saunders, *The Other Bahamas*, 263.

37. Fawkes, *Faith That Moved the Mountain*, (2003), 81–82; H. Taylor, *My Political Memoirs*, 1–15, 122–43.

38. P. Anthony White, "The Real Story of the PLP Founding Fathers," *Punch*, 11 June 2012.

39. Fawkes, *Faith That Moved the Mountain*, 2003, 85.

40. Ibid., 82.

41. White, "The Real Story of the PLP Founding Fathers," *Punch*, 11 June 2012.

42. H. Saunders, *The Other Bahamas*, 264.

43. C. Hughes, *Race and Politics*, 44; H. Taylor, *My Political Memoirs,* 123–30; H. Saunders, *The Other Bahamas*, 265).

44. Darling, *Sir Clifford Darling*, 90.

45. Roker, *Vision of Sir Lynden Pindling*, 12.

46. Interview with Sir Lynden O. Pindling, 16 July 1996.

47. *Nassau Herald*, 21 August 1954; *Tribune,* 26 October 1953; C. Hughes, *Race and Politics*, 38; H. Saunders, *The Other Bahamas*, 267–76.

48. *Tribune*, 28 October 1953; *Nassau Guardian*, 24 October 1953.

49. Eneas, *Let the Church Roll On* (1990), 49.

50. Cited in H. Saunders, *The Other Bahamas*, 278; William Cartwright, "The Coming of the PLP," *Bahamian Review Magazine* 32, no. 3 (May 1984): 55; H. Taylor, *My Political Memoirs*, 122.

51. H. Saunders, *The Other Bahamas*, 280; *Tribune*, 12 December 1953.

52. Darling, *Sir Clifford Darling*, 95–96; extract from Bahamas Political Report for September and October 1954, CO1031/1532, 157–59.

53. H. Taylor, *My Political Memoirs*, 132.

54. H. Saunders, *The Other Bahamas*, 287; interview by H. Saunders with William Cartwright, 20 October 1988, Nassau.

55. H. Saunders, *The Other Bahamas*, 282.

56. *Tribune*, 28 March 1954.

57. *Tribune,* 26 October 1953; *Nassau Guardian*, 22 October 1953. The full text of the platform was published as an advertisement in the *Guardian* of 26 October 1953; see also *Tribune*, 5 June 1954; H. Saunders, *The Other Bahamas*, 281.

58. Cited in Darling, *Sir Clifford Darling*, 96–97; extract from semiofficial letter from A.G.H. Gardiner Brown, Colonial Secretariat, Bahamas, to N. L. Mayle, 29 September 1954, CO1031/1532/160; extract from Bahamas Political Report for July 1954, CO1031/1532/161; N. L. Mayle to Gardiner Brown, 17 September 1954, CO1031/1532/162.

59. Cited in C. Hughes, *Race and Politics*, 55; *Nassau Guardian*, 31 October 1954.

60. *Nassau Guardian*, 1 October 1954.

61. *Nassau Herald,* 6 November 1954.

62. Extract from Bahamas Political Report for October 1954, Internal Political Matters, CO1031/1532/157.

63. C. Hughes, *Race and Politics*, 48.

64. H. Saunders, *The Other Bahamas*, 289.

65. Dupuch, *Tribune Story*, 140.

66. *Tribune*, 20 March 1956.

67. N. Bethel, "Navigations," 147–48.

68. Ibid., 148.

69. Ibid.

70. C. Hughes, *Race and Politics*, 49.

71. Ibid.

72. Cited in ibid., 49–50; *Nassau Guardian*, 13 May 1955.

73. Votes of the House of Assembly, 16 November 1950–18 June 1951, 593–95, ANG.

74. H. Saunders, *The Other Bahamas*, 291.

75. Ibid.

76. C. Hughes, *Race and Politics*, 45–51.

77. Ibid., 50; *Nassau Guardian*, 9 February 1954.

78. C. Hughes, *Race and Politics*, 50.

79. *Tribune*, 3 December 1953; "Policy Regarding Racial Discrimination in the Bahamas," CO1031/1041.

80. H. Foot to Lyttleton, 14 December 1953, CO1031/1041.

81. W. W. Grave to Robert Neville, 9 December 1953, Governor's Office, Secret no. 120: "Colour Bar" unofficial file, 24 September 1943–4 July 1959, Bahamas Archives, Nassau (hereafter cited as "Colour Bar" unofficial file).

82. Hugh Foot to Ranfurly, telegram, 3 December 1955, "Colour Bar" unofficial file.

83. B.G.W. Wiggett to Ranfurly, 5 December 1955, "Colour Bar" unofficial file.

84. Ranfurly to Princess Alice of Athlone, conf., 10 December 1955, "Colour Bar" unofficial file.

85. Encl. Hugh Foot to Ranfurly, 21 February 1956, "Colour Bar" unofficial file.

86. *Tribune*, 3 January 1956.

87. *Nassau Guardian*, 12 February 1956.

88. Dupuch, *Tribune Story*, 147; *Tribune*, 3 January 1956.

89. *Tribune*, 6 January 1956.

90. H. Taylor, *My Political Memoirs*, 201.

91. *Tribune*, 10 February 1956.

92. H. Taylor, *My Political Memoirs*, 201.

93. Ibid., 44; *Tribune*, 24 January 1956; Votes of the House of Assembly, 17 November 1955–17 May 1956, 163–64, 217–18, 286, 381, ANG.

94. H. Taylor, *My Political Memoirs*, 202.

95. Dupuch, *Tribune Story*, 148.

96. *Tribune*, 24 January 1956.

97. *Tribune*, 24 January 1956.

98. Dupuch, *Tribune* Story, 149.

99. *Tribune*, 24 January 1956; Dupuch, *Tribune Story*, 149.

100. C. Hughes, *Race and Politics*, 53; Dupuch, *Tribune Story*, 149; interview with Arthur D. Hanna, 1 January 1994.

101. Stafford Sands to Ranfurly, 25 January 1956, and Arthur to Etheridge, 4 July 1959, "Colour Bar" unofficial file.

102. *Tribune*, 26 and 28 January 1956.

103. Wesley T. Keenan to Ranfurly, 1 February 1956, "Colour Bar" unofficial file.

104. *Tribune*, 2 and 8 February 1956, 21 February 1956; *Nassau Guardian*, 22 February 1956; Votes of the House of Assembly, 1955–56, 217–18, ANG.

105. Dupuch, *Tribune Story*, 151–52.

106. *Tribune,* 1 March 1956.

107. Dupuch, *Tribune Story*, 153–54.

108. H. Taylor, *My Political Memoirs*, 208.

109. D. Johnson, *Quiet Revolution*, 34; C. Hughes, *Race and Politics*, 63–70.

110. Dupuch, *Tribune Story*, 151; C. Hughes, *Race and Politics*, 51–54, 63–66.

111. Dupuch, *Tribune Story*, 152; D. Johnson, *Quiet Revolution*, 34.

112. Interview with Sir Clifford Darling, 18 October 1991.

113. Interview with Winston V. Saunders, 10 December 1993.

114. Interview with Arthur Hanna, 1 January 1994.

115. Arthur to Etheridge, 2 July 1959, "Colour Bar" unofficial file.

116. PLP Programme Events, Third Annual Convention, CO 1031/1532/21.

117. Ranfurly to Lennox-Boyd, 28 May 1956, telegram (secret), CO 1031/1294/77, 114.

118. Ranfurly to Lennox-Boyd, 28 May 1956, CO1031/1294/114.

119. Lennox-Boyd to Ranfurly, 5 June 1956, CO/1031/1294/100–1.

120. H. Taylor, *My Political Memoirs*, 212.

121. *Nassau Guardian*, 28 May 1956.

122. *Nassau Guardian*, 14 June 1956; C. Hughes, *Race and Politics*, 60.

123. Bahamas Political Report of June 1956, CO1031/1294/77.

124. *Nassau Guardian*, 22 June 1956.

125. *Nassau Herald*, 2 June 1956; H. Saunders, *The Other Bahamas*, 293.

126. Extract from Bahamas Political Report, June 1956, CO 1031/1294/77.

127. H. Taylor, *My Political Mem*oirs, 222-23, 226–27, 237–38; G. Saunders, "The Making of a Leader," 168.

128. Roker, *Vision of Sir Lynden Pindling*, 12.

129. C. Hughes, *Race and Politics*, 61; *Tribune,* 30 June 1956.

130. Draft, Conf. Record of a Meeting between Representatives of the Colonial Office and the Progressive Liberal Party of the Bahamas, 8 October 1956, CO 1031/1532/72–82.

131. Conduct of Elections in the Bahamas, Regina v. Jonathan Rolle, Preliminary Hearing, Exhibit B, 20 June 1956, CO1031/2138/30; Darling, *Sir Clifford Darling*, 107–9.

132. Darling, *Sir Clifford Darling*, 109.

133. D. Johnson, *Quiet Revolution,* 41.

134. *Tribune,* 12 May 1956; H. Saunders, *The Other Bahamas*, 307–9.

135. *Nassau Guardian*, 12 and 13 May 1956.

136. Ibid.

137. Ranfurly to Rogers, 10 July 1956, CO1031/1294/87–88; Darling, *Sir Clifford Darling*, 110.

138. Ranfurly to Rogers, 12 July 1956, CO1031/1294/88; Darling, *Sir Clifford Darling*, 111.

139. Ranfurly to Rogers, 31 July 1956, CO1031/1294/75; Darling, *Sir Clifford Darling*, 112–13.

140. Ranfurly to Rogers, 31 July 1956, CO1031/1294/75.

141. H. M. Taylor, C. Stevenson, and Lynden Pindling to Lt. Secretary of State for the Colonies, 21 July 1956, CO1031/1532/150–52.

142. Ibid.

143. Ranfurly to Rogers, 31 July 1956, CO1031/1294/75.

144. Ibid.

145. Office Note, F. Kennedy, and Record of a Meeting between Representatives of the Colonial Office and of the Progressive Liberal Party (PLP) of the Bahamas, 8 October 1956, CO1031/1532/9, 72–82; see also *Tribune*, 22 October 1956.

146. Office Note, F. Kennedy, Record of Meeting with the PLP, 8 October 1956, CO 1031/1532/80; see also Office Note, Edith Mercer, 28 September 1956, CO1031/1532/8–9.

147. K. M. Walmsley to Rogers, 25 September 1956, CO1031/1532/107–10.

148. Rogers to Ranfurly, 17 October 1956, CO1031/1532/46–47.

149. Rogers to Ranfurly, 17 October 1956, CO1031/1532/47.

150. Ranfurly to Rogers, 3 December 1956, CO1031/1532/40–42.

151. Ibid.

152. Ibid.

153. Ranfurly to Rogers, 4 December 1956, CO1031/2236/139–40.

154. *Tribune*, 19 February 1957; *Nassau Guardian*, 18 February 1957; H. M. Taylor and L. O. Pindling to Sir Raynor Arthur, 19 October 1957, Activities of the Progressive Liberal Party, 1957–59, CO 1031/2477/22.

155. Taylor and Pindling to Arthur, 19 October 1957, CO1031/2477, 1–8.

156. Arthur to Lennox-Boyd, 7 August 1957, CO1031/2232/419–20.

157. H. M. Taylor to Lord Lloyd, 14 June 1957, CO1031/2232/460.

158. Rogers to Arthur, 5 July 1957, (secret and personal office note), CO1031/2232/446.

Chapter 8. The 1958 General Strike and Its Aftermath

1. C. Hughes, *Race and Politics*, 88.

2. Policy Regarding Racial Discrimination in the Bahamas 1957–59, CO1031/2416.

3. Interview with Arthur D. Hanna, Nassau, 30 December 1996.

4. Fawkes, *The Faith That Moved the Mountain* (2003), 79; Craton, *Pindling*, 45.

5. Interview with Sir Randol Fawkes, Nassau, 25 October 1991.

6. Darling, *Sir Clifford Darling*, 61–62.

7. Ibid., 238–39.

8. Ibid., 68–69.

9. Ibid., 72–74.

10. Bahamas Political Report, September 1954, CO1031/1532/158–59.

11. Darling, *Sir Clifford Darling*, 226.

12. Acting Governor to Lennox-Boyd, 6 November 1957, CO1031/2835.

13. Ibid.

14. Darling, *Sir Clifford Darling*, 227–28, 230.

15. Ibid., 230; Acting Governor to Lennox-Boyd, 6 November 1957, CO1031/2835.

16. *Tribune*, 2 November 1957.

17. Acting Governor to Lennox-Boyd, 5 November 1957, CO1031/2835; Darling, *Sir Clifford Darling*, 231.

18. Acting Governor to Lennox-Boyd, 6 November 1957, CO1031/2835.

19. Darling, *Sir Clifford Darling*, 232.

20. Ibid., 241.

21. *Tribune,* 29 November 1957.

22. *Tribune,* 30 November 1957.

23. *Tribune,* 3 December 1957; *Nassau Guardian*, 3 December 1957.

24. Darling, *Sir Clifford Darling*, 250–51.

25. Ibid., 267–68.

26. Arthur to Lennox-Boyd, 28 January 1958, CO1031/2835/1–6.

27. Fawkes, *The Faith That Moved the Mountain* (2003), 115.

28. Darling, *Sir Clifford Darling*, 269; Fawkes, *The Faith That Moved the Mountain*, 115–17; interview with James Shepherd by Tracey Thompson, 2 June 1982.

29. Darling, *Sir Clifford Darling*, 272.

30. Profumo to Roland Robinson, 30 January 1958, CO1031/2835; *Tribune*, 13 January 1958; see also Arthur to Lennox-Boyd, 13 January 1958, CO1031/2835/152.

31. Darling, *Sir Clifford Darling*, 280–81; Arthur to Commander of the Caribbean Area No. 11, Repeated to Secretary of State, 14 January 1958, CO1031/2835.

32. Intelligence Report for the month of January 1958, 27 January 1958, CO1031/2835/3.

33. *Nassau Guardian*, 15 January 1958.

34. *Nassau Guardian*, 1 January 1958; Darling, *Sir Clifford Darling*, 284.

35. *Tribune*, 14 January 1958; Darling, *Sir Clifford Darling*, 285.

36. Interview with Sir Clifford Darling, 18 October 1991, Nassau.

37. Darling, *Sir Clifford Darling*, 286.

38. Ibid., 286–87.

39. *Nassau Guardian*, 16 January 1958.

40. *Tribune*, 15 January 1958.

41. *Nassau Guardian*, 16 January 1958.

42. Arthur to Lennox-Boyd, 20 January 1958, CO1031/2835.

43. Darling, *Sir Clifford Darling*, 295.

44. *Nassau Guardian*, 21 January 1958.

45. Ibid.

46. *Tribune,* 21 January 1958.

47. *Tribune,* 16 January 1958.

48. Ibid.

49. *Tribune,* 23 January 1958; *Nassau Guardian*, 23 January 1958.

50. Arthur to Lennox-Boyd, 22 January 1958, CO1031/2835/107.

51. Darling, *Sir Clifford Darling*, 325.

52. *New York Times*, 14 January 1958.

53. Douglas Williams to John Stacpoole, Colonial Office, 29 January 1958, CO1031/2835/82. Mau Mau was a 1950s rebellion against colonial rule in Kenya.

54. Fawkes, *The Faith That Moved the Mountain* (2003), 121.

55. John McPherson to Vincent Tewson, 11 February 1958, CO1031/2835; Intelligence Report, January 1958, CO1031/2835/3–6.

56. Fawkes, *The Faith That Moved the Mountain* (2003), 131.

57. C. Hughes, *Race and Politics*, 75.

58. Darling, *Sir Clifford Darling*, 382–85.

59. Lennox-Boyd to Arthur, 28 February 1958, CO1031/2950.

60. Raynor Arthur to Philip Rogers, 9 July 1957, CO1031/2472.

61. Arthur to Rogers, 10 February 1958, CO1031/2950.

62. Rogers to Arthur, 18 February 1958, CO1031/2950.

63. Office Memorandum, Rogers to Poynton, 28 October 1959, CO1031/2950.

64. Fawkes, *The Faith That Moved the Mountain* (2003), 140; D. Johnson, *Quiet Revolution*, 36; C. Hughes, *Race and Politics*, 77.

65. *Tribune*, 18 February 1958.

66. J. McPherson to Charles Cunningham, 10 February 1958, CO1031/2232/236–37.

67. Interview with Robert H. Symonette, 4 May 1993.

68. Arthur to Lennox-Boyd, 6 February 1958, CO1031/2835.

69. Act 57 of 1958, *Statute Law of the Bahamas, 1799–1965* (ed. Hone), 6:3069–141.

70. Votes of the House of Assembly, 14 January–18 September 1958, 113–14, ANG.

71. C. Hughes, *Race and Politics*, 75–76.

72. *Tribune*, 7 February 1958.

73. *Tribune*, 14 April 1958; see also Craton, *History of the Bahamas*, 274.

74. Alan Burns to Rogers, 4 November 1957, CO1031/2232/338–40.

75. H. Houghton, *Report on Bahamian Education*; H. L. Glyn Hughes, *A Survey of Medical Services, Nassau, 1960*.

76. A. Deans Peggs to Lennox-Boyd, 1 April 1957, CO1031/2198.

77. "A Comparison of the Level of Living in the Bahamas and Other Caribbean Islands," preliminary report, December 1958, Economist Intelligence Unit, CO1031/2467.

78. Memorandum on points concerning the Bahamas made by Sir Charles Hambro, CO1031/2121; Craton, *History of the Bahamas*, 274.

79. C. Hughes, *Race and Politics*, 76–77; Craton, *History of the Bahamas*, 274; Craton and Saunders, *Islanders*, 2:311–12.

80. F. M. Collett to Secretary of State, 16 May 1956, CO1031/2140, 96, cited in Craton, *Pindling*, 91.

81. M. Bethel, "The Women's Suffrage Movement in the Bahamas, 1948–1962." See also Bethel and Govan, *Womanish Ways*.

82. In fact, some women in Trinidad and Tobago and Jamaica got the vote in the 1920s. Professor Bridget Brereton, pers. comm., November 2012.

83. Marion Bethel, "The Women's Suffrage Movement in the Bahamas, 1948–1962."

84. Ibid.

85. Outten-Stubbs, "A Chronological History of Women's Suffrage."

86. The story is told that when Rufus Ingraham lost his seat in the House of Assembly in 1949, he told his wife, Mary, that if women had the vote, he would have won his seat. Soon after that, she officially founded the Women's Suffrage Movement.

87. *Tribune*, editorial, 22 November 2012.

88. D. Johnson, *Quiet Revolution*, 36.

89. Outten-Stubbs, "A Chronological History of Women's Suffrage."

90. Votes of the House of Assembly, 1 December 1958, ANG.

91. Fawkes, *The Faith That Moved the Mountain* (2003), 203.

92. Ibid., 203–8.

93. *Tribune*, 22 November 2012.

94. Outten-Stubbs, "A Chronological History of Women's Suffrage."

95. Ibid.

96. Ibid.

97. Ibid.

98. Bahamas Acts, Election Act, 23 February 1961.

99. *Tribune,* 22 November 2012.

100. *Nassau Herald*, 10 October 1960.

101. *Nassau Guardian,* 25 May 1960; *Tribune,* 25 May 1960.

102. *Nassau Herald*, 10 October 1959.

103. *Tribune,* 14 October 1959.

104. *Nassau Guardian*, 16 October 1959.

105. C. Hughes, *Race and Politics*, 83.

106. F. Bethel and Stevenson, "The State, the Crowd, and the Heroes," 11–14, 17; see also Singham, *The Hero and the Crowd in a Colonial Polity*, 192–93; H. Taylor, *My Political Memoirs*, 244–45, 324–25.

107. Reprinted in the *Nassau Herald*, 27 February 1960; cited in C. Hughes, *Race and Politics*, 87–88.

108. C. Hughes, *Race and Politics*, 88; *Nassau Herald*, 28 June 1958.

109. *Nassau Herald*, 28 February 1959; Hughes, *Race and Politics*, 89.

110. Cited in Hughes, *Race and Politics*, 89; *Nassau Herald*, 23 May 1959.

111. *Nassau Herald*, 3 February 1960.

112. *Nassau Guardian,* 4 April 1960.

113. H. Taylor, *My Political Memoirs*, 249.

114. Interview with Jeffrey Thompson by Tracey Thompson, 18 December 1996; Interview with H.E. Sir Arthur Foulkes, 27 December 2000.

115. Interview with Jeffrey Thompson by Tracey Thompson, 18 December 1996; interview with Sir Orville Turnquest, 17 December 1996.

116. C. Hughes, *Race and Politics*, 93; *Tribune*, 10 June 1960.

117. *Nassau Herald*, 10 October 1960.

118. Ibid.; C. Hughes, *Race and Politics*, 94–95

119. Craton, *Pindling*, 164–65; Craton and Saunders, *Islanders*, 2:332–36.

120. Cited in C. Hughes, *Race and Politics*, 102–3; *Nassau Guardian*, 31 October 1962.

121. *Tribune*, 25 November 1962.

122. Interview with Dr. Eugene Newry, 2 December 2000; interview with H.E. Sir Arthur Foulkes, 27 December 2000.

123. Cited in C. Hughes, *Race and Politics*, 95; *Bahamian Times*, January 1962.

124. C. Hughes, *Race and Politics*, 97; *Tribune,* 1 February 1962.

125. *Nassau Herald*, 25 April 1962.

126. *Tribune*, 17 April 1962; see also *Tribune*, editorial, 15 December 1962.

127. *Nassau Guardian*, 31 October 1962.

128. *Tribune*, 24 November 1962.

129. C. Hughes, *Race and Politics*, 102.

130. *Nassau Guardian*, 31 October 1962.

131. C. Hughes, *Race and Politics*, 105.

132. Craton, "Bay Street, Black Power, and the Conchy Joes," 82.

133. *Nassau Herald*, 1 December 1962.

134. *Tribune*, 24 November 1962.

Chapter 9. Confronting a Divided Society

1. Report on the Census of the Bahama Islands, Taken in April 1881; Report on the Census, 15 November 1963; all census reports cited in this chapter were printed by the Nassau Guardian (ANG) and are housed in the Bahamas Archives and the Department of Statistics, Nassau.

2. Report on the Census, 15 November 1963.

3. *Bahamas Civil Service List,* 57–63; Report on the Census, 6 December 1953; Report on the Census, 15 November 1963; see also Tinker, *Migration of Peoples,* 37–59.

4. Report on the Census, April 1881; Report on the Census, 15 November 1963.

5. Report on the Census, 25 April 1943; Report on the Census, 6 December 1953.

6. Williams, *Methodist Contribution*, 99.

7. Symonette and Canzoneri, *Baptists in the Bahamas,* 17.

8. Ibid., 26–27; *Tribune*, 24 August 1953.

9. Symonette and Canzoneri, *Baptists in the Bahamas,* 50.

10. Ibid., 52–61; Williams, *Methodist Contribution,* 100.

11. Williams, *Methodist Contribution*, 105.

12. Williams, *Methodist Contribution*, 105; Eneas, *Let the Church Roll On*, 2–7.

13. Craton and Saunders, *Islanders*, 2:117.

14. Interview with Percival Hanna, 22 February 1984.

15. Hanna, *Pictorial History and Memories of Nassau's Over-the-Hill*, vii.

16. Interview with Sir Orville Turnquest, 19 March 2013.

17. Report on the Census, 6 December 1953.

18. Doran and Landis, "Origins and Persistence of an Inner-City Slum," 20.

19. Notes on the Bahamas 1951 by S.E.V. Luke, 20 April 1951, CO23/889.

20. Interview with Sir Orville Turnquest, 19 March 2013.

21. Interview with Arlene Nash Ferguson, 20 March 2013.

22. Hanna, *Pictorial History and Memories of Nassau's Over-the-Hill*, viii.

23. Report on the Census, 15 November 1963.

24. Report on the Census, 6 December 1953; Report on the Census, 15 November 1963.

25. Report on the Census, 6 December 1953; Report on the Census, 15 November 1963.

26. Out Island Commissioner's Reports, Rock Sound, Eleuthera, 1950–53; Hatchet Bay, Eleuthera, 1949; Harbour Island, 1947–53; and Bimini, 1953, Bahamas Archives, Nassau.

27. *Colonial Annual Reports, Bahamas,* 1964–65.

28. *Colonial Annual Reports, Bahamas,* 1950–51.

29. Bahamas Administrative Reports 1951, CO26/154. See also Cash, "Colonial Policies and Outside Influences," 343.

30. *Colonial Annual Reports, Bahamas,* 1964–65, 79.

31. Encl. Neville to Luke, 1 October 1951, CO23/889.

32. *Colonial Annual Reports, Bahamas,* 1952–53, 1964–65.

33. Rules Governing the Procedure to Be Adopted in Disposal of Crown Lands, encl. Murphy to Creech Jones, 14 December 1948, CO23/877.

34. McDermott, "Harold Christie," 22–23. See also *Bahamas Civil Service List.*

35. *Tribune,* 5 November 1953.

36. Ibid.

37. Judgement in the Case of the Petition of James Maxwell Mitchell Bowe under the Quieting of Titles Act, 1959, concerning the Forest Estate, Bahama Islands Supreme Court, Equity Division, no. 137 of 1961, Bahamas Archives, Nassau.

38. Report on the Census, 27 June 1891; Report on the Census, 15 November 1963, ANG.

39. *Colonial Annual Reports, Bahamas,* 1964–65, 26–32.

40. C. Hughes, *Race and Politics,* 20–31.

41. Extract from Lord Listowel's Report on the West Indies, 1949, CO23/888.

42. McDermott, "Harold Christie," 29.

43. Interview with Gurth Duncombe, 15 September 1984.

44. *Nassau Magazine* 12, no. 1 (December 1945): 11, 31; P. Albury, *Story of the Bahamas,* 212–13.

45. Interview with Lorraine Lightbourn and Arlene Nash Ferguson, 15 and 20 March 2013.

46. Personal reminiscences of the author.

47. *Tribune,* 3 September 1949; see also *Bahamas Review Magazine* 2, nos. 1–2 (April–May 1953): 33.

48. Interview with Jeanne Thompson, 22 March 2013.

49. Personal reminiscences of the author.

50. *Annual Report Board of Education, 1953,* Ministry of Education Records, Bahamas Archives.

51. H. Houghton, *Report on Bahamian Education,* 25.

52. *Year Book of the West Indies and Countries of the Caribbean,* 1948–49, 108–9.

53. *Bahamas Civil Service List,* 47.

54. Ibid., 48.

55. Ibid., 56.

56. *Tribune,* 19 December 1953.

57. "Hilda Bowen, MBE Portrait of the Week," *Tribune,* 1 November 1983.

58. *Tribune,* 21 October 1953.

59. Interview with Jeanne Thompson, 22 March 2013.

60. Public Establishment Commission of Enquiry conducted by Sir Alan Burns, 1949, CO23/844.

61. *Bahamas Civil Service List,* 12.

62. *Year Book of the West Indies and Countries of the Caribbean,* 1951, 103.

63. *Nassau Guardian,* 29 August and 1 September 1949; *Tribune,* 21 December 1953.

64. *Tribune,* 23 December 1950.

65. *Tribune,* 7 July 1953.

66. *Tribune,* 7 March 1951.

67. *Nassau Guardian,* 3 May 1949.

68. Dyer to Noble, 7 November 1953, Nassau, WMMS Papers.

69. *Bahamian Review Magazine* 2, nos. 8–9 (Winter 1953–54): 14.

70. Denyer to Noble, 10 April 1947, Governor's Harbour, Eleuthera, WMMS Papers.

71. Personal reminiscences and experience of the author, who attended a predominantly white high school.

72. Lowenthal, *West Indian Societies,* 97.

73. Interview with Winston V. Saunders, 10 November 1984.

74. Interview with Peter Graham, 8 May 2013.

75. Interview with Sir Arthur Foulkes, 24 April 2013.

76. Tull, "Colour Pride in Tarpum Bay," 69.

77. Interview with Sir Arthur Foulkes, 24 April 2013.

78. Interview with Marina D'Aguilar, 7 May 2013.

79. Lewis, *The Growth of the Modern West Indies,* 322.

80. H. Johnson, "National Identity and Bahamian Culture," 16–17; Craton and Saunders, *Islanders,* 1:xviii.

81. H. Houghton, *Report on Bahamian Education,* 31.

82. H. Johnson, "National Identity and Bahamian Culture," 17.

83. Ibid., 13.

84. C. Hughes, *Race and Politics,* 95.

85. Interview with Sir Arthur Foulkes, 24 April 2013.

86. Hanna, *Pictorial History and Memories of Nassau's Over-the-Hill,* vi.

87. Interview with the Right Reverend Gilbert A. Thompson, assistant bishop, Anglican Diocese of the Bahamas, 6 March 2013.

88. Craton, "Bay Street, Black Power, and the Conchy Joes," 82.

89. C. Hughes, *Race and Politics,* 115.

90. Interview with Jeffrey Thompson by Tracey Thompson, 18 December 1996; interview with Sir Arthur Foulkes, 27 December 2000.

91. C. Hughes, *Race and Politics,* 142, 144.

92. Ibid., 153, 170, 183.

93. *Bahamian Times,* 5 April 1957.

94. D'Albenas is said to have left for health reasons.

95. C. Hughes, *Race and Politics,* 184–85.

96. Ibid., 185; *Nassau Guardian,* 30 July 1970.

97. Craton and Saunders, *Islanders,* 2:359.

BIBLIOGRAPHY

Primary Sources

BAHAMAS ARCHIVES, COMMONWEALTH OF THE BAHAMAS, NASSAU

Armbrister Papers.

Bahamas Blue Books, 1844, 1894, 1897, 1901–2, 1908–9, 1914–15, 1918–46.

Bahamas Governor's Dispatches, original correspondence, 1881–1962, CO23/91, 138, 96, 140, 154, 163, 165, 191–92, 221–899; CO1031/138, 1041, 1294, 1532, 2121, 2140, 2198, 2232, 2416, 2467, 2472, 2477, 2835, 2950.

Colonial Annual Reports, Bahamas. London: Her Majesty's Stationery Office, 1881–1965.

Colonial Annual Reports, Bahamas, 1881–1907. London: HMSO, 1908.

Colonial Office Records, National Archives of England, Wales, and the United Kingdom, Kew, Richmond, Surrey.

Colonial Secretary Papers.

Duplicate Governor's Dispatches, 1881–87, 1887–93, 1893–97.

Eneas Collection.

Executive Council Minutes, 1860–80.

Governor's Office, Secret no. 120: "Colour Bar" unofficial file, 1889, 1891, 1896, 1907–8, 1911–14, 1923, 1936, 1951.

Magistrate's Court Records.

Methodist Missionary Society (MMS), West Indies Correspondence, Bahamas.

Ministry of Education Records.

Nassau Guardian Archives.

Neville Chamberlain Papers.

   BC 2 Correspondence between Beatrice and Neville Chamberlain 1891–1918.

   NC1 Austen and Neville Chamberlain to Joseph Chamberlain 1891–97.

   NC2 Journals and Diaries 1889–1940.

   NC3 Andros Scheme: Letters and Documents 1890–1904.

O'Brien Collection.

Out Island Commissioners' Reports.

Rawson, Sir Rawson W. *Report on the Bahamas Hurricane of October 1866 with a Description of the City of Nassau*. Nassau, 1868.

Report on the Census of the Bahama Islands, taken in April 1881.

Report on the Census of the Bahama Islands, taken on 27 June 1891.

Report on the Census of the Bahama Islands, taken on 14 April 1901.

Report on the Census of the Bahama Islands, taken on 2 April 1911.

Report on the Census of the Bahama Islands, taken on 24 April 1921.

Report on the Census of the Bahama Islands, taken on 26 April 1931.

Report on the Census of the Bahama Islands, taken on 25 April 1943.

Report on the Census of the Bahama Islands, taken on 6 December 1953.

Report on the Census of the Bahama Islands, taken on 15 November 1963.

Report of the [Russell] Commission Appointed to Enquire into Disturbances in the Bahamas which took place in June 1942, Nassau: Nassau Guardian, 1942.

Report of the Select Committee of The House of Assembly Appointed to Enquire into the Disturbances in the Bahamas which took place in June, 1942, Votes of the House of Assembly, 1942–43, Nassau, 1943.

Royal Commonwealth Society Library, Cambridge University, digital collection.

Smith, James Carmichael, Papers.

Supreme Court Records.

Synod Minutes 1890–1946, Wesleyan Methodist Missionary Society (WMMS), School of African and Oriental Studies Library, University of London, digital collection.

University of Birmingham Library, United Kingdom, digital collection.

Votes of the House of Assembly, 1883–1958.

Votes of the Legislative Council, 1907–38.

Wesleyan Methodist Missionary Society Papers, 1883–1946.

PERIODICALS AND NEWSPAPERS

Bahamas Almanac, 1892, 1894, 1901.

Bahamas Handbook, 1971–72, 1976–77, 1978–79, 1980.

Chicago Defender, 1924.

Freeman, 1886–89.

Nassau Guardian, 1886–1962.

Nassau Herald, 1944, 1954, 1959–60.

Nassau Magazine, 1934–53.

Nassau Quarterly Mission Papers, 1888–97, 1913–18.

Nassau Times, 1880–87.

Nassau Tribune, 1911–62.

Negro World, 1927.

Strombus Magazine, 1914.

Watchman, 1901, 1903, 1904–7.

INTERVIEWS (BY AUTHOR IN NASSAU, UNLESS OTHERWISE INDICATED)

Bethel, Cecil V., 1 May 1984.

Brown, Holly, 10 September 1984.

Cancino, Jennie, 12 January 1984.

Cartwright, William, interview by Hartley C. Saunders, 20 October 1988, Nassau.

Darling, Sir Clifford, 18 October 1991.

D'Aguilar, Marina, 7 May 2013.

Dumont, Dame Ivy, former governor general, 22 October 2009.

Duncombe, Gurth, 15 September 1984.

Eldon, Rowena, 3 May 1983, 8 December 1983.

Fawkes, Sir Randol, 22 November 1982, 25 October 1991.

Ferguson, Arlene Nash, 15 and 20 March 2013.

Foulkes, Sir Arthur, 27 December 2000, 24 April 2013.

Graham, Peter, 8 May 2013.

Hanna, H.E. Hon. Arthur D., 1 January 1994, 30 December 1996, 16 March 2010.

Hanna, Percival, 22 February 1984.

Higgs, Alphonso Blake, 30 June 1982.

Lightbourn, Lorraine, 15 and 20 March 2013.

Lunn, Drs. John and Sonia, 10 September 1984.

McKinney, Herbert, 8 November 1975.

Newry, Dr. Eugene, 2 December 2000.

North, Audrey V. Isaacs, 20 June 1984, 31 July 1984, 10 August 1984.

North, Edward Basil, 31 July 1984, 10 August 1984, 8 January 2004.

North, Dr. Terry, 5 August 1983, London.

Pindling, Sir Lynden O., 16 July 1996.

Podlewski, Dr. Henryk, 9 September 1984.

Saunders, Winston V., 10 November 1984, 10 December 1993.

Shepherd, James, interview by Tracey Thompson, 2 June 1982.

Stirrup, Edith, 3 July 2012.

Symonette, Robert H., 4 May 1993.

Taylor, Sir Henry M., 18 September 1984.

Thompson, Right Reverend Gilbert A., 6 March 2013.

Thompson, Jeanne, 18 December 1996, 22 March 2013.

Thompson, Jeffrey, interview by Tracey Thompson, 18 December 1996.

Thompson, Maxwell, 17 January 1984.

Thompson, Sybil, 25 April 1984.

Turnquest, Sir Orville, 17 December 1996, 19 March 2013, 23 March 2013.

Walker, Dr. C. R., 31 July 1970, Grant's Town.

Secondary Sources

Adderley, Paul. *From Pompey to Pindling* (DVD). Inaugural Sir Lynden O. Pindling Memorial Lecture, Nassau, 22 March 2001. Nassau: Bahamas Archives.

Adderley, Rosanne M. *"New Negroes from Africa": Slave Trade Abolition and Free African Settlement in the Nineteenth-Century Caribbean.* Bloomington: Indiana University Press, 2006.

Albury, Haziel. *Man-O-War, My Island Home: A History of an Outer Abaco Island.* Hockessin, Del.: Holly Press, 1977.

Albury, Paul. *The Story of the Bahamas*. London: Macmillan Education, 1975.

Aspinall, Algernon. *Pocket Guide to the West Indies*. London: Sifton Praed, 1923.

Ayearst, Morley. *The British West Indies: The Search for Self-Government*. New York: New York University Press, 1960.

Bahamas Almanac, with a Guide to the Bahamas. Nassau: Nassau Guardian, 1892, 1894, 1901.

Bahamas Archives. *The Bahamas in the Nineteenth Century, 1870–1899*. Nassau: Government Printing Department, 1987.

———. *Junkanoo*. Exhibition booklet. Nassau: Government Printing Department, 1978.

———. *The Pineapple Industry of the Bahamas*. Exhibition booklet. Nassau: Public Records Office, Archives Section, Ministry of Education and Culture, 1977.

———. *The Salt Industry of the Bahamas*. Exhibition booklet. Nassau: Government Printing Department, 1980.

———. *A Selection of Historic Buildings of the Bahamas*. Exhibition booklet. Nassau: Government Printing Department, 1975.

———. *Settlements in New Providence*. Nassau: Government Printing Department, 1982.

———. *The Sponging Industry*. Exhibition booklet. Nassau: Government Printing Department, 1974.

Bahamas Civil Service List, 1953. Nassau: Nassau Guardian, 1953.

Banton, Michael. *Race Relations*. London: Tavistock Publications, 1967.

Barratt, Peter. *Grand Bahama*. Harrisburg, Pa., Newton Abbott Devon, 1972; 2nd ed., London: Macmillan Caribbean, 1982.

Barry, Colman. *Upon These Rocks: Catholics in the Bahamas*. Collegeville, Minn.: St. John's Abbey Press, 1973.

Bell, Hugh MacLachlan. *Bahamas: Isles of June*. New York: Robert M. McBride, 1934.

Besson, Jean. "Family Land as a Model for Martha Brae's New History: Culture Building in an Afro-Caribbean Village." In *Afro-Caribbean Villages in Historical Perspective*, ed. C. V. Carnegie, 100–32. Kingston: African Caribbean Institute of Jamaica.

———. "A Paradox in Caribbean Attitudes to Land." In *Land and Development in the Caribbean*, ed. Jean Besson and Janet Momsen, 13–45. London: Macmillan Caribbean, 1987.

Bethel, E. Clement. "Music in the Bahamas: Its Roots, Developments, and Personality." MA thesis, University of California, Los Angeles, 1978.

Bethel, Felix, and Michael Stevenson. "The State, the Crowd, and the Heroes: The Struggle for Control in the Bahamas, 1958–68." Paper delivered at the 24th Conference of the Association of Caribbean Historians, Nassau, Bahamas, 1992.

Bethel, Marion. "The Women's Suffrage Movement in the Bahamas, 1948–1962." Presented at the Bahamas Historical Society, 15 November 2012.

Bethel, Marion, and Maria Govan, directors. *Womanish Ways: Freedom, Human Rights, and Democracy. A Documentary of the History of the Women's Suffrage Movement in the Bahamas*. DVD. Nassau, 2012.

Bethel, Nicolette. "Generation Property: A Consideration of Customary Land Tenure in the Bahamas." *College of the Bahamas Research Journal* 11 (2002): 11–16.

———. "Navigations: The Fluidity of National Identity in the Post-Colonial Bahamas." Ph.D. diss., Corpus Christi College, University of Cambridge, 2000.

Beveridge, Sir Wilfrid. *Report on the Public Health and on Medical Conditions in New Providence, Bahama Islands.* London: Waterlow and Sons, 1927.

Blair, Tosheena Robinson. "Baptist Preachers Helped Build a Nation." In *Bahamas Handbook*, 83–98. Nassau: Etienne Dupuch Jr. Publications, 2011.

Bloch, Michael. *The Duke of Windsor's War.* London: Weidenfeld and Nicolson, 1982.

Bolland, O. Nigel. "Historiography of Decolonization in the Anglophone Caribbean." In *Beyond Fragmentation: Perspectives on Caribbean History*, ed. Juanita de Barros, Audra Diptee, and David V. Trotman, 265–69. Princeton: Markus Wiener, 2006.

———. *The Politics of Labour in the British Caribbean: The Social Origins of Authoritarianism and Democracy in the Labour Movement.* Kingston, Jamaica: Ian Randle; Oxford: James Curry; Princeton: Markus Wiener, 2001.

Bolt, Christine. *Victorian Attitudes to Race.* London: Routledge and Kegan Paul, 1971.

Bowe, Ruth. "Honourable Percy William Armbrister, 1862–1957." *Journal of the Bahamas Historical Society* 3, no. 1 (October 1981): 20–22.

Braithwaite, Lloyd. "Stratification in Trinidad." In *Slaves, Freemen, Citizens: West Indian Perspectives*, ed. Lambos Comitas and David Lowenthal, 212–39. Garden City, N.Y.: Anchor Press–Doubleday, 1973.

Brathwaite, Kamau. *The Development of Creole Society in Jamaica, 1770–1820.* Oxford: Clarendon Press, 1971.

Bregenzer, John. *Trying to Make It: Adapting to the Bahamas.* Washington, D.C.: University Press of America, 1982.

Brereton, Bridget. "'The Development of an Identity': The Black Middle Class of Trinidad in the Late Nineteenth Century." In *Caribbean Freedom: Society and Economy from Emancipation to the Present*, ed. Hilary Beckles and Verene Shepherd. Kingston, Jamaica: Ian Randle, 1993.

———. *Race Relations in Colonial Trinidad, 1870–1900.* Cambridge: Cambridge University Press, 1979.

———. "Social Organization and Class." In *Trinidad Ethnicity*, ed. Kelvin Yelvington. Knoxville: University of Tennessee Press, 1993, 33–55.

Brodber, Erna. *A Study of Yards in the City of Kingston.* Working Paper no. 9. Mona, Jamaica: Institute of Social and Economic Research, 1975.

Bruce, Peter Henry. *Memoirs of Peter Henry Bruce, Esq.: A Military Officer in the Services of Prussia, Russia, and Great Britain: Containing an Account of His Travels in Germany, Russia, Tartary, Turkey, the West Indies, &c., as Also Several Very Interesting Private Anecdotes of the Czar, Peter I of Russia.* London: Printed for the author's widow and sold by T. Payne and Son, 1782. Republished as *Bahamian Interlude*, London: R. H. Johns, 1949.

Burn, William Laurence. *Emancipation and Apprenticeship in the British West Indies.* London: Jonathan Cape, 1937; reprint, London: Johnson Reprint, 1970.

Burns, Sir Alan. *Colonial Civil Servant*. London: Allen and Unwin, 1949.

Cash, Philip. "Colonial Policies and Outside Influences: A Study of Bahamian History, 1919–1947." MA diss., University of Wales, 1979.

Cash, Philip, Shirley Gordon, and Gail Saunders. *Sources of Bahamian History*. London: Macmillan Education, 1991.

Churton, Edward. *The Island Missionary of the Bahamas: A Manual of Instruction and Routine in Ten Practical Addresses*. London: J. Masters, 1888, 1892.

Clifford, Sir Bede. *Proconsul, Being Incidents in the Life and Career of the Honourable Sir Bede Clifford, GCMG, CB, MVO*. London: Evans Brothers, 1964.

Cottman, Evan W., with Wyatt Blassingame. *Out Island Doctor*. London: Hodder and Stoughton, 1963.

Cox, Oliver C. *Caste, Class, and Race: A Study in Social Dynamics*. New York: Monthly Review Press, 1959.

Craton, Michael. "Bay Street, Black Power, and the Conchy Joes: Race and Class in the Colony and Commonwealth of the Bahamas, 1850–2000." In *The White Minority in the Caribbean*, ed. Howard Johnson and Karl Watson, 71–94. Kingston, Jamaica: Ian Randle, 1998.

———. *A History of the Bahamas*. 3rd ed. Waterloo, Canada: San Salvador Press, 1986.

———. *The Life and Times of Lynden Oscar Pindling: First Prime Minister of the Bahamas, 1930–2000*. Oxford: Macmillan Education, 2002.

———. "White Law and Black Custom: The Evolution of Bahamian Land Tenures." In *Land and Development in the Caribbean*, ed. Jean Besson and Janet Momsen, 88–114. London: Macmillan Caribbean, 1987.

Craton, Michael, and Gail Saunders. *Islanders in the Stream: A History of the Bahamian People*. Vol. 1: *From Aboriginal Times to the End of Slavery*, and vol. 2: *From the Ending of Slavery to the Twenty-First Century*. Athens: University of Georgia Press, 1992, 1998.

Curry, Robert. *Bahamian Lore*. Paris: privately printed, 1928.

Dahl, Anthony. *Literature of the Bahamas, 1724–1992: The March towards National Identity*. Boston: University Press of America, 1995.

Darling, Sir Clifford. *Sir Clifford Darling: A Bahamian Life Story*. Vol. 1: *The Years of Struggle, 1922–1958*. Nassau: privately published, 2002.

Defries, Amelia. *In a Forgotten Colony, Being Some Studies in Nassau and at Grand Bahama during 1916*. Nassau: Nassau Guardian, 1916.

Dodge, Steve. *Abaco: The History of an Out Island and Its Cays*. Miami: Tropic Isles, 1983.

Doran, Michael F., and Renee A. Landis. "Origins and Persistence of an Inner-City Slum." *Geographical Review* 70, no. 2 (April 1980).

Dorland, W.A.N., and L. B. Arey. *Dorland's Illustrated Medical Dictionary*. 23rd ed. Philadelphia: W. B. Saunders, 1957.

Dupuch, Etienne. *Bahamas Handbook and Businessman's Annual*. Nassau: Etienne Dupuch Jr. Publications, 1960–84.

———. "Government in the Bahamas." In *Bahamas Handbook and Businessman's Annual*, 123–29. Nassau: Etienne Dupuch Jr. Publications, 1950.

———. *A Salute to Friend and Foe: My Battles, Sieges and Fortunes*. Nassau: Tribune, 1982.

———. *The Tribune Story*. London: Ernest Benn, 1967.

Eneas, Cleveland W. Sr. *Bain Town*. Nassau: Privately published, 1976, 1988.

———. *Let the Church Roll On: A Collection of Speeches and Writings*. Nassau: Written 1976, privately published, 1984, 1990.

Edwards, Charles. *Bahamas Songs and Stories*. Boston: Houghton Mifflin, 1895; reprint, New York: Stechert, 1942.

Eric, Allan. "'*Buckra Land' Land: Two Weeks in Jamaica: Details of a Voyage to the West Indies, Day by Day, and a Tour of Jamaica, Step by Step*. 2nd ed. Boston: Boston Fruit, 1897.

Farquharson, Charles. *A Relic of Slavery: Farquarson's Journal for 1831–32*. Copied from the original by Ormond J. McDonald, 1903. Nassau: Deans Peggs Research Fund, 1957.

Fawkes, Sir Randol. *The Faith That Moved the Mountain*. Nassau: Nassau Guardian, 1979; expanded memorial edition, Hialeah: Dodd, 2003.

Feiling, Keith. *The Life of Neville Chamberlain*. London: Macmillan, 1946.

Forbes, Rosita. *Appointment with Destiny*. London: Cassell, 1949.

———. *A Unicorn in the Bahamas*. London: Jenkins, 1939.

Furnivall, J. S. *Colonial Policy and Practice: A Comparative Study of Burma and Netherlands India*. Cambridge: Cambridge University Press, 1948.

———. *Netherlands India: A Study of Plural Economy*. Cambridge: Cambridge University Press, 1939.

Gelda, Beth, and Lynda Griffin. "Dyadic Relationships within the Bahamian Family." In *Strangers No More*, ed. Joel S. Savishinsky, 208–21. Ithaca, N.Y.: Ithaca College, 1978.

Glinton-Meicholas, Patricia. *From the Void to the Wonderful: A History of the Roman Catholic Church in the Bahamas*. Nassau: Guanima Press, 1995.

Gordon, Shirley. *A Century of West Indian Education*. London: Longmans, Green, 1969.

Greenberg, David. "The Contract, 'the Project,' and Work Experiences." In *Strangers No More*, ed. Joel S. Savishinsky, 170–207. Ithaca, N.Y.: Ithaca College, 1978.

Hanna, Rosemary. *Pictorial History and Memories of Nassau's Over-the-Hill*. Nassau: Media Enterprises, 2013.

Hill, Robert A., ed. *The Marcus Garvey and Universal Improvement Association Papers*. Vol. 3. Berkeley: University of California Press, 1984.

Holm, John. "African Features in White Bahamian English." *English World Wide* 1, no. 1 (1980): 53.

Holmes, Frank. *The Bahamas during the Great War*. Nassau: Tribune, 1924.

Houghton, H. *Report on Bahamian Education, 30 September 1958*. London: Colonial Office, 1958.

Hughes, Colin A. *Race and Politics in the Bahamas*. St. Lucia: University of Queensland Press, 1981; reprint, Nassau: Media Enterprises, 2010.

Hughes, H. L. Glyn. *A Survey of Medical Services, Nassau, 1960*. Nassau: Government Printing Department, 1960.

Hurston, Zora Neale. *Dust Tracks on a Road: An Autobiography.* Philadelphia: Lippincott, 1942.

———. *The Florida Negro: A Federal Writers' Project Legacy.* Edited, with an introduction, by Gary W. McDonogh. Jackson: University Press of Mississippi, 1993.

Ives, Charles. *The Isles of Summer; or, Nassau and the Bahamas.* New Haven: Privately published, 1880.

Jenkins, Olga. *Bahamian Memories: Island Voices of the Twentieth Century.* Gainesville: University Press of Florida, 2000.

Johnson, Cedric L. "The Strategic Importance of the British West Indies, 1882–1932," *Journal of Caribbean History* 6–7 (November 1973): 23–67.

Johnson, Dame Doris. *The Quiet Revolution in the Bahamas.* Nassau: Family Islands Press, 1972.

Johnson, Howard. *The Bahamas from Slavery to Servitude, 1783–1933.* Gainesville: University Press of Florida, 1996.

———. *The Bahamas in Slavery and Freedom.* Kingston, Jamaica: Ian Randle, 1991.

———. "Friendly Societies in the Bahamas, 1834–1910." *Slavery and Abolition: A Journal of Comparative Studies* 12, no. 3 (December 1991): 183–99.

———. "Labour on the Move: West Indian Migration, 1922–1930." Paper at Conference on Dimensions of Latin American and Caribbean Migration, University of Illinois, Chicago, 15–17 November 1984.

———. "National Identity and Bahamian Culture," *Yinna: Journal of the Bahamas Association for Cultural Studies* 1 (2000): 13–20.

Johnson, Whittington. *Post-Emancipation Race Relations in the Bahamas.* Gainesville: University Press of Florida, 2006.

Johnston, Wilhelmina Kemp. *Bahamian Jottings: Poems and Prose.* City: Brice, 1973.

Kiernan, V. G. *Lords of Human Kind: European Attitudes towards the Outside World in the Imperial Age.* London: Weidenfeld and Nicholson, 1969.

King, W. Francis Henry. *Addington Venables, Bishop of Nassau: A Sketch of His Life and Labours for the Church of God.* London: W. Wells Gardner, 1877.

La Flamme, Alan G. "Green Turtle Cay: A Bi-Racial Community in the Out Island Bahamas." Ph.D. diss., University of New York, Buffalo, 1972.

Lee, J. M. *Colonial Development and Good Government.* Oxford: Clarendon Press, 1967.

Lewis, Gordon K. *The Growth of the Modern West Indies.* New York: Monthly Review Press, 1968.

———. *Main Currents in Caribbean Thought.* Kingston, Jamaica: Heinemann Educational Books, 1983.

Lowenthal, David. *West Indian Societies.* Published for the Institute of Race Relations, London, in collaboration with the American Geographical Society, New York. London: Oxford University Press, 1972.

Malcolm, Harcourt Gladstone, ed. *Manual of Procedure in the Business of the General Assembly.* Nassau: House of Assembly, 1934.

Malone, Shelley Boyd, and Richard Campbell Roberts. *Nostalgic Nassau: Picture Postcards, 1900–1940.* Nassau: A.C. Graphics, 1991.

Martin, N. P., and Virgil H. Storr. "'I'se a Man': Political Awakening and the 1942 Riot in the Bahamas." *Journal of Caribbean History* 41, nos. 1–2 (2007): 72–87.

Martin, Tony. *Race First: The Ideological and Organizational Struggles of Marcus Garvey and the Universal Negro Improvement Association*. Dover, Mass.: Majority Press, 1976.

McCartney, Timothy. *Ten, Ten, the Bible Ten: Obeah in the Bahamas*. Nassau: Timpaul, 1976.

McDermott, Benson. "Harold Christie, the Man Who Put the Bahamas on the Map." In *Bahamas Handbook and Businessman's Annual*. Nassau: Etienne Dupuch Jr. Publications, 1979.

———. "L. W. Young: Formidable Force from Fox Hill." In *Bahamas Handbook and Businessman's Annual*. Nassau: Etienne Dupuch Jr. Publications, 1984.

———. "Opinionated, Warm-Hearted, Autocratic, Patriotic: Kenneth Solomon Served and Ruled the Bahamas." In *Bahamas Handbook and Businessman's Annual*. Nassau: Etienne Dupuch Jr. Publications, 1983.

Mills, T. Wesley. "The Study of a Small and Isolated Community in the Bahamas." *American Naturalist* 21, no. 10 (October 1887): 875–85.

Mohl, Raymond A. "Settlements of Blacks in South Florida." In *South Florida: The Winds of Change*, ed. Thomas D. Boswell, 112–39. Miami: Association of American Geographers, 1991.

Moseley, Mary. *The Bahamas Handbook*. Nassau: Nassau Guardian, 1926.

Myers, Robert A. "'I love my country bad, but . . .': The Historical and Contemporary Context of Migration to Dominica, West Indies." Ph.D. diss., University of North Carolina, 1976.

Noble, David W., David A. Horowitz, and Peter N. Carroll. *Twentieth Century Limited: A History of Recent America*. Boston: Houghton Mifflin, 1980.

Northcroft, G.H.J. *Sketches of Summerland: Giving Some Account of Nassau and the Bahama Islands*. Nassau: Nassau Guardian, 1902; republished, Nassau Guardian, 1906.

Otterbein, Keith. *The Andros Islanders: A Study of Family Organization in the Bahamas*. Lawrence: University of Kansas Press, 1966.

Outten-Stubbs, Kim. "A Chronological History of Women's Suffrage in the Bahamas, 1952–1962." Aspects of Bahamian History, Department of Archives, *Nassau Guardian*, 23 November 1987.

Parks, Arva Moore. "The History of Coconut Grove, Florida, 1821–1925." MA diss., University of Miami, 1971.

———. *Miami: The Magic City*. Tulsa: Continental Heritage Press, 1981.

Peggs, A. Deans. "A History of Bahamian Education." M.Ed. diss., University of Durham, 1947.

Pelling, Henry. *Modern Britain, 1885–1955*. London: W. W. Norton, 1967.

Penrose, C. A. "Sanitary Conditions in the Bahamas." In *The Bahama Islands*, ed. G. B. Shattuck, 387–416. Baltimore: Johns Hopkins University Press, 1905.

Peters, Thelma. "The American Loyalists and the Plantation Period in the Bahamas." Ph.D. diss., University of Florida, Gainesville.

Poitier, Sir Sidney. *This Life*, New York: Ballantine, 1980.

Powles, Liston D. *The Land of the Pink Pearl*. London: Lowe, Marston, Searle and Rivington, 1888.

Pye, Michael. *The King over the Water*. London: Hutchinson, 1981.

Report on Blue Book for 1887. London: Her Majesty's Stationery Office, 1888.

Richardson, J. Henry. *Review of Bahamian Economic Conditions and Post War Problems*. Nassau: Nassau Guardian, 1944.

Rogers, William B. "The Wages of Change: An Anthropological Study of the Effects of Economic Development on Some Negro Communities in the Out Islands." Ph.D. diss., Stanford University, 1965.

Roker, Patricia B., ed. *Sir Clifford Darling: A Bahamian Life Story*. Vol. 1: *The Years of Struggle, 1922–1958*. Nassau: Privately published, 2002.

——. *The Vision of Sir Lynden Pindling in His Own Words: Letters and Speeches, 1948–1997.* Nassau: Estate of Sir Lynden Pindling, 2000.

Sands, Kirkley. *The Anglican Church and Education in the Bahamas*. Nassau: Nassau Guardian, 2007.

Saunders, Gail. "The Ambiguous Admission Policy at Queen's College High School, Nassau, Bahamas, 1920s–1950s." *Yinna: Journal of the Bahamas Association for Cultural Studies* 3 (2011): 13-39.

——. *Bahamian Loyalists and Their Slaves*. London: Macmillan, 1983.

——. *Bahamian Society after Emancipation*. Kingston, Jamaica: Ian Randle, 2003.

——. "The Making of a Leader." In *Before and After 1865: Education, Politics, and Regionalism in the Caribbean*, ed. Brian L. Moore and Swithin R. Wilmot, 163–74. Kingston, Jamaica: Ian Randle, 1998.

——. "Profiles of Several Outstanding Bahamian Women." *Journal of the Bahamas Historical Society* 19 (October 1997): 50–52.

——. "Recent Developments in the Historiography of the Post-Emancipation Anglophone Caribbean." In *Beyond Fragmentation Perspectives on Caribbean History*, ed. by Juanita de Barros, Audra Diptee, and David V. Trotman, 187–209. Princeton: Markus Wiener, 2006.

——. *Slavery in the Bahamas*. Nassau: Nassau Guardian, 2000.

——. "The Social History of the Bahamas, 1890–1953." Ph.D. diss., University of Waterloo, Ontario, 1984.

——. *Social Life in the Bahamas, 1880s–1920s*. Nassau: Rosebud, 1996.

Saunders, Hartley C. *The Other Bahamas*. Nassau: BODAB (printed at the *Nassau Guardian*), 1991.

Savishinsky, Joel S., ed. *Strangers No More: Anthropological Studies of Cat Island, the Bahamas*. Ithaca, N.Y.: Ithaca College, 1978.

Sharer, Cyrus. "The Population Growth of the Bahama Islands." Ph.D. diss., University of Michigan, 1955.

Shattuck, G. B. *The Bahama Islands*. Baltimore: Johns Hopkins University Press, 1905.

Shedden, Roscow. *Ups and Downs in a West Indian Diocese*. London: A. R. Mowbray, 1927.

Singham, A. W. *The Hero and the Crowd in a Colonial Polity.* New Haven: Yale University Press, 1968.

Smith, M. G. *A Framework for Caribbean Studies.* Mona, Jamaica: University of the West Indies, 1955.

——. *The Plural Society in the British West Indies.* Berkeley: University of California Press, 1965.

——. *West Indian Family Structure.* Seattle: University of Washington Press, 1962.

Stark, James Henry. *Stark's History and Guide to the Bahama Islands, Containing Everything on or About the Bahama Islands of Which the Visitor or Resident May Desire Information. Including Their History, Inhabitants, Climate, Agriculture, Geology, Government and Resources.* Boston: Plimpton Press, 1891.

The Statute Law of the Bahama Islands, 1799–1929. 2 vols. Edited by Harcourt Gladstone Malcolm. Nassau: Government of the Colony of the Bahama Islands, 1929.

The Statute Law of the Bahamas, 1799–1965. 7 vols. Edited by Sir Ralph Hone. Nassau: Government of the Colony of the Bahama Islands, 1965.

Symonette, Michael, and Antonina Canzoneri. *Baptists in the Bahamas: An Historical Review.* El Paso: Baptist Spanish Publishing House, 1977.

Taylor, A.J.P. *English History, 1914–1945.* New York: Oxford University Press, 1965.

Taylor, Frank. "The Tourist Industry in Jamaica, 1919–1939." *Social and Economic Studies* 22 (1973): 205–28.

Taylor, Sir Henry M. *My Political Memoirs: A Political History of the Bahamas in the Twentieth Century.* Nassau: Privately published, 1987.

Themistocleous, Rosalyn. "'The Merchant Princes of Nassau': The Maintenance of Political Hegemony in the Bahamas, 1834–1948." Ph.D. diss., University of Kent at Canterbury, 2000.

Thompson, Anthony. *An Economic History of the Bahamas.* 2nd ed. Nassau: Commercial Services Group, 2008.

Thompson, Krista. *An Eye for the Tropics: Tourism, Photography, and the Framing of the Caribbean Picturesque.* Durham, N.C.: Duke University Press, 2006.

Thompson, Tracey. "Constitutional Authority in the Bahama Islands, 1946–1947: The Governor and the Assembly." *Journal of the Bahamas Historical Society* 5, no. 1 (1983): 20–28.

——. "Remembering 'the Contract': Recollections of Bahamians." *International Journal of Bahamian Studies* 18 (2012): 6–12.

Thomson, David. *England in the Twentieth Century.* With additional material by Geoffrey Warner. Harmondsworth, Middlesex: Penguin Books, 1981.

Tinker, Keith L. *The Migration of Peoples from the Caribbean to the Bahamas.* Gainesville: University Press of Florida, 2010.

Tull, Marc. "Colour Pride in Tarpum Bay: A Bahamian Community Reacts to Equality." In Garry Thomas, *Anthropological Perspectives on Eleuthera Island, 1973–1974.* Corning, N.Y.: College Center of the Finger Lakes, 1974.

Van de Water, Frederic Franklyn. *The Real McCoy.* Garden City, N.Y.: Doubleday, 1933.

Wakefield, Edward Gibbon. *A View of the Art of Colonization*. London: John W. Parker, 1849; reprint, Oxford: Clarendon Press, 1914.

Williams, Colbert. *The Methodist Contribution to Education in the Bahamas*. Gloucester, U.K.: Alan Sutton, 1982.

Williamson, James A. *A Notebook of Commonwealth History*. 3rd ed. New York: Macmillan, 1967.

Wilmot, Swithin. "Race and Justice in the Bahamas: The Case of Lewis Powles." *College Forum* 1 (1980): 15–18.

The Year Book of the West Indies and Countries of the Caribbean, 1926–27, 1929, 1948–49, 1951, 1953–54. London: Skinner 1927–63 (title and publisher vary).

Index

Figures appear after p. 142 and are indexed in *italics* as *p1*, *p2*, *p3*, and so on.

Bahamas Rejuvenation League, 111
Bahamas Timber Company, 88–90
Bahamas War Committee, 178–79
Bahamian economy, xi–xiii; cash, 68–69; gradual changes in, 68–73; in 1953, 222–28; post-emancipation period, 17–23; pre-industrial subsistence, 66; white elite controlling, 227, 293; WWI influencing, 102. *See also* Economic depression and 1930s; Labor
Bahamian Society after Emancipation (Saunders), ix–xi
Bahamian Times, 283, 300
Bailey, Robert, 169, 198
Bain, Alexander, 41–42
Bain, Clarence, 279–80, *p13*
Bain, Francis, 80–81
Bain Town, 10, 30, 41, 47, 50; police and, 80–81; segregation in, 77
Baker, Joseph, 259–60
Ballot Box Party, 116
Band of Inagua Terrors, 167–68
Baptists, 26–28, 57–58, 63, 223, *p14*; African traditions and, 48; black solidarity and, 288–89
Barbadian, 80
Barbados, xi–xii, 23–24
Barratt, Peter, 211
Barry, Colman, 134
Baxter, Guy, 210
Bay Street, 2, 11, 22, 233–34, *p10–p11*; Burma Road Riot, 1942, and, 189–95; electricity on, 82–83; in 1956 general election, 248–49, 251–56; in postwar years, 210; race and, 146, 155, 159–60, 173, 189–94, 220–21, 237, 279–80; strike and, 265–66; UBP and, 270–72, 275–78, 281–86, 300–303
B'Booky and B'Rabby stories, 50
BDL. *See* Bahamas Democratic League
Bell, H. M., 123, 125, 143
Bermuda, 23–24
Besson, Jean, 15
Bethel, Cecil, 142
Bethel, Clement, 50
Bethel, H. R., 203
Bethel, Marion, 273
Bethel, Milton, 44
Bethel, Nicolette, 15, 235–36
Bethel, Reuben, 109
Beveridge, Wilfred, 136

BFL. *See* Bahamas Federation of Labour
Bimini, 123–24
Birth control, 199
Black population: creole, 9, 76; defined, 6; in divided society, 287–91, 293–303; Garvey-related organizations of, 109–11; health problems among, 87–88; justice for, 41–42; labor system exploiting, 19–20; in late nineteenth and early twentieth centuries, 33, 43, 47–52, 54–66; middle class, 8–9, 42, 47, 157, 296–97; morality of, 46–47; in 1950s, 217–19, 223–27, 231–40, 245–46; in 1930s, 146–49, 154–73; in Out Islands, 9, 54–66; political awareness of, 12, 194–95; Prohibition benefiting, 141–43; racial pride and identity in, 10–11, 73–74; recreational activities of, 48–50; secular organizations and, 47–48, 289; social control of, 77–79; success of, 43, 47; U.S. Civil War and, 22; women's suffrage and, 273–74, 277; during WWII, 180, 183–86, 194–95, 199–200, 206–7
Black solidarity, 288–89
Black Tuesday, 300
Blake, Henry, 34, 41–43, 49, 78, 91
Bloch, Michael, 180–81
Board of Education, 29–30, 111, 214, 272
Bodie, Remelda, 202–3
Bolland, Nigel, 166–67, 169
Bootlegging, 122–25, 138–40, 143
Bosfield, George A., 42
Bosfield, Samuel, 74
Bowe, James Maxwell, 226
Bowe, Robert J., 119
Bowe case, 225–26
Boys Central School, 30–31, 133
Boy Scouts, 114, 163
Brathwaite, Kamau, 7, 33
Braynen, Alvin, 171, 216
Brereton, Bridget, 7, 157
Bribery, 250–51, 254
Britain, 35; cable communication with, 82; changes in, 67–68; Commonwealth, 68, 144–45; Depression in, 144
British: commissioned officers, 11; white elite and, 8, 35, 299
Brodber, Erna, 5
Brown, Holly, 164–65, 229–30
Brown, H. W., *p14*
Brown population, 6. *See also* Mixed-race population

Nassau Grammar School, 31, 133–34

Nassau Guardian, 35, 40, 44, 96, 100, 106, 298; Christmas described by, 51–53; politics and, 76, 116, 231, 234, 236, 240, 248, 251, 255, 265, 278–80, 284; Prohibition and, 125–26

National Archives of the Bahamas, x

National Committee for Positive Action (NCPA), 280–83, 300

National Council of Women, 275

National General Council (NGC), 280, 284

National identity, 117–19

Native Baptist churches, 27, 48, 288

NCPA. *See* National Committee for Positive Action

Negro World, 109

Neligan, William Hayes, 97

Nesbitt, C. R., 70

Nettleford, Rex, 157

Newman, John, 201, 203

New Plymouth, 56, 58

New Providence, xii, 9, 17, 30, 50, 249; air crews trained in, 11, 174, 185–86, 205; health and sanitary conditions on, 86; houses, 3; land development in, 130–31; modernized, 126, 286; population in, 1–2. *See also* Nassau

Newspaper Security Act, 164–65

New Year's, 53, 64–65, 155

New York, 95, 110–11

NGC. *See* National General Council

Nightclubs, 153–54

Noad, F. A., 255–56

Noble, Marjorie, 266

Nonwhite population. *See* Black population; Mixed-race population

North, Basil, 163

North, William B., 43, 135, 142

Northcroft, G.J.H., 39–41, 50–51

Nottage, Bernard J., 191

Nouveau riche class, 139–41, 146

No Way Out, 218

Nurses, 86, 214, 223

Oakes, Harry, 148–49, 170, 185, 207–10, *p21*

Oakes Airfield, 149, 185–86, 211, 261, 291. *See also* Burma Road Riot, 1942

Obeah, 49, 63

Oil, 213

O'Keefe, Charles George, 97

"Old Skin" (Bunce), 65

On the Shore Road, East of Nassau, p5

Orr, Charles, 116–17

Out Islands, xii–xiii, 17, 83, 233; black population in, 9, 54–66; class in, 56; development of, 126–27, 137, 180, 291–92; in economic depression and 1930s, 145, 150, 165–73; education in, 29, 31–32, 57–58, 75; industry, 54–58; land tenure in, 15–16, 22; in late nineteenth and early twentieth centuries, 34, 54–66; medical personnel on, 85–86, 214; migration from, 95, 127–28, 150–51, 177, 186, 202, 222, 225–26, 286–87; mixed-race population on, 54–55, 57–63; population of, 3, 5, 9; poverty in, 54, 66, 145, 172, 180–81; religion in, 49, 223; remittances to, 93, 95; segregation in, 57–59, 66, 291; settlements in, 5, 54; similarities among, 64, 66; sisal industry on, 70–71; socioeconomic conditions, in 1953, 223–27; sponging industry on, 20–21, 45, 65, 69; tourism, 211–12; travel to, 5–6; upward mobility in, 53, 296; white population on, 54, 56–66; during WWII, 176–77, 197–99

Outsiders, resentment of, 117–19

Over-the-Hill settlements, 3, 49, 51, 160, 190, 222, 290

Paget, E. V., 161

Pajaro, 59

Pan-Africanism, 11, 74

Partner (*asue*), 48, 227

Patton, David, 43, 47

Paul, Joseph, 26

Peasantry, 9–10, 16, 20, 172

Penny, Charles, 26

Penny Savings Bank, 221–22, 227, 246

Penrose, Clement, 60–61

Pentecostal Church, 48

Pharmacy Act of 1913, 85

Pilotage, 56

Pindling, Lynden, 195, 237, 270, 295; in PLP, 230–32, 248–54, 256, 275–77, 279–80, 284, 300–303, *p13*; strike and, 258, 261, 264–65, 269

Pineapple industry, 18–20, 57–58, 70

Pitt, William, 39, 85, 88

PLP. *See* Progressive Liberal Party

Poitier, Reginald, 177

Poitier, Sidney, 177, 218, 301

Polhemus, William, 118

Gail Saunders, pioneer Bahamian archivist at the Department of Archives of the Bahamas and presently scholar-in-residence at the College of the Bahamas, is the author and coauthor of a number of books, including *Bahamian Society after Emancipation, Sources of Bahamian History* (with Philip Cash and Shirley Gordon), *Bahamian Loyalists and Their Slaves,* and, with Michael Craton, *Islanders in the Stream: A History of the Bahamian People,* vols. 1 and 2.

9 780813 064512